# ON THE CONTRARY

## Essays by Men and Women

# ON THE CONTRARY

## Essays by Men and Women

edited by

Martha Rainbolt
DEPAUW UNIVERSITY

and

Janet Fleetwood
SCOTT, FORESMAN & CO.

STATE UNIVERSITY OF NEW YORK PRESS
Albany

Published by
State University of New York Press, Albany



Printed in the United States of America



For information, address State University of New York
Press, State University Plaza, Albany, N.Y., 12246

Library of Congress Cataloging in Publication Data
Main entry under title:
On the contrary.
1. College readers. I. Rainbolt, Martha, 1938–
II. Fleetwood, Janet, 1944–
PE1417.054 1984 808'.0427 82-19421
ISBN 0-87395-720-2 (pbk.)

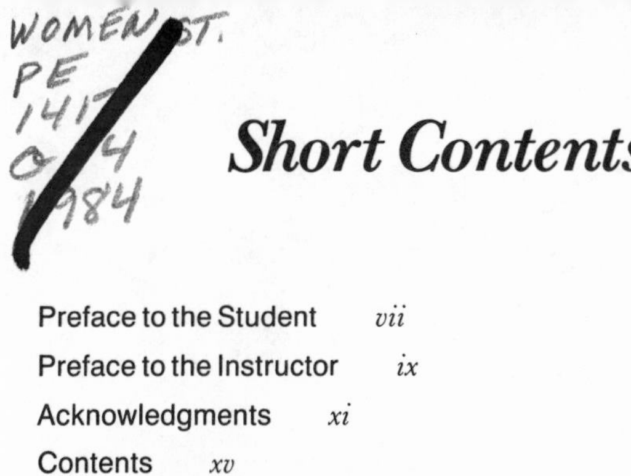

# Short Contents


Preface to the Student *vii*

Preface to the Instructor *ix*

Acknowledgments *xi*

Contents *xv*

Rhetorical Contents *xxiii*

**Part One: FRIENDS AND LOVERS** *1*

1. Concepts of Masculinity *3*
2. Concepts of Femininity *10*
3. Love *28*
4. Friendship *42*
5. Personality Clashes *56*

**Part Two: YOUTH AND MATURITY** *65*

6. The Stages of Life *67*
7. Growing Up *76*
8. Raising Children *87*
9. Growing Older *99*

**Part Three: KNOWLEDGE AND EDUCATION** *119*

10. Attitudes Toward Formal Education *121*
11. Motivation and Reluctance *130*
12. The College Atmosphere *144*
13. Ultimate Goals *156*

**Part Four: FREEDOM AND INDIVIDUALITY** *173*

14. Society and the Individual *175*
15. Minority Rights *197*
16. Prescribed Roles *215*
17. Self-Assertion *224*

**Part Five: SUCCESS AND FAILURE** *231*

18. Ambition: A Skeptical View *233*
19. Ambition: An Affirmative View *242*
20. Wealth and Acquisition *254*
21. Fame and Recognition *267*
22. Self-Fulfillment *288*
23. Barriers to Success *294*

**Appendix: ESSAYS ON THE WRITING PROCESS** *305*

Notes on Contributors

# Preface to the Student

"On the contrary," "on the other hand," "on second thought," "but what about" are all expressions commonly used in writing and speaking. We make a point and then think of a qualification or contradiction. Much of our best thinking proceeds in this dialectical direction. The thinking process is somewhat like climbing a very steep hill in that it is not possible to march straight up. Instead, the climbers must move to the right and slightly upward, then to the left, and perhaps even backward before they go forward again. In this way they finally reach the summit.

Most of us learn very effectively in this dialectical pattern. The essays in the anthology are organized to reinforce and affirm this method of thinking. There are five major parts in this work: Friends and Lovers, Youth and Maturity, Knowledge and Education, Freedom and Individuality, and Success and Failure. Instead of a random selection of essays on these general topics, this work moves logically and systematically through the categories in each topic. It examines each facet of the subject with pairs of complementary or contrasting essays. The pairs, one essay by a woman and one by a man, sometimes present radically differing perspectives, sometimes represent generalization and example, and often set up a debate on basic assumptions and underlying principles. Reading through these essays, you will be required to evaluate the various perspectives and perhaps to come to terms with some of your own ideas on the subject.

Clear writing, of course, cannot be separated from clear thinking. By the same token, vague and imprecise writing is usually an indication of fuzzy thinking. An understanding of the writing strategies in these essays will help you to think more accurately and to handle concepts more skillfully and, as a result, to express yourself more effectively in writing. In addition, the essays in this anthology exemplify a wide range of possible writing styles. They can suggest to you different types of organization, different modes of expression, and different kinds of language and tone. A study of these essays and regular practice in writing can give your compositions greater variety and complexity. It is all too easy to write the same type of essay again and again, but such formulaic writing ignores the validity and the originality which is possible when the unusual and innovative conquers the commonplace. With the help of the writers in this anthology, we the editors hope that you will learn to write with more originality, more clarity, more complexity, and more enjoyment.

# Preface

# Preface to the Instructor

The prospect of reading and analyzing one essay after another can be a bleak one for students. In a world where experiences tend to be hurried and fragmented anyway, an anthology of diverse readings may seem to present students with still another set of disconnected encounters. This collection of writings is designed to correct that situation by offering the student an integrated reading experience.

The selections in this anthology focus on five topics of major importance to college students. From "Friends and Lovers" to "Success and Failure" the organization of the book encourages a thorough examination of each subject. The essays are carefully arranged in pairs that form effective contrasts. For example, skeptical views are paired with affirmative views, satirical treatments with enthusiastic endorsements, and generalized discussions with personalized accounts. In this way the student, instead of encountering ideas in isolation, can actually see them played against each other. The challenge of contrasting ideas should stimulate students to come to grips with some of their own ideas. In addition, the rigorous organization of the contents will demonstrate some of the principles of systematic presentation so essential to good writing.

The organizational pattern of the book offers another advantage over most composition anthologies. The paired essays, one by a woman and one by a man, show women writers contributing equally with men writers. These women write on many stylistic levels — from tough, philosophical essays to light, whimsical essays. ON THE CONTRARY is neither an exclusively feminist book nor a collection containing a few token women writers. Instead, it presents a balanced perspective: women and men engaged in dialogue and debate over issues significant to all people.

Another strength of this anthology is its inclusion of classic, as well as contemporary writings. Many current collections focus almost entirely on contemporary essays, and some of these are faddish and not particularly well written. We have included writings by some of the best contemporary essayists: E. B. White, Joan Didion, Joseph Epstein, Ellen Goodman. But there are also strong and accessible writings by classic writers: Aristotle, Samuel Johnson, John Stuart Mill. The topics we have selected and the essays which discuss these topics provide college students with an opportunity to compare perspectives from former times with those of the contemporary scene.

The essays on writing in the appendix can be used at any time in the semester. These writings discuss journals and notebooks (Didion), peer evaluation (Le Guin), writer's block (Barzun and Godwin), clarity (Mitchell), and style (Gibson).

They may be used as a unit in themselves to begin the semester or as a supplement to the various sections of the course which focus on these aspects of writing. The alternate table of contents permits the organization of the essays in terms of rhetorical modes if that format is more appropriate for your course.

Most importantly, almost all of the essays in this anthology were selected for their intrinsic merit, as well as for their value in providing divergent points of view. They should help sharpen the students' ability to analyze and criticize, discourage facile and superficial thinking, and serve as good models for student papers. Finally, the interest, readability, and thoughtfulness of the writings should add to the students' general awareness and enjoyment.

# Acknowledgments

Ilse Aichinger, "The Bound Man" from *The Bound Man and Other Stories*, translated from the German by Eric Mosbacher. © 1956 by Ilse Aichinger. Reprinted by permission of Farrar, Straus and Giroux, Inc., New York, New York.

Alan Alda, "What Every Woman Should Know about Men" from *Ms* (October 1975). © 1975 by *Ms* magazine. Reprinted by permission of *Ms*.

Maya Angelou, "Mama and the Dentist" from *I Know Why the Caged Bird Sings*. © 1969 by Maya Angelou. Reprinted by permission of Random House, Inc., New York, New York.

Jacques Barzun, "A Writer's Discipline" from *On Writing, Editing, and Publishing*. © 1971 by Jacques Barzun. Published by the University of Chicago Press. Reprinted by permission of the author.

Daniel J. Boorstin, "From Hero to Celebrity" from *The Image: A Guide to Pseudo-Events in America*. © 1961 by Daniel J. Boorstin. Reprinted by permission of Atheneum Publishers, New York, New York.

Brigid Brophy, "Women: Invisible Cages" from *Don't Never Forget: Collected Views and Reviews*. © 1963 by Brigid Brophy. Published by Holt, Rinehart and Winston. Reprinted by permission of the author.

Winston Churchill, "School Days" from *A Roving Commission: My Early Life*. © 1930 by Charles Scribner's Sons. Reprinted by permission of Charles Scribner's Sons, New York, New York.

John Ciardi, "Is Everybody Happy?" from *Saturday Review* (March 14, 1964). © 1964 by *Saturday Review*. All rights reserved. Reprinted by permission of *Saturday Review*.

Eldridge Cleaver, "Prelude to Love — Three Letters" from *Soul on Ice*. © 1968 by Eldridge Cleaver. Reprinted by permission of McGraw-Hill, New York, New York.

Simone de Beauvoir, "Introduction" from *The Coming of Age*. Translation © 1972 by Andre Deutsch, Weidenfeld. Reprinted by permission of G. P. Putnam's Sons, New York, New York.

Joan Didion, "On Keeping a Notebook" from *Slouching towards Bethlehem*. © 1966, 1968 by Joan Didion. Reprinted by permission of Farrar, Straus and Giroux, Inc., New York, New York.

Ecclesiastes: Verses marked The Living Bible are taken from The Living Bible. © 1971 by Tyndale House Publishers. Reprinted by permission of Tyndale House Publishers, Wheaton, Illinois.

Loren Eiseley, "Obituary of a Bone Hunter" from *The Night Country*. © 1947, 1956, 1971 by Loren Eiseley. Reprinted by permission of Charles Scribner's Sons, New York, New York.

Nora Ephron, "A Few Words about Breasts" from *Crazy Salad: Some Things about Women.* ©1975 by Nora Ephron. Reprinted by permission of Alfred A. Knopf, Inc., New York, New York.

Joseph Epstein, "The Virtues of Ambition: Some Kind Words for Money, Fame, and Power" from *Ambition: The Secret Passion.* ©1981 by Joseph Epstein. Reprinted by permission of E. P. Dutton, Inc., New York, New York. (Article first appeared as "The Virtues of Ambition" in *Harper's* magazine, October, 1981.)

Walker Gibson, "Hearing Voices: Tough Talk, Sweet Talk, Stuffy Talk" from *Tough, Sweet and Stuffy.* ©1966 by Indiana University Press. Reprinted by permission of Indiana University Press, Bloomington, Indiana.

Gail Godwin, "The Watcher at the Gates" from *The New York Times Book Review* (January 9, 1977). ©1977 by The New York Times Company. Reprinted by permission of The New York Times Company, New York, New York.

Ellen Goodman, "Such Empty Options" from *At Large.* ©1981 by The Washington Post Company. Reprinted by permission of Summit Books, a Simon and Schuster Division of Gulf and Western Corporation, New York, New York.

Margaret Halsey, "What's Wrong with 'Me, Me, Me'" from *Newsweek* (April 17, 1978). ©1978 by Margaret Halsey. Reprinted by permission of International Creative Management, New York, New York.

Lillian Hellman, "Dashiell Hammett" from *An Unfinished Woman.* ©1969 by Lillian Hellman. Reprinted by permission of Little, Brown and Company, Boston, Mass.

Muriel James and Dorothy Jongeward, "Winners and Losers" from *Born to Win.* ©1971 by Muriel James and Dorothy Jongeward. Reprinted by permission of Addison-Wesley Publishing Co., Reading, Mass.

Suzanne Britt Jordan, "That Lean and Hungry Look," from *Newsweek* (October 9, 1978). ©1978 by Newsweek. Reprinted by permission of Newsweek, Inc., New York, New York.

Jean Kerr, "The Poet and the Peasants" from *Penny Candy.* ©1966, 1967, 1968, 1969, 1970 by Collins Publications. Reprinted by permission of Doubleday and Company, Inc., New York, New York.

Martin Luther King, Jr., "Letter from Birmingham Jail" from *Why We Can't Wait.* ©1963 by Martin Luther King, Jr. Reprinted by permission of Harper and Row, Publishers, Inc., New York, New York.

Ring Lardner, "Some Like Them Cold" from *How to Write Short Stories.* ©1924 by Charles Scribner's Sons; copyright renewed 1952 by Ellis A. Lardner. Reprinted by permission of Charles Scribner's Sons, New York, New York.

Susan Lee, "Friendship, Feminism, and Betrayal" from *The Village Voice.* ©1975 by The Village Voice, Inc. Reprinted by permission of The Village Voice, Inc., New York, New York.

Ursula K. Le Guin, "Fifteen Vultures, the Strop, and the Old Lady" from *Clarion II*, edited by Robin Scott Wilson. Published by New American Library. ©1972 by Robin Scott Wilson. Reprinted by permission of Ursula K. Le Guin and the author's agent, Virginia Kidd.

C. S. Lewis, "Friendship" from *The Four Loves*. ©1960 by Helen Joy Lewis. Reprinted by permission of Harcourt Brace Jovanovich, Inc., New York, New York.

Anne Morrow Lindbergh, "Channelled Whelk" from *Gift from the Sea*. ©1955 by Anne Morrow Lindbergh. Reprinted by permission of Pantheon Books, a Division of Random House, Inc., New York, New York.

D. Keith Mano, "Cruel Lib" from *Newsweek* (September 8, 1975). ©1975 by Newsweek, Inc. Reprinted by permission of Newsweek, Inc., New York, New York.

Milton Mayer, "Commencement Address: What You Will Be" from *What Can a Man Do?*, edited by E. Gustafson. ©1964 by the University of Chicago Press. Reprinted by permission of the University of Chicago Press, Chicago, Illinois.

Mary McCarthy, "The Vassar Girl" from *On the Contrary*. ©1946, 1947, 1949, 1950, 1951, 1952, 1953, 1954, 1955, 1958, 1959, 1960, 1961 by Mary McCarthy. ©1951 by Curtis Publishing Company. Reprinted by permission of Farrar, Straus and Giroux, Inc., New York, New York.

H. L. Mencken, "Education" from *Prejudices: Third Series*. ©1922 and renewed 1950 by H. L. Mencken. Reprinted by permission of Alfred A. Knopf, Inc., New York, New York.

Richard Mitchell, "The Worm in the Brain" from *Less Than Words Can Say*. ©1979 by Richard Mitchell. Reprinted by permission of Little, Brown and Company, Boston, Mass.

Tillie Olsen, "I Stand Here Ironing" from *Tell Me a Riddle*. ©1956 by Tillie Olsen. Reprinted by permission of Delacorte Press/Seymour Lawrence, New York, New York.

Dorothy Parker, "Good Souls" from *Vanity Fair* (June 1919). ©1919 by Vanity Fair Publications Co., Inc. Reprinted by permission of Vanity Fair.

William G. Perry, "Examsmanship and the Liberal Arts: A Study in Educational Epistemology" from *Examining in Harvard College: A Collection of Essays* by Members of the Harvard Faculty. ©1963 by Harvard University Press. Reprinted by permission of Harvard University Press, Cambridge, Mass.

Adrienne Rich, "Taking Women Students Seriously" from *On Lies, Secrets, and Silence: Selected Prose, 1966–1978*. ©1979 by W. W. Norton and Company, Inc. Reprinted by permission of W. W. Norton and Company, Inc., New York, New York.

Lissa Rotundo, "One-Year-Old Scholars" from *Newsweek* (February 2, 1981). ©1981 by Newsweek. Reprinted by permission of Newsweek, Inc., New York, New York.

Bertrand Russell, "What I Have Lived For" from *Autobiography of Bertrand Russell*. ©1969 by George Allen and Unwin. Reprinted by permission of George Allen and Unwin Publishers, Ltd., London.

Dorothy Sayers, "The Human-Not-Quite-Human" from *Unpopular Opinions*. ©1947 by Dorothy L. Sayers, renewed 1974 by Anthony Fleming. Published by Harcourt, Brace. Reprinted by permission of A. Watkins, Inc.

Manuel J. Smith, "Assertive Rights" from *When I Say No, I Feel Guilty*. ©1975 by Manuel J. Smith. Reprinted by permission of The Dial Press, New York, New York.

Susan Sontag, "The Double Standard of Aging" from *Saturday Review* (September 23,

1975). ©1975 by Saturday Review. All rights reserved. Reprinted by permission of Saturday Review, New York, New York.

Diana Trilling, "The Death of Marilyn Monroe" from *Claremont Essays*. ©1963 by Diana Trilling. Reprinted by permission of Harcourt Brace Jovanovich, Inc., New York, New York.

Esther Vilar, "What Is Man?" from *The Manipulated Man*. ©1972 by Farrar, Straus and Giroux, Inc. Reprinted by permission of Farrar, Straus and Giroux, Inc., New York, New York.

E. B. White, "Afternoon of an American Boy" from *Essays of E. B. White*. ©1947 by E. B. White. Reprinted by permission of Harper and Row Publishers, Inc., New York, New York.

Virginia Woolf, "Professions for Women" from *The Death of the Moth and Other Essays*. ©1942 by Harcourt Brace Jovanovich, Inc.; copyright renewed 1970 by Marjorie T. Parsons, Executrix. Reprinted by permission of Harcourt Brace Jovanovich, Inc., New York, New York.

William Zinsser, "College Pressures" from *Blair and Ketchum's Country Journal*. ©1979 by William K. Zinsser. Reprinted by permission of the author.

## OTHER REFERENCES

Aristotle, "Young Men and Elderly Men" from *Rhetoric,* Book II.

Andrew Carnegie, "The Gospel of Wealth" from the *North American Review* (June 1889).

Ecclesiastes (Chapters 1–3) from the King James Version.

Samuel Johnson, "The Good Sort of Woman" from *The Idler,* No. 100 (March 15, 1760).

John Stuart Mill, "Of Individuality, As One of the Elements of Well-Being" from *On Liberty.*

# Contents

**Part One FRIENDS AND LOVERS** *1*

1. CONCEPTS OF MASCULINITY *3*

   1. *Alan Alda,* "What Every Woman Should Know about Men" *3*
      "See if you can get yourself to cry by some means other than getting hit in the eye or losing a lot of money."

   2. *Esther Vilar,* "What Is Man?" *6*
      "Any qualities in a man that a woman finds useful, she calls *masculine*; all others, of no use to her or to anyone else for that matter, she chooses to call *effeminate*."

      Suggestions For Discussion *8*
      Suggestions For Writing *9*

2. CONCEPTS OF FEMININITY *10*

   1. *Dorothy Sayers,* "The Human-Not-Quite-Human" *10*
      "Probably no man has ever troubled to imagine how strange his life would appear to himself if it were unrelentingly assessed in terms of his maleness; if everything he wore, said, or did had to be justified by reference to female approval."

   2. *Ring Lardner,* "Some Like Them Cold" *14*
      "Maybe you will think that . . . I am 'jealous' of the lady in question. Well, sir, I won't tell you whether I am or not, but will keep you 'guessing.' Now, don't you wish you knew?"

      Suggestions For Discussion *26*
      Suggestions For Writing *27*

3. LOVE *28*

   1. *Eldridge Cleaver,* "Prelude to Love — Three letters" *28*
      "Getting to know someone, entering that new world, is an ultimate, irretrievable leap into the unknown. The prospect is terrifying. The stakes are high."

   2. *Lillian Hellman,* "Dashiell Hammett" *34*
      "He was the most interesting man I've ever met. I laugh at what he did say, amuse myself with what he might say, and even this many years later speak to him, often angry that he still interferes with me, still dictates the rules."

      Suggestions For Discussion *40*
      Suggestions For Writing *41*

4. FRIENDSHIP 42

1. *C. S. Lewis,* "Friendship" 43
"Friendship is unnecessary, like philosophy, like art, like the universe itself (for God did not need to create). It has no survival value; rather it is one of those things which give value to survival."

2. *Susan Lee,* "Friendship, Feminism, and Betrayal" 50
"While I, and several of my friends, too often excuse our choice of lovers as irrational or necessary acts, we take the responsibility for whom we've chosen as friends."

Suggestions For Discussion 55
Suggestions For Writing 55

5. PERSONALITY CLASHES 56

1. *Dorothy Parker,* "Good Souls" 56
"It is the Good Souls who efficiently smooth out your pillow when you have just worked it into a comfortable shape, . . . who tenderly lay on your fevered brow damp cloths which drip ceaselessly down your neck."

2. *Samuel Johnson,* "The Good Sort of Woman" 60
"When any of her acquaintance decline in the opinion of the world she always finds it inconvenient to visit them."

Suggestions For Discussion 62
Suggestions For Writing 63

**Part Two YOUTH AND MATURITY** 65

6. THE STAGES OF LIFE 67

1. *Aristotle,* "Young Men and Elderly Men" 68
"They [the elderly] are cowardly, and are always anticipating danger; unlike that of the young, who are warm-blooded, their temperament is chilly; old age has paved the way for cowardice; fear is, in fact, a form of chill."

2. *Simone de Beauvoir,* "Introduction" from *The Coming of Age* 70
"If we do not know what we are going to be, we cannot know what we are: let us recognize ourselves in this old man or in that old woman."

Suggestions For Discussion 75
Suggestions For Writing 75

7. GROWING UP 76

1. *Nora Ephron,* "A Few Words about Breasts" 77
"Even though I was outwardly a girl and had many of the trappings generally associated with the field of girldom — a girl's name, for example, and dresses, my own telephone, an autograph book — I spent the early years of my adolescence absolutely certain that I might at any point gum it up."

2. *E. B. White,* "Afternoon of an American Boy" *82*
"I never went to a school dance and I never took a girl to a drugstore for a soda. . . . What I finally did manage to do, however, and what is the subject of this memoir, was far brassier, far gaudier. As an exhibit of teen-age courage and ineptitude, it never fails to amaze me in retrospect."

Suggestions For Discussion *86*
Suggestions For Writing *86*

8. RAISING CHILDREN *87*

1. *Tillie Olsen,* "I Stand Here Ironing" *87*
"Let her be. So all that is in her will not bloom — but in how many does it? There is still enough left to live by."

2. *Robert Paul Smith,* "Let Your Kids Alone" *93*
"The kids know that any grownup who gets down on all fours and makes mudpies with them is either a spy or a fool."

Suggestions For Discussion *98*
Suggestions For Writing *98*

9. GROWING OLDER *99*

1. *Susan Sontag,* "The Double Standard of Aging" *99*
"Most men experience getting older with regret, apprehension. But most women experience it even more painfully: with shame."

2. *Milton Mayer,* "Commencement Address: What You Will Be" *112*
"You will be tempted to smile when I tell you that I am middle-aged and corrupt. You should resist the temptation. Twenty-five years from now you will be ineluctably middle-aged and, unless you hear and heed what I say today, just as ineluctably corrupt."

Suggestions For Discussion *117*
Suggestions For Writing *118*

**Part Three KNOWLEDGE AND EDUCATION** *119*

10. ATTITUDES TOWARD FORMAL EDUCATION *121*

1. *H. L. Mencken,* "Education" *121*
"The false inference is that there is any sound reason for prohibiting teaching by asses, if only the asses know how to do it, and do it well. The false assumption is that there are no asses in our schools and colleges today."

2. *Lissa Rotundo,* "One-Year-Old Scholars" *126*
"Everyone is encouraged to take courses until death is imminent, and a few years ago it even became fashionable to take courses *about* death, to be sure that one would die properly. Who would want to be caught dead without being prepared for it?"

Suggestions For Discussion *128*
Suggestions For Writing *128*

11. MOTIVATION AND RELUCTANCE *130*

1. *Winston Churchill,* "School Days" *131*
"Where my reason, imagination or interest were not engaged, I would not or I could not learn."

2. *Jean Kerr,* "The Poet and the Peasants" *134*
"As I unfolded The Plan they couldn't have been more horrified if I had suddenly suggested that all of them wear hair ribbons to football practice. Nevertheless, I was adamant."

Suggestions For Discussion *142*
Suggestions For Writing *143*

12. THE COLLEGE ATMOSPHERE *144*

1. *Mary McCarthy,* "The Vassar Girl" *144*
"Almost all of us were joyous to be leaving college, precisely because we had loved it, for Vassar had inspired us with the notion that the wide, wide world was our oyster."

2. *William Zinsser,* "College Pressures" *149*
"They want a map — right now — that they can follow unswervingly to career security, financial security, Social Security and, presumably, a prepaid grave."

Suggestions For Discussion *154*
Suggestions For Writing *155*

13. ULTIMATE GOALS *156*

1. *William G. Perry, Jr.,* "Examsmanship and the Liberal Arts: A Study in Educational Epistemology" *156*
"'But sir, I don't think I really deserve it, it was mostly bull, really.' This disclaimer from a student whose examination we have awarded a straight "A" is wondrously depressing. Alfred North Whitehead invented its only possible rejoinder: 'Yes, sir, what you wrote is nonsense, utter nonsense. But ah! Sir! it's the right *kind* of nonsense!'"

2. *Adrienne Rich,* "Taking Women Students Seriously" *165*
"What has been the student's experience of education in the inadequate . . . public school system, which rewards passivity and treats a questioning attitude or independent mind as a behavior problem?"

Suggestions For Discussion *171*
Suggestions For Writing *171*

**Part Four FREEDOM AND INDIVIDUALITY** *173*

14. SOCIETY AND THE INDIVIDUAL *175*

1. *John Stuart Mill,* "Of Individuality, As One of the Elements of Well-Being" *175*
"The demand that all other people shall resemble ourselves grows by what it feeds on. If resistance waits till life is reduced *nearly* to one uniform type, all deviation from that type will come to be considered impious, immoral, even monstrous and contrary to nature."

2. *Ilse Aichinger,* "The Bound Man" *187*
"In that he remained entirely within the limits set by his rope he was free of it, it did not confine him, but gave him wings and endowed his leaps and jumps with purpose."

Suggestions For Discussion *195*
Suggestions For Writing *196*

15. MINORITY RIGHTS *197*

1. *Martin Luther King, Jr.,* "Letter from Birmingham Jail" *197*
"Any law that uplifts human personality is just. Any law that degrades human personality is unjust. All segregation statutes are unjust because segregation distorts the soul and damages the personality."

2. *Maya Angelou,* "Mama and the Dentist" *209*
"It seemed terribly unfair to have a toothache and a headache and have to bear at the same time the heavy burden of Blackness."

Suggestions For Discussion *213*
Suggestions For Writing *214*

16. PRESCRIBED ROLES *215*

1. *Brigid Brophy,* "Women: Invisible Cages" *215*
"Modern society, like the modern zoo, has contrived to get rid of the bars without altering the fact of imprisonment."

2. *D. Keith Mano,* "Cruel Lib" *220*
"Roles don't limit people; roles protect them. And, yes, most people need protection."

Suggestions For Discussion *222*
Suggestions For Writing *223*

17. SELF-ASSERTION *224*

1. *Manuel J. Smith,* "Assertive Rights" *224*
"You have the right to offer no reasons or excuses to justify your behavior."

2. *Margaret Halsey,* "What's Wrong with 'Me, Me, Me'" *228*
"It will be argued that the cult of "I" has done some individuals a lot of good. But at whose expense? What about the people to whom these 'healthy' egotists are rude or even abusive?"

Suggestions For Discussion *230*
Suggestions For Writing *230*

## Part Five SUCCESS AND FAILURE *231*

### 18. AMBITION: A SKEPTICAL VIEW *233*

1. From Ecclesiastes, King James Version and The Living Bible translation, Chapters 1–3 *234*
"Then I looked on all the works that my hands had wrought; and on the labour that I had laboured to do: and behold, all was vanity and vexation of spirit, and there was no profit under the sun."

"But as I looked at everything I had tried, it was all so useless, a chasing of the wind, and there was nothing really worthwhile anywhere."

2. *Suzanne Britt Jordan,* "That Lean and Hungry Look" *239*
"I like to surround myself with sluggish, inert, easy-going fat people, the kind who believe that if you clean up today, it will just get dirty again tomorrow."

Suggestions For Discussion *240*
Suggestions For Writing *241*

### 19. AMBITION: AN AFFIRMATIVE VIEW *242*

1. *Muriel James* and *Dorothy Jongeward,* "Winners and Losers" *246*
"Each human being is born as something new, something that never existed before. Each is born with a capacity to win at life."

2. *Joseph Epstein,* "The Virtues of Ambition: Some Kind Words for Money, Fame, and Power" *252*
"Some dreams, begun in selflessness, end in rancor; other dreams, begun in selfishness, end in large-heartedness. The unpredictability of the outcome of dreams is no reason to cease dreaming."

Suggestions For Discussion *252*
Suggestions For Writing *253*

### 20. WEALTH AND ACQUISITION *254*

1. *Andrew Carnegie,* "The Gospel of Wealth" *254*
"While the law [of competition] may be sometimes hard for the individual, it is best for the race, because it insures the survival of the fittest."

2. *Anne Morrow Lindbergh,* "Channelled Whelk" *261*
"I mean to lead a simple life, to choose a simple shell I can carry easily — like a hermit crab. But I do not."

Suggestions For Discussion *266*
Suggestions For Writing *266*

### 21. FAME AND RECOGNITION *267*

1. *Daniel J. Boorstin,* "From Hero to Celebrity" *268*
"The hero was distinguished by his achievement; the celebrity by his image or trademark. The hero created himself; the celebrity is created by the media. The hero was a big man; the celebrity is a big name:"

2. *Diana Trilling,* "The Death of Marilyn Monroe" *278*
"The boldness with which she could parade herself and yet never be gross, her sexual flamboyance and bravado which yet breathed an air of mystery and even reticence, her voice which carried such ripe overtones of erotic excitement and yet was the voice of a shy child — these complications were integral to her gift. And they described a young woman trapped in some never-never land of unawareness."

**Suggestions For Discussion** *286*
**Suggestions For Writing** *287*

**22. SELF-FULFILLMENT** *288*

1. *Ellen Goodman,* "Such Empty Options" *288*
"He once described life to me as a kind of one-plate buffet table. If you fill up your plate at the beginning, you won't have any more room at the end of the table. What, he asked earnestly, if the shrimp cocktail is in the last dish?"

2. *John Ciardi,* "Is Everybody Happy?" *290*
"The satisfactions we get from a lifetime depend on how high we choose our difficulties . . . Whatever else happiness may be, it is neither in having nor in being, but in becoming."

**Suggestions For Discussion** *292*
**Suggestions For Writing** *292*

**23. BARRIERS TO SUCCESS** *294*

1. *Loren Eiseley,* "Obituary of a Bone Hunter" *294*
"I am a little bone hunter. I've played this game for a twenty-year losing streak. I used to think it all lay in the odds — that it was luck that made the difference between the big and little bone hunters. Now I'm not so sure any longer."

2. *Virginia Woolf,* "Professions for Women" *300*
"And all these questions, according to the Angel in the House, cannot be dealt with freely and openly by women; they must charm, they must conciliate, they must — to put it bluntly — tell lies if they are to succeed. Thus, whenever I felt the shadow of her wing or the radiance of her halo upon my page, I took up the inkpot and flung it at her."

**Suggestions For Discussion** *304*
**Suggestions For Writing** *304*

**Appendix ESSAYS ON THE WRITING PROCESS** *305*

1. *Joan Didion,* "On Keeping a Notebook" *306*
"We forget all too soon the things we thought we could never forget. . . . It is a good idea, then, to keep in touch, and I suppose that keeping in touch is what notebooks are all about."

2. *Ursula LeGuin,* "Fifteen Vultures, the Strop, and the Old Lady" *311*
"I have never found anywhere, in the domain of art, that you don't have to walk to. . . . Great artists make the roads; good teachers and good companions can point them out. But there ain't no free rides, baby. No hitchhiking."

3. *Jacques Barzun,* "A Writer's Discipline" *313*
"Convince yourself that you are working in clay not marble, on paper not eternal bronze: let that first sentence be as stupid as it wishes."

4. *Gail Godwin,* "The Watcher at the Gates" *319*
"Other writers . . . told me some of the quirks and habits of their Watchers, . . . all of whom seemed passionately dedicated to one goal: rejecting too soon and discriminating too severely."

5. *Richard Mitchell,* "The Worm in the Brain" *321*
"Grammatical forms are *exactly* the things that make us understand the world the way we understand it."

6. *Walker Gibson,* "Hearing Voices: Tough Talk, Sweet Talk, Stuffy Talk" *327*
"The Tough Talker . . . is a man dramatized as centrally concerned with himself — his style is *I*-talk. The Sweet Talker goes out of his way to be nice to us — his style is *you*-talk. The Stuffy Talker expresses no concern either for himself or his reader — his style is *it*-talk."

Notes on Contributors *335*

# Rhetorical Contents

## I. RHETORICAL MODES

### DEFINITION

1. *Esther Vilar,* "What Is Man?" *6*
2. *C. S. Lewis,* "Friendship" *43*
3. *Dorothy Parker,* "Good Souls" *56*
4. *Martin Luther King, Jr.,* "Letter from Birmingham Jail" *197*
5. *John Ciardi,* "Is Everybody Happy?" *290*
6. *Samuel Johnson,* "The Good Sort of Woman" *60*

### NARRATIVE

1. *Ring Lardner,* "Some Like Them Cold" *14*
2. *Lillian Hellman,* "Dashiell Hammett" *34*
3. *Nora Ephron,* "A Few Words about Breasts" *77*
4. *E. B. White,* "Afternoon of an American Boy" *82*
5. *Tillie Olsen,* "I Stand Here Ironing" *87*
6. *Winston Churchill,* "School Days" *131*
7. *Jean Kerr,* "The Poet and the Peasants" *134*
8. *Ilse Aichinger,* "The Bound Man" *187*
9. *Maya Angelou,* "Mama and the Dentist" *209*
10. *Loren Eiseley,* "Obituary of a Bone Hunter" *294*

### DESCRIPTION

1. *Joan Didion,* "On Keeping a Notebook" *306*
2. *Ursula Le Guin,* "Fifteen Vultures, the Strop, and the Old Lady" *311*
3. *Gail Godwin,* "The Watcher at the Gates" *319*
4. *Eldridge Cleaver,* "Prelude to Love — Three Letters" *28*
5. *Dorothy Parker,* "Good Souls" *56*
6. *Mary McCarthy,* "The Vassar Girl" *144*
7. *Suzanne Britt Jordan,* "That Lean and Hungry Look" *239*
8. *Anne Morrow Lindbergh,* "Channelled Whelk" *261*
9. *Samuel Johnson,* "The Good Sort of Woman" *60*

## COMPARISON AND CONTRAST

1. *Susan Sontag,* "The Double Standard of Aging" *99*
2. *Winston Churchill,* "School Days" *131*
3. *Suzanne Britt Jordan,* "That Lean and Hungry Look" *239*
4. *Muriel James* and *Dorothy Jongeward,* "Winners and Losers" *242*
5. *Daniel J. Boorstin,* "From Hero to Celebrity" *208*
6. *Ellen Goodman,* "Such Empty Options" *288*

## CLASSIFICATION AND DIVISION

1. *Walker Gibson,* "Hearing Voices: Tough Talk, Sweet Talk, Stuffy Talk" *327*
2. *Aristotle,* "Young Men and Elderly Men" *68*
3. *William Zinsser,* "College Pressures" *149*

## ANALYSIS

1. *Jacques Barzun,* "A Writer's Discipline" *313*
2. *Richard Mitchell,* "The Worm in the Brain" *321*
3. *Walker Gibson,* "Hearing Voices: Tough Talk, Sweet Talk, Stuffy Talk" *327*
4. *C. S. Lewis,* "Friendship" *43*
5. *Susan Lee,* "Friendship, Feminism, and Betrayal" *50*
6. *Susan Sontag,* "The Double Standard of Aging" *99*
7. *William G. Perry, Jr.,* "Examsmanship and the Liberal Arts: A Study in Educational Epistemology" *156*
8. *Joseph Epstein,* "The Virtues of Ambition: Some Kind Words for Money, Fame, and Power" *246*
9. *Daniel J. Boorstin,* "From Hero to Celebrity" *268*
10. *Diana Trilling,* "The Death of Marilyn Monroe" *278*
11. *Virginia Woolf,* "Professions for Women" *300*

## ARGUMENT AND PERSUASION

1. *Alan Alda,* "What Every Woman Should Know about Men" *3*
2. *Dorothy Sayers,* "The Human-Not-Quite-Human" *10*
3. *Simone de Beauvoir,* "The Coming of Age" *70*
4. *Robert Paul Smith,* "Let Your Kids Alone" *93*
5. *Milton Mayer,* "Commencement Address: What You Will Be" *112*
6. *H. L. Mencken,* "Education" *121*
7. *William Zinsser,* "College Pressures" *149*
8. *Adrienne Rich,* "Taking Women Students Seriously" *165*
9. *John Stuart Mill,* "Of Individuality, As One of the Elements of Well-Being" *175*
10. *Martin Luther King, Jr.,* "Letter from Birmingham Jail" *197*
11. *Brigid Brophy,* "Women: Invisible Cages" *215*
12. *D. Keith Mano,* "Cruel Lib" *220*

13. *Manuel J. Smith,* "Assertive Rights" *224*
14. *Margaret Halsey,* "What's Wrong with 'Me, Me, Me'" *228*
15. *Andrew Carnegie,* "The Gospel of Wealth" *254*
16. *Ellen Goodman,* "Such Empty Options" *288*

## II. SOME ELEMENTS OF STYLE

### IRONY AND SATIRE

1. *Alan Alda,* "What Every Woman Should Know about Men" *3*
2. *Ring Lardner,* "Some Like Them Cold" *14*
3. *Dorothy Sayers,* "The Human-Not-Quite-Human" *10*
4. *Dorothy Parker,* "Good Souls" *56*
5. *H. L. Mencken,* "Education" *121*
6. *Lissa Rotundo,* "One-Year-Old Scholars" *126*

### FIGURATIVE LANGUAGE

1. *Ursula Le Guin,* "Fifteen Vultures, the Strop, and the Old Lady" *311*
2. *Richard Mitchell,* "The Worm in the Brain" *321*
3. *Gail Godwin,* "The Watcher at the Gates" *319*
4. *Eldridge Cleaver,* "Prelude to Love — Three Letters" *28*
5. *Ilse Aichinger,* "The Bound Man" *187*
6. *Brigid Brophy,* "Women: Invisible Cages" *215*
7. Ecclesiastes, Chapters 1–3 *234*
8. *Jordan,* "That Lean and Hungry Look" *239*
9. *Anne Morrow Lindbergh,* "Channelled Whelk" *261*
10. *Virginia Woolf,* "Professions for Women" *300*

### PARALLEL STRUCTURE AND BALANCE

1. *Aristotle,* "Young Men and Elderly Men" *68*
2. *John Stuart Mill,* "Of Individuality, As One of the Elements of Well-Being" *175*
3. *Martin Luther King, Jr.,* "Letter from Birmingham Jail" *197*
4. *Joseph Epstein,* "The Virtues of Ambition: Some Kind Words for Money, Fame, and Power" *246*
5. *Daniel J. Boorstin,* "From Hero to Celebrity" *268*
6. *Samuel Johnson,* "The Good Sort of Woman" *60*

### REPETITION AND EMPHASIS

1. *Tillie Olsen,* "I Stand Here Ironing" *87*
2. *Milton Mayer,* "Commencement Address: What You Will Be" *112*
3. Ecclesiastes, Chapters 1–3 *234*
4. *Loren Eiseley,* "Obituary of a Bone Hunter" *294*

# *Part One*

# FRIENDS AND LOVERS

*The beings closest to us are often virtually our interpreters of the world.*

—GEORGE ELIOT

Each of us has a special view of the world that is, to some degree, ours alone. But our relationships with other people also influence the way we see ourselves and the way we see our surroundings. While we live as separate selves with our own unique vision, we are constantly viewing things through the eyes of others, as in a series of mirrors. Society is one of those mirrors. It offers us a view of the world and a view of ourselves that occasionally seems honest, but it often distorts the images we have. Like the mirrors at a carnival, it presents us with a series of shapes which we often view as inaccurate or only partial portrayals of reality. We are not that short, not that fat, not that angular. Life is not that easy, not that tough, not that predictable.

The other mirror in which we see ourselves and our surroundings is the image projected by our companions, friends, and lovers. We see a different world through the eyes of our friends. Sometimes that image seems true and sometimes distorted, but it always has an effect on us. In either subtle or profound ways, we must deal with the images and messages that come to us from others. We must either accept these perspectives or else combat them with alternative views of our own. This part of the book explores some of the ways in which our companions oppose, modify, or share our perceptions.

The first four essays examine various social images of men and women and the patterns of feminine and masculine behavior that often result. The essayists in this section discuss and criticize specific concepts of masculinity or femininity. The remaining six essays present personal experiences: love, friendship, and personality clashes. In this section there are witty, affectionate, philosophical, and even cynical portraits of personal relationships.

These essays remind us that all of us are many people at once: men or women, friends, enemies, companions, and lovers. The social images we confront influence us in our understanding of these special roles. And the experiences we share with other people, whether pleasant or unpleasant, become crucial factors in the shaping of our lives.

# 1

# Concepts of Masculinity

*Alan Alda*

## "WHAT EVERY WOMAN SHOULD KNOW ABOUT MEN"

*Esther Vilar*

## "WHAT IS MAN?"

Alan Alda and Esther Vilar address two totally different concepts of masculinity. Alda writes about "testosterone poisoning" and its disastrous effects on men. Using a clinical tone and spoofing self-help magazine articles, Alda constructs a test to aid in diagnosing the "ailment" called masculinity. He then proceeds to give advice to both men and women about how to cure the disease that causes men to torment women. Vilar, in contrast, presents women as the tormentors of men. She sees the concept of masculinity as one invented by women to make men take "pleasure in non-freedom." In this essay she discusses men's clothes and their obsession with work as evidence of the dominance of women.

*Alan Alda*

## "WHAT EVERY WOMAN SHOULD KNOW ABOUT MEN"

Everyone knows that testosterone, the so-called male hormone, is found in both men and women. What is not so well known is that men have an overdose.

Until now it has been thought that the level of testosterone in men is normal simply because they have it. But if you consider how abnormal their *behavior* is, then you are led to the hypothesis that almost all men are suffering from *testosterone poisoning.*

The symptoms are easy to spot. Sufferers are reported to show an early preference (while still in the crib) for geometric shapes. Later, they become obsessed with machinery and objects to the exclusion of human values. They have an intense need to rank everything, and are obsessed with size. (At some point in his life, nearly every male measures his penis.)

It is well known that men don't look like other people. They have chicken legs. This is symptomatic of the disease, as is the fact that those men with the most aviary underpinnings will rank women according to the shapeliness of *their* legs.

The pathological violence of most men hardly needs to be mentioned. They are responsible for more wars than any other leading sex.

Testosterone poisoning is particularly cruel because its sufferers usually don't know they have it. In fact, when they are most under its sway they believe that they are at their healthiest and most attractive. They even give each other medals for exhibiting the most advanced symptoms of the illness.

But there is hope.

Sufferers can change (even though it is harder than learning to walk again). They must first realize, however, that they are sick. The fact that this condition is inherited in the same way that dimples are does not make it cute.

Eventually, of course, telethons and articles in the *Reader's Digest* will dramatize the tragedy of testosterone poisoning. In the meantime, it is imperative for your friends and loved ones to become familiar with the danger signs.

*Have the men you know take this simple test for—*

## THE SEVEN WARNING SIGNS OF TESTOSTERONE POISONING

1. *Do you have an intense need to win?* When having sex, do you take pride in always finishing before your partner? Do you always ask if this time was "the best"—and gnaw on the bedpost if you get an ambiguous answer?

2. *Does violence play a big part in your life?* Before you answer, count up how many hours you watched football, ice hockey, and children's cartoons this year on television. When someone crosses you, do you wish you could stuff his face full of your fist? Do you ever poke people in your fantasies or throw them to and fro at all? When someone cuts you off in traffic, do violent, angry curses come bubbling out of your mouth before you know it? If so, you're in big trouble, fella, and this is only question number two.

3. *Are you "thing" oriented?* Do you value the parts of a woman's body more than the woman herself? Are you turned on by things that even *remind* you of those parts? Have you ever fallen in love with a really great doorknob?

4. *Do you have an intense need to reduce every difficult situation to charts and figures?* If you were present at a riot, would you tend to count the crowd? If your wife is despondent over a deeply felt setback that has left her feeling helpless, do you take her temperature?

5. *Do you tend to measure things that are really qualitative?* Are you more impressed with how high a male ballet dancer can leap than with what he does while he's up there? Are you more concerned with how long you can spend in bed, and with how many

orgasms you can have, than you are with how you or your partner feels while you're there?

**6.** *Are you a little too mechanically minded?* Would you like to watch a sunset with a friend and feel at one with nature and each other, or would you rather take apart a clock?

**7.** *Are you easily triggered into competition?* When someone tries to pass you on the highway, do you speed up a little? Do you find yourself getting into contests of crushing beer cans—with the beer still in them?

If you've answered yes to three or fewer of the above questions, you may be learning to deal with your condition. A man answering yes to more than three is considered sick and not someone you'd want to have around in a crisis — such as raising children or growing old together. Anyone answering yes to all seven of the questions should seek help immediately before he kills himself in a high-wire act.

## WHAT TO DO IF YOU SUFFER FROM TESTOSTERONE POISONING

**1.** *Don't panic.* Your first reaction may be that you are sicker than anyone else—or that you are the one man in the world able to fight it off—or, knowing that you are a sufferer, that you are the one man ordained to lead others to health (such as by writing articles about it). These are all symptoms of the disease. Just relax. First, sit back and enjoy yourself. Then find out how to enjoy somebody else.

**2.** *Try to feel something.* (Not with your hands, you oaf.) Look at a baby and see if you can appreciate it. (Not how *big* it's getting, just how nice she or he is.) See if you can get yourself to cry by some means other than getting hit in the eye or losing a lot of money.

**3.** *See if you can listen while someone is talking.* Were you the one talking? Perhaps you haven't got the idea yet.

**4.** *Practice this sentence:* "You know, I think you're right and I'm wrong." (Hint: it is useful to know what the other person thinks before you say this.)

## FOR WOMEN ONLY: WHAT TO DO IF YOU ARE LIVING WITH A SUFFERER

**1.** Remember that a little sympathy is a dangerous thing. The sufferer will be inclined to interpret any concern for him as appropriate submissiveness.

**2.** Let him know that you expect him to fight his way back to health and behave like a normal person — for his own sake, not for yours.

**3.** Only after he begins to get his condition under control and has actually begun to enjoy life should you let him know that there is no such thing as testosterone poisoning.

## *Esther Vilar*

# "WHAT IS MAN?"

A man is a human being who works. By working, he supports himself, his wife, and his wife's children. A woman, on the other hand, is a human being who does not work—or at least only occasionally. Most of her life she supports neither herself nor her children, let alone her husband.

Any qualities in a man that a woman finds useful, she calls *masculine;* all others, of no use to her or to anyone else for that matter, she chooses to call *effeminate.* A man's appearance has to be *masculine* if he wants to have success with women, and that means it will have to be geared to his one and only *raison d'être*—work. His appearance must conform to each and every task put to him, and he must always be able to fulfill it.

Except at night when the majority of men wear striped pajamas with at most two pairs of pockets, men wear a kind of uniform made of durable, stain-resistant material in brown, blue, or gray. These uniforms, or "suits," have up to ten pockets, in which men carry instruments and tools indispensable for their work. Since a woman does not work, her night or day clothes rarely have pockets.

For social events men are permitted to wear black, a color that shows marks and stains, since on those occasions men are less likely to dirty themselves. Moreover, the bright colors worn by women show to advantage against it. The occasional red or green evening jackets worn by men are acceptable, since, by contrast, all the real men present seem so much more masculine.

The rest of a man's appearance is also adapted to his situation. His hair style requires only fifteen minutes at the barber every two or three weeks. Curls, waves, and tints are not encouraged as they might hinder his work. Men often work in the open air or spend a considerable amount of time in it, hence complicated styles would be a nuisance. Furthermore, it is improbable that such styles would make a hit with women since, unlike men, they never judge the opposite sex from an aesthetic point of view. So most men, after one or two attempts at individuality, realize that women are indifferent to their efforts and revert to a standard style, short or long. The same is true of beards. Only oversensitive men—usually ones with intellectual pretensions—who want to appear mentally tough by letting their facial hair grow indiscriminately wear a full beard for any length of time. It will be tolerated by women, however, for a beard is an important indication of a man's character and therefore of the way in which he might be most easily exploited. (His field of work will usually be that of the neurotic intellectual.)

Generally a man uses an electric razor for about three minutes every morning to keep his beard in check. For his skin, soap and water are considered good enough. All that is required is cleanliness and an absence of make-up so that everyone can see what he is like. As for his fingernails, they should be as short as possible for work.

Apart from a wedding ring—worn to show that he is already being used by a particular woman for a particular purpose—a proper man wears no ornaments. His clumsy, functional watch, worn on the wrist, is hardly decorative. Heavy in design, waterproof, shock-resistant, showing the correct date, it cannot possibly be called an ornament. Usually it was given to him by the woman for whom he works.

Shirts, underwear, and socks for real men are so standardized that their only difference is one of size. They can be bought in any shop without difficulty or loss of time. Only in ties is there any degree of freedom—and then a man is usually so unused to choosing that he lets his woman buy them for him.

Anyone visiting this earth from another planet would think it each man's goal to look as much like the next as possible. Yet, to fulfill woman's purposes, masculinity and male usefulness vary to a considerable degree: necessarily, because women, who hardly ever work, need men for everything.

There are men who carefully maneuver a large limousine out of the garage at eight o'clock every morning. Others leave an hour earlier, traveling in a middle-class sedan. Still others leave when it is not yet light, wearing overalls and carrying lunch boxes, to catch buses, subways, or trains to factories or building sites. By a trick of fate, it is always the latter, the poorest, who are exploited by the least attractive women. For, unlike women (who have an eye for money), men notice only woman's external appearance. Therefore, the more desirable women in their own class are always being snatched out from under their noses by men who happen to earn more.

No matter what a particular man does or how he spends his day, he has one thing in common with all other men—he spends it in a degrading manner. And he himself does not gain by it. It is not his own livelihood that matters: he would have to struggle far less for that, since luxuries do not mean anything to him anyway. It is the fact that he does it for others that makes him so tremendously proud. He will undoubtedly have a photograph of his wife and children on his desk, and will miss no opportunity to hand it around.

No matter what a man's job may be—bookkeeper, doctor, bus driver, or managing director—every moment of his life will be spent as a cog in a huge and pitiless system—a system designed to exploit him to the utmost, to his dying day.

It may be interesting to add up figures and make them tally—but surely not year in, year out? How exciting it must be to drive a bus through a busy town! But always the same route, at the same time, in the same town, day after day, year after year? What a magnificent feeling of power to know that countless workers move at one's command! But how would one feel if one suddenly realized one was their prisoner and not their master?

We have long ceased to play the games of childhood. As children, we became bored quickly and changed from one game to another. A man is like a child who is condemned to play the same game for the rest of his life. The reason is obvious: as soon as he is discovered to have a gift for one thing, he is made to specialize. Then, because he can earn more money in that field than another, he is forced to do it forever. If he was good at arithmetic in school, if he had a "head for figures," he will be sentenced to a lifetime of figure work as bookkeeper, mathematician, or computer operator, for there lies his maximum work potential. Therefore, he will add up figures, press buttons, and add up more figures, but he will never be able to say, "I'm bored. I want to do something else!" The woman who is exploiting him will never permit him to look for something else. Driven by this woman, he may engage in a desperate struggle against competitors, to improve his position, and perhaps even become head clerk or managing director of a bank. But isn't the price he is paying for his improved salary rather too high?

A man who changes his way of life, or rather his profession (for life and profession are synonymous to him), is considered unreliable. If he does it more than once, he becomes a social outcast and remains alone.

The fear of being rejected by society must be considerable. Why else will a doctor (who as a child liked to observe tadpoles in jam jars,) spend his life opening up nauseating growths, examining and pronouncing on human excretions? Why else does he busy himself night and day with people of such repulsiveness that everyone else is driven away? Does a pianist who, as a child, liked to tinkle on the piano really enjoy playing the same Chopin nocturne over and over again all his life? Why else does a politician who as a schoolboy discovered the techniques of manipulating people successfully continue as an adult, mouthing words and phrases as a minor government functionary? Does he actually enjoy contorting his face and playing the fool and listening to the idiotic chatter of other politicians? Surely he must once have dreamed of a different kind of life. Even if he became President of the United States, wouldn't the price be too high?

No, one can hardly assume men do all this for pleasure and without feeling a desire for change. They do it because they have been *manipulated* into doing it: their whole life is nothing but a series of conditioned reflexes, a series of animal acts. A man who is no longer able to perform these acts, whose earning capacity is lessened, is considered a failure. He stands to lose everything—wife, family, home, his whole purpose in life—all the things, in fact, which give him security.

Of course one might say that a man who has lost his capacity for earning money is automatically freed from his burden and should be glad about this happy ending—but freedom is the last thing he wants. He functions, as we shall see, according to the principle of *pleasure in non-freedom*. To be sentenced to life-long freedom is a worse fate than life-long slavery.

To put it another way: man is always searching for someone or something to enslave him, for only as a slave does he feel secure—and, as a rule, his choice falls on a woman. Who or what is this creature who is responsible for his lowly existence and who, moreover, exploits him in such a way that he only feels safe as her slave, *and her slave alone?*

## SUGGESTIONS FOR DISCUSSION

1. Alda's article appeared in *Ms.* magazine, and Vilar's essay is taken from her book, *The Manipulated Man.* Think first about their purposes: What does Alda expect or hope readers will do after they read his article? What does Vilar hope her readers will do?
2. One can often determine people's values by knowing what they are *against*. Alda and Vilar are quite explicit about the forms of behavior they dislike. What human qualities do you think they admire?

3. A useful concept in writing is the *persona:* the image projected by the writer or speaker. Every knowledgeable writer chooses a role that is appropriate to the situation and audience that he or she is dealing with. The word *persona* is derived from the Greek word for "mask" and recalls the ancient Greek actors who adoped different masks as they changed roles. Similarly, a writer or speaker may adopt a light-hearted *persona* on one occasion and a *persona* that is deeply concerned on another, depending on the circumstances.

   Without rereading, jot down six adjectives that describe the *persona* of the Alda piece, then six for the Vilar piece. Now go back to each essay and try to figure out where in the text you got the impressions you did. Most of you knew who Alda was; on the other hand, few of you knew Vilar. Did those circumstances influence your understanding of how to read them?
4. Both authors define, at least indirectly, masculinity. Does Vilar treat it as a natural characteristic or as something that is socially conditioned? Compare her definition to Alda's.

## SUGGESTIONS FOR WRITING

1. Both Alda's and Vilar's essays attack the way men behave in our culture. Alda depicts them as "diseased": self-centered, insensitive, blindly macho. Vilar is more sympathetic: men are enslaved, trapped, victimized. Imagine yourself to be a kind of mediator, a person whose job it is to bring people of disparate opinions together by pointing out the similarities of their positions and helping them reach compromises on their differences. Now, in writing, address yourself to Alda and Vilar in a session where, you hope, you can produce a model for male behavior that will please both. Feel free to address them directly: "Mr. Alda, you say here that . . . "
2. Alda is obviously writing a parody of the "self-help" articles that appear in popular magazines. Write a similar parody, diagnosing what you consider to be some of the more unattractive feminine traits. (You may use the term "estrogen-poisoning" if you wish.)

# 2

# Concepts of Femininity

*Dorothy Sayers*

"THE HUMAN-NOT-QUITE-HUMAN"

*Ring Lardner*

"SOME LIKE THEM COLD"

Complementing the views of masculinity presented by Alda and Vilar, Dorothy Sayers and Ring Lardner present equally divergent views of femininity. Sayers contends that society views women as a separate species. She uses witty language and clever examples to make a serious and seemingly obvious point: women should be allowed to join the human race. Lardner's short story reveals the destructive quality of gender stereotypes. In the letters of Charles and Mabelle, the reader sees the characters acting a series of roles and never presenting themselves as they really are.

## *Dorothy Sayers*
## "THE HUMAN-NOT-QUITE-HUMAN"

The first thing that strikes the careless observer is that women are unlike men. They are the "opposite sex"—(though why "opposite" I do not know; what is the "neighbouring sex"?). But the fundamental thing is that women are more like men than anything else in the world. They are human beings. *Vir* is male and *Femina* is female: but *Homo* is male and female.

This is the equality claimed and the fact that is persistently evaded and denied. No matter what arguments are used, the discussion is vitiated from the start, because Man is always dealt with as both *Homo* and *Vir,* but Woman only as *Femina*. . . .

Probably no man has ever troubled to imagine how strange his life would appear to himself if it were unrelentingly assessed in terms of his maleness; if everything he wore, said, or did had to be justified by reference to female approval; if he were compelled to regard himself, day in day out, not as a member of society, but merely . . . as a virile member of society. If the centre of his dress-consciousness were the cod-piece, his education directed to making him a spirited lover and meek paterfamilias; his interests held to be natural only insofar as they were sexual. If from school and lecture-room, press and pulpit, he heard the persistent outpouring of a shrill and scolding voice, bidding him remember his biological function. If he were vexed by continual advice how to add a rough male touch to his typing, how to be learned without losing his masculine appeal, how to combine chemical research with education, how to play bridge without incurring the suspicion of impotence. If, instead of allowing with a smile that "women prefer cavemen," he felt the unrelenting pressure of a whole social structure forcing him to order all his goings in conformity with that pronouncement.

He would hear (and would he like hearing?) the female counterpart of Dr. Peck (Dr. Peck had disclaimed adherence to the *Kinder, Kirche, Küche* school of thought) informing him: "I am no supporter of the Horseback Hall doctrine of 'gun-tail, plough-tail and stud' as the only spheres for masculine action; but we do need a more definite conception of the nature and scope of man's life." In any book on sociology he would find, after the main portion dealing with human needs and rights, a supplementary chapter devoted to "The Position of the Male in the Perfect State." His newspaper would assist him with a "Men's Corner," telling him how, by the expenditure of a good deal of money and a couple of hours a day, he could attract the girls and retain his wife's affection; and when he had succeeded in capturing a mate, his name would be taken from him, and society would present him with a special title to proclaim his achievement. People would write books called, "History of the Male," or "Males of the Bible," or "The Psychology of the Male," and he would be regaled daily with headlines, such as "Gentleman-Doctor's Discovery," "Male-Secretary Wins Calcutta Sweep," "Men-Artists at the Academy." If he gave an interview to a reporter, or performed any unusual exploit, he would find it recorded in such terms as these: "Professor Bract, although a distinguished botanist, is not in any way an unmanly man. He has, in fact, a wife and seven children. Tall and burly, the hands with which he handles his delicate specimens are as gnarled and powerful as those of a Canadian lumberjack, and when I swilled beer with him in his laboratory, he bawled his conclusions at me in a strong, gruff voice that implemented the promise of his swaggering moustache." Or: "There is nothing in the least feminine about the home surroundings of Mr. Focus, the famous children's photographer. His 'den' is paneled in teak and decorated with rude sculptures from Easter Island; over his austere iron bedstead hangs a fine reproduction of the Rape of the Sabines." Or: "I asked M. Sapristi, the renowned chef, whether kitchen-cult was not a rather unusual occupation for a man. 'Not a bit of it!, he replied, bluffly. 'It is the genius that counts, not the sex. As they say in *la belle Écosse,* a man's a man for a' that'—and his gusty, manly guffaw blew three small patty pans from the dresser."

He would be edified by solemn discussions about "Should Men Serve in Drapery Establishments?" and acrimonious ones about "Tea-Drinking Men"; by cross-shots of public affairs, "From the Masculine Angle," and by irritable correspondence about men who expose their anatomy on beaches (so masculine of them), conceal it in dressing gowns (too feminine of them), think about nothing but women, pretend an unnatural indifference to women, exploit their sex to get jobs, lower the tone of the office by their sexless appearance, and generally fail to please a public opinion which demands the incompatible. And at dinner-parties he would hear the wheedling, unctuous, predatory female voice demand: "And why should you trouble your handsome little head about politics?"

If, after a few centuries of this kind of treatment, the male was a little self-conscious, a little on the defensive, and a little bewildered about what was required of him, I should not blame him. If he traded a little upon his sex, I could forgive him. If he presented the world with a major social problem, I would scarcely be surprised. It would be more surprising if he retained any rag of sanity and self-respect.

"The rights of woman," says Dr. Peck, "considered in the economic sphere, seem to involve her in competition with men in the struggle for jobs." It does seem so indeed, and this is hardly to be wondered at; for the competition began to appear when the men took over the women's jobs by transferring them from the home to the factory. The medieval woman had effective power and a measure of real (though not political) equality, for she had control of many industries—spinning, weaving, baking, brewing, distilling, perfumery, preserving, pickling—in which she worked with head as well as hands, in command of her own domestic staff. But now the control and direction—all the intelligent part—of those industries have gone to the men, and the women have been left, not with their "proper" *work* but with *employment* in those occupations. And at the same time, they are exhorted to be feminine and return to the home from which all intelligent occupation has been steadily removed.

There has never been any question but that the women of the poor should toil alongside their men. No angry, and no compassionate, voice has been raised to say that women should not break their backs with harvest work, or soil their hands with blacking grates and peeling potatoes. The objection is only to work that is pleasant, exciting or profitable—the work that any human being might think it worth while to do. The boast, "My wife doesn't need to soil her hands with work," first became general when the commercial middle classes acquired the plutocratic and aristocratic notion that the keeping of an idle woman was a badge of superior social status. Man must work, and woman must exploit his labour. What else are they there for? And if the woman submits, she can be cursed for her exploitation; and if she rebels, she can be cursed for competing with the male: whatever she does will be wrong, and that is a great satisfaction.

The men who attribute all the ills of *Homo* to the industrial age yet accept it as the norm for the relations of the sexes. But the brain, that great and sole true Androgyne, that can mate indifferently with male or female and beget offspring upon itself, the cold brain laughs at their perversions of history. The period from which we are emerging was like no other: a period when empty head and idle hands were qualities for which a man prized his woman and despised her. When, by an odd, sadistic twist of morality, sexual intercourse was deemed to be a marital right to be religiously enforced upon a meek reluctance—as though the insatiable appetite of wives were not one of the oldest jokes in the world. . . . When to think of sex was considered indelicate in a woman, and to think about anything else unfeminine. When to "manage" a husband by lying and the exploitation of sex was held to be honesty and virtue. When the education that Thomas More gave his daughters was denounced as a devilish indulgence, and could only be wrung from the outraged holder of the purse-strings by tears and martyrdom and desperate revolt, in the teeth of the world's mockery and the reprobation of a scandalised Church.

What is all this tenderness about women herded into factories? Is it much more than an excuse for acquiescing in the profitable herding of men? The wrong is inflicted upon *Homo*. There are temperaments suited to herding and temperaments that are not; but the dividing lines do not lie exactly along the sexual boundary. The Russians, it seems, have begun to realise this; but are revolution and blood the sole educational means for getting this plain fact into our heads?

Women are not human. They lie when they say they have human needs: warm and decent clothing; comfort in the bus; interests directed immediately to God and His universe, not intermediately through any child of man. They are far above men to inspire him, far beneath him to corrupt him; they have feminine minds and feminine natures, but their mind is not one with their nature like the minds of men; they have no human mind and no human nature. "Blessed be God," says the Jew, "that hath not made me a woman."

God, of course, may have His own opinion, but the Church is reluctant to endorse it. I think I have never heard a sermon preached on the story of Martha and Mary that did not attempt, somehow, somewhere, to explain away its text. Mary's, of course, was the better part—the Lord said so, and we must not precisely contradict Him. But we will be careful not to despise Martha. No doubt, He approved of her too. We could not get on without her, and indeed (having paid lip-service to God's opinion) we must admit that we greatly prefer her. For Martha was doing a really feminine job, whereas Mary was just behaving like any other disciple, male or female; and that is a hard pill to swallow.

Perhaps it is no wonder that the women were first at the Cradle and last at the Cross. They had never known a man like this Man—there never has been such another. A prophet and teacher who never nagged at them, never flattered or coaxed or patronised; who never made arch jokes about them, never treated them either as "The women, God help us!" or "The ladies, God bless them!"; who rebuked without querulousness and praised without condescension; who took their questions and arguments seriously; who never mapped out their sphere for them, never urged them to be feminine or jeered at them for being female; who had no axe to grind and no uneasy male dignity to defend; who took them as he found them, and was completely unself-conscious. There is no act, no sermon, no parable in the whole Gospel that borrows its pungency from female perversity; nobody could possibly guess from the words and deeds of Jesus that there was anything "funny" about woman's nature.

But we might easily deduce it from His contemporaries, and from His prophets before Him, and from His Church to this day. Women are not human; nobody shall persuade us that they are human; let them say what they like, we will not believe it, though One rose from the dead.

## *Ring Lardner*
# "SOME LIKE THEM COLD"

*N. Y., Aug. 3.*

Dear Miss Gillespie: How about our bet now as you bet me I would forget all about you the minute I hit the big town and would never write you a letter. Well girlie it looks like you lose so pay me. Seriously we will call all bets off as I am not the kind that bet on a sure thing and it sure was a sure thing that I would not forget a girlie like you and all that is worrying me is whether it may not be the other way round and you are wondering who this fresh guy is that is writeing you this letter. I bet you are so will try and refreshen your memory.

Well girlie I am the handsome young man that was wondering round the Lasalle st. station Monday and "happened" to sit down beside of a mighty pretty girlie who was waiting to meet her sister from Toledo and the train was late and I am glad of it because if it had not of been that little girlie and I would never of met. So for once I was a lucky guy but still I guess it was time I had some luck as it was certainly tough luck for you and I to both be liveing in Chi all that time and never get together till a half hour before I was leaveing town for good.

Still "better late than never" you know and maybe we can make up for lost time though it looks like we would have to do our makeing up at long distants unless you make good on your threat and come to N.Y. I wish you would do that little thing girlie as it looks like that was the only way we would get a chance to play round together as it looks like they was little or no chance of me comeing back to Chi as my whole future is in the big town. N.Y. is the only spot and specially for a man that expects to make my liveing in the song writeing game as here is the Mecca for that line of work and no matter how good a man may be they don't get no recognition unless they live in N.Y.

Well girlie you asked me to tell you all about my trip. Well I remember you saying that you would give anything to be makeing it yourself but as far as the trip itself was conserned you ought to be thankfull you did not have to make it as you would of sweat your head off. I know I did specially wile going through Ind. Monday P.M. but Monday night was the worst of all trying to sleep and finely I give it up and just layed there with the prespiration rolling off of me though I was laying on top of the covers and nothing on but my underwear.

Yesterday was not so bad as it rained most of the A.M. comeing through N.Y. state and in the P.M. we road along side of the Hudson all P.M. Some river girlie and just looking at it makes a man forget all about the heat and everything else except a certain girlie who I seen for the first time Monday and then only for a half hour but she is the kind of a girlie that a man don't need to see her only once and they would be no danger of forgetting her. There I guess I better lay off that subject or you will think I am a "fresh guy."

Well that is about all to tell you about the trip only they was one amuseing incidence that come off yesterday which I will tell you. Well they was a dame got on the train at Toledo Monday and had the birth opp. mine but I did not see nothing of her that night as I was out smokeing till late and she hit the hay early but yesterday A.M. she come in the dinner and sit at the same table with me and tried to make me and it was so raw that the dinge waiter seen it and give me the wink and of course I paid no tension and I waited till she got through so as they would be no danger of her folling me out but she stopped on the way out to get a tooth pick and when I come out she was out on the platform with it so I tried to brush right by but she spoke up and asked me what time it was and I told her and she said she guessed her watch was slow so I said maybe it just seemed slow on acct. of the company it was in.

I don't know if she got what I was driveing at or not but any way she give up trying to make me and got off at Albany. She was a good looker but I have no time for gals that tries to make strangers on a train.

Well if I don't quit you will think I am writeing a book but will expect a long letter in answer to this letter and we will see if you can keep your promise like I have kept mine. Don't dissapoint me girlie as I am all alone in a large city and hearing from you will keep me from getting home sick for old Chi though I never thought so much of the old town till I found out you lived there. Don't think that is kidding girlie as I mean it.

You can address me at this hotel as it looks like I will be here right along as it is on 47th st. right off of old Broadway and handy to everything and am only paying $21 per wk. for my rm. and could of got one for $16 but without bath but am glad to pay the differents as am lost without my bath in the A.M. and sometimes at night too.

Tomorrow I expect to commence fighting the "battle of Broadway" and will let you know how I come out that is if you answer this letter. In the mean wile girlie au reservoir and don't do nothing I would not do.

Your new friend (?)
Chas. F. Lewis.

*Chicago, Ill., Aug. 6.*

My Dear Mr. Lewis: Well, that certainly was a "surprise party" getting your letter and you are certainly a "wonder man" to keep your word as I am afraid most men of your sex are gay deceivers but maybe you are "different." Any way it sure was a surprise and will gladly pay the bet if you will just tell me what it was we bet. Hope it was not money as I am a "working girl" but if it was not more than a dollar or two will try to dig it up even if I have to "beg, borrow or steal."

Suppose you will think me a "case" to make a bet and then forget what it was, but you must remember, Mr. Man, that I had just met you and was "dazzled." Joking aside I was rather "fussed" and will tell you why. Well, Mr. Lewis, I suppose you see lots of girls like the one you told me about that you saw on the train who tried to "get acquainted" but I want to assure you that I am not one of those kind and sincerely hope you will believe me when I tell you that you was the first man I ever spoke to meeting them like that and my friends and the people who know me would simply faint if they knew I ever spoke to a man without a "proper introduction."

Believe me, Mr. Lewis, I am not that kind and I don't know now why I did it only that you was so "different" looking if you know what I mean and not at all like the kind of men that usually try to force their attentions on every pretty girl they see.

Lots of times I act on impulse and let my feelings run away from me and sometimes I do things on the impulse of the moment which I regret them later on, and that is what I did this time, but hope you won't give me cause to regret it and I know you won't as I know you are not that kind of a man a specially after what you told me about the girl on the train. But any way as I say, I was in a "daze" so can't remember what it was we bet, but will try and pay it if it does not "break" me.

Sis's train got in about ten minutes after yours had gone and when she saw me what do you think was the first thing she said? Well, Mr. Lewis, she said: "Why Mibs (That is a pet name some of my friends have given me) what has happened to you? I never seen you have as much color." So I passed it off with some remark about the heat and changed the subject as I certainly was not going to tell her that I had just been talking to a man who I had never met or she would of dropped dead from the shock. Either that or she would not of believed me as it would be hard for a person who knows me well to imagine me doing a thing like that as I have quite a reputation for "squelching" men who try to act fresh. I don't mean anything personal by that, Mr. Lewis, as am a good judge of character and could tell without you telling me that you are not that kind.

Well, Sis and I have been on the "go" ever since she arrived as I took yesterday and today off so I could show her the "sights" though she says she would be perfectly satisfied to just sit in the apartment and listen to me "rattle on." Am afraid I am a great talker, Mr. Lewis, but Sis says it is as good as a show to hear me talk as I tell things in such a different way as I cannot help from seeing the humorous side of everything and she says she never gets tired of listening to me, but of course she is my sister and thinks the world of me, but she really does laugh like she enjoyed my craziness.

Maybe I told you that I have a tiny little apartment which a girl friend of mine and I have together and it is hardly big enough to turn round in, but still it is "home" and I am a great home girl and hardly ever care to go out evenings except occasionally to the theatre or dance. But even if our "nest" is small we are proud of it and Sis complimented us on how cozy it is and how "homey" it looks and she said she did not see how we could afford to have everything so nice and Edith (my girl friend) said: "Mibs deserves all the credit for that. I never knew a girl who could make a little money go a long ways like she can." Well, of course she is my best friend and always saying nice things about me, but I do try and I hope I get results. Have always said that good taste and being careful is a whole lot more important than lots of money though it is nice to have it.

You must write and tell me how you are getting along in the "battle of Broadway" (I laughed when I read that) and whether the publishers like your songs though I know they will. Am crazy to hear them and hear you play the piano as I love good jazz music even better than classical, though I suppose it is terrible to say such a thing. But I usually say just what I think though sometimes I wish afterwards I had not of. But still I believe it is better for a girl to be her own self and natural instead of always acting. But am afraid I will never have a chance to hear you play unless you come back to Chi and pay us a visit as my "threat" to come to New York was just a "threat" and I don't see any hope of ever getting there unless some rich New Yorker should fall in love with me and take me there to live. Fine chance for poor little me, eh Mr. Lewis?

Well, I guess I have "rattled on" long enough and you will think I am writing a book unless I quit and besides, Sis has asked me as a special favor to make her a pie for dinner. Maybe you don't know it, Mr. Man, but I am quite famous for my pie and pastry, but I don't suppose a "genius" is interested in common things like that.

Well, be sure and write soon and tell me what N.Y. is like and all about it and don't forget the little girlie who was "bad" and spoke to a strange man in the station and have been blushing over it ever since.

Your friend (?)
Mabelle Gillespie.

*N. Y., Aug. 10.*

Dear Girlie: I bet you will think I am a fresh guy commenceing that way but Miss Gillespie is too cold and a man can not do nothing cold in this kind of weather specially in this man's town which is the hottest place I ever been in and I guess maybe the reason why New Yorkers is so bad is because they think they are all ready in H—— and can not go no worse place no matter how they behave themselves. Honest girlie I certainly envy you being where there is a breeze off the old Lake and Chi may be dirty but I never heard of nobody dying because they was dirty but four people died here yesterday on acct. of the heat and I seen two different women flop right on Broadway and had to be taken away in the ambulance and it could not of been because they was dressed too warm because it would be impossible for the women here to leave off any more cloths.

Well have not had much luck yet in the battle of Broadway as all the heads of the big music publishers is out of town on their vacation and the big boys is the only ones I will do business with as it would be silly for a man with the stuff I have got to waste my time on somebody that is just on the staff and have not got the final say. But I did play a couple of my numbers for the people up to Levy's and Goebel's and they went crazy over them in both places. So it looks like all I have to do is wait for the big boys to get back and then play my numbers for them and I will be all set. What I want is to get taken on the staff of one of the big firms as that gives a man the inside and they will plug your numbers more if you are on the staff. In the meanwhile have not got nothing to worry me but am just seeing the sights of the big town as have saved up enough money to play round for a wile and any way a man that can play piano like I can don't never have to worry about starveing. Can certainly make the old music box talk girlie and am always good for a $75 or $100 job.

Well have been here a week now and on the go every minute and I thought I would be lonesome down here but no chance of that as I have been treated fine by the people I have met and have sure met a bunch of them. One of the boys liveing in the hotel is a vaudeville actor and he is a member of the Friars club and took me over there to dinner the other night and some way another the bunch got wise that I could play piano so of course I had to sit down and give them some of my numbers and everybody went crazy over them. One of the boys I met there was Paul Sears the song writer but he just writes the lyrics and has wrote a bunch of hits and when he heard some of my melodies he called me over to one side and said he would like to work with me on some numbers. How is that girlie as he is one of the biggest hit writers in N.Y.

N.Y. has got some mighty pretty girlies and I guess it would not be hard to get acquainted with them and in fact several of them has tried to make me since I been here but I always figure that a girl must be something wrong with her if she tries to make a man that she don't know nothing about so I pass them all up. But I did meet a couple of pips that a man here in the hotel went up on Riverside Drive to see them and insisted on me going along and they got on some way that I could make a piano talk so they was nothing but I must play for them so I sit down and played some of my own stuff and they went crazy over it.

One of the girls wanted I should come up and see her again, and I said I might but I think I better keep away as she acted like she wanted to vamp me and I am not the kind that likes to play round with a gal just for their company and dance with them etc. but when I see the right gal that will be a different thing and she won't have to beg me to come and see her as I will camp right on her trail till she says yes. And it won't be none of these N.Y. fly by nights neither. They are all right to look at but a man would be a sucker to get serious with them as they might take you up and next thing you know you would have a wife on your hands that don't know a dish rag from a waffle iron.

Well girlie will quit and call it a day as it is too hot to write any more and I guess I will turn on the cold water and lay in the tub a wile and then turn in. Don't forget to write to

Your friend,
Chas. F. Lewis.

*Chicago, Ill., Aug. 13.*

Dear Mr. Man: Hope you won't think me a "silly Billy" for starting my letter that way but "Mr. Lewis" is so formal and "Charles" is too much the other way and any way I would not dare call a man by their first name after only knowing them only two weeks. Though I may as well confess that Charles is my favorite name for a man and have always been crazy about it as it was my father's name. Poor old dad, he died of cancer three years ago, but left enough insurance so that mother and we girls were well provided for and do not have to do anything to support ourselves though I have been earning my own living for two years to make things easier for mother and also because I simply can't bear to be doing nothing as I feel like a "drone." So I flew away from the "home nest" though mother felt bad about it as I was her favorite and she always said I was such a comfort to her as when I was in the house she never had to worry about how things would go.

But there I go gossiping about my domestic affairs just like you would be interested in them though I don't see how you could be though personly I always like to know all about my friends, but I know men are different so will try and not bore you any longer. Poor Man, I certainly feel sorry for you if New York is as hot as all that. I guess it has been very hot in Chi, too, at least everybody has been complaining about how terrible it is. Suppose you will wonder why I say "I guess" and you will think I ought to know if it is hot. Well, sir, the reason I say "I guess" is because I don't feel the heat like others do or at least I don't let myself feel it. That sounds crazy I know, but don't you think there is a good deal in mental suggestion and not letting yourself feel things? I believe that if a person simply won't allow themselves to be affected by disagreeable things, why such things won't bother them near as much. I know it works with me and that is the reason why I am never cross when things go wrong and "keep smiling" no matter what happens and as far as the heat is concerned, why I just don't let myself feel it and my friends say I don't even look hot no matter if the weather is boiling and Edith, my girl friend, often says that I am like a breeze and it cools her off just to have me come in the room. Poor Edie suffers terribly during the hot weather and says it almost makes her mad at me to see how cool and unruffled I look when everybody else is perspiring and have red faces etc.

I laughed when I read what you said about New York being so hot that people thought it was the "other place." I can appreciate a joke, Mr. Man, and that one did not go "over my head." Am still laughing at some of the things you said in the station though they probably struck me funnier than they would most girls as I always see the funny side and sometimes something is said and I laugh and the others wonder what I am laughing at as they cannot see anything in it themselves, but it is just the way I look at things so of course I cannot explain to them why I laughed and they think I am crazy. But I had rather part with almost anything rather than my sense of humour as it helps me over a great many rough spots.

Sis has gone back home though I would of liked to of kept her here much longer, but she had to go though she said she would of liked nothing better than to stay with me and just listen to me "rattle on." She always says it is just like a show to hear me talk as I always put things in such a funny way and for weeks after she has been visiting me she thinks of some of the things I said and laughs over them. Since she left Edith and I have been pretty quiet though poor Edie wants to be on the "go" all the time and tries to make me go out with her every evening to the pictures and scolds me when I say I had rather stay home and read and calls me a "book worm." Well, it is true that I had rather stay home with a good book than go to some crazy old picture and the last two nights I have been reading myself to sleep with Robert W. Service's poems. Don't you love Service or don't you care for "high-brow" writings?

Personly there is nothing I love more than to just sit and read a good book or sit and listen to somebody play the piano, I mean if they can really play and I really believe I like popular music better than the classical though I suppose that is a terrible thing to confess, but I love all kinds of music but a specially the piano when it is played by somebody who can really play.

Am glad you have not "fallen" for the "ladies" who have tried to make your acquaintance in New York. You are right in thinking there must be something wrong with girls who try to "pick up" strange men as no girl with self respect would do such a thing and when I say that, Mr. Man, I know you will think it is a funny thing for me to say on account of the way our friendship started, but I mean it and I assure you that was the first time I ever done such a thing in my life and would never of thought of doing it had I not known you were the right kind of a man as I flatter myself that I am a good judge of character and can tell pretty well what a person is like by just looking at them and I assure you I had made up my mind what kind of a man you were before I allowed myself to answer your opening remark. Otherwise I am the last girl in the world that would allow myself to speak to a person without being introduced to them.

When you write again you must tell me all about the girl on Riverside Drive and what she looks like and if you went to see her again and all about her. Suppose you will think I am a little old "curiosity shop" for asking all those questions and will wonder why I want to know. Well, sir, I won't tell you why, so there, but I insist on you answering all questions and will scold you if you don't. Maybe you will think that the reason why I am so curious is because I am "jealous" of the lady in question. Well, sir, I won't tell you whether I am or not, but will keep you "guessing." Now, don't you wish you knew?

Must close or you will think I am going to "rattle on" forever or maybe you have all ready become disgusted and torn my letter up. If so all I can say is poor little me—she was a nice little girl and meant well, but the man did not appreciate her.

There! Will stop or you will think I am crazy if you do not all ready.

Yours (?)
Mabelle.

*N. Y., Aug. 20.*

Dear Girlie: Well girlie I suppose you thought I was never going to answer your letter but have been busier than a one armed paper hanger the last week as have been working on a number with Paul Sears who is one of the best lyric writers in N.Y. and has turned out as many hits as Berlin or Davis or any of them. And believe me girlie he has turned out another hit this time that is he and I have done it together. It is all done now and we are just waiting for the best chance to place it but will not place it nowheres unless we get the right kind of a deal but maybe will publish it ourselves.

The song is bound to go over big as Sears has wrote a great lyric and I have give it a great tune or at least every body that has heard it goes crazy over it and it looks like it would go over bigger than any song since Mammy and would not be surprised to see it come out the hit of the year. If it is handled right we will make a bbl. of money and Sears says it is a cinch we will clean up as much as $25000 apiece which is pretty fair for one song but this one is not like the most of them but has got a great lyric and I have wrote a melody that will knock them out of their seats. I only wish you could hear it girlie and hear it the way I play it. I had to play it over and over about 50 times at the Friars last night.

I will copy down the lyric of the chorus so you can see what it is like and get the idea of the song though of course you can't tell much about it unless you hear it played and sang. The title of the song is When They're Like You and here is the chorus:

*"Some like them hot, some like them cold.*
*Some like them when they're not too darn old.*
*Some like them fat, some like them lean.*

*Some like them only at sweet sixteen.*
*Some like them dark, some like them light.*
*Some like them in the park, late at night.*
*Some like them fickle, some like them true,*
*But the time I like them is when they're like you."*

How is that for a lyric and I only wish I could play my melody for you as you would go nuts over it but will send you a copy as soon as the song is published and you can get some of your friends to play it over for you and I know you will like it though it is a different melody when I play it or when somebody else plays it.

Well girlie you will see how busy I have been and am libel to keep right on being busy as we are not going to let the grass grow under our feet but as soon as we have this number placed we will get busy on another one as a couple like that will put me on Easy st. even if they don't go as big as we expect but even 25 grand is a big bunch of money and if a man could only turn out one hit a year and make that much out of it I would be on Easy st. and no more hammering on the old music box in some cabaret.

Who ever we take the song to we will make them come across with one grand for advance royaltys and that will keep me going till I can turn out another one. So the future looks bright and rosey to yours truly and I am certainly glad I come to the big town though sorry I did not do it a whole lot quicker.

This is a great old town girlie and when you have lived here a wile you wonder how you ever stood for a burg like Chi which is just a hick town along side of this besides being dirty etc. and a man is a sucker to stay there all their life specially a man in my line of work as N.Y. is the Mecca for a man that has got the musical gift. I figure that all the time I spent in Chi I was just wasteing my time and never really started to live till I come down here and I have to laugh when I think of the boys out there that is trying to make a liveing in the song writeing game and most of them starve to death all their life and the first week I am down here I meet a man like Sears and the next thing you know we have turned out a song that will make us a fortune.

Well girlie you asked me to tell you about the girlie up on the Drive that tried to make me and asked me to come and see her again. Well I can assure you you have no reason to be jealous in that quarter as I have not been back to see her as I figure it is wasteing my time to play round with a dame like she that wants to go out somewheres every night and if you married her she would want a house on 5th ave. with a dozen servants so I have passed her up as that is not my idea of home.

What I want when I get married is a real home where a man can stay home and work and maybe have a few of his friends in once in a wile and entertain them or go to a good musical show once in a wile and have a wife that is in sympathy with you and not nag at you all the wile but be a real help mate. The girlie up on the Drive would run me ragged and have me in the poor house inside of a year even if I was makeing 25 grand out of one song. Besides she wears a make up that you would have to blast to find out what her face looks like. So I have not been back there and don't intend to see her again so what is the use of me telling you about her. And the only other girlie I have met is a sister of Paul Sears who I met up to his house wile we was working on the song but she don't hardly count as she has not got no use for the boys but treats them like dirt and Paul says she is the coldest proposition he ever seen.

Well I don't know no more to write and besides have got a date to go out to Paul's place for dinner and play some of my stuff for him so as he can see if he wants to set words to some more of my melodies. Well don't do nothing I would not do and have as good a time as you can in old Chi and will let you know how we come along with the song.

Chas. F. Lewis.

*Chicago, Ill., Aug 23.*

Dear Mr. Man: I am thrilled to death over the song and think the words awfully pretty and am crazy to hear the music which I know must be great. It must be wonderful to have the gift of writing songs and then hear people play and sing them and just think of making $25,000 in such a short time. My, how rich you will be and I certainly congratulate you though am afraid when you are rich and famous you will have no time for insignificant little me or will you be an exception and remember your "old" friends even when you are up in the world? I sincerely hope so.

Will look forward to receiving a copy of the song and will you be sure and put your name on it? I am all ready very conceited just to think that I know a man that writes songs and makes all that money.

Seriously I wish you success with your next song and I laughed when I read your remark about being busier than a one armed paper hanger. I don't see how you think up all those comparisons and crazy things to say. The next time one of the girls asks me to go out with them I am going to tell them I can't go because I am busier than a one armed paper hanger and then they will think I made it up and say: 'The girl is clever."

Seriously I am glad you did not go back to see the girl on the Drive and am also glad you don't like girls who makes themselves up so much as I think it is disgusting and would rather go round looking like a ghost than put artificial color on my face. Fortunately I have a complexion that does not need 'fixing" but even if my coloring was not what it is I would never think of lowering myself to "fix" it. But I must tell you a joke that happened just the other day when Edith and I were out at lunch and there was another girl in the restaurant whom Edie knew and she introduced her to me and I noticed how this girl kept staring at me and finally she begged my pardon and asked if she could ask me a personal question and I said yes and she asked me if my complexion was really "mine." I assured her it was and she said: "Well, I thought so because I did not think anybody could put it on so artistically. I certainly envy you." Edie and I both laughed.

Well, if that girl envies me my complexion, why I envy you living in New York. Chicago is rather dirty though I don't let that part of it bother me as I bathe and change my clothing so often that the dirt does not have time to "settle." Edie often says she cannot see how I always keep so clean looking and says I always look like I had just stepped out of a band box. She also calls me a fish (jokingly) because I spend so much time in the water. But seriously I do love to bathe and never feel so happy as when I have just "cleaned up" and put on fresh clothing.

Edie has just gone out to see a picture and was cross at me because I would not go with her. I told her I was going to write a letter and she wanted to know to whom and I told her and she said: "You write to him so often that a person would almost think you was in love with him." I just laughed and turned it off, but she does say the most embarrassing things and I would be angry if it was anybody but she that said them.

Seriously I had much rather sit here and write letters or read or just sit and dream than go out to some crazy old picture show except once in awhile I do like to go to the theater and see a good play and a specially a musical play if the music is catchy. But as a rule I am contented to just stay home and feel cozy and lots of evenings Edie and I sit here without saying hardly a word to each other though she would love to talk but she knows I had rather be quiet and she often says it is just like living with a deaf and dumb mute to live with me because I make so little noise round the apartment. I guess I was born to be a home body as I so seldom care to go "gadding."

Though I do love to have company once in awhile, just a few congenial friends whom I can talk to and feel at home with and play cards or have some music. My friends love to drop in here, too, as they say Edie and I always give them such nice things to eat. Though poor Edie has not much to do with it, I am afraid, as she hates anything connected with cooking which is one of the things I love best of anything and I often say that when I begin keeping house in my own home I will insist on doing most of my own work as I would take so much more interest in it than a servant, though I would want somebody to help me a little if I could afford it as I often think a woman that does all her own work is liable to get so tired that she loses interest in the bigger things of life like books and music. Though after all what bigger thing is there than home making a specially for a woman?

I am sitting in the dearest old chair that I bought yesterday at a little store on the North Side. That is my one extravagance, buying furniture and things for the house, but I always say it is economy in the long run as I will always have them and have use for them and when I can pick them up at a bargain I would be silly not to. Though heaven knows I will never be "poor" in regards to furniture and rugs and things like that as mother's house in Toledo is full of lovely things which she says she is going to give to Sis and myself as soon as we have real homes of our own. She is going to give me the first choice as I am her favorite. She has the loveliest old things that you could not buy now for love or money including lovely old rugs and a piano which Sis wanted to have a player attachment put on it but I said it would be an insult to the piano so we did not get one. I am funny about things like that, a specially old furniture and feel towards them like people whom I love.

Poor mother, I am afraid she won't live much longer to enjoy her lovely old things as she has been suffering for years from stomach trouble and the doctor says it has been worse lately instead of better and her heart is weak besides. I am going home to see her a few days this fall as it may be the last time. She is very cheerful and always says she is ready to go now as she had had enough joy out of life and all she would like would be to see her girls settled down in their own homes before she goes.

There I go, talking about my domestic affairs again and I will bet you are bored to death though personly I am never bored when my friends tell me about themselves. But I won't "rattle on" any longer, but will say good night and don't forget to write and tell me how you come out with the song and thanks for sending me the words to it. Will you write a song about me some time? I would be thrilled to death! But I am afraid I am not the kind of girl that inspires men to write songs about them, but am just a quiet "mouse" that loves home and am not giddy enough to be the heroine of a song.

Well, Mr. Man, good night and don't wait so long before writing again to

Yours (?)
Mabelle.

*N. Y., Sept. 8.*

Dear Girlie: Well girlie have not got your last letter with me so cannot answer what was in it as I have forgotten if there was anything I was supposed to answer and besides have only a little time to write as I have a date to go out on a party with the Sears. We are going to the Georgie White show and afterwards somewheres for supper. Sears is the boy who wrote the lyric to my song and it is him and his sister I am going on the party with. The sister is a cold fish that has no use for men but she is show crazy and insists on Paul takeing her to 3 or 4 of them a week.

Paul wants me to give up my room here and come and live with them as they have plenty of room and I am running a little low on money but don't know if I will do it or not as am afraid I would freeze to death in the same house with a girl like the sister as she is ice cold but she don't hang round the house much as she is always takeing trips or going to shows or somewheres.

So far we have not had no luck with the song. All the publishers we have showed it to has went crazy over it but they won't make the right kind of a deal with us and if they don't loosen up and give us a decent royalty rate we are libel to put the song out ourselves and show them up. The man up to Goebel's told us the song was O.K. and he liked it but it was more of a production number than anything else and ought to go in a show like the Follies but they won't be in N.Y. much longer and what we ought to do is hold it till next spring.

Mean wile I am working on some new numbers and also have taken a position with the orchestra at the Wilton and am going to work there starting next week. They pay good money $60 and it will keep me going.

Well girlie that is about all the news. I believe you said your father was sick and hope he is better and also hope you are getting along O.K. and take care of yourself. When you have nothing else to do write to your friend,

Chas. F. Lewis.

*Chicago, Ill., Sept. 11.*

Dear Mr. Lewis: Your short note reached me yesterday and must say I was puzzled when I read it. It sounded like you was mad at me though I cannot think of any reason why you should be. If there was something I said in my last letter that offended you I wish you would tell me what it was and I will ask your pardon though I cannot remember anything I could of said that you could take offense at. But if there was something, why I assure you, Mr. Lewis, that I did not mean anything by it. I certainly did not intend to offend you in any way.

Perhaps it is nothing I wrote you, but you are worried on account of the publishers not treating you fair in regards to your song and that is why your letter sounded so distant. If that is the case I hope that by this time matters have rectified themselves and the future looks brighter. But any way, Mr. Lewis, don't allow yourself to worry over business cares as they will all come right in the end and I always think it is silly for people to worry themselves sick over temporary troubles, but the best way is to "keep smiling" and look for the "silver lining" in the cloud. That is the way I always do and no matter what happens, I manage to smile and my girl friend, Edie, calls me Sunny because I always look on the bright side.

Remember also, Mr. Lewis, that $60 is a salary that a great many men would like to be getting and are living on less than that and supporting a wife and family on it. I always say that a person can get along on whatever amount they make if they manage things in the right way.

So if it is business troubles, Mr. Lewis, I say don't worry, but look on the bright side. But if it is something I wrote in my last letter that offended you I wish you would tell me what it was so I can apologize as I assure you I meant nothing and would not say anything to hurt you for the world.

Please let me hear from you soon as I will not feel comfortable until I know I am not to blame for the sudden change.

Sincerely,
Mabelle Gillespie.

*N. Y., Sept. 24.*

Dear Miss Gillespie: Just a few lines to tell you the big news or at least it is big news to me. I am engaged to be married to Paul Sears' sister and we are going to be married early next month and live in Atlantic City where the orchestra I have been playing with has got an engagement in one of the big cabarets.

I know this will be a surprise to you as it was even a surprise to me as I did not think I would ever have the nerve to ask the girlie the big question as she was always so cold and acted like I was just in the way. But she said she supposed she would have to marry somebody some time and she did not dislike me as much as most of the other men her brother brought round and she would marry me with the understanding that she would not have to be a slave and work round the house and also I would have to take her to a show or somewheres every night and if I could not take her myself she would "run wild" alone. Atlantic City will be O.K. for that as a lot of new shows opens down there and she will be able to see them before they get to the big town. As for her being a slave, I would hate to think of marrying a girl and then have them spend their lives in druggery round the house. We are going to live in a hotel till we find something better but will be in no hurry to start house keeping as we will have to buy all new furniture.

Betsy is some doll when she is all fixed up and believe me she knows how to fix herself up. I don't know what she uses but it is weather proof and I have been out in a rain storm with her and we both got drowned but her face stayed on. I would almost think it was real only she tells me different.

Well girlie I may write to you again once in a wile as Betsy says she don't give a damn if I write to all the girls in the world just so I don't make her read the answers but that is all I can think of to say now except good bye and good luck and may the right man come along soon and he will be a lucky man getting a girl that is such a good cook and got all that furniture etc.

But just let me give you a word of advice before I close and that is don't never speak to strange men who you don't know nothing about as they may get you wrong and think you are trying to make them. It just happened that I knew better so you was lucky in my case but the luck might not last.

Your friend,
Chas. F. Lewis.

*Chicago, Ill., Sept. 27.*

My Dear Mr. Lewis: Thanks for your advice and also thank your fiance for her generosity in allowing you to continue your correspondence with her "rivals," but personly I have no desire to take advantage of that generosity as I have something better to do than read letters from a man like you, a specially as I have a man friend who is not so generous as Miss Sears and would strongly object to my continuing a correspondence with another man. It is at his request that I am writing this note to tell you not to expect to hear from me again.

Allow me to congratulate you on your engagement to Miss Sears and I am sure she is to be congratulated too, though if I met the lady I would be tempted to ask her to tell me her secret, namely how she is going to "run wild" on $60.

Sincerely,
Mabelle Gillespie.

## SUGGESTIONS FOR DISCUSSION

1. There are three *personae*, three adopted roles, in these two pieces: Sayers in her essay, and Charles's and Mabelle's in Lardner's story. In both pieces, too, the personae change fairly radically. Go back through each piece and locate those changing points. Try to figure out what in the text is different.
2. Lardner's choice of form can be called epistolary fiction—a narrative that progresses through the exchange of correspondence. Why do you suppose he decided to tell the story in this form? What would it be like if it were told in other ways—with the action, perhaps, shuttling back and forth from Chicago to New York? Or as told in retrospect by one or both of the characters?
3. One of the turning points in Sayers's essay comes in the third paragraph from the end, when she mentions the gospel story of Martha and Mary. Read that New Testament passage (Luke, Ch. 10). Why does Sayers invoke it? How does it change the mood of the essay?
4. The styles in both these pieces rely heavily on mechanics to achieve certain effects; Sayers uses a wide variety of punctuation in acceptable ways, while Lardner often ignores punctuation, usage, and spelling rules altogether. Go through the Sayers essay looking for ten different uses of punctuation other than commas or periods (semi-colons, colons, dashes, ellipses, italics, quotation marks, parentheses, question marks, exclamation points, titles). Describe the

function of each mark. Next go through Lardner's story looking for the absence or misuse of mechanical features: misspelled words, mistaken comma use, incorrect abbreviations, etc. Keep track of which character uses which, and again try to describe the impact of such features.

## SUGGESTIONS FOR WRITING

1. Pick three jobs or professions: lumberjacking, law, professional athlete. Now make a series of ten statements about the qualities necessary for anyone who wants to pursue such a career, set in the form "He must be ——." When you have ten, go back and reread all the *He*'s as *She*'s. Does the change make any difference?
2. Choose a classmate with whom you will exchange a series of letters. Write that correspondent a letter in which you try to present yourself as a person he or she will like. Deliver the letter. Next have your correspondent write a response; his or her job is to present a person that *you* will like. Now you respond to his/her letter, adjusting the self you present to be more attractive. And, finally, have your correspondent write to you one last time. How did you decide on a *persona*? How did you decide what to tell, and what to leave out? How did your response shift after reading your partner's letter?
3. Imagine the conversation between Charles and Mabelle when they first met at the railroad station. Write this exchange in the form of a dialogue.

# 3

# Love

*Eldridge Cleaver*

"PRELUDE TO LOVE—THREE LETTERS"

*Lillian Hellman*

"DASHIELL HAMMETT"

In contrast to the earlier essays, which emphasize societal views of men and women, these writings describe individual relationships. In the first selection, Eldridge Cleaver describes the new love which is growing between him and Beverly Axelrod as an exciting and irrational force. He is writing these letters from prison and views his love as a kind of liberation. Lillian Hellman presents a more complex relationship as she describes her love for Dashiell Hammett. Her account, which is reflective and mellow, forms a strong contrast to Cleaver's intense involvement.

## *Eldridge Cleaver*
## "PRELUDE TO LOVE—THREE LETTERS"

[*Note:* Eldridge Cleaver had been in prison in California for nearly nine years. Beverly Axelrod is a San Francisco lawyer. Prior to the time the following letters were written, Mr. Cleaver had written to Mrs. Axelrod for legal assistance. She had visited him three times before the following exchange of letters took place.]

Eldridge Cleaver
Folsom Prison
Represa, California
September 5, 1965

Dear Beverly Axelrod:

For two charged days and restless nights after you left, I loafed in the case of my skull, feeling prematurely embalmed in some magical ethered mist dispensed by the dialetic of our contact. When I left you sitting in that little glass cage, which I must somehow learn to respect because it has a special, eternal meaning now, I did not stop or pause. Including the door to that glass cage, and counting the door of my cell, I passed through twelve assorted gates and doors before collapsing on my narrow bed, staggering under the weight of the DAY. The doors and gates swung open before me as I advanced upon them, as I charged down on them, as if they were activated by photoelectric cells responding to my approach. I walked swiftly, but I felt myself to be running, stumbling, thrashing and flailing with my arms to clear a passage through dense, tangled vines. I spoke to no one, recognized no one, and I felt that no one could see or recognize me (wrong: I was accused next day of walking past a couple of henchmen as if they weren't even there. I kept telling them that, in fact, as far as I was concerned, they weren't there, but they refuse to believe in their own non-existence or invisibility).

On the third day I arose again from the damned. No, that's going too far!

What a transfusion! I don't believe I can stand you in such massive doses. It may prove lethal.

I am almost afraid to return to my manuscripts — which themselves seem to cringe from me — after talking with you. I know I shall remain immobile, transfixed, until I've gotten this letter off to you. Then. . . .

I really have no sense of myself and I have always suffered under the compliments of others, especially my friends. I panic. I ran for an office in the Folsom Gavel Club recently. One of my boosters poured lavish praise upon me and my qualifications for the job. I squirmed in my seat and felt oppressed. Does this mean that I do not have the ego for a compliment? No, it does not. It's hypocritical of me, but whenever someone says something nice about me, it sort of knocks me for a loop. And you? The things you said sent me spinning. But don't stop, let me suffer—and overcome.

I feel impelled to express myself to you extravagantly, and words, phrases, sentences, paragraphs leap in my mind. But I beat them down, refuse to write them, because it all seems so predictable and trite. I feel humiliated by the words you inspire me to write to you. I refuse to write them. What right have you to summon my soul from its slumber? But it's all golden and I write this from a sense of the sweetness of irony, the better to marvel at the unbelievable sequence of chance events which brought us face to face in a little glass cage in the office of the Warden of Folsom Prison.

You have tossed me a lifeline. If you only knew how I'd been drowning, how I'd considered that I'd gone down for the third time long ago, how I kept thrashing around in the water simply because I still felt the impulse to fight back and the tug of a distant shore, how I sat in a rage that night with the polysyllabic burden of your name pounding in my brain—Beverly Axelrod, Beverly Axelrod—and out of what instinct did I decide to write to you? It was a gamble on an equation constructed in delirium, and it was right.

Let me say this. I was 22 when I came to prison and of course I have changed tremendously over the years. But I had always had a strong sense of myself and in the last few years I felt I was losing my identity. There was a deadness in my body that eluded me, as though I could not exactly locate its site. I would be aware of this numbness, this feeling of atrophy, and it haunted the back of my mind. Because of this numb spot, I felt peculiarly off balance, the awareness of something missing, of a blank spot, a certain intimation of emptiness. Now I know what it was. And since encountering you, I feel life strength flowing back into that spot. My step, the tread of my stride, which was becoming tentative and uncertain, has begun to recover and take on a new definiteness, a confidence, a boldness which makes me want to kick over a few tables. I may even swagger a little, and, as I read in a book somewhere, "push myself forward like a train."

NOW TURN THE RECORD OVER AND PLAY THE OTHER SIDE

I have tried to mislead you. I am not humble at all. I have no humility and I do not fear you in the least. If I pretend to be shy, if I appear to hesitate, it is only a sham to deceive. By playing the humble part, I sucker my fellow men in and seduce them of their trust. And then, if it suits my advantage, I lower the boom—mercilessly. I lied when I stated that I had no sense of myself. I am very well aware of my style. My vanity is as vast as the scope of a dream, my heart is that of a tyrant, my arm is the arm of the Executioner. It is only the failure of my plots that I fear. Whereas in the past we have had Prophets of Doom, in my vanity I wish to be the Voice of Doom itself. I am angry at the insurgents of Watts. They have pulled the covers off me and revealed to all what potential may lie behind my Tom Smile. I had planned to run for President of the United States. My slogan?

PUT A BLACK FINGER ON THE NUCLEAR TRIGGER.

400 years of docility, of being calm, cool and collected under stress and strain would go to prove that I was the man for the job, that I would not panic in a crisis and push the button. I could be counted on to be cool. It was a cinch, I had it made — but then came Watts! All my plans went up in smoke! And so, with worn-out tools, I stoop to begin again.

Please take care of yourself.

Until something happens, I shall remain, because I have no other choice—and even if I had another choice I would still remain—

Most Emphatically Yours,
*Eldridge*

Beverly Axelrod
Attorney-at-Law
San Francisco, Calif.
September 10, 1965

Dear Eldridge Cleaver:

. . . The need for expression is now upon me, having finished the legal matters, and I'm getting panicky. I'm not strong enough to take the safest course, which would be to not widen the subject matter of our correspondence, and I'm having a terrible time trying to say what I want knowing it will be read by the censors.

Your letter, which I keep rereading, shows you're going through the same turmoil I am; but I bear the onus of having allowed it. You talk about it being lethal, and then about life coming back—and I know that both are true.

I'm going purely on instinct now, which is not usual for me, but somehow I know I'm right, or maybe it's just that it's so important that I don't care about the risk of being wrong. Am I coming through to you? I'm writing I know in an obscure kind of way because of the damnable lack of privacy in our communications.

Believe this: I accept you. I know you little and I know you much, but whichever way it goes, I accept you. Your manhood comes through in a thousand ways, rare and wonderful. I'm out in the world, with an infinity of choices. You don't have to wonder if I'm grasping at something because I have no real measuring stick. I accept you.

About that other side of the record: Did you really think I didn't know? Another facet of the crystal might be an apter term; I have a few facets myself. I do not fear you, I know you will not hurt me. Your hatred is large, but not nearly so vast as you sometimes imagine; it can be used, but it can also be soothed and softened.

What an enormous amount of exploring we have to do! I feel as though I'm on the edge of a new world.

Memo to me: Be rational. It cannot be resolved. The choices: 1. He believes everything he says, but he cannot know, he has no choice; or 2. It's a beautiful put-on because he doesn't know that you would do exactly what you are doing for him anyway; or 3. It's a game to relieve the monotony, conscious or not. Answer: It doesn't make a damn bit of difference, because I can't find out, he can't find out, and it's too late anyway. The only important thing is to get him out, and that was obvious from the first letter, with all lawyerlike objectivity.

What an awesome thing it is to feel oneself on the verge of the possibility of really knowing another person. Can it ever happen? I'm not sure. I don't know that any two people can really strip themselves that naked in front of each other. We're so filled with fears of rejection and pretenses that we scarcely know whether we're being fraudulent or real ourselves.

Of all the dangers we share, probably the greatest comes from our fantasizing about each other. Are we making each other up? We have no way of testing the reality of it.

I can't write any more. I'm thunderstruck at having written this much. I'm afraid to read it over, because it's likely I would tear it up, so I'll send it as is. Can you imagine how much I haven't said?

Sincerely yours,
*Beverly Axelrod*

Eldridge Cleaver
Folsom Prison
Represa, California
September 15, 1965

Dear Beverly Axelrod:

Your letters to me are living pieces—chunks!—of you, and are the most important things in my life. This is fantastic. It only happens in books—or in the dreams of inmates of insane asylums—and with people who are for real. I share with you the awesome feeling of being on the verge of really knowing another person.

I place a great deal of emphasis on people really listening to each other, to what the person has to say, because one seldom encounters a person capable of taking either you or themselves seriously. But I was not *really* like this when I was out of prison—although the seeds were there, but there was too much confusion and madness mixed in. I was not too interested in communicating with other people—that is not true. What I mean is, I had a profound desire for communicating with and getting to know other people, but I was incapable of doing so, I didn't know how.

Do you know what shameless thought just bullied its way into my consciousness? That I deserve you, that I deserve to know you and to communicate with you, that I deserve to have all this happening. What have I done to merit this? I don't believe in the merit system. I Am That I Am. No, I will not hurt you.

Memo to us: 1. He believes everything he says and knows what he is saying; 2. Put-ons are cruel, and how could I be cruel to you? 3. He does not play games, and he does not find life monotonous, conscious or not. He has plans and dreams, and he is deadly serious. Answer: It makes every bit of difference, and I hope to help you find out, he is already finding out; taking it like you find it is a burn, it sells yourself short: be discerning and take only after you spot what you like—but I'm hoping that it is too late for you to flip over on me because it is certainly much too late for me.

Your thought, "Of all the dangers we share, probably the greatest comes from our fantasizing about each other. Are we making each other up?" bothers me. It would be very simple if that were the case: I could arrange (and how easy it would be!) to spend the rest of my life in prison and we could live happily ever after. But it is not that easy, is it? I seek a lasting relationship, something permanent in a world of change, in which all is transitory, ephemeral, and full of pain. We humans, we are too frail creatures to handle such titanic emotions and deep magnetic yearnings, strivings and impulses.

The reason two people are reluctant to really strip themselves naked in front of each other is because in doing so they make themselves vulnerable and give enormous power over themselves one to the other. How awful, how deadly, how catastrophically they can hurt each other, wreck and ruin each other forever! How often, indeed, they end by inflicting pain and torment upon each other. Better to maintain shallow, superficial affairs; that way the scars are not too deep, no blood is hacked from the soul. You beautifully—O, how beautifully!!—spoke, in your letter, of "What an awesome thing it is to feel oneself on the verge of the possibility of really knowing another person . . ." and "I feel as though I am on the edge of a new world." Getting to know someone, entering that new world, is an ultimate, irretrievable leap into the unknown. The prospect is terrifying. The stakes are high. The emotions are overwhelming. In human experience, only the perennial themes can move us to such an extent. Death. Birth. The Grave. Love. Hate.

I do not believe that a beautiful relationship has to always end in carnage. I do not believe that we have to be fraudulent and pretentious, because that is the source of future difficulties and ultimate failure. If we project fraudulent, pretentious images, or if we fantasize each other into distorted caricatures of what we really are, then, when we awake from the trance and see beyond the sham and front, all will dissolve, all will die and transform into bitterness and hate. I know that sometimes people fake on each other out of genuine motives to hold onto the object of their tenderest feelings. They see themselves as so inadequate that they feel forced to wear a mask in order to continuously impress the other. I do not want to "hold" you, I want you to "stay" out of your own need for me.

I seek the profound. Contrary to the advice of the Prophet, I'll take the credit and let the cash go. What I feel for you is profound. Beverly, there is something happening between us that is way out of the ordinary. Ours is one for the books, for the poets to draw new inspiration from, one to silence the cynics, and one to humble us by reminding us of how little we know about human beings, about ourselves. I did not know that I had all these feelings inside me. They have never been aroused before. Now they cascade down upon my head and threaten to beat me down to the ground, into the dust. But because of the strength of the magnetic pull I feel toward you, I am not fazed and I know that I can stand against the tide.

I even respect you behind your back. I have a bad habit, when speaking of women while only men are present, of referring to women as bitches. This bitch this and this bitch that, you know. A while back I was speaking of you to a couple of cutthroats and I said, "this bitch . . ." And I felt very ashamed of myself about that. I passed judgement upon myself and suffered spiritually for days afterward. This may seem insignificant, but I attach great importance to it because of the chain of thought kicked off by it. I care about you, I am concerned about you, which is all very new for, and a sharp departure from, Eldridge X.

Your persistent query, "How can he tell? He has no choices," deserves an answer. But it is not the type of question that can be answered by words. It takes time and deeds, and this involves trust, it involves making ourselves vulnerable to each other, to strip ourselves naked, to become sitting ducks for each other—and if one of the ducks is shamming, then the sincere duck will pay in pain—but the deceitful duck, I feel, will be the loser. (If both ducks are shamming, what a lark, what a fiasco, what a put-on, what a despicable thought! I laugh at it because it has no power over me, I do not feel vulnerable to it, I feel protected by the flashing eyes of Portia. I extended my trust to you. I am vulnerable and defenseless and I make myself a duck for you.)

Listen: Your letter is very beautiful, and you came through with rockets on. You came through and landed on your feet, with spiked shoes on, right on my heart. It is not that we are making each other up and it is not ourselves alone who are involved in what is happening to us. It is really a complex movement taking place of which we are mere parts. We represent historical forces and it is really these forces that are coalescing and moving toward each other. And it is not a fraud, forced out of desperation. We live in a disoriented, deranged social structure, and we have transcended its barriers in our own ways and have stepped psychologically outside its madness and repressions. It is lonely out here. We recognize each other. And, having recognized each other, is it any wonder that our souls hold hands and cling together even while our minds equivocate, hesitate, vacillate, and tremble?

Peace. Don't panic, and don't wake up.
Dream on. I am
Yours,
*Eldridge*

## *Lillian Hellman*
## "DASHIELL HAMMETT"

For years we made jokes about the day I would write about him. In the early years, I would say, "Tell me more about the girl in San Francisco. The silly one who lived across the hall in Pine Street."

And he would laugh and say, "She lived across the hall in Pine Street and was silly."

"Tell more than that. How much did you like her and how—?"

He would yawn. "Finish your drink and go to sleep."

But days later, maybe even that night, if I was on the find-out kick, and I was, most of the years, I would say, "O.K., be stubborn about the girls. So tell me about your grandmother and what you looked like as a baby."

"I was a very fat baby. My grandmother went to the movies every afternoon. She was very fond of a movie star called Wallace Reid and I've told you all this before."

I would say I wanted to get everything straight for the days after his death when I would write his biography and he would say that I was not to bother writing his biography because it would turn out to be the history of Lillian Hellman with an occasional reference to a friend called Hammett.

The day of his death came on January 10, 1961. I will never write that biography because I cannot write about my closest, my most beloved friend. And maybe, too, because all those questions through all the thirty-one on and off years, and the sometimes answers, got muddled, and life changed for both of us and the questions and answers became one in the end, flowing together from the days when I was young to the days when I was middle-aged. And so this will be no attempt at a biography of Samuel Dashiell Hammett, born in St. Mary's County, Maryland, on May 27, 1894. Nor will it be a critical appraisal of his work. In 1966 I edited and published a collection of his stories. There was a day when I thought all of them very good. But all of them are not good, though most of them, I think, are very good. It is only right to say immediately that by publishing them at all I did what Hammett did not want to do: he turned down all offers to republish the stories, although I never knew the reason and never asked. I did know, from what he said about "Tulip," the unfinished novel that I included in the book, that he meant to start a new literary life and maybe didn't want the old work to get in the way. But sometimes I think he was just too ill to care, too worn out to listen to plans or read contracts. The fact of breathing, just breathing, took up all the days and nights.

In the First World War, in camp, influenza led to tuberculosis and Hammett was to spend years after in army hospitals. He came out of the Second World War with emphysema, but how he ever got into the Second World War at the age of forty-eight still bewilders me. He telephoned me the day the army accepted him to say it was the happiest day of his life, and before I could finish saying it wasn't the happiest day of mine and what about the old scars on his lungs, he laughed and hung up. His death was caused by cancer of the lungs, discovered only two months before he died. It was not operable—I doubt that he would have agreed to an operation even if it had been—and so I decided not to tell him about the cancer. The doctor said that when the pain came, it would come in the right chest and arm, but that the pain might never come. The doctor was wrong: only a few hours after he told me, the pain did come. Hammett had had self-diagnosed rheumatism in the right arm and had always said that was why he had given up hunting. On the day I heard about the cancer, he said his gun shoulder hurt him again, would I rub it for him. I remember sitting behind him, rubbing the shoulder and hoping he would always think it was rheumatism and remember only the autumn hunting days. But the pain never came again, or if it did he never mentioned it, or maybe death was so close that the shoulder pain faded into other pains.

He did not wish to die and I like to think he didn't know he was dying. But I keep from myself even now the possible meaning of a night, very late, a short time before his death. I came into his room, and for the only time in the years I knew him there were tears in his eyes and the book was lying unread. I sat down beside him and waited a long time before I could say, "Do you want to talk about it?"

He said, almost with anger, "No. My only chance is not to talk about it."

And he never did. He had patience, courage, dignity in those last, awful months. It was as if all that makes a man's life had come together to prove itself: suffering was a private matter and there was to be no invasion of it. He would seldom even ask for anything he needed, and so the most we did—my secretary and Helen, who were devoted to him, as most women always had been—was to carry up the meals he barely touched, the books he now could hardly read, the afternoon coffee, and the martini that I insisted upon before the dinner that wasn't eaten.

One night of that last year, a bad night, I said, "Have another martini. It will make you feel better."

"No," he said, "I don't want it."

I said, "O.K., but I bet you never thought I'd urge you to have another drink."

He laughed for the first time that day. "Nope. And I never thought I'd turn it down."

Because on the night we had first met he was getting over a five-day drunk and he was to drink very heavily for the next eighteen years, and then one day, warned by a doctor, he said he would never have another drink and he kept his word except for the last year of the one martini, and that was my idea.

We met when I was twenty-four years old and he was thirty-six in a restaurant in Hollywood. The five-day drunk had left the wonderful face looking rumpled, and the very tall thin figure was tired and sagged. We talked of T. S. Eliot, although I no longer remember what we said, and then went and sat in his car and talked at each other and over each other until it was daylight. We were to meet again a few weeks later and, after that, on and sometimes off again for the rest of his life and thirty years of mine.

Thirty years is a long time, I guess, and yet as I come now to write about them the memories skip about and make no pattern and I know only certain of them are to be trusted. I know about that first meeting and the next, and there are many other pictures and sounds, but they are out of order and out of time, and I don't seem to want to put them into place. (I could have done a research job, I have on other people, but I didn't want to do one on Hammett, or to be a bookkeeper of my own life.) I don't want modesty for either of us, but I ask myself now if it can mean much to anybody but me that my second sharpest memory is of a day when we were living on a small island off the coast of Connecticut. It was six years after we had first met: six full, happy, unhappy years during which I had, with help from Hammett, written *The Children's Hour,* which was a success, and *Days to Come,* which was not. I was returning from the mainland in a catboat filled with marketing and Hammett had come down to the dock to tie me up. He had been sick that summer—the first of the sicknesses—and he was even thinner than usual. The white hair, the white pants, the white shirt made a straight, flat surface in the late sun. I thought: Maybe that's the handsomest sight I ever saw, that line of a man, the knife for a nose, and the sheet went out of my hand and the wind went out of the sail. Hammett laughed as I struggled to get back the sail. I don't know why, but I yelled angrily, "So you're a Dostoevsky sinner-saint. So you are." The laughter stopped, and when I finally came in to the dock we didn't speak as we carried up the packages and didn't speak through dinner.

Later that night, he said, "What did you say that for? What does it mean?"

I said I didn't know why I had said it and I didn't know what it meant.

Years later, when his life had changed, I did know what I had meant that day: I had seen the sinner—whatever is a sinner—and sensed the change before it came. When I told him that, Hammett said he didn't know what I was talking about, it was all too religious for him. But he did know what I was talking about and he was pleased.

But the fat, loose, wild years were over by the time we talked that way. When I first met Dash he had written four of the five novels and was the hottest thing in Hollywood and New York. It is not remarkable to be the hottest thing in either city—the hottest kid changes for each winter season—but in his case it was of extra interest to those who collect people that the ex-detective who had bad cuts on his legs and an indentation in his head from being scrappy with criminals was gentle in manner, well educated, elegant to look at, born of early settlers, was eccentric, witty, and spent so much money on women that they would have liked him even if he had been none of the good things. But as the years passed from 1930 to 1948, he wrote only one novel and a few short stories. By 1945, the drinking was no longer gay, the drinking bouts were longer and the moods darker. I was there off and on for most of those years, but in 1948 I didn't want to see the drinking anymore. I hadn't seen or spoken to Hammett for two months until the day when his devoted cleaning lady called to say she thought I had better come down to his apartment. I said I wouldn't, and then I did. She and I dressed a man who could barely lift an arm or a leg and brought him to my house, and that night I watched delirium tremens, although I didn't know what I was watching until the doctor told me the next day at the hospital. The doctor was an old friend. He said, "I'm going to tell Hammett that if he goes on drinking he'll be dead in a few months. It's my duty to say it, but it won't do any good." In a few minutes he came out of Dash's room and said, "I told him. Dash said O.K., he'd go on the wagon forever, but he can't and he won't."

But he could and he did. Five or six years later, I told Hammett that the doctor had said he wouldn't stay on the wagon.

Dash looked puzzled. "But I gave my word that day."

I said, "Have you always kept your word?"

"Most of the time," he said, "maybe because I've so seldom given it."

He had made up honor early in his life and stuck with his rules, fierce in the protection of them. In 1951 he went to jail because he and two other trustees of the bail bond fund of the Civil Rights Congress refused to reveal the names of the contributors to the fund. The truth was that Hammett had never been in the office of the Congress, did not know the name of a single contributor.

The night before he was to appear in court, I said, "Why don't you say that you don't know the names?"

"No," he said, "I can't say that."

"Why?"

"I don't know why. I guess it has something to do with keeping my word, but I don't want to talk about that. Nothing much will happen, although I think we'll go to jail for a while, but you're not to worry because"—and then suddenly I couldn't understand him because the voice had dropped and the words were coming in a most untypical nervous rush. I said I couldn't hear him, and he raised his voice and dropped his head. "I hate this damn kind of talk, but maybe I better tell you that if it were more than jail, if it were my life, I would give it for what I think democracy is, and I don't let cops or judges tell me what I think democracy is." Then he went home to bed, and the next day he went to jail.

*July 14, 1965*

It is a lovely summer day. Fourteen years ago on another lovely summer day the lawyer Hammett said he didn't need, didn't want, but finally agreed to talk to because it might make me feel better, came back from West Street jail with a message from Hammett that the lawyer had written on the back of an old envelope. "Tell Lilly to go away. Tell her I don't need proof she loves me and don't want it." And so I went to Europe, and wrote a letter almost every day, not knowing that about one letter in ten was given to him, and never getting a letter from him because he wasn't allowed to write to anybody who wasn't related to him. (Hammett had, by this time, been moved to a federal penitentiary in West Virginia.) I had only one message that summer: that his prison job was cleaning bathrooms, and he was cleaning them better than I had ever done.

I came back to New York to meet Hammett the night he came out of jail. Jail had made a thin man thinner, a sick man sicker. The invalid figure was trying to walk proud, but coming down the ramp from the plane he was holding tight to the railing, and before he saw me he stumbled and stopped to rest. I guess that was the first time I knew he would now always be sick. I felt too bad to say hello, and so I ran back into the airport and we lost each other for a few minutes. But in a week, when he had slept and was able to eat small amounts of food, an irritating farce began and was to last for the rest of his life: jail wasn't bad at all. True, the food was awful and sometimes even rotted, but you could always have milk; the moonshiners and car thieves were dopes but their conversation was no sillier than a New York cocktail party; nobody liked cleaning toilets, but in time you came to take a certain pride in the work and an interest in the different cleaning materials; jail homosexuals were nasty-tempered, but no worse than the ones in any bar, and so on. Hammett's form of boasting was always to make fun of trouble or pain. We had once met Howard Fast on the street and he told us about his to-be-served jail sentence. As we moved away, Hammett said, "It will be easier for you, Howard, and you won't catch cold, if you first take off the crown of thorns." So I should have guessed that Hammett would talk about his own time in jail the way many of us talk about college.

I do not wish to avoid the subject of Hammett's political beliefs, but the truth is that I do not know if he was a member of the Communist party and I never asked him. If that seems an odd evasion between two people we did not mean it as an evasion: it was, probably, the product of the time we lived through and a certain unspoken agreement about privacy. Now, in looking back, I think we had rather odd rules about privacy, unlike other peoples' rules. We never, for example, asked each other about money, how much something cost or how much something earned, although each of us gave to the other as, through the years, each of us needed it. It does not matter much to me that I don't know if Hammett was a Communist party member: most certainly he was a Marxist. But he was a very critical Marxist, often contemptuous of the Soviet Union in the same hick sense that many Americans are contemptuous of foreigners. He was often witty and biting sharp about the American Communist party, but he was, in the end, loyal to them. Once, in an argument with me, he said that of course a great deal about Communism worried him and always had and that when he found something better he intended to change his opinions. And then he said, "Now please don't let's ever argue about it again because we're doing each other harm." And so we did not argue again, and I suppose that itself does a kind of harm or leaves a moat too large for crossing, but it was better than the arguments we had been having—they had started in the 1940's —when he knew that I could not go his way. I think that must have pained him, but he never said so. It pained me, too, but I knew that, unlike many radicals, whatever he believed in, whatever he had arrived at, came from reading and thinking. He took time to find out what he thought, and he had an open mind and a tolerant nature.

. . . . . . . . . . . . . . . . . .

In 1952 I had to sell the farm. I moved to New York and Dash rented a small house in Katonah. I went once a week to see him, he came once a week to New York, and we talked on the phone every day. But he wanted to be alone — or so I thought then, but am now not so sure because I have learned that proud men who can ask for nothing may be fine characters, but they are difficult to live with or to understand. In any case, as the years went on he became a hermit, and the ugly little country cottage grew uglier with books piled on every chair and no place to sit, the desk a foot high with unanswered mail. The signs of sickness were all around: now the phonograph was unplayed, the typewriter untouched, the beloved, foolish gadgets unopened in their packages. When I went for my weekly visits we didn't talk much and when he came for his weekly visits to me he was worn out from the short journey.

Perhaps it took me too long to realize that he couldn't live alone anymore, and even after I realized it I didn't know how to say it. One day, immediately after he had made me promise to stop reading "L'il Abner," and I was laughing at his vehemence about it, he suddenly looked embarrassed—he always looked embarrassed when he had something emotional to say—and he said, "I can't live alone anymore. I've been falling. I'm going to a Veterans Hospital. It will be O.K., we'll see each other all the time, and I don't want any tears from you." But there were tears from me, two days of tears, and finally he consented to come and live in my apartment. (Even now, as I write this, I am still angry and amused that he always had to have things on his own terms: a few minutes ago I got up from the typewriter and railed against him for it, as if he could still hear me. I know as little about the nature of romantic love as I knew when I was eighteen, but I do know about the deep pleasure of continuing interest, the excitement of wanting to know what somebody else thinks, will do, will not do, the tricks played and unplayed, the short cord that the years make into rope and, in my case, is there, hanging loose, long after death. I am not sure what Hammett would feel about the rest of these notes about him, but I am sure that he would be pleased that I am angry with him today.) And so he lived with me for the last four years of his life. Not all of that time was easy, indeed some of it was very bad, but it was an unspoken pleasure that having come together so many years before, ruined so much, and repaired a little, we had endured. Sometimes I would resent the understated or seldom stated side of us and, guessing death wasn't too far away, I would try for something to have afterwards. One day I said, "We've done fine, haven't we?"

He said, "Fine's too big a word for me. Why don't we just say we've done better than most people?"

On New Year's Eve, 1960, I left Hammett in the care of a pleasant practical nurse and went to spend a few hours with friends. I left their house at twelve-thirty, not knowing that the nurse began telephoning for me a few minutes later. As I came into Hammett's room, he was sitting at his desk, his face as eager and excited as it had been in the drinking days. In his lap was the heavy book of Japanese prints that he had bought and liked many years before. He was pointing to a print and saying to the nurse, "Look at it, darling, it's wonderful." As I came toward him, the nurse moved away, but he caught her hand and kissed it, in the same charming, flirtatious way of the early days, looking up to wink at me. The book was lying upside down and so the nurse didn't need to mumble the word "irrational." From then on—we took him to the hospital the next morning—I never knew and will now not ever know what irrational means. Hammett refused all medication, all aid from nurses and doctors in some kind of mysterious wariness. Before the night of the upside-down book our plan had been to move to Cambridge because I was to teach a seminar at Harvard. An upside-down book should have told me the end had come, but I didn't want to think that way, and so I flew to Cambridge, found a nursing home for Dash, and flew back that night to tell him about it. He said, "But how are we going to get to Boston?" I said we'd take an ambulance and I guess for the first time in his life he said, "That will cost too much." I said, "If it does, then we'll take a covered wagon." He smiled and said, "Maybe that's the way we should have gone places anyway."

And so I felt better that night, sure of a postponement. I was wrong. Before six o'clock the next morning the hospital called me. Hammett had gone into a coma. As I ran across the room toward his bed there was a last sign of life: his eyes opened in shocked surprise and he tried to raise his head. He was never to think again and he died two days later.

But I do not wish to end this book on an elegiac note. It is true that I miss Hammett, and that is as it should be. He was the most interesting man I've ever met. I laugh at what he did say, amuse myself with what he might say, and even this many years later speak to him, often angry that he still interferes with me, still dictates the rules.

But I am not yet old enough to like the past better than the present, although there are nights when I have a passing sadness for the unnecessary pains, the self-made foolishness that was, is, and will be. I do regret that I have spent too much of my life trying to find what I called "truth," trying to find what I called "sense." I never knew what I meant by truth, never made the sense I hoped for. All I mean is that I left too much of me unfinished because I wasted too much time. However.

## SUGGESTIONS FOR DISCUSSION

1. Consider that any piece of writing can be said to have one of four aims: referential (to tell about the world in a factual way); persuasive (to change readers' opinions); literary (to create something beautiful or truthful for its own sake); and expressive (to represent on paper what the writer feels). The writings of all three authors here can best be considered expressive: that is, their *primary* aim is for the author to express his or her feelings. But Hellman's audience is a large, public one; this essay is taken from her memoirs. Axelrod and Cleaver are writing for one another. How do these different audiences seem to affect the way the writers pursue their aims?
2. The first four essays in this part view the social images of men and women with a critical eye. Do the considerations raised in these essays apply to the men and women presented here? Would Alda approve of Hammett? Would Vilar? Would they—or Dorothy Sayers—approve of what we can see of the Cleaver-Axelrod relationship?
3. Here again we have three *personae* to deal with: Hellman's, Axelrod's, and Cleaver's. The word *personae* itself, you might remember, is the Greek word for "mask." What sort of masks do these writers wear? Which do you like best? Least?
4. At one point Cleaver suddenly interrupts himself to write, "Now turn the record

over and play the other side." Axelrod objects to his choice of words, saying, "Another facet of the crystal might be an apter term." Why does she want to change his metaphor? What does her metaphor suggest that his does not?

## SUGGESTIONS FOR WRITING

1. In their letters, both Cleaver and Axelrod are terribly, even painfully, self-conscious: they interrupt themselves constantly to contradict, second-guess, restate. Few people ever try to write that way. Compose a letter—*which you will show to no one*—about someone for whom you have very deep, complex feelings. Try to capture the chaos and turmoil of your thoughts and feelings, writing with the kind of self-consciousness shown by Cleaver and Axelrod. When you finish, be ready to talk about the experience. Did it help you sort out your feelings?
2. Explain the basis of Hellman's love for Hammett. In your analysis focus on the early incidents which Hellman describes. Cleaver speaks of his letters as "a prelude to love"; what is the prelude to love of Hellman and Hammett?

# 4

# Friendship

*C. S. Lewis*

## "FRIENDSHIP"

*Susan Lee*

## "FRIENDSHIP, FEMINISM, AND BETRAYAL"

These essays present friendship from two perspectives. C. S. Lewis writes a definition essay which shows how friendship differs from affection and love. He sees friendship as a bond that develops from shared perspectives and values, and he analyzes it primarily as a masculine experience. Susan Lee, on the other hand, discusses the difficulties inherent in friendships between women. She also distinguishes friendship from love: "A friend is someone I can be myself with; with a lover, I'm all too often someone else, someone I'd rather be." While Lewis focuses on the advantages and joys of friendship, Lee emphasizes the barriers between friends.

### WRITE BEFORE READING

The next pair of essays deals directly with friendship: what it is, where it comes from, how it changes. Before you read them, try defining it yourself. After all, everyone has had enough experience with friendship to be at least a minor authority on the subject. You will have to decide for yourself who your audience is, what your purpose will be, and what *persona* you will adopt.

# *C. S. Lewis*
# "FRIENDSHIP"

When either Affection or Eros is one's theme, one finds a prepared audience. The importance and beauty of both have been stressed and almost exaggerated again and again. Even those who would debunk them are in conscious reaction against this laudatory tradition and, to that extent, influenced by it. But very few modern people think Friendship a love of comparable value or even a love at all. I cannot remember that any poem since *In Memoriam,* or any novel, has celebrated it. Tristan and Isolde, Antony and Cleopatra, Romeo and Juliet, have innumerable counterparts in modern literature: David and Jonathan, Pylades and Orestes, Roland and Oliver, Amis and Amile, have not. To the Ancients, Friendship seemed the happiest and most fully human of all loves; the crown of life and the school of virtue. The modern world, in comparison, ignores it. We admit of course that besides a wife and family a man needs a few "friends." But the very tone of the admission, and the sort of acquaintanceships which those who make it would describe as "friendships," show clearly that what they are talking about has very little to do with that *Philia* which Aristotle classified among the virtues or that *Amicitia* on which Cicero wrote a book. It is something quite marginal; not a main course in life's banquet; a diversion; something that fills up the chinks of one's time. How has this come about?

The first and most obvious answer is that few value it because few experience it. And the possibility of going through life without the experience is rooted in that fact which separates Friendship so sharply from both the other loves. Friendship is—in a sense not at all derogatory to it—the least *natural* of loves; the least instinctive, organic, biological, gregarious and necessary. It has least commerce with our nerves; there is nothing throaty about it; nothing that quickens the pulse or turns you red and pale. It is essentially between individuals; the moment two men are friends they have in some degree drawn apart together from the herd. Without Eros none of us would have been begotten and without Affection none of us would have been reared; but we can live and breed without Friendship. The species, biologically considered, has no need of it. The pack or herd—the community—may even dislike and distrust it. Its leaders very often do. Headmasters and Headmistresses and Heads of religious communities, colonels and ships' captains, can feel uneasy when close and strong friendships arise between little knots of their subjects.

This (so to call it) "non-natural" quality in Friendship goes far to explain why it was exalted in ancient and medieval times and has come to be made light of in our own. The deepest and most permanent thought of those ages was ascetic and world-renouncing. Nature and emotion and the body were feared as dangers to our souls, or despised as degradations of our human status. Inevitably that sort of love was most prized which seemed most independent, or even defiant, of mere nature. Affection and Eros were too obviously connected with our nerves, too obviously shared with the brutes. You could feel these tugging at your guts and fluttering in your diaphragm. But in Friendship—in that luminous, tranquil, rational world of relationships freely chosen—you got away from all that. This alone, of all the loves, seemed to raise you to the level of gods or angels.

But then came Romanticism and "tearful comedy" and the "return to nature" and the exaltation of Sentiment; and in their train all that great wallow of emotion which, though often criticized, has lasted ever since. Finally, the exaltation of instinct, the dark gods in the blood; whose hierophants may be incapable of male friendship. Under this new dispensation all that had once commended this love now began to work against it. It had not tearful smiles and keepsakes and baby-talk enough to please the sentimentalists. There was not blood and guts enough about it to attract the primitivists. It looked thin and etiolated; a sort of vegetarian substitute for the more organic loves.

Other causes have contributed. To those—and they are now the majority—who see human life merely as a development and complication of animal life all forms of behaviour which cannot produce certificates of an animal origin and of survival value are suspect. Friendship's certificates are not very satisfactory. Again, that outlook which values the collective above the individual necessarily disparages Friendship; it is a relation between men at their highest level of individuality. It withdraws men from collective "togetherness" as surely as solitude itself could do; and more dangerously, for it withdraws them by two's and three's. Some forms of democratic sentiment are naturally hostile to it because it is selective and an affair of the few. To say "These are my friends" implies "Those are not." For all these reasons if a man believes (as I do) that the old estimate of Friendship was the correct one, he can hardly write a chapter on it except as a rehabilitation.

This imposes on me at the outset a very tiresome bit of demolition. It has actually become necessary in our time to rebut the theory that every firm and serious friendship is really homosexual.

The dangerous word *really* is here important. To say that every Friendship is consciously and explicitly homosexual would be too obviously false; the wiseacres take refuge in the less palpable charge that it is *really*—unconsciously, cryptically, in some Pickwickian sense—homosexual. And this, though it cannot be proved, can never of course be refuted. The fact that no positive evidence of homosexuality can be discovered in the behaviour of two Friends does not disconcert the wiseacres at all: "That," they say gravely, "is just what we should expect." The very lack of evidence is thus treated as evidence; the absence of smoke proves that the fire is very carefully hidden. Yes—if it exists at all. But we must first prove its existence. Otherwise we are arguing like a man who should say "If there were an invisible cat in that chair, the chair would look empty; but the chair does look empty; therefore there is an invisible cat in it."

A belief in invisible cats cannot perhaps be logically disproved, but it tells us a good deal about those who hold it. Those who cannot conceive Friendship as a substantive love but only as a disguise or elaboration of Eros betray the fact that they have never had a Friend. The rest of us know that though we can have erotic love and friendship for the same person yet in some ways nothing is less like a Friendship than a love-affair. Lovers are always talking to one another about their love; Friends hardly ever about their Friendship. Lovers are normally face to face, absorbed in each other; Friends, side by side, absorbed in some common interest. Above all,

Eros (while it lasts) is necessarily between two only. But two, far from being the necessary number for Friendship, is not even the best. And the reason for this is important.

Lamb says somewhere that if, of three friends (A, B, and C), A should die, then B loses not only A but "A's part in C," while C loses not only A but "A's part in B." In each of my friends there is something that only some other friend can fully bring out. By myself I am not large enough to call the whole man into activity; I want other lights than my own to show all his facets. Now that Charles is dead, I shall never again see Ronald's reaction to a specifically Caroline joke. Far from having more of Ronald, having him "to myself" now that Charles is away, I have less of Ronald. Hence true Friendship is the least jealous of loves. Two friends delight to be joined by a third, and three by a fourth, if only the newcomer is qualified to become a real friend. They can then say, as the blessed souls say in Dante, "Here comes one who will augment our loves." For in this love "to divide is not to take away." Of course the scarcity of kindred souls—not to mention practical considerations about the size of rooms and the audibility of voices—set limits to the enlargement of the circle; but within those limits we possess each friend not less but more as the number of those with whom we share him increases. In this, Friendship exhibits a glorious "nearness by resemblance" to Heaven itself where the very multitude of the blessed (which no man can number) increases the fruition which each has of God. For every soul, seeing Him in her own way, doubtless communicates that unique vision to all the rest. That, says an old author, is why the Seraphim in Isaiah's vision are crying "Holy, Holy, Holy" *to one another* (Isaiah VI, 3). The more we thus share the Heavenly Bread between us, the more we shall all have. . . .

I have said that Friendship is the least biological of our loves. Both the individual and the community can survive without it. But there is something else, often confused with Friendship, which the community does need; something which, though not Friendship, is the matrix of Friendship.

In early communities the co-operation of the males as hunters or fighters was no less necessary than the begetting and rearing of children. A tribe where there was no taste for the one would die no less surely than a tribe where there was no taste for the other. Long before history began we men have got together apart from the women and done things. We had to. And to like doing what must be done is a characteristic that has survival value. We not only had to do the things, we had to talk about them. We had to plan the hunt and the battle. When they were over we had to hold a *post mortem* and draw conclusions for future use. We liked this even better. We ridiculed or punished the cowards and bunglers, we praised the star-performers. We revelled in technicalities. ("He might have known he'd never get near the brute, not with the wind that way" . . . "You see, I had a lighter arrowhead; that's what did it" . . . "What I always say is——" . . . "stuck him just like that, see? Just the way I'm holding this stick" . . .) In fact, we talked shop. We enjoyed one another's society greatly: we Braves, we hunters, all bound together by shared skill, shared dangers and hardships, esoteric jokes—away from the women and children. As some wag has said, palaeolithic man may or may not have had a club on his shoulder but he certainly had a club of the other sort. It was probably part of his religion; like that sacred smoking-club where the savages in Melville's *Typee* were "famously snug" every evening of their lives.

What were the women doing meanwhile? How should I know? I am a man and never spied on the mysteries of the Bona Dea. They certainly often had rituals from which men were excluded. When, as sometimes happened, agriculture was in their hands, they must, like the men, have had common skills, toils and triumphs. Yet perhaps their world was never as emphatically feminine as that of their menfolk was masculine. The children were with them; perhaps the old men were there too. But I am only guessing. I can trace the pre-history of Friendship only in the male line.

This pleasure in co-operation, in talking shop, in the mutual respect and understanding of men who daily see one another tested, is biologically valuable. You may, if you like, regard it as a product of the "gregarious instinct." To me that seems a roundabout way of getting at something which we all understand far better already than anyone has ever understood the word *instinct*—something which is going on at this moment in dozens of ward-rooms, bar-rooms, common-rooms, messes and golf-clubs. I prefer to call it Companionship—or Clubbableness.

This Companionship is, however, only the matrix of Friendship. It is often called Friendship, and many people when they speak of their "friends" mean only their companions. But it is not Friendship in the sense I give to the word. By saying this I do not at all intend to disparage the merely Clubbable relation. We do not disparage silver by distinguishing it from gold.

Friendship arises out of mere Companionship when two or more of the companions discover that they have in common some insight or interest or even taste which the others do not share and which, till that moment, each believed to be his own unique treasure (or burden). The typical expression of opening Friendship would be something like, "What? You too? I thought I was the only one." We can imagine that among those early hunters and warriors single individuals—one in a century? one in a thousand years?—saw what others did not; saw that the deer was beautiful as well as edible, that hunting was fun as well as necessary, dreamed that his gods might be not only powerful but holy. But as long as each of these percipient persons dies without finding a kindred soul, nothing (I suspect) will come of it; art or sport or spiritual religion will not be born. It is when two such persons discover one another, when, whether with immense difficulties and semi-articulate fumblings or with what would seem to us amazing and elliptical speed, they share their vision—it is then that Friendship is born. And instantly they stand together in an immense solitude.

Lovers seek for privacy. Friends find this solitude about them, this barrier between them and the herd, whether they want it or not. They would be glad to reduce it. The first two would be glad to find a third.

In our own time Friendship arises in the same way. For us of course the shared activity and therefore the companionship on which Friendship supervenes will not often be a bodily one like hunting or fighting. It may be a common religion, common studies, a common profession, even a common recreation. All who share it will be our companions; but one or two or three who share something more will be our Friends. In this kind of love, as Emerson said, *Do you love me?* means *Do you see the same truth?*—Or at least, "Do you *care about* the same truth?" The man who agrees with us that some question, little regarded by others, is of great importance can be our Friend. He need not agree with us about the answer.

Notice that Friendship thus repeats on a more individual and less socially necessary level the character of the Companionship which was its matrix. The Companionship was between people who were doing something together—hunting, studying, painting or what you will. The Friends will still be doing something together, but something more inward, less widely shared and less easily defined; still hunters, but of some immaterial quarry; still collaborating, but in some work the world does not, or not yet, take account of; still travelling companions, but on a different kind of journey. Hence we picture lovers face to face but Friends side by side; their eyes look ahead.

That is why those pathetic people who simply "want friends" can never make any. The very condition of having Friends is that we should want something else besides Friends. Where the truthful answer to the question *Do you see the same truth?* would be "I see nothing and I don't care about the truth; I only want a Friend," no Friendship can arise—though Affection of course may. There would be nothing for the Friendship to be *about;* and Friendship must be about something, even if it were only an enthusiasm for dominoes or white mice. Those who have nothing can share nothing; those who are going nowhere can have no fellow-travellers.

When the two people who thus discover that they are on the same secret road are of different sexes, the friendship which arises between them will very easily pass—may pass in the first half-hour—into erotic love. Indeed, unless they are physically repulsive to each other or unless one or both already loves elsewhere, it is almost certain to do so sooner or later. And conversely, erotic love may lead to Friendship between the lovers. But this, so far from obliterating the distinction between the two loves, puts it in a clearer light. If one who was first, in the deep and full sense, your Friend, is then gradually or suddenly revealed as also your lover you will certainly not want to share the Beloved's erotic love with any third. But you will have no jealousy at all about sharing the Friendship. Nothing so enriches an erotic love as the discovery that the Beloved can deeply, truly and spontaneously enter into Friendship with the Friends you already had: to feel that not only are we two united by erotic love but we three or four or five are all travellers on the same quest, have all a common vision.

The co-existence of Friendship and Eros may also help some moderns to realise that Friendship is in reality a love, and even as great a love as Eros. Suppose you are fortunate enough to have "fallen in love with" and married your Friend. And now suppose it possible that you were offered the choice of two futures: "*Either* you two will cease to be lovers but remain forever joint seekers of the same God, the same beauty, the same truth, *or else,* losing all that, you will retain as long as you live the raptures and ardours, all the wonder and the wild desire of Eros. Choose which you please." Which should we choose? Which choice should we not regret after we had made it?

I have stressed the "unnecessary" character of Friendship, and this of course requires more justification than I have yet given it.

It could be argued that Friendships are of practical value to the Community. Every civilised religion began in a small group of friends. Mathematics effectively began when a few Greek friends got together to talk about numbers and lines and angles. What is now the Royal Society was originally a few gentlemen meeting in their spare time to discuss things which they (and not many others) had a fancy for. What we now call "the Romantic Movement" once *was* Mr. Wordsworth and Mr. Coleridge talking incessantly (at least Mr. Coleridge was) about a secret vision of their own. Communism, Tractarianism, Methodism, the movement against slavery, the Reformation, the Renaissance, might perhaps be said, without much exaggeration, to have begun in the same way.

There is something in this. But nearly every reader would probably think some of these movements good for society and some bad. The whole list, if accepted, would tend to show, at best, that Friendship is both a possible benefactor and a possible danger to the community. And even as a benefactor it would have, not so much survival value, as what we may call "civilisation-value"; would be something (in Aristotelian phrase) which helps the community not to live but to live well. Survival value and civilisation value coincide at some periods and in some circumstances, but not in all. What at any rate seems certain is that when Friendship bears fruit which the community can use it has to do so accidentally, as a by-product. Religions devised for a social purpose, like Roman emperor-worship or modern attempts to "sell" Christianity as a means of "saving civilisation," do not come to much. The little knots of Friends who turn their backs on the "World" are those who really transform it. Egyptian and Babylonian Mathematics were practical and social, pursued in the service of Agriculture and Magic. But the free Greek Mathematics, pursued by Friends as a leisure occupation, have mattered to us more.

Others again would say that Friendship is extremely useful, perhaps necessary for survival, to the individual. They could produce plenty of authority: "bare is back without brother behind it" and "there is a friend that sticketh closer than a brother." But when we speak thus we are using *friend* to mean "ally." In ordinary usage *friend* means, or should mean, more than that. A Friend will, to be sure, prove himself to be also an ally when alliance becomes necessary; will lend or give when we are in need, nurse us in sickness, stand up for us among our enemies, do what he can for our widows and orphans. But such good offices are not the stuff of Friendship. The occasions for them are almost interruptions. They are in one way relevant to it, in another not. Relevant, because you would be a false friend if you would not do them when the need arose; irrelevant, because the role of benefactor always remains accidental, even a little alien, to that of Friend. It is almost embarrassing. For Friendship is utterly free from Affection's need to be needed. We are sorry that any gift or loan or night-watching should have been necessary—and now, for heaven's sake, let us forget all about it and go back to the things we really want to do or talk of together. Even gratitude is no enrichment to this love. The stereotyped "Don't mention it" here expresses what we really feel. The mark of perfect Friendship is not that help will be given when the pinch comes (of course it will) but that, having been given, it makes no difference at all. It was a distraction, an anomaly. It was a horrible waste of the time, always too short, that we had together. Perhaps we had only a couple of hours in which to talk and, God bless us, twenty minutes of it has had to be devoted to *affairs!*

For of course we do not want to know our Friend's affairs at all. Friendship, unlike Eros, is uninquisitive. You become a man's Friend without knowing or caring whether he is married or single or how he earns his living. What have all these "unconcerning things, matters of fact" to do with the real question, *Do you see the same truth?* In a circle of true Friends each man is simply what he is: stands for nothing but himself. No one cares twopence about any one else's family, profession, class, income, race, or previous history. Of course you will get to know about most of these in the end. But casually. They will come out bit by bit, to furnish an illustration or an analogy, to serve as pegs for an anecdote; never for their own sake. That is the kingliness of Friendship. We meet like sovereign princes of independent states, abroad, on neutral ground, freed from our contexts. This love (essentially) ignores not only our physical bodies but that whole embodiment which consists of our family, job, past and connections. At home, besides being Peter or Jane, we also bear a general character; husband or wife, brother or sister, chief, colleague or subordinate. Not among our Friends. It is an affair of disentangled, or stripped, minds. Eros will have naked bodies; Friendship naked personalities.

Hence (if you will not misunderstand me) the exquisite arbitrariness and irresponsibility of this love. I have no duty to be anyone's Friend and no man in the world has a duty to be mine. No claims, no shadow of necessity. Friendship is unnecessary, like philosophy, like art, like the universe itself (for God did not need to create). It has no survival value; rather it is one of those things which give value to survival.

When I spoke of Friends as side by side or shoulder to shoulder I was pointing a necessary contrast between their posture and that of the lovers whom we picture face to face. Beyond that contrast I do not want the image pressed. The common quest or vision which unites Friends does not absorb them in such a way that they remain ignorant or oblivious of one another. On the contrary it is the very medium in which their mutual love and knowledge exist. One knows nobody so well as one's "fellow." Every step of the common journey tests his metal; and the tests are tests we fully understand because we are undergoing them ourselves. Hence, as he rings true time after time, our reliance, our respect and our admiration blossom into an Appreciative love of a singularly robust and well-informed kind. If, at the outset, we had attended more to him and less to the thing our Friendship is "about," we should not have come to know or love him so well. You will not find the warrior, the poet, the philosopher or the Christian by staring in his eyes as if he were your mistress: better fight beside him, read with him, argue with him, pray with him.

In a perfect Friendship this Appreciative love is, I think, often so great and so firmly based that each member of the circle feels, in his secret heart, humbled before all the rest. Sometimes he wonders what he is doing there among his betters. He is lucky beyond desert to be in such company. Especially when the whole group is together, each bringing out all that is best, wisest, or funniest in all the others. Those are the golden sessions; when four or five of us after a hard day's walking have come to our inn; when our slippers are on, our feet spread out towards the blaze and our drinks at our elbows; when the whole world, and something beyond the world, opens itself to our minds as we talk; and no one has any claim on or any responsibility for another, but all are free-men and equals as if we had first met an hour ago, while at the same time an Affection mellowed by the years enfolds us. Life—natural life—has no better gift to give. Who could have deserved it?

*Susan Lee*

## "FRIENDSHIP, FEMINISM, AND BETRAYAL"

Home for Christmas my first year in college, I spoke to my best friend from high school. Elizabeth and I stayed on the phone for 45 minutes, but we had nothing very much to say to each other. After the conversation, I was upset. I remember wanting to tell my mother, who asked what the matter was, about the weirdness of discovering that this woman and I, who had talked every school day for five years, no longer had anything in common. All I could do was cry.

Except for a brief, awkward visit to my house a month later when my father died, a church wedding where Elizabeth married a man I'd gone out with in seventh grade, and two short stopovers in southern New Jersey, I don't remember ever seeing or speaking to her again.

We used to spend hours talking about our relationships with boys. We never discussed our relationship with each other. Except for the few minutes with my mother, who told me she thought Elizabeth and I never had anything in common, and my once making a distinction between acquaintances and friends, I'd never spoken about what I considered a real friendship.

Many people have expressed agreement with Cicero that "friendship can only exist between good men." I'm not one of them. As a 30-year-old woman who has had friends since grade school, I have been very concerned with those friendships. Yet only in the last few years have such relationships been acknowledged as being as important as they've always been.

It was always commonplace for girls in my high school to spend a great deal of time together. It was also commonplace for a girl to spend Saturdays with another girl listening to Johnny Mathis albums, trying on clothes to find something that fit right, or babysitting and then having the evening that was planned together usurped by some boy calling up for a date. When this happened to me, I felt betrayed. I never said anything. It didn't occur to me that this wasn't the natural order of things. I didn't know anyone who complained, nor do I remember anyone who ever turned down a boy because she'd already made plans with a girl.

One woman I know said that if as a teenager she had told her parents she'd prefer being with a girl than a boy, they would have sent her to a doctor.

Even now, this past summer, when I was home for a few weeks because my mother was sick, my mother only asked questions about the men who called. One night when I was coming into the city, she discovered I was going to see a woman instead of the man who had just called.

All she said was, "Oh?" Within that one word was more archness than I'd ever heard placed in such a small space.

A male friend of mine suggested that, as kids, if a girl could turn down another girl for a boy, maybe the girls weren't friends. What he didn't understand is how power works, how it matters who gets to set the dates, how important one telephone call can be, and how helpless someone can feel waiting for it.

But girls didn't deny each other because we weren't friends. We could only do it because we were and because boys weren't, and because they got to make the call and we didn't.

Still, a friend of mine recently remembered that she once was leaving a girl to go out on a date. Her girlfriend's mother, who was very hurt for her daughter, stopped her and said that when she was young, girls knew the value of friendship.

Now, each of us knows what this woman meant. We might express it in terms of a heightened woman's consciousness. We might talk of it in terms of respect for each of our relationships. My friend didn't. She went out on her date. She knew what was flexible in her life and what wasn't. The given of having friends then was that we understood the same rules. The same given remains except that some of the rules are changing.

* * *

Friendship has become so institutionalized in our culture that a recent book combined the notion that everyone should have a good friend with the alienated sense that each person should be her or his own best friend.

My guess is that as the family breaks down, friendships will grow in importance. In my own life, as I have relied less and less on the idea of marriage for myself, the more I've come to see the friendships that I've had for years and years as the ongoing relationships in my life.

College was a relatively easy place to find people I liked. Condescending as it might have sounded to me then, we each had our futures ahead of us. It seemed possible to get on with a large number of people. Still, most of my college friends and acquaintances disappeared from my life almost as soon as I left the campus. Like Elizabeth and me, we had little more in common than living near each other.

I used to think affection was enough for friendship, but I no longer believe that. Affection can be sufficient for lovers in a way it isn't for friends. But then, people "fall in" love. Someone is a lover after a few days. A friendship, where love develops, often takes years.

A friend is someone I can be myself with; with a lover, I'm all too often someone else, someone I'd rather be.

I can only be myself when there is a shared community of interests between the other person and me. I began to realize how important this was when I got to graduate school in San Francisco and met other people who cared intimately about the same work I did. No longer was someone's impending wedding date the ongoing center of a conversation.

I found people who perceived what went on outside of them and how they acted in the world in many of the same ways I did. I was not as aware of the need for loyalty to friends as I am now. If I fall under the illusion that I was particularly unusual in the way that I treated other women, I remind myself of the green rocking chair in my San Francisco living room. I gave this chair up to any man who came into my house and kept it for myself if another woman was there.

One relationship developed into something more than shared after classroom time. Both Linda and I were dedicated to writing fiction and to working out our lives so that we'd be able to write. And, however different Linda and I were, I was conscious that our friendship had a loyalty and a respect for each other that other friendly relationships did not have.

We spent hours discussing our lives, our work, our dailyness. Where a lover and I take endless time concerning ourselves with ourselves and our specific relationship, Linda and I were spectators at the landscapes of each other's lives. We were more like adjacent lands sharing common borders than the same property itself. It seemed to me that not only did I have my life, but I had hers as well, to see the working out of our goal to become the best writers we possibly could.

A friend like Linda is a reflection of what I value, in a way a lover is not necessarily. I like to be friends, with what is best in me and with what I'm interested in. While I, and several of my friends, too often excuse our choice of lovers as irrational or necessary acts, we take the responsibility for whom we've chosen as friends.

Still, I'm far more conscious of lovers than I am of friends. Though this is changing, I usually think about friends when something is wrong between us. When I'm in love, I'm almost always aware of my lover.

When I was in California and Linda didn't call or was late for an appointment, I assumed there was a good reason. When a lover messes up, I'm quick to think it's our relationship. Friends don't take things as personally as lovers do. There's less expectation and more politeness with friends, who are taken far more for granted than lovers. Yet the reality in my life is that friends are more constant. Lovers come and go except for those who become my friends and stay near me.

Even understanding this, it didn't occur to me to stay in California because of my friends. Linda, abiding by the same implicit rules I did, never mentioned my remaining to me; I don't know if she thought of it. Another friend confronted me; he asked how I could leave the people I freely acknowledged loving more than anyone else. It was enough for me that I was bored and dissatisfied in San Francisco and wanted to come back to New York.

The following year, I returned to the West Coast for Linda's wedding to another writer. Our relationship had deepened into the assumption that we were each other's friend. Although I had fears about the marriage which Linda was all too aware of, I didn't think of not going to give support. I hoped that if any woman could manage writing and a marriage, Linda would.

I tried seeing her for several weeks yearly in Italy or France where she lived. What I didn't admit to myself after one visit to Praiano was how the three of us were developing. I was writing; Thomas, Linda's husband, was writing; only Linda wasn't.

A year and a half later in Paris, I couldn't help seeing what I hadn't wanted to see in Italy. Thomas wrote constantly, and Linda talked about writing. When he worked, we had to whisper. One night when Linda went into her study to work, Thomas interrupted her. I expected her to tell him to leave her alone as she so assiduously left him. Instead, he talked her out of doing anything but spending time with him and me. She acceded to him as she did in much else of what he wanted. She had become a wife.

My visit to Paris was disastrous. Whenever I tried talking about what I found appalling, Linda turned the discussion to my love relationships of the previous year which had not been ones she would have liked to have had. My anger at what I construed as her growing passivity remained unarticulated and high.

I came home and didn't answer a cheery letter ignoring the realities of my stay. A few months later, I wrote a very disturbed explanatory response and did not hear from Linda again.

I knew she'd stopped speaking to her childhood best friend because the woman had once flirted with Thomas. I was aware she'd given me up because of what she thought was an opposite reaction to the man she chose to live with and to the way she led her life.

Six months later, I was speaking to an editor in the publishing house which had signed Thomas's novel and found out Linda and Thomas were in New York for a few weeks.

Sorting out my resentment at having lost my closest friendship, I called them. Linda answering, we talked awkwardly and arranged dinner for that night. I thought the two of us might be able to resolve our difficulties. Perhaps I had been wrong. Deep friendship is hard to come by, and I was prepared to do what I could to salvage this one.

When Linda arrived at the restaurant, she said Thomas would be there with some of his friends within half an hour. I was dumbfounded. She and I were to have dinner alone.

By the next day, I was furious. Living outside English-speaking countries, Linda might have missed the American women's movement. Still, she taught a college course on women in Paris. She couldn't be as unaware of turning into a passive, dependent person as she seemed to be. If she and I weren't going to be friends, I at least wanted to make clear what bothered me.

But she didn't want to hear it. As far as she was concerned, I was hostile. Finally, she agreed to meet.

There we were at the Buffalo Road House: I, with a tennis racket, T-shirt, and dungarees; she, with the latest long Parisian swirl skirt. We were surrounded by four booths of male couples who all stopped talking as we began.

I gathered they all thought we were the lovers Thomas had believed we were years before. I wanted to turn around and say, "No, no. This is worse. We were friends, and now we're not going to be."

We drank wine and were each very upset. Surprising me, she told me that I had betrayed her. She, who long before defined a friend as someone who knew you and loved you anyway, said I didn't trust her. On my side, I was sure she was the one who betrayed our original friendship. She was the one who'd given up her life for someone else's needs.

I argued, somewhat disingenuously, that I was never hostile to her but to her role as wife. I remember thinking that we were never as close as I had thought.

Linda said, "If Thomas ever was as nasty about you as you've been about him, I would have divorced him a long time ago."

I thought this was not only untrue but gratuitous. Thomas, whose novel includes such lines as, "He stuck his throbbing cock into her Hawaiian cunt," could afford to be magnanimous. There was little reason for him to complain. I could talk all I wanted of the need for women to struggle. While he and his friends discussed how liberated they were, he knew Linda's allegiance and investment were more and more in him and his future and less so in her own.

Then she said that since she and I had stopped corresponding, she'd started a novel about the friendship between two women and had gotten more than 100 pages into it.

She and I haven't spoken since. I've hoped she would finish that novel. Not only do I want her to write, I want to read about a friendship through her eyes, and I want something to come out of our relationship.

But I'm being disingenuous again. While acting as an external conscience to a friend might sound touching and be theoretically correct, the reshaping of people, luckily for friendship, is traditionally—and usually without success—left to lovers. Linda knew what I was upset about. At one point when I was in Paris talking to Thomas about each of our projects, Linda burst out, "Don't you both see? *I'm* the one in trouble." Thomas denied what I perceived was true. Linda didn't need me to be tiresome or belligerent about it. Even more, she didn't need someone who she sensed didn't trust her enough to overcome it.

While I now know I can no longer be friendly with someone who acts like a "wife," I think Linda was right about my betraying her. I acted like one of the Plymouth Bay colonists. In effect, I said that specific beliefs and actions meant more than our history together.

Still, I'm angry. I know very well that other people's supposedly durable friendships turn out unexpectedly fragile and break fairly easily. Yet, however necessary my betrayal was, this woman and I had made a commitment to each other, the alternative was not to have gone on being friends. We were too on edge with each other to do that. All we could have done was to fade away from each other without having had the courage to talk about our differences at all.

When I was young, I thought my friends *had* to act as they did. As a result, I overlooked many decisions that I fundamentally disagreed with. Now, due to the women's movement, I assume each of my friends takes responsibility for her life. Because I no longer consider us powerless, I no longer can forgive acting as if we were.

While a heightened women's consciousness has resulted in our openly valuing friendships more highly than we did before, this same conciousness has caused me, and other women, to demand more of these relationships. The validity of each of our lives has become an issue that might have been passed by before and now can no longer be.

Often, these new pressures are too great for many of these friendships to bear. I know there are no models to go by to put them back together. I know we have to develop new models of not only keeping friendships but having them at all.

Yet to venture that friendships often break apart because of social and political dislocations doesn't alleviate my wanting friendships that last or my being hurt that this relationship with Linda, which I had assumed would be one of these, no longer exists.

Looking back on what happened between us, I can understand the pressures on her to choose as she did. I can wish her well. I can understand my own development which made me make demands that others might find unreasonable. I can do a lot of things, but what I feel—not by Linda so much as by historical circumstance—is cheated.

## SUGGESTIONS FOR DISCUSSION

1. One fundamental difference between these two essays is that Lee writes from and illustrates heavily with personal experience, while Lewis, though probably an experienced "friend," relies on more academic illustrations. Which tack did you take? What are the advantages and disadvantages of each approach?
2. Both Lewis and Lee have "friendship" in their titles. Lee, however, adds to hers "Feminism" and "Betrayal." Who are their audiences? Can you make inferences, for example, about the age of their audiences? About their sex? About their education? Do you think they see their audiences as hostile or sympathetic?
3. Susan Lee writes of broken friendships that "I know there are no models to go by to put them back together. I know we have to develop new models of not only keeping friendships but having them at all." The "we," of course, are women. Why does Lee think the old models are outmoded? Would C. S. Lewis agree? Can you tell what Lee's purpose in writing this essay is? How does her point about friendship models serve her purpose.

## SUGGESTIONS FOR WRITING

1. Now you have had a chance to read two definitions of friendship other than your own. What is important for your purposes, though, is not so much *what* C. S. Lewis and Susan Lee say about friendship, but *how* they say it, how they construct their essays. Decide which writer your essay is most unlike, and then try to revise it in that direction. For example, if, like Lewis, you tended to be abstract and academic, try to be more personal and concrete. If you tended to be more like Lee—anecdotal, expressive—try to adopt a more detached, intellectualized perspective.

# 5

# Personality Clashes

*Dorothy Parker*
"GOOD SOULS"

*Samuel Johnson*
"THE GOOD SORT OF WOMAN"

While the essays on love and friendship describe primarily positive relationships, the last two essays in this part offer accounts of sour associations. Dorothy Parker provides a satirical portrait of a common character type—the self-sacrificing individual whose good deeds are oppressive to other people. Samuel Johnson's essay takes the form of an imaginary letter from one of his readers. The "letter" describes another "good sort" of person—the woman who is superficially charming, tolerant, and gracious but who has no real principles and no real convictions. Parker makes her point by constructing a generalized personality type, while Johnson describes the quirks of a specific individual.

## *Dorothy Parker*
## "GOOD SOULS"

*Their Characteristics, Habits, and Innumerable Methods of Removing the Joy from Life*

*June 1919*

All about us, living in our very families, it may be, there exists a race of curious creatures. Outwardly, they possess no marked peculiarities; in fact, at a hasty glance, they may be readily mistaken for regular human beings. They are built after the popular design; they have the usual number of features, arranged in the conventional manner; they offer no variations on the general run of things in their habits of dressing, eating, and carrying on their business.

Yet, between them and the rest of the civilized world, there stretches an impassable barrier. Though they live in the very thick of the human race, they are forever isolated from it. They are fated to go through life, congenital pariahs. They live out their little lives, mingling with the world, yet never a part of it.

They are, in short, Good Souls.

And the piteous thing about them is that they are wholly unconscious of their condition. A Good Soul thinks he is just like anyone else. Nothing could convince him otherwise. It is heartrending to see him, going cheerfully about, even whistling or humming as he goes, all unconscious of his terrible plight. The utmost he can receive from the world is an attitude of good-humored patience, a perfunctory word of approbation, a praising with faint damns, so to speak—yet he firmly believes that everything is all right with him.

There is no accounting for Good Souls.

They spring up anywhere. They will suddenly appear in families which, for generations, have had no slightest stigma attached to them. Possibly they are throwbacks. There is scarcely a family without at least one Good Soul somewhere in it at the present moment—maybe in the form of an elderly aunt, an unmarried sister, an unsuccessful brother, an indigent cousin. No household is complete without one.

The Good Soul begins early; he will show signs of his condition in extreme youth. Go now to the nearest window, and look out on the little children playing so happily below. Any group of youngsters that you may happen to see will do perfectly. Do you observe the child whom all the other little dears make "it" in their merry games? Do you follow the child from whom the other little ones snatch the cherished candy, to consume it before his streaming eyes? Can you get a good look at the child whose precious toys are borrowed for indefinite periods by the other playful youngsters, and are returned to him in fragments? Do you see the child upon whom all the other kiddies play their complete repertory of childhood's winsome pranks—throwing bags of water on him, running away and hiding from him, shouting his name in quaint rhymes, chalking coarse legends on his unsuspecting back?

Mark that child well. He is going to be a Good Soul when he grows up.

Thus does the doomed child go through early youth and adolescence. So does he progress towards the fulfillment of his destiny. And then, some day, when he is under discussion, someone will say of him, "Well, he means well, anyway." That settles it. For him, that is the end. Those words have branded him with the indelible mark of his pariahdom. He has come into his majority; he is a full-fledged Good Soul.

The activities of the adult of the species are familiar to us all. When you are ill, who is it that hastens to your bedside bearing molds of blanc-mange, which, from infancy, you have hated with unspeakable loathing? As usual, you are way ahead of me, gentle reader—it is indeed the Good Soul. It is the Good Souls who efficiently smooth out your pillow when you have just worked it into the comfortable shape, who creak about the room on noisy tiptoe, who tenderly lay on your fevered brow damp cloths which drip ceaselessly down your neck. It is they who ask, every other minute, if there isn't something that they can do for you. It is they who, at great personal sacrifice, spend long hours sitting beside your bed, reading aloud the continued stories in the *Woman's Home Companion,* chatting cozily on the increase in the city's death rate.

In health, as in illness, they are always right there, ready to befriend you. No sooner do you sit down, than they exclaim that they can see you aren't comfortable in that chair, and insist on your changing places with them. It is the Good Souls who just *know* that you don't like your tea that way, and who bear it masterfully away from you to alter it with cream and sugar until it is a complete stranger to you. At the table, it is they who always feel that their grapefruit is better than yours and who have to be restrained almost forcibly from exchanging with you. In a restaurant the waiter invariably makes a mistake and brings them something which they did not order—and which they refuse to have changed, choking it down with a wistful smile. It is they who cause traffic blocks, by standing in subway entrances arguing altruistically as to who is to pay the fare.

At the theater, should they be members of a box-party, it is the Good Souls who insist on occupying the rear chairs; if the seats are in the orchestra, they worry audibly, all through the performance, about their being able to see better than you, until finally in desperation you grant their plea and change seats with them. If, by so doing, they can bring a little discomfort on themselves—sit in a draught, say, or behind a pillar—then their happiness is complete. To feel the genial glow of martyrdom—that is all they ask of life.

Good Souls are punctilious in their observation of correct little ceremonies. If, for example, they borrow a postage stamp, they immediately offer two pennies in return for it—they insist upon this business transaction. They never fail to remember birthdays—their little gift always brings with it a sharp stab of remembrance that you have blissfully ignored their own natal day. At the last moment, on Christmas Eve, comes a present from some Good Soul whose existence, in the rush of holiday shopping you have completely overlooked. When they go away, be it only for an overnight stay, they never neglect to send postcards bearing views of the principal buildings of the place to all their acquaintances; to their intimates, they always bring back some local souvenir—a tiny dish, featuring the gold-lettered name of the town; a thimble in an appropriate case, both bearing the name of their native city; a tie-rack with the name of its place of residence burned decoratively on its wood; or some such useful novelty.

The lives of Good Souls are crowded with Occasions, each with its own ritual which must be solemnly followed. On Mothers' Day, Good Souls conscientiously wear carnations; on St. Patrick's Day, they faithfully don boutonnieres of shamrocks; on Columbus Day, they carefully pin on miniature Italian flags. Every feast must be celebrated by the sending out of cards—Valentine's Day, Arbor Day, Groundhog Day, and all the other important festivals, each is duly observed. They have a perfect genius for discovering appropriate cards of greeting for the event. It must take hours of research.

If it's too long a time between holidays, then the Good Soul will send little cards or little mementoes, just by way of surprises. He is strong on surprises, anyway. It delights him to drop in unexpectedly on his friends. Who has not known the joy of those evenings when some Good Soul just runs in, as a surprise? It is particularly effective when a chosen company of other guests happens to be present—enough for two tables of bridge, say. This means that the Good Soul must sit wistfully by, patiently watching the progress of the rubber, or else must cut in at intervals, volubly voicing his desolation at causing so much inconvenience, and apologizing constantly during the evening.

His conversation, admirable though it is, never receives its just due of attention and appreciation. He is one of those who believe and frequently quote the exemplary precept that there is good in everybody; hanging in his bedchamber is the whimsically phrased, yet vital, statement, done in burned leather—"There is so much good in the worst of us and so much bad in the best of us that it hardly behooves any of us to talk about the rest of us." This, too, he archly quotes on appropriate occasions. Two or three may be gathered together, intimately discussing some mutual acquaintance. It is just getting really absorbing, when comes the Good Soul, to utter his dutiful, "We mustn't judge harshly—after all, we must always remember that many times our own actions may be misconstrued." Somehow, after several of these little reminders, there seems to be a general waning of interest; the little gathering breaks up, inventing quaint excuses to get away and discuss the thing more fully, adding a few really good details, some place where the Good Soul will not follow. While the Good Soul, pitifully ignorant of their evil purpose, glows with the warmth of conscious virtue, and settles himself to read the Contributors Club, in the *Atlantic Monthly,* with a sense of duty well done.

Yet it must not be thought that their virtue lifts Good Souls above the enjoyment of popular pastimes. Indeed, it does not; they are enthusiasts on the subject of good, wholesome fun. They lavishly patronize the drama, in its cleaner forms. They flock to the plays of Miss Rachel Crothers, Miss Eleanor Porter, and Mr. Edward Childs Carpenter. They are passionate admirers of the art of Mr. William Hodge. In literature, they worship at the chaste shrines of Harold Bell Wright, Gene Stratton-Porter, Eleanor Hallowell Abbott, Alice Hegan Rice, and the other triple-named apostles of optimism. They have never felt the same towards Arnold Bennett since he sprung "The Pretty Lady" on them; they no longer give "The Human Machine" and "How to Live on Twenty-four Hours a Day" as birthday offerings to their friends. In poetry, though Tennyson, Whittier, and Longfellow stand for the highest, of course, they have marked leaning toward the later works of Mrs. Ella Wheeler Wilcox. They are continually meeting people who know her, encounters of which they proudly relate. Among humorists, they prefer Mr. Ellis Parker Butler.

Good Souls, themselves, are no mean humorists. They have a time-honored formula of fun-making, which must be faithfully followed. Certain words or phrases must be whimsically distorted every time they are used. "Over the river," they dutifully say, whenever they take their leave. "Don't you cast any asparagus on me," they warn, archly; and they never fail to speak of "three times in concussion." According to their ritual, these screaming phrases must be repeated several times, for the most telling effect, and are invariably followed by hearty laughter from the speaker, to whom they seem eternally new.

Perhaps the most congenial role of the Good Soul is that of advice-giver. He loves to take people aside and have serious little personal talks, all for their own good. He thinks it only right to point out faults or bad habits which are, perhaps unconsciously, growing on them. He goes home and laboriously writes long, intricate letters, invariably beginning, "Although you may feel that this is no affair of mine, I think that you really ought to know," and so on, indefinitely. In his desire to help, he reminds one irresistibly of Marcelline, who used to try so pathetically and so fruitlessly to be of some assistance in arranging the circus arena, and who brought such misfortunes on his own innocent person thereby.

The Good Souls will, doubtless, gain their reward in Heaven; on this earth, certainly, theirs is what is technically known as a rough deal. The most hideous outrages are perpetrated on them. "Oh, he won't mind," people say. "He's a Good Soul." And then they proceed to heap the rankest impositions upon him. When Good Souls give a party, people who have accepted weeks in advance call up at the last second and refuse, without the shadow of an excuse save that of a subsequent engagement. Other people are invited to all sorts of entertaining affairs; the Good Soul, unasked, waves them a cheery good-bye and hopes wistfully that they will have a good time. His is the uncomfortable seat in the motor; he is the one to ride backwards in the train; he is the one who is always chosen to solicit subscriptions and make up deficits. People borrow his money, steal his servants, lose his golf balls, use him as a sort of errand boy, leave him flat whenever something more attractive offers—and carry it all off with their cheerful slogan, "Oh, he won't mind—he's a Good Soul."

And that's just it—Good Souls never do mind. After each fresh atrocity they are more cheerful, forgiving and virtuous, if possible, than they were before. There is simply no keeping them down—back they come, with their little gifts, and their little words of advice, and their little endeavors to be of service, always anxious for more.

Yes, there can be no doubt about it—their reward will come to them in the next world.

Would that they were even now enjoying it!

## *Samuel Johnson*
## "THE GOOD SORT OF WOMAN"

*Saturday, 15 March 1760.*

SIR,

The uncertainty and defects of language have produced very frequent complaints among the learned; yet there still remain many words among us undefined, which are very necessary to be rightly understood, and which produce very mischievous mistakes when they are erroneously interpreted.

I lived in a state of celibacy beyond the usual time. In the hurry first of pleasure and afterwards of business, I felt no want of a domestick companion; but becoming weary of labour I soon grew more weary of idleness, and thought it reasonable to follow the custom of life, and to seek some solace of my cares in female tenderness, and some amusement of my leisure in female cheerfulness.

The choice which has been long delayed is commonly made at last with great caution. My resolution was to keep my passions neutral, and to marry only in compliance with my reason. I drew upon a page of my pocket book a scheme of all female virtues and vices, with the vices which border upon every virtue, and the virtues which are allied to every vice. I considered that wit was sarcastick, and magnanimity imperious; that avarice was economical, and ignorance obsequious; and having estimated the good and evil of every quality, employed my own diligence and that of my friends to find the lady in whom nature and reason had reached that happy mediocrity which is equally remote from exuberance and deficience.

Every woman had her admirers and her censurers, and the expectations which one raised were by another quickly depressed: yet there was one in whose favour almost all suffrages concurred. Miss Gentle was universally allowed to be a good sort of woman. Her fortune was not large, but so prudently managed, that she wore finer cloaths and saw more company than many who were known to be twice as rich. Miss Gentle's visits were every where welcome, and whatever family she favoured with her company, she always left behind her such a degree of kindness as recommended her to others; every day extended her acquaintance, and all who knew her declared that they never met with a better sort of woman.

To Miss Gentle I made my addresses, and was received with great equality of temper. She did not in the days of courtship assume the privilege of imposing rigorous commands, or resenting slight offences. If I forgot any of her injunctions I was gently reminded, if I missed the minute of appointment I was easily forgiven. I foresaw nothing in marriage but a halcyon calm, and longed for the happiness which was to be found in the inseparable society of a good sort of woman.

The jointure was soon settled by the intervention of friends, and the day came in which Miss Gentle was made mine for ever. The first month was passed easily enough in receiving and repaying the civilities of our friends. The bride practised with great exactness all the niceties of ceremony, and distributed her notice in the most punctilious proportions to the friends who surrounded us with their happy auguries.

But the time soon came when we were left to ourselves, and were to receive our pleasures from each other, and I then began to perceive that I was not formed to be much delighted by a good sort of woman. Her great principle is, that the orders of a family must not be broken. Every hour of the day has its employment inviolably appropriated, nor will any importunity persuade her to walk in the garden, at the time which she has devoted to her needlework, or to sit up stairs in that part of the forenoon, which she has accustomed herself to spend in the back parlour. She allows herself to sit half an hour after breakfast, and an hour after dinner; while I am talking or reading to her, she keeps her eye upon her watch, and when the minute of departure comes, will leave an argument unfinished, or the intrigue of a play unravelled. She once called me to supper when I was watching an eclipse, and summoned me at another time to bed when I was going to give directions at a fire.

Her conversation is so habitually cautious, that she never talks to me but in general terms, as to one whom it is dangerous to trust. For discriminations of character she has no names; all whom she mentions are honest men and agreeable women. She smiles not by sensation but by practice. Her laughter is never excited but by a joke, and her notion of a joke is not very delicate. The repetition of a good joke does not weaken its effect; if she has laughed once, she will laugh again.

She is an enemy to nothing but ill nature and pride, but she has frequent reason to lament that they are so frequent in the world. All who are not equally pleased with the good and bad, with the elegant and gross, with the witty and the dull, all who distinguish excellence from defect she considers as ill-natured; and she condemns as proud all who repress impertinence or quell presumption, or expect respect from any other eminence than that of fortune, to which she is always willing to pay homage.

There are none whom she openly hates; for if once she suffers, or believes herself to suffer, any contempt or insult, she never dismisses it from her mind but takes all opportunities to tell how easily she can forgive. There are none whom she loves much better than others; for when any of her acquaintance decline in the opinion of the world she always finds it inconvenient to visit them; her affection continues unaltered but it is impossible to be intimate with the whole town.

She daily exercises her benevolence by pitying every misfortune that happens to every family within her circle of notice; she is in hourly terrors lest one should catch cold in the rain, and another be frighted by the high wind. Her charity she shews by lamenting that so many poor wretches should languish in the streets, and by wondering what the great can think on that they do so little good with such large estates.

Her house is elegant and her table dainty though she has little taste of elegance, and is wholly free from vicious luxury; but she comforts herself that nobody can say that her house is dirty, or that her dishes are not well drest.

This, Mr. Idler, I have found by long experience to be the character of a good sort of woman, which I have sent you for the information of those by whom "a good sort of woman" and "a good woman" may happen to be used as equivalent terms, and who may suffer by the mistake like

Your humble servant,
TIM WARNER.

## SUGGESTIONS FOR DISCUSSION

1. Essays describing certain character types were once popular forms of writing. Johnson's essay belongs to this tradition, and Parker's essay is clearly inspired by an older tradition. What indications does Parker give that she is consciously imitating an older literary form?
2. Both of these essays rely heavily on specific details. Why does the reader need to know that the Good Soul likes gifts such as "a tie-rack with the name of its place of residence burned decoratively on its wood" or that the "good sort of woman" once announced supper in the middle of an eclipse? What is the cumulative effect of these minute details?
3. In both of these essays we are presented with negative definitions of goodness, something that commonly passes for goodness but which, on closer inspection, turns out to be a kind of neurotic behavior. How do you think Johnson and Parker

would define genuine goodness?

4. Parker and Johnson rely heavily on the repetition of parallel grammatical items for effect. Johnson, for instance, speaks of "the vices which border upon every virtue, and the virtues which are allied to every vice." Find other examples of parallel structure in both essays and discuss the effect.

## SUGGESTIONS FOR WRITING

1. Write your own sketch of a negative character type. You might want to consider one of the following: the gossip, the miser, the extrovert or introvert, the follower, the braggart, the optimist or pessimist, the slob, the crusader, the go-getter.

   Or consider something a bit more difficult. Write a letter to someone who fits the description of Parker's Good Soul or Johnson's "good sort of woman." Adopt an understanding tone rather than a critical one, and try to explain to that person why his or her behavior annoys other people.

# *Part Two*

# YOUTH AND MATURITY

*They who would be young when they are old*
*must be old when they are young.*

—JOHN RAY

There are two radically different, even contradictory, metaphors for the process of developing from youth to maturity. One of these metaphors is Aristotle's description of the acorn which contains the potential to become an oak tree. This image implies that all of us are born with the essence of our individuality and that maturity is primarily a process by which that individuality is fulfilled. The other metaphor, most fully delineated by John Locke, is that of the *tabula rasa*, the blank tablet. In this view of human development, individuals have no identity until they assimilate experiences and knowledge. These two views are still at odds with each other today. Some people see the transition from youth to maturity as a basic continuity, an unfolding of powers that come from within. Others see the human personality as something subject to drastic change, something acted upon by outside forces or written upon like an empty page. Our view of human growth colors the way we see ourselves, the way we raise our children, and the way we imagine the future.

The essays in this part explore seriously and humorously some of these ideas. They discuss childhood, adolescence, and old age. They mock some youthful behavior and warn against some threats to integrity in the later stages of life. Growing up and growing old are much more than physical processes; they also constitute a series of mental and emotional stages through which we pass. From the classic essay by Aristotle to the contemporary writings of Susan Sontag and Simone de Beauvoir, these essayists examine carefully and compellingly various aspects of these stages. They require their readers to be conscious of personal development in a variety of ways and to be aware of some of the damaging attitudes which may accompany different stages of life.

The passage from youth to maturity to old age, then, is more than just an inescapable journey through life. The subject of human growth raises crucial questions about human identity itself. Is the growth of an individual primarily a realization of potential? Or is it a process of assimilation, reaction, and change? Finally, what are the major ways in which each stage of life offers challenges or threats to personal development?

# 6

# The Stages of Life

*Aristotle*

## "YOUNG MEN AND ELDERLY MEN"

*Simone de Beauvoir*

## "INTRODUCTION" FROM *THE COMING OF AGE*

This first pair of essays discusses the stages of life from youth to old age. A selection from Aristotle's *Rhetoric,* "Young Men and Elderly Men," classifies and describes the personality traits of people in three different stages of life: youth, middle age, and old age. Aristotle sees a sharp discrepancy between the behavior and beliefs of young people and those of old people, with middle age forming a happy medium between the two extremes. Simone de Beauvoir, on the other hand, objects to this tendency to separate life into distinct parts. The result, she argues, is that we dissociate ourselves from old people and refuse to recognize ourselves as "already being the dwelling-place of our own future old age."

### WRITE BEFORE READING

1. The next two essays—indeed, this whole section—treat the issues of youth and maturity, what it means to grow up and to grow old. Prepare for it by writing two profiles—character sketches, if you will. Pick two people, one a young person, one a person over sixty, both of whom you admire for the way they handle their age. Describe them for an audience of the sort that reads newspaper feature pages. Be sure to detail just what you admire about them.

*Aristotle*
# "YOUNG MEN AND ELDERLY MEN"

Young men have strong passions, and tend to gratify them indiscriminately. Of the bodily desires, it is the sexual by which they are most swayed and in which they show absence of self-control. They are changeable and fickle in their desires, which are violent while they last, but quickly over: their impulses are keen but not deep-rooted, and are like sick people's attacks of hunger and thirst. They are hot-tempered and quick-tempered, and apt to give way to their anger; bad temper often gets the better of them, for owing to their love of honour they cannot bear being slighted, and are indignant if they imagine themselves unfairly treated. While they love honour, they love victory still more; for youth is eager for superiority over others, and victory is one form of this. They love both more than they love money, which indeed they love very little, not having yet learnt what it means to be without it—this is the point of Pittacus' remark about Amphiaraus.* They look at the good side rather than the bad, not having yet witnessed many instances of wickedness. They trust others readily, because they have not yet often been cheated. They are sanguine; nature warms their blood as though with excess of wine; and besides that, they have as yet met with few disappointments. Their lives are mainly spent not in memory but in expectation; for expectation refers to the future, memory to the past, and youth has a long future before it and a short past behind it: on the first day of one's life one has nothing at all to remember, and can only look forward. They are easily cheated, owing to the sanguine disposition just mentioned. Their hot tempers and hopeful dispositions make them more courageous than older men are; the hot temper prevents fear, and the hopeful disposition creates confidence; we cannot feel fear so long as we are feeling angry, and any expectation of good makes us confident. They are shy, accepting the rules of society in which they have been trained, and not yet believing in any other standard of honour. They have exalted notions, because they have not yet been humbled by life or learnt its necessary limitations; moreover, their hopeful disposition makes them think themselves equal to great things—and that means having exalted notions. They would always rather do noble deeds than useful ones: their lives are regulated more by moral feeling than by reasoning; and whereas reasoning leads us to choose what is useful, moral goodness leads us to choose what is noble. They are fonder of their friends, intimates, and companions than older men are, because they like spending their days in the company of others, and have not yet come to value either their friends or anything else by their usefulness to themselves. All their mistakes are in the direction of doing things excessively and vehemently. They disobey Chilon's precept† by overdoing everything; they love too much and hate too much, and the same with everything else. They think they know everything, and are always quite sure about it; this, in fact, is why they overdo everything. If they do wrong to others, it is because they mean to insult them, not to do them actual harm. They are ready to pity others, because they think every one an honest man, or

* The remark is unknown.—Eds.

† Nothing in excess.—Eds.

anyhow better than he is: they judge their neighbour by their own harmless natures, and so cannot think he deserves to be treated in that way. They are fond of fun and therefore witty, wit being well-bred insolence.

Such, then, is the character of the Young. The character of Elderly Men—men who are past their prime—may be said to be formed for the most part of elements that are the contrary of all these. They have lived many years; they have often been taken in, and often made mistakes; and life on the whole is a bad business. The result is that they are sure about nothing and *under-do* everything. They 'think', but they never 'know'; and because of their hesitation they always add a 'possibly' or a 'perhaps', putting everything this way and nothing positively. They are cynical; that is, they tend to put the worse construction on everything. Further, their experience makes them distrustful and therefore suspicious of evil. Consequently they neither love warmly nor hate bitterly, but following the hint of Bias they love as though they will some day hate and hate as though they will some day love. They are small-minded, because they have been humbled by life: their desires are set upon nothing more exalted or unusual than what will help them to keep alive. They are not generous, because money is one of the things they must have, and at the same time their experience has taught them how hard it is to get and how easy to lose. They are cowardly, and are always anticipating danger; unlike that of the young, who are warm-blooded, their temperament is chilly; old age has paved the way for cowardice; fear is, in fact, a form of chill. They love life; and all the more when their last day has come, because the object of all desire is something we have not got, and also because we desire most strongly that which we need most urgently. They are too fond of themselves; this is one form that small-mindedness takes. Because of this, they guide their lives too much by considerations of what is useful and too little by what is noble—for the useful is what is good for oneself, and the noble what is good absolutely. They are not shy, but shameless rather; caring less for what is noble than for what is useful, they feel contempt for what people may think of them. They lack confidence in the future; partly through experience—for most things go wrong, or anyhow turn out worse than one expects; and partly because of their cowardice. They live by memory rather than by hope; for what is left to them of life is but little as compared with the long past; and hope is of the future, memory of the past. This, again, is the cause of their loquacity; they are continually talking of the past, because they enjoy remembering it. Their fits of anger are sudden but feeble. Their sensual passions have either altogether gone or have lost their vigour: consequently they do not feel their passions much, and their actions are inspired less by what they do feel than by the love of gain. Hence men at this time of life are often supposed to have a self-controlled character; the fact is that their passions have slackened, and they are slaves to the love of gain. They guide their lives by reasoning more than by moral feeling; reasoning being directed to utility and moral feeling to moral goodness. If they wrong others, they mean to injure them, not to insult them. Old men may feel pity, as well as young men, but not for the same reason. Young men feel it out of kindness; old men out of weakness, imagining that anything that befalls any one else might easily happen to them, which, as we saw, is a thought that excites pity. Hence they are querulous, and not disposed to jesting or laughter—the love of laughter being the very opposite of querulousness.

Such are the characters of Young Men and Elderly Men. People always think well of speeches adapted to, and reflecting, their own character: and we can now see how to compose our speeches so as to adapt both them and ourselves to our audiences.

As for Men in their Prime, clearly we shall find that they have a character between that of the young and that of the old, free from the extremes of either. They have neither that excess of confidence which amounts to rashness, nor too much timidity, but the right amount of each. They neither trust everybody nor distrust everybody, but judge people correctly. Their lives will be guided not by the sole consideration either of what is noble or of what is useful, but by both; neither by parsimony nor by prodigality, but by what is fit and proper. So, too, in regard to anger and desire; they will be brave as well as temperate, and temperate as well as brave; these virtues are divided between the young and the old; the young are brave but intemperate, the old temperate but cowardly. To put it generally, all the valuable qualities that youth and age divide between them are united in the prime of life, while all their excesses or defects are replaced by moderation and fitness.

## *Simone de Beauvoir*
# "INTRODUCTION" FROM *THE COMING OF AGE*

When Buddha was still Prince Siddartha he often escaped from the splendid palace in which his father kept him shut up and drove about the surrounding countryside. The first time he went out he saw a tottering, wrinkled, toothless, white-haired man, bowed, mumbling and trembling as he propped himself along on his stick. The sight astonished the prince and the charioteer told him just what it meant to be old. "It is the world's pity," cried Siddartha, "that weak and ignorant beings, drunk with the vanity of youth, do not behold old age! Let us hurry back to the palace. What is the use of pleasures and delights, since I myself am the future dwelling-place of old age?"

Buddha recognized his own fate in the person of a very aged man, because, being born to save humanity, he chose to take upon himself the entirety of the human state. In this he differed from the rest of mankind, for they evade those aspects of it that distress them. And above all they evade old age. The Americans have struck the word death out of their vocabulary—they speak only of "the dear departed": and in the same way they avoid all reference to great age. It is a forbidden subject in present-day France, too. What a furious outcry I raised when I offended against this taboo at the end of *La Force des choses*! Acknowledging that I was on the threshold of old age was tantamount to saying that old age was lying there in wait for every woman, and that it had already laid hold upon many of them. Great numbers of people, particularly old people, told me, kindly or angrily but always at great length and again and again, that old age simply did not exist! There were some who were less young than others, and that was all it amounted to. Society looks upon old age as a kind of shameful secret that it is unseemly to mention. There is a copious literature dealing with women, with children, and with young people in all their aspects: but apart from specialized works we scarcely ever find any reference whatsoever to the old. A comic-strip artist once had to re-draw a whole series because he had included a pair of grandparents among his characters. "Cut out the old folks," he was ordered.* When I say that I am working on a study of old age people generally exclaim, "What an extraordinary notion! . . . But you aren't old! . . . What a dismal subject."

And that indeed is the very reason why I am writing this book. I mean to break the conspiracy of silence. Marcuse observes that the consumers' society has replaced a troubled by a clear conscience and that it condemns all feelings of guilt. But its peace of mind has to be disturbed. As far as old people are concerned this society is not only guilty but downright criminal. Sheltering behind the myths of expansion and affluence, it treats the old as outcasts. In France, where twelve per cent of the population are over sixty-five and where the proportion of old people is the highest in the world, they are condemned to poverty, decrepitude, wretchedness and despair. In the United States their lot is no happier. To reconcile this barbarous treatment with the humanist morality they profess to follow, the ruling class adopts the convenient plan of refusing to consider them as real people: if their voices were heard, the hearers would be forced to acknowledge that these were human voices. I shall compel my readers to hear them. I shall describe the position that is allotted to the old and the way in which they live: I shall tell what in fact happens inside their minds and their hearts; and what I say will not be distorted by the myths and the clichés of bourgeois culture.

Then again, society's attitude towards the old is deeply ambivalent. Generally speaking, it does not look upon the aged as belonging to one clearly-defined category. The turning-point of puberty allows the drawing of a line between the adolescent and the adult—a division that is arbitrary only within narrow limits; and at eighteen or perhaps twenty-one youths are admitted to the community of grown men. This advancement is nearly always accompanied by initiation rites. The time at which old age begins is ill-defined; it varies according to the era and the place, and nowhere do we find any initiation ceremonies that confirm the fresh status.† Throughout his life the individual retains the same political rights and duties: civil law makes not the slightest difference between a man of forty and one of a hundred. For the lawyers an aged man is as wholly responsible for his crimes as a young one, except in pathological cases.‡ In practice the aged are not looked upon as a class apart, and in any case they would not wish so to be regarded. There are books, periodicals, entertainments, radio and television programmes for children and young people: for the old there are

* Reported by François Garrigue in *Dernières Nouvelles d'Alsace,* 12 October 1968.—Au.

† The feasts with which some societies celebrate people's sixtieth or eightieth birthdays are not of an initiatory character.—Au.

‡ Mornet, the public prosecutor, began his indictment of Petain by reminding his hearers that the law takes no account of age. In recent years the "inquiry into personality" that comes before the trial can emphasize the age of the accused: but only as one feature among all the rest.—Au.

none.* Where all these things are concerned, they are looked upon as forming part of the body of adults less elderly than themselves. Yet on the other hand, when their economic status is decided upon, society appears to think that they belong to an entirely different species: for if all that is needed to feel that one has done one's duty by them is to grant them a wretched pittance, then they have neither the same needs nor the same feelings as other men. Economists and legislators endorse this convenient fallacy when they deplore the burden that the "non-active" lay upon the shoulders of the active population, just as though the latter were not potential non-actives and as though they were not insuring their own future by seeing to it that the aged are taken care of. For their part, the trades-unionists do not fall into this error: whenever they put forward their claims the question of retirement always plays an important part in them.

The aged do not form a body with any economic strength whatsoever and they have no possible way of enforcing their rights: and it is to the interest of the exploiting class to destroy the solidarity between the workers and the unproductive old so that there is no one at all to protect them. The myths and the clichés put out by bourgeois thought aim at holding up the elderly man as someone who is different, as *another being*. "Adolescents who last long enough are what life makes old men out of," observes Proust. They still retain the virtues and the faults of the men they were and still are: and this is something that public opinion chooses to overlook. If old people show the same desires, the same feelings and the same requirements as the young, the world looks upon them with disgust: in them love and jealousy seem revolting or absurd, sexuality repulsive and violence ludicrous. They are required to be a standing example of all the virtues. Above all they are called upon to display serenity: the world asserts that they possess it, and this assertion allows the world to ignore their unhappiness. The purified image of themselves that society offers the aged is that of the white-haired and venerable Sage, rich in experience, planing high above the common state of mankind: if they vary from this, then they fall below it. The counterpart of the first image is that of the old fool in his dotage, a laughing-stock for children. In any case, either by their virtue or by their degradation they stand outside humanity. The world, therefore, need feel no scruple in refusing them the minimum of support which is considered necessary for living like a human being.

We carry this ostracism so far that we even reach the point of turning it against ourselves: for in the old person that we must become, we refuse to recognize ourselves. "Of all realities [old age] is perhaps that of which we retain a purely abstract notion longest in our lives," says Proust with great accuracy. All men are mortal: they reflect upon this fact. A great many of them become old: almost none ever foresees this state before it is upon him. Nothing should be more expected than old age; nothing is more unforeseen. When young people, particularly girls, are asked about their future, they set the utmost limit of life at sixty. Some say, "I shan't get that far: I'll die first." Others even go so far as to say "I'll kill myself first." The adult behaves as though he will never grow old. Working men are often amazed, stupefied

* *La Bonne Presse* has recently launched a periodical intended for old people. It confines itself to giving information and practical advice.—Au.

when the day of their retirement comes. Its date was fixed well beforehand; they knew it; they ought to have been ready for it. In fact, unless they have been thoroughly indoctrinated politically, this knowledge remains entirely outside their ken.

When the time comes nearer, and even when the day is at hand, people usually prefer old age to death. And yet at a distance it is death that we see with a clearer eye. It forms part of what is immediately possible for us: at every period of our lives its threat is there: there are times when we come very close to it and often enough it terrifies us. Whereas no one ever becomes old in a single instant: unlike Buddha, when we are young or in our prime we do not think of ourselves as already being the dwelling-place of our own future old age. Age is removed from us by an extent of time so great that it merges with eternity: such a remote future seems unreal. Then again the dead are *nothing*. This nothingness can bring about a metaphysical vertigo, but in a way it is comforting—it raises no problems. "I shall no longer exist." In a disappearance of this kind I retain my identity.* Thinking of myself as an old person when I am twenty or forty means thinking of myself as someone else, as *another* than myself. Every metamorphosis has something frightening about it. When I was a little girl I was amazed and indeed deeply distressed when I realized that one day I should turn into a grown-up. But when one is young the real advantages of the adult status usually counterbalance the wish to remain oneself, unchanged. Whereas old age looms ahead like a calamity: even among those who are thought well preserved, age brings with it a very obvious physical decline. For of all species, mankind is that in which the alterations caused by advancing years are the most striking. Animals grow thin; they become weaker: they do not undergo a total change. We do. It wounds one's heart to see a lovely young woman and then next to her her reflection in the mirror of the years to come—her mother. Levi-Strauss says that the Nambikwara Indians have a single word that means "young and beautiful" and another that means "old and ugly." When we look at the image of our own future provided by the old we do not believe it: an absurd inner voice whispers that *that* will never happen to us—when *that* happens it will no longer be ourselves that it happens to. Until the moment it is upon us old age is something that only affects other people. So it is understandable that society should manage to prevent us from seeing our own kind, our fellow-men, when we look at the old.

We must stop cheating: the whole meaning of our life is in question in the future that is waiting for us. If we do not know what we are going to be, we cannot know what we are: let us recognize ourselves in this old man or in that old woman. It must be done if we are to take upon ourselves the entirety of our human state. And when it is done we will no longer acquiesce in the misery of the last age; we will no longer be indifferent, because we shall feel concerned, as indeed we are. This misery vehemently indicts the system of exploitation in which we live. The old person who can no longer provide for himself is always a burden. But in those societies where there is some degree of equality—within a rural community, for example, or among certain primitive nations—the middle-aged man is aware, in spite of himself, that his state tomorrow will be the same as that which he allots to the old today. That is the mean-

* This identity is all the more strongly guaranteed to those who believe they have an immortal soul.—Au.

ing of Grimm's tale, versions of which are to be found in every countryside. A peasant makes his old father eat out of a small wooden trough, apart from the rest of the family: one day he finds his son fitting little boards together. "It's for you when you are old," says the child. Straight away the grandfather is given back his place at the family table. The active members of the community work out compromises between their long-term and their immediate interests. Imperative necessity compels some primitive tribes to kill their aged relatives, even though they themselves have to suffer the same fate later on. In less extreme cases selfishness is moderated by foresight and by family affection. In the capitalist world, long-term interests no longer have any influence: the ruling class that determines the fate of the masses has no fear of sharing that fate. As for humanitarian feelings, they do not enter into account at all, in spite of the flood of hypocritical words. The economy is founded upon profit; and in actual fact the entire civilization is ruled by profit. The human working stock is of interest only in so far as it is profitable. When it is no longer profitable it is tossed aside. At a congress a little while ago, Dr. Leach, a Cambridge anthropologist, said, in effect, "In a changing world, where machines have a very short run of life, men must not be used too long. Everyone over fifty-five should be scrapped."*

The word "scrap" expresses his meaning admirably. We are told that retirement is the time of freedom and leisure: poets have sung "the delights of reaching port."† These are shameless lies. Society inflicts so wretched a standard of living upon the vast majority of old people that it is almost tautological to say "old and poor": again, most exceedingly poor people are old. Leisure does not open up new possibilities for the retired man; just when he is at last set free from compulsion and restraint, the means of making use of his liberty are taken from him. He is condemned to stagnate in boredom and loneliness, a mere throw-out. The fact that for the last fifteen or twenty years of his life a man should be no more than a reject, a piece of scrap, reveals the failure of our civilization: if we were to look upon the old as human beings, with a human life behind them, and not as so many walking corpses, this obvious truth would move us profoundly. Those who condemn the maiming, crippling system in which we live should expose this scandal. It is by concentrating one's efforts upon the fate of the most unfortunate, the worst-used of all, that one can successfully shake a society to its foundations. In order to destroy the caste system, Gandhi tackled the status of the pariahs: in order to destroy the feudal family, Communist China liberated the women. Insisting that men should remain men during the last years of their life would imply a total upheaval of our society. The result cannot possibly be obtained by a few limited reforms that leave the system intact: for it is the exploitation of the workers, the pulverization of society, and the utter poverty of a culture confined to the privileged, educated few that leads to this kind of dehumanized old age. And it is this old age that makes it clear that everything has to be reconsidered, recast from the very beginning. That is why the whole problem is so carefully passed over in silence: and that is why this silence has to be shattered. I call upon my readers to help me in doing so.

* This was written in December 1968.—Au.

† Racan's phrase.—Au.

## SUGGESTIONS FOR DISCUSSION

1. How does Simone de Beauvoir's view of life stages differ from that of Aristotle? Does she tend to emphasize the continuity between youth and old age or the contrast? Which does Aristotle emphasize? How are these different emphases related to their different purposes?
2. Most of you fall into Aristotle's "young" category—if we make allowance, that is, for his discussing only young men. Do you agree with his characterization of you? Now think of people you know who fit his "elderly" category. Do they match his description? Reverse some of the attributes. (For example: The old love honour and victory more than they love money, which indeed they love little, having learnt how quickly money can come and go.) Can you think of people who fit the reversed characterizations? Are Aristotle's generalizations valid?
3. Some individuals have attempted to elevate the status of older people by using such terms as "senior citizens" and "gray panthers." How do you think Simone de Beauvoir would react to this practice? Would she see it as part of the solution or part of the problem?

## SUGGESTIONS FOR WRITING

1. Simone de Beauvoir is an impassioned advocate trying to shock an apathetic society out of its held beliefs. To do so, as she says, she is willing to "shake it to its foundations." The result, reform in our dealing with old age, "cannot possibly be obtained by a few limited reforms that leave the system intact: for it is the exploitation of the workers, the pulverization of society, and the utter poverty of a culture confined to the privileged, educated few that leads to this kind of dehumanized old age."

   She attacks the problem head on, confrontationally. How did you react to her assault? Write a response to her essay—a letter to her, if you like—explaining how you responded to her call to "shatter" the silence.
2. Aristotle's essay is taken from his *Rhetoric,* a book about the art of persuasion. Aristotle's overriding purpose in comparing young and old is to help speakers approach their audience most effectively. Assume, for the moment, that his distinctions between youth and old age are valid. Choose a contemporary issue that interests you and write two short essays—one designed to persuade older readers and another designed to persuade younger readers.

# 7

# Growing Up

*Nora Ephron*

## "A FEW WORDS ABOUT BREASTS"

*E. B. White*

## "AFTERNOON OF AN AMERICAN BOY"

Nora Ephron and E. B. White both describe episodes from their adolescent years that convey the confusion and pain of growing up. Ephron's essay, "A Few Words about Breasts," emphasizes the pressure on high school girls to conform to certain arbitrary standards of beauty. Ephron mocks these standards and, at the same time, mocks her own capacity for taking them seriously and allowing them to damage her self-esteem. White's essay, "Afternoon of an American Boy," offers a mellow contrast to Ephron's bitter experience. White recalls his "ineptitude" on his first date with a certain degree of fondness and suggests that something vital is lost as one gains social competence.

### WRITE BEFORE READING

1. The next two essays are based on the writers' recollections of adolescence. For this writing assignment, think back over your own adolescent years. Find some event or development—a first date, a change in voice, a crush on some "unattainable" person—that still makes you blush when you recall it. Now picture as your audience a sympathetic group of people your own age, people who will ease your embarrassment by telling a story of their own. Your purpose should be mainly to entertain, to tell a good story, one that makes people laugh or cry. Remember to supply as much detail as you can: dialogue, real names, real places, physical descriptions, and so on.

# *Nora Ephron*
# "A FEW WORDS ABOUT BREASTS"

I have to begin with a few words about androgyny. In grammar school, in the fifth and sixth grades, we were all tyrannized by a rigid set of rules that supposedly determined whether we were boys or girls. The episode in *Huckleberry Finn* where Huck is disguised as a girl and gives himself away by the way he threads a needle and catches a ball—that kind of thing. We learned that the way you sat, crossed your legs, held a cigarette, and looked at your nails—the way you did these things instinctively was absolute proof of your sex. Now obviously most children did not take this literally, but I did. I thought that just one slip, just one incorrect cross of my legs or flick of an imaginary cigarette ash would turn me from whatever I was into the other thing; that would be all it took, really. Even though I was outwardly a girl and had many of the trappings generally associated with girldom—a girl's name, for example, and dresses, my own telephone, an autograph book—I spent the early years of my adolescence absolutely certain that I might at any point gum it up. I did not feel at all like a girl. I was boyish. I was athletic, ambitious, outspoken, competitive, noisy, rambunctious. I had scabs on my knees and my socks slid into my loafers and I could throw a football. I wanted desperately not to be that way, not to be a mixture of both things, but instead just one, a girl, a definite indisputable girl. As soft and as pink as a nursery. And nothing would do that for me, I felt, but breasts.

I was about six months younger than everyone else in my class, and so for about six months after it began, for six months after my friends had begun to develop (that was the word we used, develop), I was not particularly worried. I would sit in the bathtub and look down at my breasts and know that any day now, any second now, they would start growing like everyone else's. They didn't. "I want to buy a bra," I said to my mother one night. "What for?" she said. My mother was really hateful about bras, and by the time my third sister had gotten to the point where she was ready to want one, my mother had worked the whole business into a comedy routine. "Why not use a Band-Aid instead?" she would say. It was a source of great pride to my mother that she had never even had to wear a brassiere until she had her fourth child, and then only because her gynecologist made her. It was incomprehensible to me that anyone could ever be proud of something like that. It was the 1950s, for God's sake. Jane Russell. Cashmere sweaters. Couldn't my mother see that? *"I am too old to wear an undershirt."* Screaming. Weeping. Shouting. "Then don't wear an undershirt," said my mother. "But I want to buy a bra." "What for?"

I suppose that for most girls, breasts, brassieres, that entire thing, has more trauma, more to do with the coming of adolescence, with becoming a woman, than anything else. Certainly more than getting your period, although that, too, was traumatic, symbolic. But you could see breasts; they were there; they were visible. Whereas a girl could claim to have her period for months before she actually got it and nobody would ever know the difference. Which is exactly what I did. All you had to do was make a great fuss over having enough nickels for the Kotex machine and walk around clutching your stomach and moaning for three to five days a month about The Curse and you could convince anybody. There is a school of thought somewhere in the women's lib/women's mag/gynecology establishment that claims that menstrual cramps are purely psychological, and I lean towards it. Not that I didn't have them finally. Agonizing cramps, heating-pad cramps, go-down-to-the-school-nurse-and-lie-on-the-cot cramps. But, unlike any pain I had ever suffered, I adored the pain of cramps, welcomed it, wallowed in it, bragged about it. "I can't go. I have cramps." "I can't do that. I have cramps." And most of all, gigglingly, blushingly: "I can't swim. I have cramps." Nobody ever used the hard-core word. Menstruation. God, what an awful word. Never that. "I have cramps."

The morning I first got my period, I went into my mother's bedroom to tell her. And my mother, my utterly-hateful-about-bras mother, burst into tears. It was really a lovely moment, and I remember it so clearly not just because it was one of the two times I ever saw my mother cry on my account (the other was when I was caught being a six-year-old kleptomaniac), but also because the incident did not mean to me what it meant to her. Her little girl, her firstborn, had finally become a woman. That was what she was crying about. My reaction to the event, however, was that I might well be a woman in some scientific, textbook sense (and could at least stop faking every month and stop wasting all those nickels). But in another sense—in a visible sense—I was as androgynous and as liable to tip over into boyhood as ever.

I started with a 28 AA bra. I don't think they made them any smaller in those days, although I gather that now you can buy bras for five-year-olds that don't have any cups whatsoever in them; trainer bras they are called. My first brassiere came from Robinson's Department Store in Beverly Hills. I went there alone, shaking, positive they would look me over and smile and tell me to come back next year. An actual fitter took me into the dressing room and stood over me while I took off my blouse and tried the first one on. The little puffs stood out on my chest. "Lean over," said the fitter. (To this day, I am not sure what fitters in bra departments do except to tell you to lean over.) I leaned over, with the fleeting hope that my breasts would miraculously fall out of my body and into the puffs. Nothing.

"Don't worry about it," said my friend Libby some months later, when things had not improved. "You'll get them after you're married."

"What are you talking about?" I said.

"When you get married," Libby explained, "your husband will touch your breasts and rub them and kiss them and they'll grow."

That was the killer. Necking I could deal with. Intercourse I could deal with. But it had never crossed my mind that a man was going to touch my breasts, that breasts had something to do with all that, petting, my God, they never mentioned petting in my little sex manual about the fertilization of the ovum. I became dizzy. For I knew instantly—as naive as I had been only a moment before—that only part of what she was saying was true: the touching, rubbing, kissing part, not the growing part. And I knew that no one would ever want to marry me. I had no breasts. I would never have breasts.

My best friend in school was Diana Raskob. She lived a block from me in a house full of wonders. English muffins, for instance. The Raskobs were the first people in Beverly Hills to have English muffins for breakfast. They also had an apricot tree in the back, and a badminton court, and a subscription to *Seventeen* magazine, and hundreds of games, like Sorry and Parcheesi and Treasure Hunt and Anagrams. Diana and I spent three or four afternoons a week in their den reading and playing and eating. Diana's mother's kitchen was full of the most colossal assortment of junk food I have ever been exposed to. My house was full of apples and peaches and milk and homemade chocolate-chip cookies—which were nice, and good for you, but-not-right-before-dinner-or-you'll-spoil-your-appetite. Diana's house had nothing in it that was good for you, and what's more, you could stuff it in right up until dinner and nobody cared. Bar-B-Q potato chips (they were the first in them, too), giant bottles of ginger ale, fresh popcorn with melted butter, hot fudge sauce on Baskin-Robbins jamoca ice cream, powdered-sugar doughnuts from Van de Kamp's. Diana and I had been best friends since we were seven; we were about equally popular in school (which is to say, not particularly), we had about the same success with boys (extremely intermittent), and we looked much the same. Dark. Tall. Gangly.

It is September, just before school begins. I am eleven years old, about to enter the seventh grade, and Diana and I have not seen each other all summer. I have been to camp and she has been somewhere like Banff with her parents. We are meeting, as we often do, on the street midway between our two houses, and we will walk back to Diana's and eat junk and talk about what has happened to each of us that summer. I am walking down Walden Drive in my jeans and my father's shirt hanging out and my old red loafers with the socks falling into them and coming toward me is . . . I take a deep breath . . . a young woman. Diana. Her hair is curled and she has a waist and hips and a bust and she is wearing a straight skirt, an article of clothing I have been repeatedly told I will be unable to wear until I have the hips to hold it up. My jaw drops, and suddenly I am crying, crying hysterically, can't catch my breath sobbing. My best friend has betrayed me. She has gone ahead without me and done it. She has shaped up.

Here are some things I did to help:

Bought a Mark Eden Bust Developer.

Slept on my back for four years.

Splashed cold water on them every night because some French actress said in *Life* magazine that that was what *she* did for her perfect bustline.

Ultimately, I resigned myself to a bad toss and began to wear padded bras. I think about them now, think about all those years in high school I went around in them, my three padded bras, every single one of them with different-sized breasts. Each time I changed bras I changed sizes: one week nice perky but not too obstrusive breasts, the next medium-sized slightly pointy ones, the next week knockers, true knockers; all the time, whatever size I was, carrying around this rubberized appendage on my chest that occasionally crashed into a wall and was poked inward and had to be poked outward—I think about all that and wonder how anyone kept a straight face through it. My parents, who normally had no restraints about needling me—why did they say nothing as they watched my chest go up and down? My friends, who would periodically inspect my breasts for signs of growth and reassure me—why didn't they at least counsel consistency?

And the bathing suits. I die when I think about the bathing suits. That was the era when you could lay an uninhabited bathing suit on the beach and someone would make a pass at it. I would put one on, an absurd swimsuit with its enormous bust built into it, the bones from the suit stabbing me in the rib cage and leaving little red welts on my body, and there I would be, my chest plunging straight downward absolutely vertically from my collarbone to the top of my suit and then suddenly, wham, out came all that padding and material and wiring absolutely horizontally.

Buster Klepper was the first boy who ever touched them. He was my boyfriend my senior year of high school. There is a picture of him in my high-school yearbook that makes him look quite attractive in a Jewish, horn-rimmed-glasses sort of way, but the picture does not show the pimples, which were air-brushed out, or the dumbness. Well, that isn't really fair. He wasn't dumb. He just wasn't terribly bright. His mother refused to accept it, refused to accept the relentlessly average report cards, refused to deal with her son's inevitable destiny in some junior college or other. "He was tested," she would say to me, apropos of nothing, "and it came out a hundred and forty-five. That's near-genius." Had the word "underachiever" been coined, she probably would have lobbed that one at me, too. Anyway, Buster was really very sweet—which is, I know, damning with faint praise, but there it is. I was the editor of the front page of the high-school newspaper and he was editor of the back page; we had to work together, side by side, in the print shop, and that was how it started. On our first date, we went to see *April Love*, starring Pat Boone. Then we started going together. Buster had a green coupe, a 1950 Ford with an engine he had hand-chromed until it shone, dazzled, reflected the image of anyone who looked into it, anyone usually being Buster polishing it or the gas-station attendants he constantly asked to check the oil in order for them to be overwhelmed by the sparkle on the valves. The car also had a boot stretched over the back seat for reasons I never understood; hanging from the rearview mirror, as was the custom, was a pair of angora dice. A previous girl friend named Solange, who was famous throughout Beverly Hills High School for having no pigment in her right eyebrow, had knitted them for him. Buster and I would ride around town, the two of us seated to the left of the sterring wheel. I would shift gears. It was nice.

There was necking. Terrific necking. First in the car, overlooking Los Angeles from what is now the Trousdale Estates. Then on the bed of his parents' cabana at Ocean House. Incredibly wonderful, frustrating necking, I loved it, really, but no further than necking, please don't, please, because there I was absolutely terrified of the general implications of going-a-step-further with a near-dummy and also terrified of his finding out there was next to nothing there (which he knew, of course; he wasn't that dumb).

I broke up with him at one point. I think we were apart for about two weeks. At the end of that time, I drove down to see a friend at a boarding school in Palos Verdes Estates and a disc jockey played "April Love" on the radio four times during the trip. I took it as a sign. I drove straight back to Griffith Park to a golf tournament

Buster was playing in (he was the sixth-seeded teen-age golf player in southern California) and presented myself back to him on the green of the 18th hole. It was all very dramatic. That night we went to a drive-in and I let him get his hand under my protuberances and onto my breasts. He really didn't seem to mind at all.

*"Do you want to marry my son?" the woman asked me.*

*"Yes," I said.*

*I was nineteen years old, a virgin, going with this woman's son, this big strange woman who was married to a Lutheran minister in New Hampshire and pretended she was gentile and had this son, by her first husband, this total fool of a son who ran the hero-sandwich concession at Harvard Business School and whom for one moment one December in New Hampshire I said—as much out of politeness as anything else—that I wanted to marry.*

*"Fine," she said. "Now, here's what you do. Always make sure you're on top of him so you won't seem so small. My bust is very large, you see, so I always lie on my back to make it look smaller, but you'll have to be on top most of the time."*

*I nodded. "Thank you," I said.*

*"I have a book for you to read," she went on. "Take it with you when you leave. Keep it." She went to the bookshelf, found it, and gave it to me. It was a book on frigidity.*

*"Thank you," I said.*

That is a true story. Everything in this article is a true story, but I feel I have to point out that that story in particular is true. It happened on December 30, 1960. I think about it often. When it first happened, I naturally assumed that the woman's son, my boyfriend, was responsible. I invented a scenario where he had had a little heart-to-heart with his mother and had confessed that his only objection to me was that my breasts were small; his mother then took it upon herself to help out. Now I think I was wrong about the incident. The mother was acting on her own, I think: that was her way of being cruel and competitive under the guise of being helpful and maternal. You have small breasts, she was saying; therefore you will never make him as happy as I have. Or you have small breasts; therefore you will doubtless have sexual problems. Or you have small breasts; therefore you are less woman than I am. She was, as it happens, only the first of what seems to me to be a never-ending string of women who have made competitive remarks to me about breast size. "I would love to wear a dress like that," my friend Emily says to me, "but my bust is too big." Like that. Why do women say these things to me? Do I attract these remarks the way other women attract married men or alcoholics or homosexuals? This summer, for example. I am at a party in East Hampton and I am introduced to a woman from Washington. She is a minor celebrity, very pretty and Southern and blond and outspoken, and I am flattered because she has read something I have written. We are talking animatedly, we have been talking no more than five minutes, when a man comes up to join us. "Look at the two of us," the woman says to the man, indicating me and her. "The two of us together couldn't fill an A cup." Why does she say that? It isn't even true, dammit, so why? Is she even more addled than I am on this subject? Does she honestly believe there is something wrong with her size breasts, which, it seems to me, now that I look hard at them, are just right? Do I unconsciously bring out competitiveness in women? In that form? What did I do to deserve it?

As for men.

There were men who minded and let me know that they minded. There were men who did not mind. In any case, *I* always minded.

And even now, now that I have been countlessly reassured that my figure is a good one, now that I am grown-up enough to understand that most of my feelings have very little to do with the reality of my shape, I am nonetheless obsessed by breasts. I cannot help it. I grew up in the terrible fifties—with rigid stereotypical sex roles, the insistence that men be men and dress like men and women be women and dress like women, the intolerance of androgyny—and I cannot shake it, cannot shake my feelings of inadequacy. Well, that time is gone, right? All those exaggerated examples of breast worship are gone, right? Those women were freaks, right? I know all that. And yet here I am, stuck with the psychological remains of it all, stuck with my own peculiar version of breast worship. You probably think I am crazy to go on like this: here I have set out to write a confession that is meant to hit you with the shock of recognition, and instead you are sitting there thinking I am thoroughly warped. Well, what can I tell you? If I had had them, I would have been a completely different person. I honestly believe that.

After I went into therapy, a process that made it possible for me to tell total strangers at cocktail parties that breasts were the hang-up of my life, I was often told that I was insane to have been bothered by my condition. I was also frequently told, by close friends, that I was extremely boring on the subject. And my girl friends, the ones with nice big breasts, would go on endlessly about how their lives had been far more miserable than mine. Their bra straps were snapped in class. They couldn't sleep on their stomachs. They were stared at whenever the word "mountain" cropped up in geography. And *Evangeline,* good God what they went through every time someone had to stand up and recite the Prologue to Longfellow's *Evangeline:* ". . . stand like druids of eld . . . / With beards that rest on their bosoms." It was much worse for them, they tell me. They had a terrible time of it, they assure me. I don't know how lucky I was, they say.

I have thought about their remarks, tried to put myself in their place, considered their point of view. I think they are full of shit.

## *E. B. White*
## "AFTERNOON OF AN AMERICAN BOY"

When I was in my teens, I lived in Mount Vernon, in the same block with J. Parnell Thomas, who grew up to become chairman of the House Committee on Un-American Activities. I lived on the corner of Summit and East Sidney, at No. 101 Summit Avenue, and Parnell lived four or five doors north of us on the same side of the avenue, in the house the Diefendorfs used to live in.

Parnell was not a playmate of mine, as he was a few years older, but I used to greet him as he walked by our house on his way to and from the depot. He was a good-looking young man, rather quiet and shy. Seeing him, I would call "Hello, Parnell!" and he would smile and say "Hello, Elwyn!" and walk on. Once I remember dashing out of our yard on roller skates and executing a rink turn in front of Parnell, to show off, and he said, "Well! Quite an artist, aren't you?" I remember the words. I was delighted at praise from an older man and sped away along the flagstone sidewalk, dodging the cracks I knew so well.

The thing that made Parnell a special man in my eyes in those days was not his handsome appearance and friendly manner but his sister. Her name was Eileen. She was my age and she was a quiet, nice-looking girl. She never came over to my yard to play, and I never went over there, and, considering that we lived so near each other, we were remarkably uncommunicative; nevertheless, she was the girl I singled out, at one point, to be of special interest to me. Being of special interest to me involved practically nothing on a girl's part—it simply meant that she was under constant surveillance. On my own part, it meant that I suffered an astonishing disintegration when I walked by her house, from embarrassment, fright, and the knowledge that I was in enchanted territory.

In the matter of girls, I was different from most boys of my age. I admired girls a lot, but they terrified me. I did not feel that I possessed the peculiar gifts or accomplishments that girls liked in their male companions—the ability to dance, to play football, to cut up a bit in public, to smoke, and to make small talk. I couldn't do any of these things successfully, and seldom tried. Instead, I stuck with the accomplishments I was sure of: I rode my bicycle sitting backward on the handle bars, I made up poems, I played selections from *Aida* on the piano. In winter, I tended goal in the hockey games on the frozen pond in the dell. None of these tricks counted much with girls. In the four years I was in the Mount Vernon High School, I never went to a school dance and I never took a girl to a drugstore for a soda or to the Westchester Playhouse or to Proctor's. I wanted to do these things but did not have the nerve. What I finally did manage to do, however, and what is the subject of this memoir, was far brassier, far gaudier. As an exhibit of teen-age courage and ineptitude, it never fails to amaze me in retrospect. I am not even sure it wasn't un-American.

My bashfulness and backwardness annoyed my older sister very much, and at about the period of which I am writing she began making strong efforts to stir me up. She was convinced that I was in a rut, socially, and she found me a drag in her own social life, which was brisk. She kept trying to throw me with girls, but I always bounced. And whenever she saw a chance she would start the phonograph and grab me, and we would go charging around the parlor in the toils of the one-step, she gripping me as in a death struggle, and I hurling her finally away from me through greater strength. I was a skinny kid but my muscles were hard, and it would have taken an unusually powerful woman to have held me long in the attitude of the dance.

One day, through a set of circumstances I have forgotten, my sister managed to work me into an afternoon engagement she had with some others in New York. To me, at that time, New York was a wonderland largely unexplored. I had been to the Hippodrome a couple of times with my father, and to the Hudson-Fulton Celebration, and to a few matinées; but New York, except as a setting for extravaganzas, was unknown. My sister had heard tales of tea-dancing at the Plaza Hotel. She and a girl friend of hers and another fellow and myself went there to give it a try. The expedition struck me as a slick piece of arrangement on her part. I was the junior member of the group and had been roped in, I imagine, to give symmetry to the occasion. Or perhaps Mother had forbidden my sister to go at all unless another member of the family was along. Whether I was there for symmetry or for decency I can't really remember, but I was there.

The spectacle was a revelation to me. However repulsive the idea of dancing was, I was filled with amazement at the setup. Here were tables where a fellow could sit so close to the dance floor that he was practically on it. And you could order cinnamon toast and from the safety of your chair observe girls and men in close embrace, swinging along, the music playing while you ate the toast, and the dancers so near to you that they almost brushed the things off your table as they jogged by. I was impressed. Dancing or no dancing, this was certainly high life, and I knew I was witnessing a scene miles and miles ahead of anything that took place in Mount Vernon. I had never seen anything like it, and a ferment must have begun working in me that afternoon.

Incredible as it seems to me now, I formed the idea of asking Parnell's sister Eileen to accompany me to a tea dance at the Plaza. The plan shaped up in my mind as an expedition of unparalleled worldliness, calculated to stun even the most blasé girl. The fact that I didn't know how to dance must have been a powerful deterrent, but not powerful enough to stop me. As I look back on the affair, it's hard to credit my own memory, and I sometimes wonder if, in fact, the whole business isn't some dream that has gradually gained the status of actuality. A boy with any sense, wishing to become better acquainted with a girl who was "of special interest," would have cut out for himself a more modest assignment to start with—a soda date or a movie date—something within reasonable limits. Not me. I apparently became obsessed with the notion of taking Eileen to the Plaza and not to any darned old drugstore. I had learned the location of the Plaza, and just knowing how to get to it gave me a feeling of confidence. I had learned about cinnamon toast, so I felt able to cope with the waiter when he came along. And I banked heavily on the general splendor of the surroundings and the extreme sophistication of the function to carry the day, I guess.

I was three days getting up nerve to make the phone call. Meantime, I worked out everything in the greatest detail. I heeled myself with a safe amount of money. I looked up trains. I overhauled my clothes and assembled an outfit I believed would meet the test. Then, one night at six o'clock, when Mother and Father went downstairs to dinner, I lingered upstairs and entered the big closet off my bedroom where the wall phone was. There I stood for several minutes, trembling, my hand on the receiver, which hung upside down on the hook. (In our family, the receiver always hung upside down, with the big end up.)

I had rehearsed my first line and my second line. I planned to say, "Hello, can I please speak to Eileen?" Then, when she came to the phone, I planned to say, "Hello, Eileen, this is Elwyn White." From there on, I figured I could ad-lib it.

At last, I picked up the receiver and gave the number. As I had suspected, Eileen's mother answered.

"Can I please speak to Eileen?" I asked, in a low, troubled voice.

"Just a minute," said her mother. Then, on second thought, she asked, "Who is it, please?"

"It's Elwyn," I said.

She left the phone, and after quite a while Eileen's voice said, "Hello, Elwyn." This threw my second line out of whack, but I stuck to it doggedly.

"Hello, Eileen, this is Elwyn White," I said.

In no time at all I laid the proposition before her. She seemed dazed and asked me to wait a minute. I assume she went into a huddle with her mother. Finally, she said yes, she would like to go tea-dancing with me at the Plaza, and I said fine, I would call for her at quarter past three on Thursday afternoon, or whatever afternoon it was—I've forgotten.

I do not know now, and of course did not know then, just how great was the mental and physical torture Eileen went through that day, but the incident stacks up as a sort of unintentional un-American activity, for which I was solely responsible. It all went off as scheduled: the stately walk to the depot; the solemn train ride, during which we sat staring shyly into the seat in front of us; the difficult walk from Grand Central across Forty-second to Fifth, with pedestrians clipping us and cutting in between us; the bus ride to Fifty-ninth Street; then the Plaza itself, and the cinnamon toast, and the music, and the excitement. The thundering quality of the occasion must have delivered a mental shock to me, deadening my recollection, for I have only the dimmest memory of leading Eileen onto the dance floor to execute two or three unspeakable rounds, in which I vainly tried to adapt my violent sister-and-brother wrestling act into something graceful and appropriate. It must have been awful. And at six o'clock, emerging, I gave no thought to any further entertainment, such as dinner in town. I simply herded Eileen back all the long, dreary way to Mount Vernon and deposited her, a few minutes after seven, on an empty stomach, at her home. Even if I had attempted to dine her, I don't believe it would have been possible; the emotional strain of the afternoon had caused me to perspire uninterruptedly, and any restaurant would have been justified in rejecting me solely on the ground that I was too moist.

Over the intervening years, I've often felt guilty about my afternoon at the Plaza, and many years ago, during Parnell's investigation of writers, my feeling sometimes took the form of a guilt sequence in which I imagined myself on the stand, in the committee room, being questioned. It went something like this:

PARNELL: Have you ever written for the screen, Mr. White?

ME: No, sir.

PARNELL: Have you ever been, or are you now, a member of the Screen Writers' Guild?

ME: No, sir.

PARNELL: Have you ever been, or are you now, a member of the Communist Party?

ME: No, sir.

Then, in this imaginary guilt sequence of mine, Parnell digs deep and comes up with the big question, calculated to throw me.

PARNELL: Do you recall an afternoon, along about the middle of the second decade of this century, when you took my sister to the Plaza Hotel for tea under the grossly misleading and false pretext that you knew how to dance?

And as my reply comes weakly, "Yes, sir," I hear the murmur run through the committee room and see reporters bending over their notebooks, scribbling hard. In my dream, I am again seated with Eileen at the edge of the dance floor, frightened, stunned, and happy—in my ears the intoxicating drumbeat of the dance, in my throat the dry, bittersweet taste of cinnamon.

I don't know about the guilt, really. I guess a good many girls might say that an excursion such as the one I conducted Eileen on belongs in the un-American category. But there must be millions of aging males, now slipping into their anecdotage, who recall their Willie Baxter period with affection, and who remember some similar journey into ineptitude, in that precious, brief moment in life before love's pages, through constant reference, had become dog-eared, and before its narrative, through sheer competence, had lost the first, wild sense of derring-do.

## SUGGESTIONS FOR DISCUSSION

1. What was your reaction to Nora Ephron's essay? to E. B. White's? If you laughed aloud at either—or even if you smiled— go back and try to remember where and why. Writing humor is among the most difficult assignments. How did these two do it? (Note: If you were angered or disgusted by either essay, you can locate the passages that made you react so.) If you felt nothing, reread: you might have missed something.
2. Ephron and White are two of the most admired stylists in contemporary American prose. What do they do, how do they write, that wins them that reputation? To begin finding out, select a fair-sized paragraph from each and try a kind of stylistic analysis. How many sentences in the paragraph? How many words per sentence? What kind of variety is there in sentence construction? Are there sentence fragments? Sentences beginning with conjunctions? One-word sentences? Are two or three attempts made to clarify a given point? How do these apparently minor decisions add up to a style?
3. In both these essays, most readers are aware of a friendly, almost intimate *persona*—someone human, warm, and witty, who at the same time is as vulnerable as anyone else. What techniques or devices do these writers use that create the impression that they're having a confidential chat with us? Do they use similar techniques? How do the *personae* differ?

## SUGGESTIONS FOR WRITING

1. If you did the writing assignment that preceded this pair of essays, you will already have tried writing a personal essay similar to White's and Ephron's. Try now to write about a sensitive topic from a more detached perspective. Using the same topic, write about it as an adult writing to other adults (parents of teenagers, for example), offering an explanation of the problem and suggestions for dealing with it.

# 8

# Raising Children

*Tillie Olsen*

"I STAND HERE IRONING"

*Robert Paul Smith*

"LET YOUR KIDS ALONE"

In the preceding essays, Ephron and White looked back at their adolescent problems with a certain amount of amusement and expressed themselves in a rather whimsical tone. In contrast, the essays by Olsen and Smith deal earnestly with the confrontation between youth and maturity that occurs during the raising of children. Tillie Olsen's narrative, "I Stand Here Ironing," sensitively explores the puzzling combination of innate and environmental factors that make up a child's identity. Robert Paul Smith, in an essay entitled "Let Your Kids Alone," argues that "we are doing things we do not really want to do for kids who do not really want to have them done." Both Olsen and Smith feel that growing up is a highly individual process that cannot be predicted or controlled. Olsen, however, demonstrates the tragedy of parental neglect, while Smith reveals the comedy of parental over-concern.

## *Tillie Olsen*
## "I STAND HERE IRONING"

I stand here ironing, and what you asked me moves tormented back and forth with the iron.

"I wish you would manage the time to come in and talk with me about your daughter. I'm sure you can help me understand her. She's a youngster who needs help and whom I'm deeply interested in helping."

"Who needs help"... Even if I came, what good would it do? You think because

I am her mother I have a key, or that in some way you could use me as a key? She has lived for nineteen years. There is all that life that has happened outside of me, beyond me.

And when is there time to remember, to sift, to weigh, to estimate, to total? I will start and there will be an interruption and I will have to gather it all together again. Or I will become engulfed with all I did or did not do, with what should have been and what cannot be helped.

She was a beautiful baby. The first and only one of our five that was beautiful at birth. You do not guess how new and uneasy her tenancy in her now-loveliness. You did not know her all those years she was thought homely, or see her poring over her baby pictures, making me tell her over and over how beautiful she had been—and would be, I would tell her—and was now, to the seeing eye. But—the seeing eyes were few or nonexistent. Including mine.

I nursed her. They feel that's important nowadays. I nursed all the children, but with her, with all the fierce rigidity of first motherhood, I did like the books then said. Though her cries battered me to trembling and my breasts ached with swollenness, I waited till the clock decreed.

Why do I put that first? I do not even know if it matters, or if it explains anything.

She was a beautiful baby. She blew shining bubbles of sound. She loved motion, loved light, loved color and music and textures. She would lie on the floor in her blue overalls patting the surface so hard in ecstasy her hands and feet would blur. She was a miracle to me, but when she was eight months old I had to leave her daytimes with the woman downstairs to whom she was no miracle at all, for I worked or looked for work and for Emily's father, who "could no longer endure" (he wrote in his goodbye note) "sharing want with us."

I was nineteen. It was the pre-relief, pre-WPA world of the depression. I would start running as soon as I got off the streetcar, running up the stairs, the place smelling sour, and awake or asleep to startle awake, when she saw me she would break into a clogged weeping that could not be comforted, a weeping I can hear yet.

After a while I found a job hashing at night so I could be with her days, and it was better. But it came to where I had to bring her to his family and leave her.

It took a long time to raise the money for her fare back. Then she got chicken pox and I had to wait longer. When she finally came, I hardly knew her, walking quick and nervous like her father, looking like her father, thin, and dressed in a shoddy red that yellowed her skin and glared at the pockmarks. All the baby loveliness gone.

She was two. Old enough for nursery school they said, and I did not know then what I know now—the fatigue of the long day, and the lacerations of group life in the kinds of nurseries that are only parking places for children.

Except that it would have made no difference if I had known. It was the only place there was. It was the only way we could be together, the only way I could hold a job.

And even without knowing, I knew. I knew the teacher that was evil because all these years it has curdled into my memory, the little boy hunched in the corner, her rasp, "why aren't you outside, because Alvin hits you? that's no reason, go out, scaredy." I knew Emily hated it even if she did not clutch and implore "don't go Mommy" like the other children, mornings.

She always had a reason why we should stay home. Momma, you look sick. Momma, I feel sick. Momma, the teachers aren't there today, they're sick. Momma, we can't go, there was a fire there last night. Momma, it's a holiday today, no school, they told me.

But never a direct protest, never rebellion. I think of our others in their three- , four-year-oldness—the explosions, the tempers, the denunciations, the demands—and I feel suddenly ill. I put the iron down. What in me demanded that goodness in her? And what was the cost, the cost to her of such goodness?

The old man living in the back once said in his gentle way: "You should smile at Emily more when you look at her." What *was* in my face when I looked at her? I loved her. There were all the acts of love.

It was only with the others I remembered what he said, and it was the face of joy, and not of care or tightness or worry I turned to them—too late for Emily. She does not smile easily, let alone almost always as her brothers and sisters do. Her face is closed and sombre, but when she wants, how fluid. You must have seen it in her pantomimes, you spoke of her rare gift for comedy on the stage that rouses a laughter out of the audience so dear they applaud and applaud and do not want to let her go.

Where does it come from, that comedy? There was none of it in her when she came back to me that second time, after I had had to send here away again. She had a new daddy now to learn to love, and I think perhaps it was a better time.

Except when we left her alone nights, telling ourselves she was old enough.

"Can't you go some other time, Mommy, like tomorrow?" she would ask. "Will it be just a little while you'll be gone? Do you promise?"

The time we came back, the front door open, the clock on the floor in the hall. She rigid awake. "It wasn't just a little while. I didn't cry. Three times I called you, just three times, and then I ran downstairs to open the door so you could come faster. The clock talked loud. I threw it away, it scared me what it talked."

She said the clock talked loud again that night I went to the hospital to have Susan. She was delirious with the fever that comes before red measles, but she was fully conscious all the week I was gone and the week after we were home when she could not come near the new baby or me.

She did not get well. She stayed skeleton thin, not wanting to eat, and night after night she had nightmares. She would call for me, and I would rouse from exhaustion to sleepily call back: "You're all right, darling, go to sleep, it's just a dream," and if she still called, in a sterner voice, "now go to sleep, Emily, there's nothing to hurt you." Twice, only twice, when I had to get up for Susan anyhow, I went in to sit with her.

Now when it is too late (as if she would let me hold and comfort her like I do the others) I get up and go to her at once at her moan or restless stirring. "Are you awake, Emily? Can I get you something?" And the answer is always the same: "No, I'm all right, go back to sleep, Mother."

They persuaded me at the clinic to send her away to a convalescent home in the country where "she can have the kind of food and care you can't manage for her, and you'll be free to concentrate on the new baby." They still send children to that place. I see pictures on the society page of sleek young women planning affairs to raise money for it, or dancing at the affairs, or decorating Easter eggs or filling Christmas stockings for the children.

They never have a picture of the children so I do not know if the girls still wear those gigantic red bows and the ravaged looks on the every other Sunday when parents can come to visit "unless otherwise notified"—as we were notified the first six weeks.

Oh it is a handsome place, green lawns and tall trees and fluted flower beds. High up on the balconies of each cottage the children stand, the girls in their red bows and white dresses, the boys in white suits and giant red ties. The parents stand below shrieking up to be heard and the children shriek down to be heard, and between them the invisible wall "Not to Be Contaminated by Parental Germs or Physical Affection."

There was a tiny girl who always stood hand in hand with Emily. Her parents never came. One visit she was gone. "They moved her to Rose Cottage," Emily shouted in explanation. "They don't like you to love anybody here."

She wrote once a week, the labored writing of a seven-year-old. "I am fine. How is the baby. If I write my leter nicly I will have a star. Love." There never was a star. We wrote every other day, letters she could never hold or keep but only hear read—once. "We simply do not have room for children to keep any personal possessions," they patiently explained when we pieced one Sunday's shrieking together to plead how much it would mean to Emily, who loved so to keep things, to be allowed to keep her letters and cards.

Each visit she looked frailer. "She isn't eating," they told us.

(They had runny eggs for breakfast or mush with lumps, Emily said later, I'd hold it in my mouth and not swallow. Nothing ever tasted good, just when they had chicken.)

It took us eight months to get her released home, and only the fact that she gained back so little of her seven lost pounds convinced the social worker.

I used to try to hold and love her after she came back, but her body would stay stiff, and after a while she'd push away. She ate little. Food sickened her, and I think much of life too. Oh she had physical lightness and brightness, twinkling by on skates, bouncing like a ball up and down up and down over the jump rope, skimming over the hill; but these were momentary.

She fretted about her appearance, thin and dark and foreign-looking at a time when every little girl was supposed to look or thought she should look a chubby blonde replica of Shirley Temple. The doorbell sometimes rang for her, but no one seemed to come and play in the house or be a best friend. Maybe because we moved so much.

There was a boy she loved painfully through two school semesters. Months later she told me how she had taken pennies from my purse to buy him candy. "Licorice was his favorite and I brought him some every day, but he still liked Jennifer better'n me. Why, Mommy?" The kind of question for which there is no answer.

School was a worry to her. She was not glib or quick in a world where glibness and quickness were easily confused with ability to learn. To her overworked and exasperated teachers she was an overconscientious "slow learner" who kept trying to catch up and was absent entirely too often.

I let her be absent, though sometimes the illness was imaginary. How different from my now-strictness about attendance with the others. I wasn't working. We had a new baby, I was home anyhow. Sometimes, after Susan grew old enough, I would keep her home from school, too, to have them all together.

Mostly Emily had asthma, and her breathing, harsh and labored, would fill the house with a curiously tranquil sound. I would bring the two old dresser mirrors and her boxes of collections to her bed. She would select beads and single earrings, bottle tops and shells, dried flowers and pebbles, old postcards and scraps, all sorts of oddments; then she and Susan would play Kingdom, setting up landscapes and furniture, peopling them with action.

Those were the only times of peaceful companionship between her and Susan. I have edged away from it, that poisonous feeling between them, that terrible balancing of hurts and needs I had to do between the two, and did so badly, those earlier years.

Oh there are conflicts between the others too, each one human, needing, demanding, hurting, taking—but only between Emily and Susan, no, Emily toward Susan that corroding resentment. It seems so obvious on the surface, yet it is not obvious. Susan, the second child, Susan, golden—and curly-haired and chubby, quick and articulate and assured, everything in appearance and manner Emily was not; Susan, not able to resist Emily's precious things, losing or sometimes clumsily breaking them; Susan telling jokes and riddles to company for applause while Emily sat silent (to say to me later: that was *my* riddle, Mother, I told it to Susan); Susan, who for all the five years' difference in age was just a year behind Emily in developing physically.

I am glad for that slow physical development that widened the difference between her and her contemporaries, though she suffered over it. She was too vulnerable for that terrible world of youthful competition, of preening and parading, of constant measuring of yourself against every other, of envy, "If I had that copper hair," "If I had that skin. . . ." She tormented herself enough about not looking like the others, there was enough of the unsureness, the having to be conscious of words before you speak, the constant caring—what are they thinking of me? without having it all magnified by the merciless physical drives.

Ronnie is calling. He is wet and I change him. It is rare there is such a cry now. That time of motherhood is almost behind me when the ear is not one's own but must always be racked and listening for the child cry, the child call. We sit for a while and I hold him, looking out over the city spread in charcoal with its soft aisles of light. "*Shoogily*," he breathes and curls closer. I carry him back to bed, asleep. *Shoogily*. A funny word, a family word, inherited from Emily, invented by her to say: *comfort*.

In this and other ways she leaves her seal, I say aloud. And startle at my saying it. What do I mean? What did I start to gather together, to try and make coherent? I was at the terrible, growing years. War years. I do not remember them well. I was working, there were four smaller ones now, there was not time for her. She had to help be a mother, and housekeeper, and shopper. She had to set her seal. Mornings of crisis and near hysteria trying to get lunches packed, hair combed, coats and shoes found, everyone to school or Child Care on time, the baby ready for transportation. And always the paper scribbled on by a smaller one, the book looked at by Susan then mislaid, the homework not done. Running out to that huge school where she was lost, she was a drop; suffering over the unpreparedness, stammering and unsure in her classes.

There was so little time left at night after the kids were bedded down. She would struggle over books, always eating (it was in those years she developed her enormous appetite that is legendary in our family) and I would be ironing, or preparing food for the next day, or writing V-mail to Bill, or tending the baby. Sometimes, to make me laugh, or out of her despair, she would imitate happenings or types at school.

I think I said once: "Why don't you do something like this in the school amateur show?" One morning she phoned me at work, hardly understandable through the weeping: "Mother, I did it. I won, I won; they gave me first prize; they clapped and clapped and wouldn't let me go."

Now suddenly she was Somebody, and as imprisoned in her difference as she had been in anonymity.

She began to be asked to perform at other high schools, even in colleges, then at city and statewide affairs. The first one we went to, I only recognized her that first moment when thin, shy, she almost drowned herself into the curtains. Then: Was this Emily? The control, the command, the convulsing and deadly clowning, the spell, then the roaring, stamping audience, unwilling to let this rare and precious laughter out of their lives.

Afterwards: You ought to do something about her with a gift like that—but without money or knowing how, what does one do? We have left it all to her, and the gift has as often eddied inside, clogged and clotted, as been used and growing.

She is coming. She runs up the stairs two at a time with her light graceful step, and I know she is happy tonight. Whatever it was that occasioned your call did not happen today.

"Aren't you ever going to finish the ironing, Mother? Whistler painted his mother in a rocker. I'd have to paint mine standing over an ironing board." This is one of her communicative nights and she tells me everything and nothing as she fixes herself a plate of food out of the icebox.

She is so lovely. Why did you want me to come in at all? Why were you concerned? She will find her way.

She starts up the stairs to bed. "Don't get me up with the rest in the morning." "But I thought you were having midterms." "Oh, those," she comes back in, kisses me, and says quite lightly, "in a couple of years when we'll all be atom-dead they won't matter a bit."

She has said it before. She *believes* it. But because I have been dredging the past, and all that compounds a human being is so heavy and meaningful in me, I cannot endure it tonight.

I will never total it all. I will never come in to say: She was a child seldom smiled at. Her father left me before she was a year old. I had to work her first six years when there was work, or I sent her home and to his relatives. There were years she had care she hated. She was dark and thin and foreign-looking in a world where the prestige went to blondeness and curly hair and dimples, she was slow where glibness was prized. She was a child of anxious, not proud, love. We were poor and could not afford for her the soil of easy growth. I was a young mother, I was a distracted mother. There were the other children pushing up, demanding. Her younger sister seemed all that she was not. There were years she did not want me to touch her. She kept too much in herself, her life was such she had to keep too much in herself. My wisdom came too late. She has much to her and probably little will come of it. She is a child of her age, of depression, of war, of fear.

Let her be. So all that is in her will not bloom—but in how many does it? There is still enough left to live by. Only help her to know—help make it so there is cause for her to know—that she is more than this dress on the ironing board, helpless before the iron.

## *Robert Paul Smith*
## "LET YOUR KIDS ALONE"

When I was a kid, the way we got to play baseball was this: school was out, we ran home and hooked a handful of cookies, hollered, "I'm home, goin' out on the block," grabbed a beat-up fielder's glove, went out on the block and met a friend who had an old first baseman's mitt and a ball, went down the block a little and hollered at the kid who had the bat. So we proceeded until we had rounded up all those kids who were not chained to piano practice, making model airplanes, lying on their backs studying the ceiling, feeding their rabbits or writing out one thousand times, "I will not put blotting paper in the inkwell." We went to the vacant lot and played a game resembling major league baseball only in that it was played with a bat and bases. It was fun.

My kid went to play soccer the other day. The way you play soccer now is this: you bring home from school a mimeographed schedule for the Saturday morning soccer league. There are six teams, named after colleges, and the schedule is so arranged that at the end of the season, by a mathematical process of permutations and combinations that would take me six weeks to figure out, every team has played every other team and every kid has shown up at the right hour the right number of times. There are always exactly eleven men on each team, the ball is regulation size, the games are played on a regulation-size field with regulation-size soccer goals, and there is a regulation-size adult to referee.

After the game I asked my kid, "Was it fun?" "Yes," he said, but he didn't sound sure. "We lost 3-0." When I was a kid, we lost 3–0 too—and also 16–2 and 135–3 at soccer or baseball or kick-the-can—but by the time we had fought about where the strike zone was, what was out of bounds and who was offside, we could wind up winning the argument, if not the game.

Because, you see, it was *our* game. I think that my kid was playing someone else's game. I think he was playing Big Brother's game.

Big Brother, in this case, is all the parents who cannot refrain from poking their snoots into a world where they have no business to be, into the whole wonderful world of a kid, which is wonderful precisely because there are no grownups in it. In come today's parents, tramping down the underbrush, cutting down the trees, driving away the game, making the place hideous with mimeographed sheets and names and regulations. They are into everything. They refuse to let anything alone if there is a kid connected with it. They have invented a whole new modern perversion: child-watching.

There are two main groups of child-watchers. The first, which includes the PTA's and the child study leagues and the children's mental hygiene groups, watches but does not touch. These are the peepers through one-way glass, the keepers of notebooks, the givers of tests.

The second group watches *and* touches—and also coaches and uniforms and proliferates rulebooks. This group manages such things as the soccer leagues and the Little Leagues and the Cub Scouts and the Boy Scouts and the Girl Scouts and the Brownies and the Sea Scouts and the Explorer Scouts and, I'd bet, the Satellite Scouts. These are the getters down on all fours, the spies in the children's world, the ones who cannot be sure whether they wish the kids to be as grownup as themselves, or wish themselves to be as childish as the kids.

All this child-watching and child-helping and child-pushing has made it tough for the kids to do anything without a complete set of instructions. Of course, once in a while they do break through the instruction barrier. The afternoon following the soccer game, my kid went off on his own business. This consisted of assembling an arrangement of batteries and resistors and what I have learned are called capacitors [not condensers], which makes five tiny neon tubes blink in a manner I can only describe as infuriating. Obviously this was fun for him. There are no plans for constructing such a machine. Indeed, it may be the first time such a machine has been built. So he built it. But he did not go outside and do the idle footling of a soccer ball which I used to do because the kid next door happened to have a soccer ball, and he did not play one-o-cat or throw a football around or even watch squirrels.

He did not do this because, although Big Brother has organized every league known to man and issued a rule book therefor, he has not yet put out a mimeographed sheet of instructions on watching squirrels. There are no books on how to be a lousy right fielder (it came to me natural), and in no book does it say that when you go to make a tackle, of course you shut your eyes and lie about it later. No doubt these books are being written.

Perhaps the finest single example of an organization that is devoted to not leaving the kids alone is the Scouts. It is not my intention to knock the Scouts as a whole. It is a well-meaning organization devoted to salutary works. I am sure that its officials are high-principled, admirable people. I merely wish to point out that the name of the organization is the *Boy* Scouts. It is for *boys*. And yet there is a small, wallet-sized card printed by the Boy Scouts of America entitled "The Scout Parent's Opportunity." Among the exhortations on this card are these:

"Be a companion to your own son." "Weave Cub Scouting into home-life pattern." "Use the program to draw the family closer." "Be with your son at all pack meetings." "Work closely with the Den Mother."

The day an organization, *any* organization, tells me how to be a companion to my son is the day I am going to take a good hard look at that organization, and if they mean it for real, I am going to prepare to mount the barricades. I find "The Scout Parent's Opportunity" a terrifying document, but it is as nothing compared to another communiqué from the same organization. This is a sheet of yellow paper headed HERE ARE THE THINGS YOU DO TO BECOME A BOBCAT.

Well, the very first thing you do to become a Bobcat is learn and take the Cub Scout promise: "I promise to DO MY BEST to do my DUTY to GOD and my COUNTRY, to be SQUARE, and to OBEY the Law of the Pack." (The capital letters are *not* mine.) Only after you have said you will OBEY the Law of the Pack do you find out what the Law of the Pack is. The very first article of the Law is, "The Cub Scout FOLLOWS Akela." Then you hear that "Akela means 'Good Leader'—your mother and father, your teacher, your Cubmaster, and many other people who have shown that they are the kind of people who are able and willing to help you." Follow this reasoning carefully: first you say you will do something; then you find out what it is that you have promised to do; and then you find out what the thing you have promised to do means.

Before I let my kid subscribe to this, he is going to have a little talk with OLD FATHER, who is going to HOLLER at him GOOD AND LOUD. And what OLD FATHER is going to TELL him is never sign a BLANK CHECK, and before he goes off following Akela, he better take a GOOD HARD LOOK at all these people who have shown that they are "able and willing" to help him and find out where they are able and willing to lead him TO.

Bobcats, I have news for you. I know who Akela is, and he is not all those people. He is the old leader of the wolves in Kipling's Mowgli stories, and during wolf meetings he lies quietly on the Council Rock, interpreting the law and keeping order by means of dignity and aloofness. He spends a great deal of time keeping his mouth shut and he spends absolutely no time at all down in the grass with the young cubs playing Pin the Tail on the Hartebeest or Ring Around the Cobra.

I know a father in Connecticut whose kid FOLLOWED Akela to a Den, and after several sessions the kid wanted out. He did not know how to convey this horrible intelligence to Akela, so instead he went to his father. Apparently he thought quitting the Scouts was like breaking with the Communist party, or trying to get away from George Raft and being cut down by a machine gun at the corner of Fifth and Main.

The thing that drove this boy away from the Cub Scouts grew out of the little joker in one corner of the Bobcats' contract. It is called the "Parents' O.K." and it says: "We have had an active part in our son's first Cub Scout experience—becoming a Bobcat. We have tried to see things through his eyes and not expect too much. On the other hand, we haven't been too easy. We have helped him complete all the Bobcat requirements and we are satisfied that he has done his best."

This sounds mawkish but fairly harmless. The way my friend from Connecticut tells it, it isn't harmless at all. "Your kid brings you a book called the Wolf Cub Scout Book. If, Lord help us, you're a Good Scout Dad, you read a little of the book. On page 18 is something called 'Feats of Skill,' and your kid has to do any three of them to pass. He can choose a frontward, backward and falling somersault, or playing catch with someone twenty feet away, or climbing at least twelve feet up a tree, or swimming thirty feet in shallow water, or walking a two-by-four forward, sideways and backward. Now I'm for this, so I watch my kid practice. He tries and he doesn't get anywhere near twelve feet up the tree. I say, 'No, that's about five feet. You didn't do it.' When he tries to walk backward on the two-by-four, he falls off, so I say, 'Give it a little more work.' After all, I'm the one who's got to sign a paper saying he passed the test."

I could see why my friend was concerned: when he signs contracts, he fulfills them.

"So there's this pack meeting," my friend continued, "and they start giving kids badges because they have done their feats of skill. After a while, my boy and I see this one kid from our block who we *know* can't find his bottom with both hands in the dark, and he's getting a badge because he did the feats of skill. It's 'proven.' His mother signed the pledge. My kid looks at me. Something is very fishy here, is what he is thinking. That goof climbed twelve feet up a tree? Then why can't he climb stairs very good? It didn't take my kid long to figure it out: mothers lie and scoutmasters believe them. So he quit.

"That summer my kid took a look at an island in the middle of a lake at a kind of farm he goes to. He was the littlest kid there. He swam out and back and wrote a letter home, and in the envelope was a weed from the island. I didn't have to tell him it was a feat of skill and the weed was a badge. He knew it."

I suggested to my friend that he tell his kid that Akela—Mr. Kipling's Akela—would have known it, too, and so would Dan Beard, whose concern in helping found the Boy Scouts was to get kids out on their own in the country where they could learn to be independent.

I hear that things are bad in the Brownie world too. One Boston mother complains that she was required to learn to do everything her daughter had to learn to do to become a Brownie. At what cost to her self-esteem she cannot say, she even had to learn to sing, with gestures, the "Brownie Smile Song," which includes the words, "I have something in my pocket." And what mother has in her pocket is a smile, which she takes out and puts on her face. I ask you.

A New York City mother swears that when her daughter was "invested" in the Brownies, all the mothers had to be invested too. "I went to the investiture," this mother says, "and before I knew it, I and all the other mothers were standing up in a line, reciting the Brownie oath, and having badges pinned on us."

Well, what's the point? The real point is that this kind of jazz doesn't fool anyone but the parents. The kids know that any grownup who gets down on all fours and makes mudpies with them is either a spy or a fool. Not that kids don't like spending time with grownups, but what they want is for the grownup to take them into his world. They are familiar with the child's world, they can handle themselves there. But a grownup can take them to a new place, an exciting world of cigars and restaurants with linen napkins and automobiles and tall people. But do parents do this today? No, they are too busy being Real Dandy Scout Dads and True Blue Brownie Moms.

The Scouts, of course, are only an example. This same attitude is found everywhere that parents and children get together. Anybody who thinks that the kids don't understand what is going on is living in a dream. These kids watch their parents making spectacles of themselves, and they reach conclusions. All parents who are now, or ever have been, down on all fours should give careful thought to the conclusions that they invite their kids to reach.

It seems to me that we are doing things we do not really want to do for kids who do not really want to have them done. Perhaps the saddest proof of all is provided by the town of Proctor, Minnesota, where members of the Duluth, Missabe and Iron Range Railway Employees Association actually go out on the street to try to get kids to use their bowling alleys, golf course, ball park, football field, rifle range, skating rink and tennis courts. No sale. The Proctor Moose Lodge offered to give away quarters to all the children of its 450 members on the Fourth of July. All the kids had to do was show up and hold out their hands. The first year only 50 kids bothered to show and the next year fewer than 25. The project was abandoned. And when Proctor sponsored a safety contest open to all the school kids in town, only one boy entered. Naturally he won first prize, a watch, but since he already had a watch he asked for $10 instead.

For reasons of their own the kids of Proctor don't want to use the bowling alleys, don't want to walk that far for a quarter, don't care very much about safety. I suspect that the main reason is that they never asked for any of these things and would rather be left alone. What is true for the kids of Proctor is going to be true for the kids of San Francisco and Chicago and New York and Ashtabula. The thing to do, I think, is for us to stop pestering them.

To this end I have formed an organization called Modern Parents Anonymous, or MPA (not under any circumstances to be confused with a recently formed Seattle organization known as PPPTA, or Proud Papas of the Parent-Teachers Associations). MPA got its start one night when four supposedly adult persons—my wife and I and another couple—were sitting in moderately comfortable chairs in our moderately well-heated, well-lighted living room. All four of us read books and magazines, we have minds to think with and an enormous world to think about. So for two hours we talked about—children.

The actions of our children seemed more sensible to me than our own. They had looked into the living room some time before, seen that grownups were in tedious conclave, said hello and good-by and left. They were not wasting their time talking about us. The moment I realized this, MPA was born.

The principal goal of MPA is to encourage parents to think and worry and talk about something other than their own offspring. I have a list of things that might be talked about: freedom, liberty, the mating habits of Eskimos, the difference between Conté crayon and charcoal, the difference between voltage and amperage, religion, Ralph De Palma, the inflation of a basketball, the principle of a two-stroke engine, money, marbles and chalk. These intelligent areas of discourse I obtained from my kids. The care and handling of parents is not, of course, on their list. They stay away from this topic with consummate ease.

Last year I wrote a book which suggested, in the mildest possible ways, that if people remembered what a nuisance grownups were when they were kids, perhaps now that they were in turn presumably grownups they might like to get off the kids' backs. The mail has been fantastic, all in agreement, and most fantastic of all have been the communications from PTA groups asking me to come and holler at them.

I am booked for one such PTA talk in the near future, and I have a letter on the subject from the program chairman. "We need you, Mr. Smith," the letter says. "We want to stimulate our parents to think seriously about the probable risk of too many set designs for living and about the possible triumphs of unstressed, unconformist ways of growing."

Translating from the PTA-ese, I take this to mean that they want me to tell them how to leave their kids alone to grow up in peace. Well, I will go, and if I do not lose my nerve I will tell them that the way to leave kids alone is to leave them alone.

## Suggestions for Discussion

1. To whom is the story, "I Stand Here Ironing," addressed? In other words, who is the "you" in such statements as "You did not know her all those years she was thought homely"? What is the narrator's attitude toward this person? Why? How does this fictitious audience affect the way we read the story?
2. Robert Paul Smith does not create a fictitious audience as Olsen does. He does, of course, have a definite audience in mind. The first three paragraphs are anecdotal. How do they recruit his audience? Do you think that Smith could find a genuinely hostile audience for what he has to say?
3. Consider the implications of the following statements from Olsen's story: (1) "Where does it come from, that comedy?" (2) "I will never total it all." (3) "All that compounds a human being is so heavy." What do these statements all have in common? Do they tend to support or refute the idea that children are basically the products of their environment and upbringing?
4. What assumptions does Smith make about human beings and the ideal conditions under which they grow? How do these assumptions differ from those of the scout masters and PTA leaders? How do they differ from Olsen's?

## Suggestions for Writing

1. Both these readings deal with an adult's view of children's situations, an adult perspective on parents' roles. For this assignment, try to write from the other, the child's, perspective. You have two options. Under the first, imagine yourself to be either Emily or one of Robert Paul Smith's children, and write a letter to your "parent" offering your version of the role they did or should have played in your life. Under the second option, write from your own experience, to your own parents, evaluating, in a sense, the job they did in raising you.
2. Or you might want to attempt this imaginative stance: Pretend you are Emily's mother's closest friend, and that you know her thoughts and feelings about Emily. Write a letter to the high school counselor explaining as clearly and persuasively as you can why Emily's mother refuses to come in and talk.

# 9

# Growing Older

*Susan Sontag*

"THE DOUBLE STANDARD OF AGING"

*Milton Mayer*

"COMMENCEMENT ADDRESS: WHAT YOU WILL BE"

The final pair of essays in this part explores the challenges and problems of growing older. Susan Sontag's "The Double Standard of Aging" is a rigorous analysis of the different ways in which women and men experience maturity and old age. Sontag sees old age as a more unpleasant period in life for women than for men, mainly because the social environment defines women more rigidly. The qualities that are considered admirable in a woman are just those qualities that disappear with the passing of youth. Milton Mayer's commencement address to college students also paints a grim picture of growing older, but not because of the social climate. Mayer sees maturity and middle age as a period of gradual moral decline which individuals bring on themselves. His dramatic argument seeks to expose the tiny compromises which many of us make that will eventually add up to moral corruption.

## *Susan Sontag*
## "THE DOUBLE STANDARD OF AGING"

"How old are you?" The person asking the question is anybody. The respondent is a woman, a woman "of a certain age," as the French say discreetly. That age might be anywhere from her early twenties to her late fifties. If the question is impersonal—routine information requested when she applies for a driver's license, a credit card, a passport—she will probably force herself to answer truthfully. Filling out a marriage license application, if her future husband is even slightly her junior, she may long to subtract a few years; probably she won't. Competing for a job, her chances often partly depend on being the "right age," and if hers isn't right, she will lie if she thinks she can get away with it. Making her first visit to a new doctor, perhaps feeling particularly vulnerable at the moment she's asked, she will probably hurry through the correct answer. But if the question is only what people call personal—if she's asked by a new friend, a casual acquaintance, a neighbor's child, a co-worker in an office, store, factory—her response is harder to predict. She may side-step the question with a joke or refuse it with playful indignation. "Don't you know you're not supposed to ask a woman her age?" Or, hesitating a moment, embarrassed but defiant, she may tell the truth. Or she may lie. But neither truth, evasion, nor lie relieves the unpleasantness of that question. For a woman to be obliged to state her age, after "a certain age," is always a miniature ordeal.

If the question comes from a woman, she will feel less threatened than if it comes from a man. Other women are, after all, comrades in sharing the same potential for humiliation. She will be less arch, less coy. But she probably still dislikes answering and may not tell the truth. Bureaucratic formalities excepted, whoever asks a woman this question—after a "certain age"—is ignoring a taboo and possibly being impolite or downright hostile. Almost everyone acknowledges that once she passes an age that is, actually, quite young, a woman's exact age ceases to be a legitimate target of curiosity. After childhood the year of a woman's birth becomes her secret, her private property. It is something of a dirty secret. To answer truthfully is always indiscreet.

The discomfort a woman feels each time she tells her age is quite independent of the anxious awareness of human mortality that everyone has, from time to time. There is a normal sense in which nobody, men and women alike, relishes growing older. After thirty-five any mention of one's age carries with it the reminder that one is probably closer to the end of one's life than to the beginning. There is nothing unreasonable in that anxiety. Nor is there any abnormality in the anguish and anger that people who are really old, in their seventies and eighties, feel about the implacable waning of their powers, physical and mental. Advanced age is undeniably a trial, however stoically it may be endured. It is a shipwreck, no matter with what courage elderly people insist on continuing the voyage. But the objective, sacred pain of old age is of another order than the subjective, profane pain of aging. Old age is a genuine ordeal, one that men and women undergo in a similar way. Growing older is mainly an ordeal of the imagination—a moral disease, a social pathology—intrinsic to which is the fact that it afflicts women much more than men. It is particularly women who experience growing older (everything that comes *before* one is actually old) with such distaste and even shame.

The emotional privileges this society confers upon youth stir up some anxiety about getting older in everybody. All modern urbanized societies—unlike tribal, rural societies—condescend to the values of maturity and heap honors on the joys of youth. This revaluation of the life cycle in favor of the young brilliantly serves a secular society whose idols are ever-increasing industrial productivity and the unlimited cannibalization of nature. Such a society must create a new sense of the rhythms of life in order to incite people to buy more, to consume and throw away faster.

People let the direct awareness they have of their needs, of what really gives them pleasure, be overruled by commercialized *images* of happiness and personal well-being; and, in this imagery designed to stimulate ever more avid levels of consumption, the most popular metaphor for happiness is "youth." (I would insist that it is a metaphor, not a literal description. Youth is a metaphor for energy, restless mobility, appetite: for the state of "wanting.") This equating of well-being with youth makes everyone naggingly aware of exact age—one's own and that of other people. In primitive and pre-modern societies people attach much less importance to dates. When lives are divided into long periods with stable responsibilities and steady ideals (and hypocrisies), the exact number of years someone has lived becomes a trivial fact; there is hardly any reason to mention, even to know, the year in which one was born. Most people in nonindustrial societies are not sure exactly how old they are. People in industrial societies are haunted by numbers. They take an almost obsessional interest in keeping the score card of aging, convinced that anything above a low total is some kind of bad news. In an era in which people actually live longer and longer, what now amounts to the latter *two-thirds* of everyone's life is shadowed by a poignant apprehension of unremitting loss.

The prestige of youth afflicts everyone in this society to some degree. Men, too, are prone to periodic bouts of depression about aging—for instance, when feeling insecure or unfulfilled or insufficiently rewarded in their jobs. But men rarely panic about aging in the way women often do. Getting older is less profoundly wounding for a man, for in addition to the propaganda for youth that puts both men and women on the defensive as they age, there is a double standard about aging that denounces women with special severity. Society is much more permissive about aging in men, as it is more tolerant of the sexual infidelities of husbands. Men are "allowed" to age, without penalty, in several ways that women are not.

This society offers even fewer rewards for aging to women than it does to men. Being physically attractive counts much more in a woman's life than in a man's, but beauty, identified, as it is for women, with youthfulness, does not stand up well to age. Exceptional mental powers can increase with age, but women are rarely encouraged to develop their minds above dilettante standards. Because the wisdom considered the special province of women is "eternal," an age-old, intuitive knowledge about the emotions to which a repertoire of facts, worldly experience, and the methods of rational analysis have nothing to contribute, living a long time does not promise women an increase in wisdom either. The private skills expected of women are exercised early and, with the exception of a talent for making love, are not the kind that enlarge with experience. "Masculinity" is identified with competence, autonomy, self-control—qualities which the disappearance of youth does not threaten. Competence in most of the activities expected from men, physical sports excepted, increases with age. "Femininity" is identified with incompetence, helplessness, passivity, noncompetitiveness, being nice. Age does not improve these qualities. . . .

The double standard about aging shows up most brutally in the conventions of sexual feeling, which presuppose a disparity between men and women that operates permanently to women's disadvantage. In the accepted course of events a woman anywhere from her late teens through her middle twenties can expect to attract a man more or less her own age. (Ideally, he should be at least slightly older.) They marry and raise a family. But if her husband starts an affair after some years of marriage, he customarily does so with a woman much younger than his wife. Suppose, when both husband and wife are already in their late forties or early fifties, they divorce. The husband has an excellent chance of getting married again, probably to a younger woman. His ex-wife finds it difficult to remarry. Attracting a second husband younger than herself is improbable; even to find someone her own age she has to be lucky, and she will probably have to settle for a man considerably older than herself, in his sixties or seventies. Women become sexually ineligible much earlier than men do. A man, even an ugly man, can remain eligible well into old age. He is an acceptable mate for a young, attractive woman. Women, even good-looking women, become ineligible (except as partners of very old men) at a much younger age.

Thus, for most women, aging means a humiliating process of gradual sexual disqualification. Since women are considered maximally eligible in early youth, after which their sexual value drops steadily, even young women feel themselves in a desperate race against the calendar. They are old as soon as they are no longer very young. In late adolescence some girls are already worrying about getting married. Boys and young men have little reason to anticipate trouble because of aging. What makes men desirable to women is by no means tied to youth. On the contrary, getting older tends (for several decades) to operate in men's favor, since their value as lovers and husbands is set more by what they do than how they look. Many men have more success romantically at forty than they did at twenty or twenty-five; fame, money, and, above all, power are sexually enhancing. (A woman who has won power in a competitive profession or business career is considered less, rather than more, desirable. Most men confess themselves intimidated or turned off sexually by such a woman, obviously because she is harder to treat as just a sexual "object.") As they age, men may start feeling anxious about actual sexual performance, worrying about a loss of sexual vigor or even impotence, but their sexual eligibility is not abridged simply by getting older. Men stay sexually possible as long as they can make love. Women are at a disadvantage because their sexual candidacy depends on meeting certain much stricter "conditions" related to looks and age.

Since women are imagined to have much more limited sexual lives than men do, a woman who has never married is pitied. She was not found acceptable, and it is assumed that her life continues to confirm her unacceptability. Her presumed lack of sexual opportunity is embarrassing. A man who remains a bachelor is judged much less crudely. It is assumed that he, at any age, still has a sexual life—or the chance of one. For men there is no destiny equivalent to the humiliating condition of being an old maid, a spinster. "Mr.," a cover from infancy to senility, precisely exempts men from the stigma that attaches to any woman, no longer young, who is still "Miss." (That women are divided into "Miss" and "Mrs.," which calls unrelenting attention to the situation of each woman with respect to marriage, reflects the belief that being single or married is much more decisive for a woman than it is for a man.)

For a woman who is no longer very young, there is certainly some relief when she has finally been able to marry. Marriage soothes the sharpest pain she feels about the passing years. But her anxiety never subsides completely, for she knows that should she re-enter the sexual market at a later date—because of divorce, or the death of her husband, or the need for erotic adventure—she must do so under a handicap far greater than any man of her age (*whatever* her age may be) and regardless of how good-looking she is. Her achievements, if she has a career, are no asset. The calendar is the final arbiter. . . .

The rules of this society are cruel to women. Brought up to be never fully adult, women are deemed obsolete earlier than men. In fact, most women don't become relatively free and expressive sexually until their thirties. (Women mature sexually this late, certainly much later than men, not for innate biological reasons but because this culture retards women. Denied most outlets for sexual energy permitted to men, it takes many women *that* long to wear out some of their inhibitions.) The time at which they start being disqualified as sexually attractive persons is just when they have grown up sexually. The double standard about aging cheats women of those years, between thirty-five and fifty, likely to be the best of their sexual life.

That women expect to be flattered often by men, and the extent to which their self-confidence depends on this flattery, reflects how deeply women are psychologically weakened by this double standard. Added on to the pressure felt by everybody in this society to look young as long as possible are the values of "femininity," which specifically identify sexual attractiveness in women with youth. The desire to be the "right age" has a special urgency for a woman it never has for a man. A much greater part of her self-esteem and pleasure in life is threatened when she ceases to be young. Most men experience getting older with regret, apprehension. But most women experience it even more painfully: with shame. Aging is a man's destiny, something that must happen because he is a human being. For a woman, aging is not only her destiny. Because she is that more *narrowly* defined kind of human being, a woman, it is also her vulnerability.

To be a woman is to be an actress. Being feminine is a kind of theater, with its appropriate costumes, *décor,* lighting, and stylized gestures. From early childhood on, girls are trained to care in a pathologically exaggerated way about their appearance and are profoundly mutilated (to the extent of being unfitted for first-class adulthood) by the extent of the stress put on presenting themselves as physically attractive objects. Women look in the mirror more frequently than men do. It is, virtually, their duty to look at themselves—to look often. Indeed, a woman who is not narcissistic is considered unfeminine. And a woman who spends literally *most* of her time caring for, and making purchases to flatter, her physical appearance is not regarded in this society as what she is: a kind of moral idiot. She is thought to be quite normal and is envied by other women whose time is mostly used up at jobs or caring for large families. The display of narcissism goes on all the time. It is expected that women will disappear several times in an evening—at a restaurant, at a party, during a theater intermission, in the course of a social visit—simply to check their appearance, to see that nothing has gone wrong with their make-up and hairstyling, to make sure that their clothes are not spotted or too wrinkled or not hanging properly.

It is even acceptable to perform this activity in public. At the table in a restaurant, over coffee, a woman opens a compact mirror and touches up her make-up and hair without embarrassment in front of her husband or her friends.

All this behavior, which is written off as normal "vanity" in women, would seem ludicrous in a man. Women are more vain than men because of the relentless pressure on women to maintain their appearance at a certain high standard. What makes the pressure even more burdensome is that there are actually several standards. Men present themselves as face-and-body, a physical whole. Women are split, as men are not, into a body and a face—each judged by somewhat different standards. What is important for a face is that it be beautiful. What is important for a body is two things, which may even be (depending on fashion and taste) somewhat incompatible: first, that it be desirable and, second, that it be beautiful. Men usually feel sexually attracted to women much more because of their bodies than their faces. The traits that arouse desire—such as fleshiness—don't always match those that fashion decrees as beautiful. (For instance, the ideal woman's body promoted in advertising in recent years is extremely thin: the kind of body that looks more desirable clothed than naked.) But women's concern with their appearance is not simply geared to arousing desire in men. It also aims at fabricating a certain image by which, as a more indirect way of arousing desire, women state their value. A woman's value lies in the way she *represents* herself, which is much more by her face than her body. In defiance of the laws of simple sexual attraction, women do not devote most of their attention to their bodies. The well-known "normal" narcissism that women display—the amount of time they spend before the mirror—is used primarily in caring for the face and hair.

Women do not simply have faces, as men do; they are identified with their faces. Men have a naturalistic relation to their faces. Certainly they care whether they are good-looking or not. They suffer over acne, protruding ears, tiny eyes; they hate getting bald. But there is a much wider latitude in what is esthetically acceptable in a man's face than what is in a woman's. A man's face is defined as something he basically doesn't need to tamper with; all he has to do is keep it clean. He can avail himself of the options for ornament supplied by nature: a beard, a mustache, longer or shorter hair. But he is not supposed to disguise himself. What he is "really" like is supposed to show. A man lives through his face; it records the progressive stages of his life. And since he doesn't tamper with his face, it is not separate from but is completed by his body—which is judged attractive by the impression it gives of virility and energy. By contrast, a woman's face is potentially separate from her body. She does not treat it naturalistically. A woman's face is the canvas upon which she paints a revised, corrected portrait of herself. One of the rules of this creation is that the face *not* show what she doesn't want it to show. Her face is an emblem, an icon, a flag. How she arranges her hair, the type of make-up she uses, the quality of her complexion—all these are signs, not of what she is "really" like, but of how she asks to be treated by others, especially men. They establish her status as an "object."

For the normal changes that age inscribes on every human face, women are much more heavily penalized than men. Even in early adolescence, girls are cautioned to protect their faces against wear and tear. Mothers tell their daughters (but never their sons): You look ugly when you cry. Stop worrying. Don't read too much.

Crying, frowning, squinting, even laughing—all these human activities make "lines." The same usage of the face in men is judged quite positively. In a man's face lines are taken to be signs of "character." They indicate emotional strength, maturity—qualities far more esteemed in men than in women. (They show he has "lived.") Even scars are often not felt to be unattractive; they too can add "character" to a man's face. But lines of aging, any scar, even a small birthmark on a woman's face, are always regarded as unfortunate blemishes. In effect, people take character in men to be different from what constitutes character in women. A woman's character is thought to be innate, static—not the product of her experience, her years, her actions. A woman's face is prized so far as it remains unchanged by (or conceals the traces of) her emotions, her physical risk-taking. Ideally, it is supposed to be a mask—immutable, unmarked. The model woman's face is Garbo's. Because women are identified with their faces much more than men are, and the ideal woman's face is one that is "perfect," it seems a calamity when a woman has a disfiguring accident. A broken nose or a scar or a burn mark, no more than regrettable for a man, is a terrible psychological wound to a woman; objectively, it diminishes her value. (As is well known, most clients for plastic surgery are women.)

Both sexes aspire to a physical ideal, but what is expected of boys and what is expected of girls involves a very different moral relation to the self. Boys are encouraged to *develop* their bodies, to regard the body as an instrument to be improved. They invent their masculine selves largely through exercise and sport, which harden the body and strengthen competitive feelings; clothes are of only secondary help in making their bodies attractive. Girls are not particularly encouraged to develop their bodies through any activity, strenuous or not; and physical strength and endurance are hardly valued at all. The invention of the feminine self proceeds mainly through clothes and other signs that testify to the very effort of girls to look attractive, to their commitment to please. When boys become men, they may go on (especially if they have sedentary jobs) practicing a sport or doing exercises for a while. Mostly they leave their appearance alone, having been trained to accept more or less what nature has handed out to them. (Men may start doing exercises again in their forties to lose weight, but for reasons of health—there is an epidemic fear of heart attacks among the middle-aged in rich countries—not for cosmetic reasons.) As one of the norms of "femininity" in this society is being preoccupied with one's physical appearance, so "masculinity" means *not* caring very much about one's looks.

This society allows men to have a much more affirmative relation to their bodies than women have. Men are more "at home" in their bodies, whether they treat them casually or use them aggressively. A man's body is defined as a strong body. It contains no contradiction between what is felt to be attractive and what is practical. A woman's body, so far as it is considered attractive, is defined as a fragile, light body. (Thus, women worry more than men do about being overweight.) When they do exercises, women avoid the ones that develop the muscles, particularly those in the upper arms. Being "feminine" means looking physically weak, frail. Thus, the ideal woman's body is one that is not of much practical use in the hard work of this world, and one that must continually be "defended." Women do not develop their bodies, as men do. After a woman's body has reached its sexually acceptable form by late adolescence, most further development is viewed as negative. And it is thought irresponsible for women to do what is normal for men: simply leave their appearance alone. During early youth they are likely to come as close as they ever will to the ideal image—slim figure, smooth firm skin, light musculature, graceful movements. Their task is to try to maintain that image, unchanged, as long as possible. Improvement as such is not the task. Women care for their bodies—against toughening, coarsening, getting fat. They *conserve* them. (Perhaps the fact that women in modern societies tend to have a more conservative political outlook than men originates in their profoundly conservative relation to their bodies.)

In the life of women in this society the period of pride, of natural honesty, of unself-conscious flourishing is brief. Once past youth women are condemned to inventing (and maintaining) themselves against the inroads of age. Most of the physical qualities regarded as attractive in women deteriorate much earlier in life than those defined as "male." Indeed, they perish fairly soon in the normal sequence of body transformation. The "feminine" is smooth, rounded, hairless, unlined, soft, unmuscled—the look of the very young; characteristics of the weak, of the vulnerable; eunuch traits, as Germaine Greer has pointed out. Actually, there are only a few years—late adolescence, early twenties—in which this look is physiologically natural, in which it can be had without touching-up and covering-up. After that, women enlist in a quixotic enterprise, trying to close the gap between the imagery put forth by society (concerning what is attractive in a woman) and the evolving facts of nature.

Women have a more intimate relation to aging than men do, simply because one of the accepted "women's" occupations is taking pains to keep one's face and body from showing the signs of growing older. Women's sexual validity depends, up to a certain point, on how well they stand off these natural changes. After late adolescence women become the caretakers of their bodies and faces, pursuing an essentially defensive strategy, a holding operation. A vast array of products in jars and tubes, a branch of surgery, and armies of hairdressers, masseuses, diet counselors, and other professionals exist to stave off, or mask, developments that are entirely normal biologically. Large amounts of women's energies are diverted into this passionate, corrupting effort to defeat nature: to maintain an ideal, static appearance against the progress of age. The collapse of the project is only a matter of time. Inevitably, a woman's physical appearance develops beyond its youthful form. No matter how exotic the creams or how strict the diets, one cannot indefinitely keep the face unlined, the waist slim. Bearing children takes its toll: the torso becomes thicker; the skin is stretched. There is no way to keep certain lines from appearing, in one's mid-twenties, around the eyes and mouth. From about thirty on, the skin gradually loses its tonus. In women this perfectly natural process is regarded as a humiliating defeat, while nobody finds anything remarkably unattractive in the equivalent physical changes in men. Men are "allowed" to look older without sexual penalty.

Thus, the reason that women experience aging with more pain than men is not simply that they care more than men about how they look. Men also care about their looks and want to be attractive, but since the business of men is mainly being and doing, rather than appearing, the standards for appearance are much less exacting.

The standards for what is attractive in a man are permissive; they conform to what is possible or "natural" to most men throughout most of their lives. The standards for women's appearance go against nature, and to come anywhere near approximating them takes considerable effort and time. Women must try to be beautiful. At the least, they are under heavy social pressure not to be ugly. A woman's fortunes depend, far more than a man's, on being at least "acceptable" looking. Men are not subject to this pressure. Good looks in a man is a bonus, not a psychological necessity for maintaining normal self-esteem.

Behind the fact that women are more severely penalized than men are for aging is the fact that people, in this culture at least, are simply less tolerant of ugliness in women than in men. An ugly woman is never merely repulsive. Ugliness in a woman is felt by everyone, men as well as women, to be faintly embarrassing. And many features or blemishes that count as ugly in a woman's face would be quite tolerable on the face of a man. This is not, I would insist, just because the esthetic standards for men and women are different. It is rather because the esthetic standards for women are much higher, and narrower, than those proposed for men.

Beauty, women's business in this society, is the theater of their enslavement. Only one standard of female beauty is sanctioned: the *girl*. The great advantage men have is that our culture allows two standards of male beauty: the *boy* and the *man*. The beauty of a boy resembles the beauty of a girl. In both sexes it is a fragile kind of beauty and flourishes naturally only in the early part of the life-cycle. Happily, men are able to accept themselves under another standard of good looks—heavier, rougher, more thickly built. A man does not grieve when he loses the smooth, unlined, hairless skin of a boy. For he has only exchanged one form of attractiveness for another: the darker skin of a man's face, roughened by daily shaving, showing the marks of emotion and the normal lines of age. There is no equivalent of this second standard for women. The single standard of beauty for women dictates that they must go on having clear skin. Every wrinkle, every line, every grey hair, is a defeat. No wonder that no boy minds becoming a man, while even the passage from girlhood to early womanhood is experienced by many women as their downfall, for all women are trained to want to continue looking like girls.

This is not to say there are no beautiful older women. But the standard of beauty in a woman of any age is how far she retains, or how she manages to simulate, the appearance of youth. The exceptional woman in her sixties who is beautiful certainly owes a large debt to her genes. Delayed aging, like good looks, tends to run in families. But nature rarely offers enough to meet this culture's standards. Most of the women who successfully delay the appearance of age are rich, with unlimited leisure to devote to nurturing along nature's gifts. Often they are actresses. (That is, highly paid professionals at doing what all women are taught to practice as amateurs.) Such women as Mae West, Dietrich, Stella Adler, Dolores Del Rio, do not challenge the rule about the relation between beauty and age in women. They are admired precisely because they *are* exceptions, because they have managed (at least so it seems in photographs) to outwit nature. Such miracles, exceptions made by nature (with the help of art and social privilege), only confirm the rule, because what makes these women seem beautiful to us is precisely that they do not look their real age. Society allows no place in our imagination for a beautiful old woman who does look like an old woman—a woman who might be like Picasso at the age of ninety, being photographed outdoors on his estate in the south of France, wearing only shorts and sandals. No one imagines such a woman exists. Even the special exceptions—Mae West & Co.—are always photographed indoors, cleverly lit, from the most flattering angle and fully, artfully clothed. The implication is they would not stand a closer scrutiny. The idea of an old woman in a bathing suit being attractive, or even just acceptable looking, is inconceivable. An older woman is, by definition, sexually repulsive—unless, in fact, she doesn't look old at all. The body of an old woman, unlike that of an old man, is always understood as a body that can no longer be shown, offered, unveiled. At best, it may appear in costume. People still feel uneasy, thinking about what they might see if her mask dropped, if she took off her clothes.

Thus, the point for women of dressing up, applying make-up, dyeing their hair, going on crash diets, and getting face-lifts is not just to be attractive. They are ways of defending themselves against a profound level of disapproval directed toward women, a disapproval that can take the form of aversion. The double standard about aging converts the life of women into an inexorable march toward a condition in which they are not just unattractive, but disgusting. The profoundest terror of a woman's life is the moment represented in a statue by Rodin called *Old Age:* a naked old woman, seated, pathetically contemplates her flat, pendulous, ruined body. Aging in women is a process of becoming obscene sexually, for the flabby bosom, wrinkled neck, spotted hands, thinning white hair, waistless torso, and veined legs of an old woman are felt to be obscene. In our direst moments of the imagination, this transformation can take place with dismaying speed—as in the end of *Lost Horizon*, when the beautiful young girl is carried by her lover out of Shangri-La and, within minutes, turns into a withered, repulsive crone. There is no equivalent nightmare about men. This is why, however much a man may care about his appearance, that caring can never acquire the same desperateness it often does for women. When men dress according to fashion or now even use cosmetics, they do not expect from clothes and make-up what women do. A face-lotion or perfume or deodorant or hairspray, used by a man, is not part of a disguise. Men, as men, do not feel the need to disguise themselves to fend off morally disapproved signs of aging, to outwit premature sexual obsolescence, to cover up aging as obscenity. Men are not subject to the barely concealed revulsion expressed in this culture against the female body—except in its smooth, youthful, firm, odorless, blemish-free form.

One of the attitudes that punish women most severely is the visceral horror felt at aging female flesh. It reveals a radical fear of women installed deep in this culture, a demonology of women that has crystallized in such mythic caricatures as the vixen, the virago, the vamp, and the witch. Several centuries of witch-phobia, during which one of the cruelest extermination programs in Western history was carried out, suggest something of the extremity of this fear. That old women are repulsive is one of the most profound esthetic and erotic feelings in our culture. Women share it as much as men do. (Oppressors, as a rule, deny oppressed people their own "native" standards of beauty. And the oppressed end up being convinced that they *are* ugly.) How women are psychologically damaged by this misogynistic idea of what is beautiful parallels the way in which blacks have been deformed in a society that has up to now defined beautiful as white. Psychological tests made on young black children in the United States some years ago showed how early and how thoroughly they incorporate the white standard of good looks. Virtually all the children expressed fantasies that indicated they considered black people to be ugly, funny looking, dirty, brutish. A similar kind of self-hatred infects most women. Like men, they find old age in women "uglier" than old age in men.

This esthetic taboo functions, in sexual attitudes, as a racial taboo. In this society most people feel an involuntary recoil of the flesh when imagining a middle-aged woman making love with a young man—exactly as many whites flinch viscerally at the thought of a white woman in bed with a black man. The banal drama of a man of fifty who leaves a wife of forty-five for a girlfriend of twenty-eight contains no strictly sexual outrage, whatever sympathy people may have for the abandoned wife. On the contrary. Everyone "understands." Everyone knows that men like girls, that young women often want middle-aged men. But no one "understands" the reverse situation. A woman of forty-five who leaves a husband of fifty for a lover of twenty-eight is the makings of a social and sexual scandal at a deep level of feeling. No one takes exception to a romantic couple in which the man is twenty years or more the woman's senior. The movies pair Joanne Dru and John Wayne, Marilyn Monroe and Joseph Cotten, Audrey Hepburn and Cary Grant, Jane Fonda and Yves Montand, Catherine Deneuve and Marcello Mastroianni; as in actual life, these are perfectly plausible, appealing couples. When the age difference runs the other way, people are puzzled and embarrassed and simply shocked. (Remember Joan Crawford and Cliff Robertson in *Autumn Leaves?* But so troubling is this kind of love story that it rarely figures in the movies, and then only as the melancholy history of a failure.) The usual view of why a woman of forty and a boy of twenty, or a woman of fifty and a man of thirty, marry is that the man is seeking a mother, not a wife; no one believes the marriage will last. For a woman to respond erotically and romantically to a man who, in terms of his age, could be her father is considered normal. A man who falls in love with a woman who, however attractive she may be, is old enough to be his mother is thought to be extremely neurotic (victim of an "Oedipal fixation" is the fashionable tag), if not mildly contemptible.

The wider the gap in age between partners in a couple, the more obvious is the prejudice against women. When old men, such as Justice Douglas, Picasso, Strom Thurmond, Onassis, Chaplin, and Pablo Casals, take brides thirty, forty, fifty years younger than themselves, it strikes people as remarkable, perhaps an exaggeration—but still plausible. To explain such a match, people enviously attribute some special virility and charm to the man. Though he can't be handsome, he is famous; and his fame is understood as having boosted his attractiveness to women. People imagine that his young wife, respectful of her elderly husband's attainments, is happy to become his helper. For the man a late marriage is always good public relations. It adds to the impression that, despite his advanced age, he is still to be reckoned with; it is the sign of a continuing vitality presumed to be available as well to his art, business activity, or political career. But an elderly woman who married a young man would be greeted quite differently. She would have broken a fierce taboo, and she would get no credit for her courage. Far from being admired for her vitality, she would probably be condemned as predatory, willful, selfish, exhibitionistic. At the same time she would be pitied, since such a marriage would be taken as evidence that she was in her dotage. If she had a conventional career or were in business or held public office, she would quickly suffer from the current of disapproval. Her very credibility as a professional would decline, since people would suspect that her young husband might have an undue influence on her. Her "respectability" would certainly be compromised. Indeed, the well-known old women I can think of who dared such unions, if only at the end of their lives—George Eliot, Colette, Edith Piaf—have all belonged to that category of people, creative artists and entertainers, who have special license from society to behave scandalously. It is thought to be a scandal for a woman to ignore that she is old and therefore too ugly for a young man. Her looks and a certain physical condition determine a woman's desirability, not her talents or her needs. Women are not supposed to be "potent." A marriage between an old woman and a young man subverts the very ground rule of relations between the two sexes, that is: whatever the variety of appearances, men remain dominant. Their claims come first. Women are supposed to be the associates and companions of men, not their full equals—and never their superiors. Women are to remain in the state of a permanent "minority."

The convention that wives should be younger than their husbands powerfully enforces the "minority" status of women, since being senior in age always carries with it, in any relationship, a certain amount of power and authority. There are no laws on the matter, of course. The convention is obeyed because to do otherwise makes one feel as if one is doing something ugly or in bad taste. Everyone feels intuitively the esthetic rightness of a marriage in which the man is older than the woman, which means that any marriage in which the woman is older creates a dubious or less gratifying mental picture. Everyone is addicted to the visual pleasure that women give by meeting certain esthetic requirements from which men are exempted, which keeps women working at staying youthful-looking while men are left free to age. On a deeper level everyone finds the signs of old age in women esthetically offensive, which conditions one to feel automatically repelled by the prospect of an elderly woman marrying a much younger man. The situation in which women are kept minors for life is largely organized by such conformist, unreflective preferences. But taste is not free, and its judgments are never merely "natural." Rules of taste enforce structures of power. The revulsion against aging in women is the cutting edge of a whole set of oppressive structures (often masked as gallantries) that keep women in their place.

The ideal state proposed for women is docility, which means not being fully grown up. Most of what is cherished as typically "feminine" is simply behavior that is childish, immature, weak. To offer so low and demeaning a standard of fulfillment in itself constitutes oppression in an acute form—a sort of moral neo-colonialism. But women are not simply condescended to by the values that secure the dominance of men. They are repudiated. Perhaps because of having been their oppressors for so long, few men really *like* women (though they love individual women), and few men ever feel really comfortable or at ease in women's company. This malaise arises because relations between the two sexes are rife with hypocrisy, as men manage to love those they dominate and therefore don't respect. Oppressors always try to justify their privileges and brutalities by imagining that those they oppress belong to a lower order of civilization or are less than fully "human." Deprived of part of their ordinary human dignity, the oppressed take on certain "demonic" traits. The oppressions of large groups have to be anchored deep in the psyche, continually renewed by partly unconscious fears and taboos, by a sense of the obscene. Thus, women arouse not only desire and affection in men but aversion as well. Women are thoroughly domesticated familiars. But, at certain times and in certain situations, they become alien, untouchable. The aversion men feel, so much of which is covered over, is felt most frankly, with least inhibition, toward the type of woman who is most taboo "esthetically," a woman who has become—with the natural changes brought about by aging—obscene.

Nothing more clearly demonstrates the vulnerability of women than the special pain, confusion, and bad faith with which they experience getting older. And in the struggle that some women are waging on behalf of all women to be treated (and treat themselves) as full human beings—not "only" as women—one of the earliest results to be hoped for is that women become aware, indignantly aware, of the double standard about aging from which they suffer so harshly.

It is understandable that women often succumb to the temptation to lie about their age. Given society's double standard, to question a woman about her age is indeed often an aggressive act, a trap. Lying is an elementary means of self-defense, a way of scrambling out of the trap, at least temporarily. To expect a woman, after "a certain age," to tell exactly how old she is—when she has a chance, either through the generosity of nature or the cleverness of art, to pass for being somewhat younger than she actually is—is like expecting a landowner to admit that the estate he has put up for sale is actually worth less than the buyer is prepared to pay. The double standard about aging sets women up as property, as objects whose value depreciates rapidly with the march of the calendar.

The prejudices that mount against women as they grow older are an important arm of male privilege. It is the present unequal distribution of adult roles between the two sexes that gives men a freedom to age denied to women. Men actively administer the double standard about aging because the "masculine" role awards them the initiative in courtship. Men choose; women are chosen. So men choose younger women. But although this system of inequality is operated by men, it could not work if women themselves did not acquiesce in it. Women reinforce it powerfully with their complacency, with their anguish, with their lies.

Not only do women lie more than men do about their age but men forgive them for it, thereby confirming their own superiority. A man who lies about his age is thought to be weak, "unmanly." A woman who lies about her age is behaving in a quite acceptable, "feminine" way. Petty lying is viewed by men with indulgence, one of a number of patronizing allowances made for women. It has the same moral unimportance as the fact that women are often late for appointments. Women are not expected to be truthful, or punctual, or expert in handling and repairing machines, or frugal, or physically brave. They are expected to be second-class adults, whose natural state is that of a grateful dependence on men. And so they often are, since that is what they are brought up to be. So far as women heed the stereotypes of "feminine" behavior, they *cannot* behave as fully responsible, independent adults.

Most women share the contempt for women expressed in the double standard about aging—to such a degree that they take their lack of self-respect for granted. Women have been accustomed so long to the protection of their masks, their smiles, their endearing lies. Without this protection, they know, they would be more vulnerable. But in protecting themselves as women, they betray themselves as adults. The model corruption in a woman's life is denying her age. She symbolically accedes to all those myths that furnish women with their imprisoning securities and privileges, that create their genuine oppression, that inspire their real discontent. Each time a woman lies about her age she becomes an accomplice in her own underdevelopment as a human being.

Women have another option. They can aspire to be wise, not merely nice; to be competent, not merely helpful; to be strong, not merely graceful; to be ambitious for themselves, not merely for themselves in relation to men and children. They can let themselves age naturally and without embarrassment, actively protesting and disobeying the conventions that stem from this society's double standard about aging. Instead of being girls, girls as long as possible, who then age humiliatingly into middle-aged women and then obscenely into old women, they can become women much earlier—and remain active adults, enjoying the long, erotic career of which women are capable, far longer. Women should allow their faces to show the lives they have lived. Women should tell the truth.

## *Milton Mayer*
## "COMMENCEMENT ADDRESS: WHAT YOU WILL BE"

As you are now, so I once was; as I am now, so you will be. You will be tempted to smile when I tell you that I am middle-aged and corrupt. You should resist the temptation. Twenty-five years from now you will be ineluctably middle-aged and, unless you hear and heed what I say today, just as ineluctably corrupt. You will not believe me, and you should not, because what I say at my age should be unbelievable at yours. But you should hear me out because I know more than you do in one respect: you know only what it is to be young, while I know what it is to be both young and old. In any case, I will not lie to you in order to make you feel good. You will be old much longer than you are young, and I would rather that you believed me the longer time than the shorter.

I tell you today that instantly is not a moment too soon if you are going to escape the fate I predict for you and embody myself. For what was said long ago is still true, that corruption runs faster than death and the faster runner overtakes the slower. It may indeed be too late already, unless you mend your ways this least of all likely moments. I once heard Robert Hutchins tell a graduating class that they were closer to the truth that day than they would ever be again. I did not believe him. But I have seen most of the members of that class since, and I regret to inform you that Hutchins was right. Mind you, he did not say that they were close to the truth; he only said that they would never be so close again. They had been taught what right and wrong were and had not yet had a chance to do what e. e. cummings calls "up grow and down forget." If my own history and the history of the race is instructive, this commencement is for nearly every last one of you the commencement of disintegration. A cynic once said that he would not give a hang for a man who wasn't a socialist before he was twenty or who was one after that. I do not know if socialism is a good ideal, but I know that it is an ideal and I know that the cynic was confident that you would lose your ideals. You may even have trifled, in your springtime, with such radical aberrations as pacifism. But you will soon stop trifling; and when, at thirty, you have already begun to molder, your friends will tell you that you have mellowed.

All societies are deplorable, and history indicates that they always will be. You have lived twenty years in a deplorable society. You have lived sheltered lives, but you have had no one to shelter you from your parents and teachers. Your parents have done what they could to adjust you to the deplorable society to which they, as their advanced age testifies, have successfully adjusted themselves. When they said you were improving, they meant that you were getting to be like them. When they said they hoped you would keep out of trouble, they meant that you should not do anything that they wouldn't do. But some of the things that they wouldn't do should have been done. The condition of the society to which they have accommodated their lives is the proof of their criminal negligence. Your teachers have been no better, and no better an influence on you, than your parents. They may have had higher ideals; it takes higher ideals to teach children than to have them. But your teachers' survival (like your parents') testifies to their adjustability. They have done as they were told, and in a deplorable society there are some things that men are told to do that no man should do. A high-school teacher in California told me that not one of his colleagues wanted to take the anti-Communist oath required of teachers in that state, and neither did he; but every one of them took it in order to hold his job and escape the national black list. As they are now, so you will be.

Like your teachers and your parents before you, you will be told to do bad things in order to hold your job. In college you may have quit the campus daily or defied the old fraternity on principle. It will be harder to quit the metropolitan daily or defy the old country on principle; it will be easier to forget the principle. And if, in addition to holding your job, you want to be promoted, you will think of bad things to do on your own. And you will have good reasons for doing them. You will have wives (at least one apiece) and children to maintain. You will have a home and mortgage to enlarge. And life insurance, purchased against the certainty of death, dread of which in turn adds preciousness to staying alive at any price. And neighbors who are having their children's teeth straightened. Your dentists' bills alone will corrupt you. You will have doctors' bills to pay, and they will increase as you grow older, becoming extremely heavy when you are moribund and powerless to earn money. You will have lusts, as you have now, to gratify, but the lusts you have now are relatively inexpensive and they will give way to more expensive if less gratifying lusts. You will have worthy philanthropies to support and the respect of people whose respect depends on your supporting those philanthropies. You will have an automobile (if you are so wretched as to be a one-car family), and you might as well turn it in every year because the new model will be so revolutionary that it will depreciate the old one to the point where there's no point in keeping it.

Some of the things you will be expected to do (or will expect yourself to do) for the sake of your wife and children, your community, your health, or your burial are bad things. You will have to have good reasons for doing them; and, thanks to your education, you will have them. The trouble with education is that it teaches you rhetoric while you are young. When, for rhetorical purposes, you embrace the doctrine of the lesser evil, you ignore its fatal flaw of present certainty and future contingency; being young, you think you will live forever, so that you may do bad things today in order to do good things tomorrow. But today is certain, tomorrow contingent; and this night an old man's soul may be required of him. When you are old, and too tired to embrace doctrines for rhetorical purposes, you will find that the doctrine of the lesser evil has embraced you and destroyed you. You protest my melancholy prediction, but the Great Actuarial Table is against you. Twenty-five years from now nine out of ten of you (or all ten) will tolerate an existence which, if you could foresee it now, you would call intolerable. If such an existence has any virtue at all, it has only one: it will give you a wistful old age. You will look back to your springtime, fifty years gone, and say, "Those were the days." And you will be right.

The only thing that will save you from wistfulness is the one talent whose lack now redeems you—the talent for self-deception. You won't even know that you are corrupt. You will be no worse than your neighbors, and you will be sure to have some that you won't be as bad as. You will have friends who praise in you the characteristics you have in common with them. They will persuade you that there is nothing wrong with either hoarding or squandering as much money as you can get legally. And if, some sudden night, you go berserk and bawl out that life is a sell, they will put you to bed with the assurance that you will be all right in the morning. And you will be. Worse than being corrupt, you will be contented in your corruption.

Twenty-five years from now you will celebrate your twentieth wedding anniversary. Because you love your wife—still more if you don't—you will want to celebrate it in style. You will reserve a window table for two at the choicest restaurant in town, and the champagne bucket will be at the table when you arrive. You will not be the cynosure of all eyes, but you will think you are. The head waiter (or maitre de, as he is known here) will address you by name. As your eye travels down the menu it will be distracted by something outside the window, which will prove to be a hungry man. What will you do? Do you know what you will do then, twenty-five years from now? You will call the maitre de and tell him to have the drapes pulled, and he will tell the waiter, and he will tell the bus boy, who will do it.

Your table, even before you have ordered, will be laden with rolls and crackers (of several sorts) and butter pats on butter plates. Hungry, and a little nervous, as you should be, you will break up a roll and butter it and eat it as you wait for your wife to make up her confounded mind. The waiter will ask you if you want the champagne poured, and you will say yes; and he will open it with a pop which, beneath the dinner din, will be unheard by the rest of the diners (but you won't know that). Thirsty, and a little nervous still, you will sip your glass, forgetting to toast your wife, and resume your study of the menu. And then, for the first time, you will see, in fine italic print at the bottom, the words "The Management reserves the right to refuse service to anyone." And then you will know (for you will be an educated man) that you are sitting in a Jim Crow restaurant—that being the meaning of the words "The Management, etc."

Now the country in which you were raised calls itself a Christian country, and the parents who raised you up called themselves Christian people, and the church whose vestry has just elected you calls itself a Christian church, and you call yourself a Christian. Jim Crowism is un-Christian. It is also un-American, and you call yourself an American. What will you do? What will you do then, twenty-five years from now?

The champagne is open and sipped. The roll is buttered, half-eaten. Will you get up from the table and tell your wife to get up and tell her why, and tell the waiter and the maitre de, and maybe the management, that you are leaving the restaurant and why, and pay for the champagne and the rolls and the butter pats and, if necessary, for the dinner, but refuse to eat there? Or will you pretend, as the management (by printing the notice in fine italic type) intended you to pretend, that you did not see the notice. You will stay at the table and order your dinner and eat it.

You will have been measured for corruption and found to fit. You may be the man who raised the flag on Iwo Jima—a hero abroad but not at home, where it's harder to be a hero. At Iwo Jima you had either to raise the flag or drop it. It was publicly shameful to drop it. But the night of your anniversary dinner it would have been publicly shameful to *raise* the flag by leaving the restaurant. And public shame was what you could not bear, either at Iwo Jima or in the restaurant.

There are a lot of involuntary, non-voluntary or reflexive heroes. I am one myself. I do not doubt that I would have raised the flag at Iwo Jima rather than let it drop in public. But I was the man who took his wife to dinner at the Jim Crow restaurant. Believe me, there is no contradiction between the corruption which will consume you, day by day, in the face of unpopularity or public shame and the heroism of the moment accompanied by public praise. And when you have been measured often enough and long enough for corruption, you will like what you see in the mirror. I don't mean that you won't continue to have good impulses. You will. But you will have persuasive reasons for suppressing them. From time to time, as the vestige of your springtime idealism stirs you, you will want to do the right thing. But you will have to put off doing it until you have buried your father, and then your mother, your brother, your children, and your grandchildren. You may live to be very old, but you will not outlive the last descendant for whose sake you will suppress your good impulses.

What life did to me, because there was no one to tell me what I am telling you now, it will do to you if you do not at once adopt *Principiis obsta* as your motto and spurn every other. "Resist the beginnings." At twenty I was what you are; I had had all the middle-class care that a middle-class society and a middle-class home could provide. My parents wanted me to have what they took to be advantages, and I had them. But my advantages were of no use to me at all when life came down on me, as it will upon you, like a ton of bricks. I had studied morality, just as you have, but it was the easy morality designed to sustain my character in an easy world. I would not steal another man's watch unless my children were starving, and my children would never be starving. Nor will yours if, with what your parents call your advantages, you do as you are told and get to the top. The reason your children will not be starving is that you will have been corrupted. Your corruption will save you from having to decide whether to steal another man's watch. I was prepared, like you, to be a hero the instant heroism was required of me. I saw myself at Iwo Jima, at Gettysburg, at Concord. But I did not see myself at home, so weakened by the corrosive years ahead that I would not be able to stand up on my hind legs and say no when I had to do it alone. Never knowing—as you do not know—that my needs would be limitless, I never imagined that my surrender would be complete.

My education prepared me to say no to my enemies. It did not prepare me to say no to my friends, still less to myself, to my own limitless need for a little more status, a little more security, and a little more of the immediate pleasure that status and security provide. Corruption is accompanied by immediate pleasure. When you feel good, you are probably, if not necessarily, doing bad. But happiness is activity in accordance with virtue, and the practice of virtue is painful. The pursuit of happiness requires a man to undertake suffering. Your intelligence, or your psychiatrist's, will tell you whether you are suffering for the right reason. But it will not move you to undertake the suffering.

God is said to come to us in little things. The Devil is no fool: he comes that way too. The Devil has only one objective, and if he can persuade you to justify your derelictions by saying "I'm only human," he has achieved it. He will have got you to deny the Christ within you, and that is all he wants. If you are only human you are his. The Devil will keep you quiet when you ought to talk by reminding you that nobody asked you to say anything. He will keep you in your chair when you ought to get up and out by reminding you that you love your wife and it's your twentieth anniversary. He will give you the oath to take and say, "As long as you're loyal, why not say so?" He will tell you that the beggar outside the restaurant would only spend the money on whiskey. The Devil has come to me in little things for twenty-five years—and now I say and do the things in which, when he first began coming, he had to instruct me.

I tell you that you are in mortal jeopardy today, and anyone who tells you differently is selling you to the Devil. It is written on Plato's ring that it is easier to form good habits than to break bad ones. Your habits are not yet fully formed. You are, in some measure still, only potentially corrupt. Life will actualize and habitualize every bit of your corruptibility. If you do not begin to cultivate the habit of heroism today—and habits are formed by acts—you never will. You may delude yourselves, as I did, by setting about to change the world. But for all that you do or do not do, you will leave the world, as I do, no better than you found it and yourselves considerably worse. For the world will change you faster, more easily, and more durably than you will change it. If you undertake only to keep the world from changing you—not to lick 'em but to avoid j'ining 'em—you will have your hands full.

Other, more agreeable commencement orators have warned you of life's pitfalls. I tell you that you are marked for them. I believe you will not escape them because I see nothing in your environment that has prepared you even to recognize them. Your elders tell you to compare yourselves with the Russians and see how much worse the Russians are; this is not the way to prepare you to recognize pitfalls. Your elders tell you to be technologists because the Russians are technologists and your country is technologically backward; this is no way to prepare you to recognize pitfalls. You are marked for the pit. The Great Actuarial Table is against you.

What you need (and the Russians with you) is neither pharisaism nor technology. What you need is what the psalmist knew he needed—a heart, not a head, of wisdom. What you need is what Bismarck said was the only thing the Germans needed—civilian courage. I do not know where you will get it. If I did, I would get it myself. You were divinely endowed to know right and to do right, and you have before you, in the tradition of your country and of human history, the vision to help you if you will turn to it. But no one will compel you to turn to it, and no one can. The dictates of your society, of any society, will not serve you. They are dictates that corrupted your parents and your teachers. If Socrates did not know where virtue came from—and he didn't—neither do I. He pursued it earlier and harder than anyone else and concluded that it was the gift of God. In despair of your parents and your society, of your teachers and your studies, of your neighbors and your friends, and above all of your fallen nature and the Old Adam in you, I bespeak for you the gift of God.

## SUGGESTIONS FOR DISCUSSION

1. Both Mayer and Sontag adopt what could be called hostile *personae:* they purposely, aggressively, take positions that go against their audience's preconceptions. What devices or techniques do they use to convey this hostility? How do they manage not to alienate their audiences? Or do they alienate them?
2. Both Mayer and Sontag make growing older, at least as it is currently experienced, seem rather horrible, though for different reasons: Sontag is concerned with physical changes and their psychological and social context, Mayer with moral changes in a social context. Can you make any connections between their arguments? What would Mayer say about Sontag's concern? Sontag about Mayer's?
3. "The Double Standard of Aging" is an argument based on evidence drawn from the writer's own observations. In an essay of this nature the reader can usually evaluate the evidence by asking two questions:

   (a) Are there enough examples to justify the conclusion?

   (b) Are there any important exceptions that the writer neglected to mention?

   How would you answer these questions with respect to Sontag's essay? Mayer's speech?

4. Mayer makes frequent use of repetition in his speech. In the last paragraph, for example, he begins three sentences with the words, "What you need is. . . ." Some statements, such as "As I am now, so you will be," recur with variations several times over. What is the purpose of these refrains?

## SUGGESTIONS FOR WRITING

1. Milton Mayer does at least three interesting things in his commencement address. First, he goes directly against his audience's expectations about what commencement speakers say; he will not, as he says, "lie to make you feel good." Second, he presents himself as mortal, as a flawed and fallen man. Third, in spite of the terrible and dire warnings he gives, he offers no solutions, no upbeat endings; the best he can manage is "to bespeak for you the gift of God." Imagine yourself in some similar position, namely, speaking to an audience with certain expectations about the kind of remarks you'll make on some subject where upbeat, pat remarks are the norm. You could be an after-dinner speaker at a sports dinner or a chamber of commerce meeting; a high school commencement speaker; a teacher making opening remarks to a new class. Then do what Mayer does: violate expectations, present yourself as something other than what your audience wants, and frighten them with the inescapable danger of their situation.

# Part Three

# KNOWLEDGE AND EDUCATION

*Education is that which remains after one has forgotten everything he learned in school.*
—ALBERT EINSTEIN

In one high school history class, the teacher requires the students to read the chapter on the Civil War and answer the questions at the end of the chapter. These students then take a test in which they are asked to discuss the causes of the war, name the major generals of the north, and explain the significance of the burning of Atlanta. In another class each student chooses a representative individual who lived during the war: a slave in North Carolina, a plantation owner from Georgia, a minister in Boston, or a woman whose home is a sanctuary for runaway slaves. After reading some of the documents about the period, the student writes a journal that describes one week in the life of this person.

The first method, which emphasizes the subject matter and the authority of the teacher, is the more traditional approach. The second method, which stresses the student's role in the learning process, is a more recent development. Educational theory has changed dramatically in the last few decades, creating strong disagreement about the most effective teaching strategies. Modern educators often contend that it is more important to engage the students than to present the subtleties of the subject. They encourage students to express their own responses rather than submit to structured procedures. But many people question the wisdom of this newer approach. They feel that students are not being asked to master the subject matter in a thorough and responsible way.

The essays in this part either criticize or defend modern educational practices. These writers approach the subject of education in various ways, from familiar accounts of individual learning experiences to philosophical analyses of the thinking process. In the first section H.L. Mencken and Lissa Rotundo question the method and the scope of formal education. The writers in the second section examine what motivates people to learn. The next two essays describe markedly different college atmospheres, one which is almost idyllic and another which creates only tension and frustration. Finally, William Perry and Adrienne Rich discuss the ultimate goals of education.

Education is universally regarded as a road to knowledge, but there is disagreement about what kind of knowledge is most worth having. The role of the schools is therefore unclear. To what extent should schools mold us and to what extent should they allow us to pursue our own inclinations? What are the proper roles of students and teachers? The way we see these issues is a highly individual matter, but the way our society resolves them will have a far-reaching impact.

# 10

# Attitudes Toward Formal Education

*H. L. Mencken*
"EDUCATION"

*Lissa Rotundo*
"ONE-YEAR-OLD SCHOLARS"

H. L. Mencken and Lissa Rotundo disagree with many popular attitudes toward formal education. Mencken attacks almost every aspect of the present educational system. He particularly deplores the emphasis on method and calls for a return to the teaching by "asses" who are passionately devoted to their subject matter, especially if that subject includes essential skills. Equally satirical but aiming at a different target, Rotundo objects to the insistence on structured learning at the expense of first-hand experience. With clarity and wit, she mocks the omnipresent educational system which threatens to engulf every stage of life from birth to death. She ironically suggests that perhaps we can eventually have classes for the fetus in the womb.

## *H. L. Mencken*
## "EDUCATION"

Next to the clerk in holy orders, the fellow with the worst job in the world is the schoolmaster. Both are underpaid, both fall steadily in authority and dignity, and both wear out their hearts trying to perform the impossible. How much the world asks of them, and how little they can actually deliver! The clergyman's business is to save the human race from hell: if he saves one eighth of one per cent, even within the limits of his narrow flock, he does magnificently. The schoolmaster's is to spread the enlightenment, to make the great masses of the plain people intelligent—and intelligence is precisely the thing that the great masses of the plain people are congenitally and eternally incapable of.

Is it any wonder that the poor birchman, facing this labor that would have staggered Sisyphus Aeolusohn,* seeks refuge from its essential impossibility in a Chinese maze of empty technic? The ghost of Pestalozzi†, once bearing a torch and beckoning toward the heights, now leads down stairways into black and forbidding dungeons. Especially in America, where all that is bombastic and mystical is most esteemed, the art of pedagogics becomes a sort of puerile magic, a thing of preposterous secrets, a grotesque compound of false premises and illogical conclusions. Every year sees a craze for some new solution of the teaching enigma, at once simple and infallible—manual training, playground work, song and doggerel lessons, the Montessori method, the Gary system—an endless series of flamboyant arcanums. The worst extravagances of *privat dozent*‡ experimental psychology are gravely seized upon; the uplift pours in its ineffable principles and discoveries; mathematical formulae are worked out for every emergency; there is no sure-cure so idiotic that some superintendent of schools will not swallow it.

A couple of days spent examining the literature of the New Thought in pedagogy are enough to make the judicious weep. Its aim seems to be to reduce the whole teaching process to a sort of automatic reaction, to discover some master formula that will not only take the place of competence and resourcefulness in the teacher but that will also create an artificial receptivity in the child. The merciless application of this formula (which changes every four days) now seems to be the chief end and aim of pedagogy. Teaching becomes a thing in itself, separable from and superior to the thing taught. Its mastery is a special business, a transcendental art and mystery, to be acquired in the laboratory. A teacher well grounded in this mystery, and hence privy to every detail of the new technic (which changes, of course, with the formula), can teach anything to any child, just as a sound dentist can pull any tooth out of any jaw.

All this, I need not point out, is in sharp contrast to the old theory of teaching. By that theory mere technic was simplified and subordinated. All that is demanded of the teacher told off to teach, say, geography, was that he master the facts in the geography book and provide himself with a stout rattan. Thus equipped, he was ready for a test of his natural pedagogical genius. First he exposed the facts in the book, then he gilded them with whatever appearance of interest and importance he could conjure up, and then he tested the extent of their transference to the minds of his pupils. Those pupils who had ingested them got apples; those who had failed got fanned with the rattan. Followed the second round, and the same test again, with a second noting of results. And then the third, and fourth, and the fifth, and so on until the last and least pupil had been stuffed to his subnormal and perhaps moronic brim.

I was myself grounded in the underlying delusions of what is called knowledge

* Sisyphus—a legendary king of Corinth who was condemned to roll a heavy stone repeatedly up a steep hill in Hades. Each time he neared the top, the stone rolled down again. (By extension, a person who persists in an impossible task.)—Eds.

† Pestalozzi—a Swiss educator (1746-1827).—Eds.

‡ *privat dozent*—an unsalaried teacher in German-speaking countries who is paid directly by student fees.—Eds.

by this austere process, and despite the eloquence of those who support newer ideas, I lean heavily in favor of it, and regret to hear that it is no more. It was crude, it was rough, and it was often not a little cruel, but it at least had two capital advantages over all the systems that have succeeded it. In the first place, its machinery was simple; even the stupidest child could understand it; it hooked up cause and effect with the utmost clarity. And in the second place, it tested the teacher as and how he ought to be tested—that is, for his actual capacity to teach, not for his mere technical virtuosity. There was, in fact, no technic for him to master, and hence none for him to hide behind. He could not conceal a hopeless inability to impart knowledge beneath a correct professional method.

That ability to impart knowledge, it seems to me, has very little to do with technical method. It may operate at full function without any technical method at all, and contrariwise, the most elaborate of technical methods, whether out of Switzerland, Italy or Gary, Ind., cannot make it operate when it is not actually present. And what does it consist of? It consists, first, of a natural talent for dealing with children, for getting into their minds, for putting things in a way that they can comprehend. And it consists, secondly, of a deep belief in the interest and importance of the thing taught, a concern about it amounting to a sort of passion. A man who knows a subject thoroughly, a man so soaked in it that he eats it, sleeps it and dreams it—this man can always teach it with success, no matter how little he knows of technical pedagogy. That is because there is enthusiasm in him, and because enthusiasm is almost as contagious as fear or the barber's itch. An enthusiast is willing to go to any trouble to impart the glad news bubbling within him. He thinks that it is important and valuable for him to know; given the slightest glow of interest in a pupil to start with, he will fan that glow to a flame. No hollow formalism cripples him and slows him down. He drags his best pupils along as fast as they can go, and he is so full of the thing that he never tires of expounding its elements to the dullest.

This passion, so unordered and yet so potent, explains the capacity for teaching that one frequently observes in scientific men of high attainments in their specialties—for example, Huxley, Ostwald, Karl Ludwig, Virchow, Billroth, Jowett, William G. Sumner, Halsted and Osler—men who knew nothing whatever about the so-called science of pedagogy, and would have derided its alleged principles if they had heard them stated. It explains, too, the failure of the general run of high-school and college teachers—men who are undoubtedly competent, by the professional standards of pedagogy, but who nevertheless contrive only to make intolerable bores of the things they presume to teach. No intelligent student ever learns much from the average drove of undergraduates; what he actually carries away has come out of his textbooks, or is the fruit of his own reading and inquiry. But when he passes to the graduate school, and comes among men who really understand the subjects they teach, and, what is more, who really love them, his store of knowledge increases rapidly, and in a very short while, if he has any intelligence at all, he learns to think in terms of the thing he is studying.

So far, so good. But an objection still remains, the which may be couched in the following terms: that in the average college or high school, and especially in the elementary school, most of the subjects taught are so bald and uninspiring that it is difficult to imagine them arousing the passion I have been describing—in brief, that only an ass could be enthusiastic about them. In witness, think of the four elementals: reading, penmanship, arithmetic and spelling. This objection, at first blush, seems salient and dismaying, but only a brief inspection is needed to show that it is really of very small validity. It is made up of a false assumption and a false inference. The false inference is that there is any sound reason for prohibiting teaching by asses, if only the asses know how to do it, and do it well. The false assumption is that there are no asses in our schools and colleges today. The facts stand in almost complete antithesis to these notions. The truth is that the average schoolmaster, on all the lower levels, is and always must be essentially an ass, for how can one imagine an intelligent man engaging in so puerile an avocation? And, the truth is that it is precisely his inherent asininity, and not his technical equipment as a pedagogue, that is responsible for whatever modest success he now shows.

I here attempt no heavy jocosity, but mean exactly what I say. Consider, for example, penmanship. A decent handwriting, it must be obvious, is useful to all men, and particularly to the lower orders of men. It is one of the few things capable of acquirement in school that actually helps them to make a living. Well, how is it taught today? It is taught, in the main, by schoolmarms so enmeshed in a complex and unintelligible technic that, even supposing them able to write clearly themselves, they find it quite impossible to teach their pupils. Every few years sees a radical overhauling of the whole business. First the vertical hand is to make it easy; then certain curves are the favorite magic; then there is a return to slants and shadings. No department of pedagogy sees a more hideous cavorting of quacks. In none is the natural talent and enthusiasm of the teacher more depressingly crippled. And the result? The result is that our American school children write abominably—that a clerk or stenographer with a simple, legible hand becomes almost as scarce as one with Greek.

Go back, now, to the old days. Penmanship was then taught, not mechanically and ineffectively, by unsound and shifting formulae, but by passionate penmen with curly patent-leather hair and far-away eyes—in brief, by the unforgettable professors of our youth, with their flourishes, their heavy down-strokes and their lovely birds-with-letters-in-their-bills. You remember them, of course. Asses all! Preposterous popinjays* and numskulls! Pathetic idiots! But they loved penmanship, they believed in the glory and beauty of penmanship, they were fanatics, devotees, almost martyrs of penmanship—and so they got some touch of that passion into their pupils. Not enough, perhaps, to make more flourishers and bird-blazoners, but enough to make sound penmen. Look at your old writing book; observe the excellent legibility, the clear strokes of your "Time is money." Then look at your child's.

Such idiots, despite the rise of "scientific" pedagogy, have not died out in the world. I believe that our schools are full of them, both in pantaloons and in skirts. There are fanatics who love and venerate spelling as a tom-cat loves and venerates catnip. There are grammatomaniacs; schoolmarms who would rather parse† than

* popinjay—a strutting, arrogant person.—Eds.

† parse—to divide a sentence into grammatical parts.—Eds.

eat; specialists in an objective case that doesn't exist in English; strange beings, otherwise sane and even intelligent and comely, who suffer under a split infinitive as you or I would suffer under gastro-enteritis. There are geography cranks, able to bound Mesopotamia and Beluchistan. There are zealots for long division, experts in the multiplication table, lunatic worshipers of the binomial theorem. But the system has them in its grip. It combats their natural enthusiasm diligently and mercilessly. It tries to convert them into mere technicians, clumsy machines. It orders them to teach, not by the process of emotional osmosis which worked in the days gone by, but by formulae that are as baffling to the pupil as they are paralyzing to the teacher. Imagine what would happen to one of them who stepped to the blackboard, seized a piece of chalk, and engrossed a bird that held the class spellbound—a bird with a thousand flowing feathers, wings bursting with parabolas and epicycloids,* and long ribbons streaming from its bill! Imagine the fate of one who began "Honesty is the best policy" with an H as florid and—to a child—as beautiful as the initial of a mediaeval manuscript! Such a teacher would be cashiered and handed over to the secular arm; the very enchantment of the assembled infantry would be held as damning proof against him. And yet it is just such teachers that we should try to discover and develop. Pedagogy needs their enthusiasm, their naive belief in their own grotesque talents, their capacity for communicating their childish passion to the childish.

But this would mean exposing the children of the Republic to contact with monomaniacs, half-wits, defectives? Well, what of it? The vast majority of them are already exposed to contact with half-wits in their own homes; they are taught the word of God by half-wits on Sundays; they will grow up into Knights of Pythias, Odd Fellows, Red Men and other such half-wits in the days to come. Moreover, as I have hinted, they are already face to face with half-wits in the actual schools, at least in three cases out of four. The problem before us is not to dispose of this fact, but to utilize it. We cannot hope to fill the schools with persons of high intelligence, for persons of high intelligence simply refuse to spend their lives teaching such banal things as spelling and arithmetic. Among the teachers male we may safely assume that 95 per cent are of low mentality, else they would depart for more appetizing pastures. And even among the teachers female the best are inevitably weeded out by marriage, and only the worst (with a few romantic exceptions) survive. The task before us, as I say, is not to make a vain denial of this cerebral inferiority of the pedagogue, nor to try to combat and disguise it by concocting a mass of technical hocus-pocus, but to search out and put to use the value lying concealed in it. For even stupidity, it must be plain, has its uses in the world, and some of them are uses that intelligence cannot meet. One would not tell off a Galileo or a Pasteur to drive an ash-cart or an Ignatius Loyola to be a stockbroker, or a Brahms to lead the orchestra in a Broadway cabaret. By the same token, one would not ask a Herbert Spencer or a Duns Scotus to instruct sucklings. Such men would not only be wasted at the job; they would also be incompetent. The business of dealing with children, in fact, demands a certain childishness of mind. The best teacher, until one comes to adult

* epicycloid—a curve traced by a point that rolls on the outside of a fixed circle.—Eds.

pupils, is not the one who knows most, but the one who is most capable of reducing knowledge to that simple compound of the obvious and the wonderful which slips easiest into the infantile comprehension. A man of high intelligence, perhaps, may accomplish the thing by a conscious intellectual feat. But it is vastly easier to the man (or woman) whose habits of mind are naturally on the plane of a child's. The best teacher of children, in brief, is one who is essentially childlike.

I go so far with this notion that I view the movement to introduce female bachelors of arts into the primary schools with the utmost alarm. A knowledge of Bergsonism, the Greek aorist, sex hygiene and the dramas of Percy Mackaye is not only no help to the teaching of spelling, it is a positive handicap to the teaching of spelling, for it corrupts and blows up that naive belief in the glory and portentousness of spelling which is at the bottom of all successful teaching of it. If I had my way, indeed, I should expose all candidates for berths in the infant grades to the Binet-Simon test, and reject all those who revealed the mentality of more than fifteen years. Plenty would still pass. Moreover, they would be secure against contamination by the new technic of pedagogy. Its vast wave of pseudo-psychology would curl and break against the hard barrier of their innocent and passionate intellects—as it probably does, in fact, even now. They would know nothing of cognition, perception, attention, the sub-conscious and all the other half-fabulous fowl of the pedagogic aviary. But they would see in reading, writing and arithmetic the gaudy charms of profound and esoteric knowledge, and they would teach these ancient branches, now so abominably in decay, with passionate gusto, and irresistible effectiveness, and a gigantic success.

## *Lissa Rotundo*
## "ONE-YEAR-OLD SCHOLARS"

The other day a friend of long standing watched as I tied my shoe, and was overcome with laughter at the method I used. Ever since I was a wee lass, people have made fun of the way I tie my shoes and no doubt this has left deep emotional scars. But years of self-analysis have finally illuminated the root of the problem: I did not go to nursery school, where most children learn the proper execution of this skill. Not only did I not go to nursery school, I did not learn to read until the first grade and I was deprived of watching "Sesame Street" because it had not yet been invented. The underprivileged background considered, it is amazing that I have survived this long.

In these progressive times the little child who stays home with his mother has become so rare that I would like to nominate the American pre-schooler as the newest vanishing species, like the California condor, the timber wolf and the whale.

I now have a year-old son. When he was four months old, a solicitous neighbor called, urging me to enroll my 15-pound wonder in the next session of the pre-nursery school co-op before all the places were filled. This, it seems, is crucial for three reasons. The first is that the co-op will provide intellectual stimulation and speed motor development. This can't be managed adequately at home because (1) I couldn't possibly match the school's collection of educational materials (expensive toys, to the uninitiated), and (2) I don't have a degree in Early Childhood Education, and must therefore be incapable of teaching my son much of anything.

Then, of course, there's the matter of social interaction: the baby needs someone to play with. Remember playing with the neighborhood children when you were a preschooler? Well, your kid can't do that, for the simple reason that all his peers are tucked away in school. One lady I know tried to buck the system and keep her daughter home until she was 4. Lacking human companions of her own age, this 2½-year-old became a great friend of the family Airedales, which no one minded until the day she lined up with them on the window seat and barked at the mailman. By the next week she, too, had begun her formal education.

The third reason for enrolling my baby in pre-nursery school is that it would help him find a place in nursery school when the time comes. You may not have realized it (I didn't), but there is fierce competition for these places. Many nursery schools have long waiting lists, and it is not at all uncommon for mothers of 2- and 3-year-old toddlers to interview at several schools before finding one that will both fit a child's personality and accept the child. A friend recently interviewed a local Montessori school for her 4-year-old, who had already attended another school for a year. The director of the school was horrified that this mother had let her son's education slide so shamefully. "Well," he said, "we can try to do something with him, but it's so late now. He should have been coming here for two years by this time." Imagine my friend's guilt: 4 years old, and her son was hopelessly behind, due to her negligence.

Of course, it follows from this that if your 2-year-old does not go to the "right" nursery school, his chances of attending the "right" kindergarten dwindle. The child of a neighbor recently had to take an entrance exam to determine whether he would be admitted to a certain kindergarten a year from now. (Among the items tested was reading readiness. It is a most unusual education system we have that may require some level of literacy for entry into kindergarten, but not for graduation from high school.) Fortunately, the child had a strong enough nursery-school background to pass the exam. His parents can breathe a sigh of relief: the doors of the "right" elementary school, and therefore, the right junior high, high school, college and law school are still open to their boy. The message is clear: if you want your kid to work for the "right" law firm 30 years hence, you'd better be darned careful in your choice of pre-nursery school now.

I have my own little theory about how this strange situation has come to exist. We all know that more and more education has become necessary to maintain a given position in society. The status accorded a high-school graduate a century ago is now denied to the average Ph.D., who has spent about ten years longer in school. And so Ph.D.'s must have postdoctoral training and, naturally, two postdocs are better than one. Everyone is encouraged to take courses until death is imminent, and a few years ago it even became fashionable to take courses *about* death, to be sure that one would die properly. Who would want to be caught dead without being prepared for it? Short of taking a cue from pharaohs of old and equipping each tomb with a library of educational videotapes and a television set on which to play them, we have reached the end of the line. The only way to utilize the army of unemployed education majors is to reverse the direction, at first offering but gradually requiring organized education of younger and younger children. In twenty more years, when everyone who's anyone has at least one Ph.D., the key question asked on job applications will no longer be "What is the highest level of education you have completed?" but "How early did your start school?"

All that remains now is for someone to figure out how to teach the fetus while it still resides in its mother's uterus. Universities will immediately establish departments of Fetal Education, and this fertile field will sprout a large crop of doctoral candidates, all eager to pack those prenatal months with valuable learning experiences. Expectant parents will be able to sleep better at night, knowing that they are wasting none of their children's precious time in the race to the best university. Just think—when your great-grandchild enters the world, his initial statement will not be simply the predictable "Wah!" He may greet his parents with "Hic, haec, hoc."

## SUGGESTIONS FOR DISCUSSION

1. Satire is an artistic attack on human error. Both Mencken and Rotundo have satiric elements in their essays. What is the "error" which Rotundo is ridiculing? Is Mencken directing his attack against the same ills?
2. Satire is often divided into two types, named after the Roman writers Horace and Juvenal. Horatian satire is gentle and mocking; it works through sympathetic laughter. Juvenalian satire is harsh and bitter; it expresses contemptuous anger or indignation. Which type is Mencken's? Rotundo's? Find examples to support your answer.
3. Mencken's style is marked by some interesting features like his penchant for archaic or irregular syntax and his habit of interrupting sentences to insert himself ("I need not point out," "it seems to me"). Another is his diction, his word choice. Go through and circle ten of his words or phrases that strike you as particularly exotic. Once you've determined what they mean, try to replace them with simpler, more pedestrian choices. What is the effect?
4. One necessary rhetorical tactic is recognizing and refuting the opposition's arguments. How does Mencken refute the opposition? How well does he present their arguments? Find at least three different ways he manages his refutations.
5. One of Rotundo's stylistic devices is hyperbole, a conscious exaggeration which is not meant to be taken literally. Find several examples of hyperbole in this essay? What is accomplished by this kind of exaggeration?
6. Mencken praises teachers who have a passion for their subject and who can impart knowledge, even when they are "fanatical." Schools of education today are more likely to stress respect for students and a good classroom atmosphere. In other words, there is a definite contrast being made between teachers who are devoted to their subject and those who are devoted to their students. Examine the teacher evaluation form used at your school. Which type of teacher would receive the highest rating on that form?

## SUGGESTIONS FOR WRITING

1. Almost everybody likes to write satirically; it is a relatively easy form of writing to pick up, even if novices don't always have much grace or subtlety. Using either

Mencken or Rotundo as a model, write satirically about something that bothers you. Don't be overly concerned with making constructive suggestions to go along with your criticisms. Assume that your audience knows as much about the topic as you do; your purpose is to get them to see the subject in as negative a light as you can manage. It helps if you can be witty along the way.

# 11

# Motivation and Reluctance

*Winston Churchill*

## "SCHOOL DAYS"

*Jean Kerr*

## "THE POET AND THE PEASANTS"

In contrast to the more general discussions of Mencken and Rotundo, Winston Churchill and Jean Kerr present personal accounts of their educational struggles. Churchill describes his inability or unwillingness to learn unless he was genuinely interested in the subject. He argues that motivation to learn is primarily an internal quality, not one which can be imposed by others. Kerr disagrees with Churchill. She describes her unpopular efforts to make her four sons learn poetry when they would have much preferred baseball, soccer, or tree houses. In spite of their loud protests, she persisted, and the result was that they came to love and appreciate poetry. What began as an enforced task finally became a pleasure and an enrichment.

### WRITE BEFORE READING

Both the essays here are about education—Kerr's about education in the home and Churchill's about education in school. In preparation for reading them, think back over your own education in those two places. Pick a subject that, at least at the time, you really *hated.* Write an account of your experience as though you were telling it to a patient listener in some comfortable setting. As you tell the story, make clear how you remember feeling at the time: bored, angry, embarrassed. When you finish with the story itself, reflect on the experience as you see it now, across time. Was it worthwhile after all? Or were you justified in hating it?

## *Winston Churchill*
# "SCHOOL DAYS"

The school my parents had selected for my education was one of the most fashionable and expensive in the country. It modelled itself upon Eton and aimed at being preparatory for that Public School above all others. It was supposed to be the very last thing in schools. Only ten boys in a class; electric light (then a wonder); a swimming pond; spacious football and cricket grounds; two or three school treats, or "expeditions" as they were called, every term; the masters all M.A.'s in gowns and mortar-boards; a chapel of its own; no hampers allowed; everything provided by the authorities. It was a dark November afternoon when we arrived at this establishment. We had tea with the Headmaster, with whom my mother conversed in the most easy manner. I was preoccupied with the fear of spilling my cup and so making "a bad start." I was also miserable at the idea of being left alone among all these strangers in this great, fierce, formidable place. After all I was only seven, and I had been so happy in my nursery with all my toys. I had such wonderful toys: a real steam engine, a magic lantern, and a collection of soldiers already nearly a thousand strong. Now it was to be all lessons. Seven or eight hours of lessons every day except half-holidays, and football or cricket in addition.

When the last sound of my mother's departing wheels had died away, the Headmaster invited me to hand over any money I had in my possession. I produced my three half-crowns which were duly entered in a book, and I was told that from time to time there would be a "shop" at the school with all sorts of things which one would like to have, and that I could choose what I liked up to the limit of the seven and sixpence. Then we quitted the Headmaster's parlour and the comfortable private side of the house, and entered the more bleak apartments reserved for the instruction and accommodation of the pupils. I was taken into a Form Room and told to sit at a desk. All the other boys were out of doors, and I was alone with the Form Master. He produced a thin greeny-brown-covered book filled with words in different types of print.

"You have never done any Latin before, have you?" he said.

"No, sir."

"This is a Latin grammar." He opened it at a well-thumbed page. "You must learn this," he said, pointing to a number of words in a frame of lines. "I will come back in half an hour and see what you know."

Behold me then on a gloomy evening, with an aching heart, seated in front of the First Declension.

| | |
|---|---|
| Mensa | a table |
| Mensa | O table |
| Mensam | a table |
| Mensae | of a table |
| Mensae | to or for a table |
| Mensa | by, with or from a table |

What on earth did it mean? Where was the sense of it? It seemed absolute rigmarole to me. However, there was one thing I could always do: I could learn by heart. And I thereupon proceeded, as far as my private sorrows would allow, to memorise the acrostic-looking task which had been set me.

In due course the Master returned.

"Have you learnt it?" he asked.

"I think I can *say* it, sir," I replied; and I gabbled it off.

He seemed so satisfied with this that I was emboldened to ask a question.

"What does it mean, sir?"

"It means what it says. Mensa, a table. Mensa is a noun of the First Declension. There are five declensions. You have learnt the singular of the First Declension."

"But," I repeated, "what does it mean?"

"Mensa means a table," he answered.

"Then why does mensa also mean O table," I enquired, "and what does O table mean?"

"Mensa, O table, is the vocative case," he replied.

"But why O table?" I persisted in genuine curiosity.

"O table,—you would use that in addressing a table, in invoking a table." And then seeing he was not carrying me with him, "You would use it in speaking to a table."

"But I never do," I blurted out in honest amazement.

"If you are impertinent, you will be punished, and punished, let me tell you, very severely," was his conclusive rejoinder.

Such was my first introduction to the classics from which, I have been told, many of our cleverest men have derived so much solace and profit.

The Form Master's observations about punishment were by no means without their warrant at St. James's School. Flogging with the birch in accordance with the Eton fashion was a great feature in its curriculum. But I am sure no Eton boy, and certainly no Harrow boy of my day, ever received such a cruel flogging as this Headmaster was accustomed to inflict upon the little boys who were in his care and power. They exceeded in severity anything that would be tolerated in any of the Reformatories under the Home Office. My reading in later life has supplied me with some possible explanations of his temperament. Two or three times a month the whole school was marshalled in the Library, and one or more delinquents were haled off to an adjoining apartment by the two head boys, and there flogged until they bled freely, while the rest sat quaking, listening to their screams. This form of correction was strongly reinforced by frequent religious services of a somewhat High Church character in the chapel. Mrs. Everest was very much against the Pope. If the truth were known, she said, he was behind the Fenians. She was herself Low Church, and her dislike of ornaments and ritual, and generally her extremely unfavourable opinion of the Supreme Pontiff, had prejudiced me strongly against that personage and all religious practices supposed to be associated with him. I therefore did not derive much comfort from the spiritual side of my education at this juncture. On the other hand, I experienced the fullest applications of the secular arm.

How I hated this school, and what a life of anxiety I lived there for more than two years. I made very little progress at my lessons, and none at all at games. I counted the days and the hours to the end of every term, when I should return home from this hateful servitude and range my soldiers in line of battle on the nursery floor. The greatest pleasure I had in those days was reading. When I was nine and a half my father gave me *Treasure Island,* and I remember the delight with which I devoured it. My teachers saw me at once backward and precocious, reading books beyond my years and yet at the bottom of the Form. They were offended. They had large resources of compulsion at their disposal, but I was stubborn. Where my reason, imagination or interest were not engaged, I would not or I could not learn. In all the twelve years I was at school no one ever succeeded in making me write a Latin verse or learn any Greek except the alphabet. I do not at all excuse myself for this foolish neglect of opportunities procured at so much expense by my parents and brought so forcibly to my attention by my Preceptors. Perhaps if I had been introduced to the ancients through their history and customs, instead of through their grammar and syntax, I might have had a better record.

I fell into a low state of health at St. James's School, and finally after a serious illness my parents took me away. Our family doctor, the celebrated Robson Roose, then practised at Brighton; and as I was now supposed to be very delicate, it was thought desirable that I should be under his constant care. I was accordingly, in 1883, transferred to a school at Brighton kept by two ladies. This was a smaller school than the one I had left. It was also cheaper and less pretentious. But there was an element of kindness and of sympathy which I had found conspicuously lacking in my first experiences. Here I remained for three years; and though I very nearly died from an attack of double pneumonia, I got gradually much stronger in that bracing air and gentle surroundings. At this school I was allowed to learn things which interested me: French, History, lots of Poetry by heart, and above all Riding and Swimming. The impression of those years makes a pleasant picture in my mind, in strong contrast to my earlier schoolday memories.

My partiality for Low Church principles which I had acquired from Mrs. Everest led me into one embarrassment. We often attended the service in the Chapel Royal at Brighton. Here the school was accommodated in pews which ran North and South. In consequence, when the Apostles' Creed was recited, everyone turned to the East. I was sure Mrs. Everest would have considered this practice Popish, and I conceived it my duty to testify against it. I therefore stood stolidly to my front. I was conscious of having created a "sensation." I prepared myself for martyrdom. However, when we got home no comment of any kind was made upon my behaviour. I was almost disappointed, and looked forward to the next occasion for a further demonstration of my faith. But when it came, the school was shown into different pews in the Chapel Royal facing East, and no action was called for from any one of us when the Creed was said. I was puzzled to find my true course and duty. It seemed excessive to turn away from the East. Indeed I could not feel that such a step would be justified. I therefore became willy-nilly a passive conformist.

It was thoughtful and ingenious of these old ladies to have treated my scruples so tenderly. The results repaid their care. Never again have I caused or felt trouble on such a point. Not being resisted or ill-treated, I yielded myself complacently to a broad-minded tolerance and orthodoxy.

# *Jean Kerr*
# "THE POET AND THE PEASANTS"

We have made mistakes with our children, which will undoubtedly become clearer as they get old enough to write their own books. But here I would like to be serious for a few minutes about the one thing we did that was right. We taught them not to be afraid of poetry.

For a number of years, or until the older boys went away to school, we gathered the protesting brood in the living room every Sunday evening, right after dinner, for what the children scornfully referred to as "Culture Hour." Each boy would recite a poem he had memorized during the week, after which we would play some classical music on the hi-fi for twenty minutes or so. This will sound simple and easy only to those who refuse to grasp that if there is an irresistible force there are most definitely immovable objects.

Actually the program came about by accident. One night I went into the den and turned on a light which promptly burned out. Then when I turned on a second light the same thing happened. Cursing the darkness, I muttered "When I consider how my light is spent. . ."

My husband surprised me by asking, "What's that from?" I recoiled as though he had just announced that he couldn't remember the colors of the American flag. "It's not possible," I said, "that you don't know what that's from. Everybody knows what that's from."

His look was short-suffering. "You don't have to sound so superior," he said. "The first present I ever gave you was a book of poetry." (I was eighteen and it was *The Collected Poems of Stephen Crane.*) "I know that's a poem, I just don't know *which* poem."

"Well," I continued, fatuous as before, "that is Milton's *Sonnet on His Blindness* and it's inconceivable to me that a man who used to be a teacher wouldn't remember." But he had left to get two new light bulbs and out of the range of my voice.

That started me mulling, which is one of the things I do best. Were our five boys going to grow up knowing all about such folk heroes as Joe Namath and Vince Lombardi and nothing whatsoever about Milton or Keats or Yeats or even Ogden Nash? Steps, I felt, had to be taken.

When I first proposed the idea to my husband his enthusiasm was less contagious than I might have hoped. "I don't suppose it will kill them" is what he said. "Them" at that point were Chris, aged fourteen, the twins, Colin and John, aged ten, and Gilbert, aged seven. There was also Gregory, aged two, who could recite "I love Bosco, that's the drink for me," but I didn't suppose his talents could be pushed further at that juncture.

I did suppose that we could plunge ahead with the four older boys. But if their father felt it wouldn't kill them, they had no such confidence. As I unfolded The Plan they couldn't have been more horrified if I had suddenly suggested that all of them wear hair ribbons to football practice. Nevertheless, I was adamant, and, as it turned out, rather obtuse. At that stage of my life I was still in good voice and bigger than they were. And I was used to giving commands. "Go," I would say to one, and he would goeth, "Come," I would say to another and he would cometh. (Occasionally he would runneth out the back door.)

I always tried (and still do try) to be very specific. To say to a ten-year-old boy, "If you don't start keeping that room tidy, I am going to go absolutely crazy" is a waste of time and breath. To begin with, he doesn't know what the word "tidy" means and he won't find out until he marries the right girl. And since he considers that you are already crazy, he will not believe that his actions are likely to worsen the situation. It may not be infallible, but it surely is more practical to say, "You don't leave this room until I say it is *perfect* and I do mean all those Good Humor sticks under the bed."

Anyway, it was with this sense of being totally explicit that I told the boys one Monday morning, "I want you to find a poem that you like and I want you to learn it so you can say it out loud next Sunday night. Is that clear?" The sighs and the groaning reassured me. I had been perfectly clear. During the week I nudged them from time to time, "How is that poem coming, do you know it yet?"

On Sunday evening there was the usual hassle over whose turn it was to dry the silver and whose turn it was to line the kitchen waste basket, etc. My own mother used to solve this problem by saying, "Just don't bother, I'll do it myself," but I am too judicious for that and also too lazy. So getting the dishes put away is always a long-drawn-out process. Tonight it was a longer-drawn-out process. But eventually the victims presented themselves in the living room, and the recital began. Three of the boys had selected limericks and poor limericks at that (imagine anybody rhyming "breakfast" with "steadfast") while the fourth recited a lengthy and truly dreadful verse about a Cookie Jar Elf. My husband, more than most men of his generation, has seen some pretty horrendous performances, but this was in a class by itself. He polished his glasses, presumably to make sure that these *were* his children. As for me, I had intended to make a few illuminating comments. Instead I was left as slackjawed and as speechless as those television commentators who were picked up by the camera minutes after President Johnson announced he would *not* run again.

In the vacuum I put a record, *The Nutcracker Suite*, on the hi-fi and warned the boys they were not to talk, they were to listen. They were not to whisper, they were to listen. The boys kept to the letter, if not the spirit, of the instructions, with the result that I was the one who talked and talked all through the music: "Stop kicking him in the ankle, take that ashtray off the top of your head, I know you can hear the music from there but get out from under the coffee table."

The whole thing was a disaster but, while I was definitely daunted, I was not yet ready to give up. (Remember that *Hello, Dolly!* looked like a failure when it opened in Detroit.) Eventually I was able to identify Mistake Number One. Asking the boys to find a poem they "liked" made about as much sense as asking me to select a Rock Group that I liked. Of course they didn't like poems, any poems. How could they, why should they? When I was the age of our oldest and was required at school to learn whole passages of *The Lady of the Lake,* I thought 'The stag at eve had drunk his fill/Where danced the moon on Monan's rill" was pretty ghastly stuff. (To tell the truth, I still think it's pretty ghastly.) Once, as a senior in high school, I got sixty on an English exam because of the way I answered a forty-point question which read: "Discuss Wordsworth's *The World Is Too Much with Us* and explain what it means to you." You will not have to remember the poem to grasp that I was not only saucy but asking for trouble when I wrote that, whatever Wordsworth was looking for as he stood on that pleasant lea, the *last* thing I wanted was to see Proteus rising from the sea, or, for that matter, hear old Triton blow his wreathed horn. I mention this only to make it clear that I was not among those prodigies who are reading Shakespeare's sonnets for pleasure at the age of five. Poetry struck me as an arbitrary and capricious method of avoiding clarity, and where my betters heard lyricism I kept hearing foolishness. If the poem said, "Go, lovely rose!" I found myself thinking "Scram, rose. On the double. Take a powder, rose."

What happened to open my eyes and shut my mouth was quite simple. I was a freshman in college when a Jesuit poet named Alfred Barrett came to lecture. I attended with the same enthusiasm that characterized my presence in Advanced Algebra, sitting way at the back of the hall behind a pillar on the theory that I could live through it if I could sleep through it.

It's hard for me to remember, all these years later, what Father Barrett said about poetry, if indeed he said anything. What he did was to read poetry—some of his own, a great deal of Gerard Manley Hopkins (whose existence I was unaware of), Yeats, Shelley, Donne, and Housman. He read with such clarity, such melody, and, above all, such directness that even I—sixteen-year-old skeptic—was converted on the spot. It wasn't so much that I cried "Eureka—I see!" I felt like a woman I know who swears she didn't get her first kiss until she was twenty-three and who exclaimed, on that occasion, "Hey, why didn't somebody *tell* me?" Later in my life I was to meet a teacher and a director, Josephine Callan, who read poetry even better than Father Barrett did but by that time I was already a believer.

Okay, that was *my* story. To get back to the indoctrination of our boys, it was clear that their taste was decidedly peccable and that we would have to select the poems for them, keeping in mind the difference in the boys' ages. (My husband was quick to point out that fortunately there was no difference in the ages of the twins.) We went through the bookshelves, leafed and leafed, and gave each of the boys a book with the poem he was to learn. This was another error because by the end of the week our good books were dog-eared or rateared, depending upon the age and irresponsibility of the boy. For a while after that we typed out copies of the poems, but that was a chore and a nuisance (why is poetry harder to type than *anything?*) so eventually we did in the last place what we should have done in the first place, which was to go out and buy a pile of cheap paperback anthologies (these are widely available and often surprisingly good).

The second, or return, engagement of "Culture" night was hardly an improvement on the first. The fact that the poems were of better quality and somewhat longer made the recitations even more agonizing, if that were possible. The younger boys stared at the rug and mumbled like altar boys answering their first Mass in Latin, while Chris stared at the ceiling and chanted in a loud, dum-de-dum see-saw-Margery-Daw rhythm (banging on every end-rhyme until I could definitely feel my inlays ache).

As I see it now, the surprising thing is that I should have been surprised. Even granting that I was much younger then (I was, you will be able to surmise, over twenty-one), there was no excuse for my being so dim-witted. Did I really believe that we were harboring a gaggle of Laurence Oliviers? (Ellen Terry heard Olivier in a school play when he was eleven and instantly announced, "That young man is already an actor.") Not, heaven forbid, that we were trying to develop actors. In my opinion, young people who wish to become actors have an addiction only a little less dangerous than heroin. No, we didn't want them to qualify for a Tony or an Emmy, we just wanted them to feel at home with language that was different from and better than the colloquial speech they heard every day. We wanted them to accept poetry without embarrassment and perhaps finally to realize that a good poem is an emotional short-cut and not just the long way around.

My husband gave a deep sigh as he faced up to the obvious. "We're just going to have to work on them," he said. And so we did. One week he'd work on two of them while I worked on the other two (the following week we alternated so that the hostility engendered would be evenly divided). Getting a boy and his poem together (a not inconsiderable feat), we read the poem aloud to him, slowly. Ignoring giggles and glassy-eyed boredom, we read it again at the proper speed and then asked questions: What do you think this poem means, is it happy or sad, and so on? Even a piece of verse as simple as "Little Boy Blue" holds mysteries for a seven-year-old. He may not know what the word "staunch" means, or even "musket." Perhaps he may not get the point at all and will be as perplexed as the little toy soldier and the little toy dog as to "what has become of our Little Boy Blue since he kissed them and put them there."

Once we determined that the child actually understood the whole poem, we got *him* to read it aloud, correcting him when he mispronounced words, correcting him when he misread phrases, persuading him not to say the rhyming word louder than any other word in the line. Two of the boys were very quick to grasp inflections; the other two were so slow that rehearsing them was like the Chinese Water Torture and I found myself wondering if there was some way to withdraw from the whole plan—with honor. What kept me resolute was the conviction I read in all those clear blue eyes that I would soon come to my senses, that this madness too would pass.

On the third Sunday night the boys were not exactly ready to cut a tape for Angel Records but they were definitely improved. In fact, the session was almost endurable, and we had some general discussion afterward about what the four poems meant, with even Gilbert making a contribution: "When the angel waked him up with a song it means he was dead, stupid."

Thereafter the Sunday hour became just another fact of life around this house and the boys seemed to accept it with hardly more resentment than they accepted baths or sweaters or my notion that a present that came in the mail required a thank-you letter. And, of course, they did get better. The day finally came when they were really able to tackle a poem without our having to tell them "What Tennyson is trying to say here is. . ." They knew. And if they made mistakes, these were fewer and fewer. Sometimes they came up with an unusual interpretation that was, we had to concede, quite possibly valid.

But this didn't happen until we'd been through years of poetry, yards of poetry, volumes of poetry. We made a number of discoveries along the way. Christopher in his mid-teens and already a little world-weary had a particular affinity for the cynical or sardonic, whether it was in a simple lyric form like Housman's

When I was one and twenty
  I heard a wise man say
'Give crowns and pounds and guineas
  But not your heart away;
  . . . . . . . . . . . .
'Tis paid with sighs a-plenty
  And sold for endless rue.
And I am two and twenty
  And oh, 'tis true, 'tis true.

or in the rich resonance of Arnold's *Dover Beach:*

Ah, love, let us be true
To one another! for the world, which seems
To lie before us like a land of dreams,
So various, so beautiful, so new
Hath really neither joy, nor love, nor light,
Nor certitude, nor peace, nor help for pain;
And we are here as on a darkling plain
Swept with confused alarms of struggle and flight,
Where ignorant armies clash by night.

I can still see him — he must have been fifteen, messy and mussed with dirty sneakers and a deplorable shirt—reciting Browning with all the hauteur and severity of George Sanders:

That's my last Duchess painted on the wall,
Looking as if she were alive. . . .
                                        She had
A heart . . . how shall I say? . . . too soon made glad,
Too easily impressed; she liked whate'er
She looked on, and her looks went everywhere.

George Sanders chilled into George C. Scott as he came to the lines:

. . . This grew; I gave commands;
Then all smiles stopped together.

Colin was a very serious ten-year-old (he's now six feet five and a very serious Harvard junior) and it seemed to us that he did better with the dark and the dire. "Out of the night that covers me, black as pitch from pole to pole," he would say in a voice that was at once sweet and piercing, "I thank whatever gods may be for my unconquerable soul." He was downright threatening as he recited John Donne's:

Death, be not proud, though some have called thee
Mighty and dreadful, for thou art not so:
For those whom thou think'st thou dost overthrow
Die not, poor Death; nor yet canst thou kill me.

John had a good voice, a trace of ham, and a total lack of inhibition that made him a natural for the more flamboyant ballads. His early pièce de résistance was *The Highwayman* by Alfred Noyes. I'm sure he couldn't do it as well today as he could when he was twelve. But then I don't honestly think *anybody* can do *The Highwayman* the way John could when he was twelve. John began the opening lines with a sense of excitement that never flagged:

The wind was a torrent of darkness among the gusty trees.
The moon was a ghostly galleon tossed upon cloudy seas.
The road was a ribbon of moonlight over the purple moor,
And the highwayman came riding—
  Riding—riding—
The highwayman came riding, up to the old inn door.

And he handled the love story of the highwayman and the innkeeper's daughter with great tenderness. Describing how she loosened her hair in the casement window, he would pause before saying, ever so gently, "Oh, sweet black waves in the moonlight!" and then flash with the fire of a prosecuting attorney as the highwayman went

  Down like a dog on the highway
And he lay in his blood on the highway, with a bunch
  Of lace at his throat.

With John's passion, one felt that the body was there on the living-room floor. Another of his early hits was *Barbara Fritchie*, and if you think that one is just another chestnut ("Who touches a hair of yon grey head dies like a dog, he said") you haven't heard it read by someone who doesn't *know* it's a chestnut and who believes he was there and is giving you an eyewitness account. John was always awfully good with people who died, or were about to die, like dogs.

Having tried the tried and the true, John gradually moved on to the intricacies of Hopkins, where he could be majestic:

The world is charged with the grandeur of God.
It will flame out, like shining from shook foil. . . .

Or filled with righteous indignation:

Thou art indeed just, Lord, if I contend
With thee, but, sir, so what I plead is just.
Why do sinners' ways prosper? and why must
Disappointment all I endeavor end?

Or rueful, as in *Spring and Fall,* which he recited often because it's a particular favorite of mine:

Margaret, are you grieving over goldengrove unleaving?
Leaves, like the things of man, you
With your fresh thoughts care for, can you?
Ah! As the heart grows older
It will come to such sights colder
By and by, nor spare a sigh
Though worlds of wanwood leafmeal lie;
And yet you will weep and know why.
Now no matter, child, the name:
Sorrow's springs are the same.
Nor mouth had, no nor mind, expressed
What heart heard of, ghost guessed:
It is the blight man was born for,
It is Margaret you mourn for.

Gilbert, being much younger, was limited to what we thought was "easy," which meant that he got relatively cheerful poems and we got some relief. As I remember it, in his poems he was always planning to go someplace. He was going to see the cherry filled with snow, he was going to go down to the lonely seas again, he was going to arise and go to Innisfree. He was also going to leave Lucasta and go to war, but that was later.

During these evenings we continued to play twenty minutes of music. This became more bearable after I stopped trying to make the boys *look* attentive; it had occurred to me, after many a grinding play and many a dull sermon, that no matter how hard you try *not* to listen, something sticks to you anyway. And some nights we broke the pattern by running the films Leonard Bernstein had made for *Omnibus*. My husband had worked for *Omnibus* and was able to borrow kinescopes of the Bernstein talks on Modern Music, Jazz, The Beethoven Manuscripts, The Art of Conducting, and so on. I think these programs are as exhilarating as anything ever done on television. What the children thought was harder to fathom, since they remained totally noncommittal. Clearly, though, Bernstein made some impression on them. I know this because, months after we had played the last of the series, I discovered that Colin had built a new fort in the backyard. It was a crude affair made from two old card tables, an abandoned playpen, and some tar paper. However, insubstantial as it was, the fort appeared to have a name. A tattered banner floating over the entrance bore the legend: *Fort Issimo*.

We also began to get evidence that gallons of nineteenth-century poetry hadn't washed over them in vain. I recall one night—the twins were twelve—when John was made an Eagle Scout. Driving home from this awe-inspiring ceremony (oh, the Nobel people could take lessons!), I started to tease John. "Well," I said, "you've reached the top. Now what are you going to do?" The answer came from Colin in the back seat. "Oh," he announced briskly, "I expect he will go down to the vile dust from whence he sprung, unwept, unhonored, and unsung."

Sometimes, I must confess, this readiness with the apt quotation could be quite maddening. I think of another night when the two smaller boys were supposed to have gone to bed but had, against all orders, slipped outside to bat a few balls directly under the living-room window. Suddenly there was a splatter of broken glass and a baseball on the rug. Chris grinned cheerfully as he said, "Come to the window, sweet is the night air."

During all the years we continued our program I never at any time was given any hint that the boys approved. Not ever, not once. So I was thunderstruck one summer, after they'd all returned from school, when the boys themselves suggested that we resume "Culture Hour" for the weeks they were to be at home. I couldn't have been more startled if they had suddenly volunteered to clean out the attic. In fact, it occurred to me that they were making an elaborate joke (irony is frequently wasted on me), so I pressed for an explanation. It turned out that they thought it was time for Gregory to have "his turn." This might have been taken as further evidence that the older children felt they had been made the guinea pigs of the system while their younger siblings got off scot-free, but here they were volunteering to suffer right along with him. Now I believed them capable of altruism, particularly where Gregory was concerned, but not heroism. It had to be, it just had to be that they enjoyed it.

So we started over with Gregory, who, at seven, was already as complex as John Kenneth Galbraith. Not necessarily smart, you understand, just complex. Some days he'd come bursting in the back door with the air of one who'd just been rescued from a burning building and call out for his father, "Where's Mr. Kerr? I need him." (No, no, no, none of the other boys ever called their father Mister.) The next day he'd drift in as slowly as smoke, like a character out of Chekhov who has just lost his country estates.

Certainly *we* didn't understand him, but he did seem to have certain intimations about himself. Let me explain. On the opening night of the cultural revival, Gregory—with much prompting—struggled and stammered his way through no more than six lines of *The Gingham Dog and the Calico Cat.* It wasn't just that he was confused about gingham and calico. I began to wonder if he knew what dog and cat meant.

I don't remember what the other boys recited that evening, but Chris recited a long section of T. S. Eliot's *Prufrock.* The next morning I was passing through the garage and came upon Gregory building a birdhouse. He was also muttering something to himself. What with the noise of the saw, he wasn't aware that I had come up behind him, so I was able to overhear him. What he was saying, thoughtfully and precisely, was "I am not Prince Hamlet, nor was meant to be."

Soon the summer was over, school began, the Captains and the Kings departed, and the program was dropped. It was never to resume again because the following summer the older boys all had jobs away from home. It was never to resume and something special, I realized, had gone out of our lives. You lose not only your own youth but the youth of your children. Sweet things vanish and brightness falls from the air.

Now all those Sunday nights blur in memory like the ghost of birthdays past. But if there is one night that remains more vivid than the others it is because of my own strange behavior. Colin was just finishing *John Anderson My Jo.* Do you remember it all?

John Anderson my jo, John,
When we were first acquent,
Your locks were like the raven,
Your bonnie brow was brent;
But now your brow is beld, John,
Your locks are like the snaw;
But blessings on your frosty pow,
John Anderson, my jo.

John Anderson my jo, John,
We clamb the hill thegither;
And monie a canty day, John,
We've had wi' ane anither:
Now we maun totter down, John,
And hand in hand we'll go,
And sleep thegither at the foot,
John Anderson, my jo.

I already knew the poem by heart, so how it happened that I heard new meanings in it I cannot exactly explain. All I can say is that after Colin had finished, to the horror of the boys and to my own acute embarrassment, I burst into tears. An uneasy silence prevailed until John said, very quietly, "Mom, it is Margaret you mourn for."

And he was right, you know. He was absolutely right.

## SUGGESTIONS FOR DISCUSSION

1. In this kind of autobiographical writing, we respond as much to the narrator—the person telling the story—as to the story itself. Do you find that you like Winston Churchill? Jean Kerr? What do you like about them? Dislike? Can you figure out what feature or combinations of features in the text influenced you to like them or dislike them? Did their names lead you to expect anything particular in the readings?
2. Kerr uses humor throughout her essay. For example, she writes: "I was used to giving commands. 'Go,' I would say to one and he would goeth. 'Come,' I would say to another and he would cometh. Occasionally he would runneth out the back door." Find other examples of her humor in this essay. How does the humor affect your response to the essay? What does it do for your sense of the essay's *persona*?
3. Sometimes, when reading something, we get a sense of intimacy with the writer, a sense that the writer has bared his or her soul and become genuinely open and vulnerable. In this collection, probably the most powerful example of such a piece is Olsen's "I Stand Here Ironing," which is, of course, fiction. How "vulnerable" do you think Kerr and Churchill are here? What, if anything, do you think keeps them protected?
4. Both Kerr and Churchill suggest that learning is rather a private thing, something that happens when the time is right and when there is genuine interest. As Churchill puts it: "Where my reason, imagination, or interest were not engaged, I

would not or could not learn." Both of them, though, give hints about how to deal with reluctant students. How do their ideas differ? What assumptions about human psychology influence their thinking?

## SUGGESTIONS FOR WRITING

1. If you wrote the assignment given before these two readings, you have already selected an educational experience that you hated and written about it. If you didn't write that assignment, you will need to pick such an experience now. In either case, what you need to do is to propose a plan for teaching the subject you learned so painfully to someone else. Your audience should be the relevant authority—parents, school board, a specific teacher—and your aim should be to present a persuasive plan reforming the way your hated subject is taught. Your strongest credentials, of course, are your own experiences, but your recommendations should be couched in broader terms. In other words, you will need to generalize on the basis of your experience.

# 12

# The College Atmosphere

*Mary McCarthy*
"THE VASSAR GIRL"

*William Zinsser*
"COLLEGE PRESSURES"

Mary McCarthy and William Zinsser discuss college education in particular. McCarthy describes the liberating atmosphere that once prevailed at Vassar, a place which encouraged the leisurely exploration of ideas. Zinsser, however, emphasizes the fierce and even destructive pressure on college students at Yale. He views the contemporary college student as a "driven creature who is largely ignoring the blithe spirit inside." These two descriptions raise several questions about the value of a goal-oriented course of study as opposed to a liberal arts education.

## *Mary McCarthy*
## "THE VASSAR GIRL"

Bucolically set in rolling orchard country just outside the town of Poughkeepsie, with the prospect of long walks and rides along curving back roads and cold red apples to bite; framed by two mirror-like lakes, by a lively off-campus street full of dress shops, antique stores, inns, which were brimming now with parents, brothers, and fiancés, Vassar, still warm and summery, gave the impression of a cornucopia overflowing with promises. The bareheaded Yale boys in roadsters parked outside Taylor Gate; the tall, dazzling girls, upperclassmen, in pale sweaters and skirts, impeccable, with pearls at the throat and stately walks, like goddesses; the vaulted library; the catalogue already marked and starred for courses like Psychology and Philosophy ("The Meaning of Morals, Beauty, Truth, God—open to freshmen by special permission"); the trolley tracks running past the spiked fence downtown to further shopping, adventure, the railroad station, New York, plays, concerts, night clubs, Fifth Avenue bus rides—all this seemed to foretell four years of a Renaissance lavishness, in an academy that was a Forest of Arden and a Fifth Avenue department store combined.

The dean, in her opening address, told us that we were the smallest class ever to be admitted (in recent years, I presume) and hence the most highly selected. She spoke to us of the responsibilities that thereby devolved on us, but to this part I hardly listened, being so filled with the pride and glory of belonging to the very best class in the very best college in America. This feeling did not really leave me during four years in college; Vassar has a peculiar power of conveying a sense of excellence.

After October, 1929, some of us had smaller allowances; my roommate and I no longer went off campus every night for a dinner beginning with *canapé* of anchovies and going on to artichokes and mushrooms under glass. More of us were on scholarships or using some form of self-help. Typing papers for others, waking friends in the morning, for the first time became regular industries. Some students' fathers were rumored to have shot themselves or to have had nervous breakdowns, but the off-campus shops still prospered, selling grape lemonade, bacon-and-tomato sandwiches, and later 3.2 beer. New York department stores brought dress exhibitions once or twice a year to the tearooms; we bought more than we could afford and charged it. Yale boys came down weekly for the Saturday-night "J" dance, at which the girls were stags and cut in on them. At these times the more prosperous went out to eat at roadhouses, tearooms, or inns in twos, fours, sixes, or eights. The boys carried whiskey in flasks, and sometimes there were gin picnics. One of my friends had an airplane; another girl kept a pet goat, very white and pretty; in the spring of senior year, when cars were permitted, a few roadsters appeared. In New York, we went to plays, musicals, and speakeasies, two or three girls together on a Saturday day leave; on weekends, alone with our beaux. Many of us were engaged.

During our junior year, the word "Communist" first assumed an active reality: a plain girl who was a science major openly admitted to being one. But most of our radicals were Socialists, and throughout that election year they campaigned for Norman Thomas, holding parades and rallies, though in most cases they were too young to vote. We of the "aesthetic" camp considered them jejune and naive; we were more impressed when we heard, after a poll, that a plurality (as I recall) of the faculty were voting for Thomas that year.

The inert mass of the student body was, as usual, Republican; we aesthetes did not believe in politics, but slightly favored the Democrats. Then our trustee, Franklin Roosevelt, was elected President. Miss Newcomer of the Economics Department went off to serve on a committee at Albany. Doctor MacCracken, our president, had lunch with Roosevelt off a tray in the White House—and we undergraduates felt more than ever that Vassar was at the center of everything.

With the impetus of the New Deal and memories of the breadlines behind us, even we aesthetes began reading about Sacco and Vanzetti and Mooney. We wrote papers for Contemporary Prose Fiction on Dos Passos. The pretty blue-eyed Republican girls looked troubled when you talked to them about these things; *their* favorite book was *Of Human Bondage,* which we despised. The Socialists made friends with us, though they swore by Miss Lockwood's press course, and we by Miss Sandison's Renaissance or by Miss Rindge's art or by a course in Old English or in verse writing: our group, being aesthetes, was naturally more individualistic. But by the end of our senior year the Socialists, the aesthetes, and the pretty Republican girls had been drawn closer together.

We all drank 3.2 beer at night in Mrs. Cary's tearoom, discussed term papers and politics, sang songs of farewell to each other in half-mocking, half-tender accents. We were happy to be together, our differences of origin and opinion reconciled in the fresh May darkness, but our happiness rested on the sense that all this was provisional and transitory. "Lost now in the wide, wide world," we sang fervently, but actually almost all of us were joyous to be leaving college, precisely because we had loved it, for Vassar had inspired us with the notion that the wide, wide world was our oyster.

A few years later, a census was taken, and it was discovered that the average Vassar graduate had two-plus children and was married to a Republican lawyer.

This finding took by surprise even that section of the alumnae—Vassar Club activists, organizers of benefits and fund-raising drives—who looked upon it as providential. Here, at last, they felt, was something concrete to offset newspaper stories of students picketing during a strike in nearby Beacon, students besieging the state legislature in Albany, that would put an end to the rumors of immorality, faddishness, and Bohemianism that, because of a few undergraduates, had clung to the college's public persona for two decades or more. What these figures proved, the alumnae apologists were really implying, was that the Vassar education had not "taken" or had taken only on a small group who were not at all typical of Vassar and who by their un-Vassarish behavior were getting the college a bad name. And yet the statistical Average herself would have been the first to protest (with that touch of apology so characteristic of Vassar women who had not "done" anything later on) that she was not at all representative of Vassar standards and point to some more unconventional classmate as the real Vassar thing.

A wistful respect for the unorthodox is ingrained in the Vassar mentality. The Vassar freshman still comes through Taylor Gate as I did, with the hope of being made over, redirected, vivified. The daughter of a conservative lawyer, doctor, banker, or businessman, she will have chosen Vassar in all probability with the idea of transcending her background. And if she does not have such plans for herself, her teachers have them for her. If she is, say, a Vassar daughter or a girl from a preparatory school like Chapin or Madeira who chose Vassar because her friends did, her teachers, starting freshman year, will seek to "shake her up," "emancipate" her, make her "think for herself." This dynamic conception of education is Vassar's hallmark.

The progressive colleges have something similar, but there the tendency is to orient the student in some preconceived direction—toward the modern dance or toward "progressive" political thinking, while at Vassar, by and large, the student is almost forbidden to take her direction from the teacher. "What do *you* think?" is the question that ricochets on the student if she asks the teacher's opinion; and the difference between Vassar and the traditional liberal college (where the teacher is also supposed to keep his own ideas in the background) is that at Vassar the student is obliged, every day, to proffer hers.

Thus at a freshman English class I recently visited, the students were discussing Richard Hughes' *The Innocent Voyage,* a book whose thesis is that children are monsters, without moral feelings in the adult sense, insane, irresponsible, incapable of conventional grief or remorse. This idea was very shocking to perhaps half the class, well-brought-up little girls who protested that children were not "like that," indignant hands waved in the air, anguished faces grimaced, while a more detached student in braids testified that her own experience as a baby-sitter bore Mr. Hughes out. The teacher took no sides but merely smiled and encouraged one side and then the other, raising a hand for quiet when the whole class began shouting at once, and interrupting only to ask, "Do you really know children? Are you speaking from what you have seen or remember, or from what you think *ought* to be so?" This book plainly was chosen not because it was a favorite with the professor or even because of its literary merits but because it challenged preconceptions and disturbed set ideas.

The effect of this training is to make the Vassar student, by the time she has reached her junior year, look back upon her freshman self with pity and amazement. When you talk to her about her life in college, you will find that she sees it as a series of before-and-after snapshots: "When I came to Vassar, I thought like Mother and Daddy. . . I was conservative in my politics. . . I had race prejudice. . . I liked academic painting." With few exceptions, among those who are articulate and who feel that the college has "done something" for them, the trend is, from the conservative to the liberal, from the orthodox to the heterodox, with stress on the opportunities Vassar has provided for getting to know "different" people, of opposite opinions and from different backgrounds.

Yet the statistical fate of the Vassar girl, thanks to Mother and Dad and the charge account, is already decreed. And the result is that the Vassar alumna, uniquely among American college women, is two persons—the housewife or matron, and the yearner and regretter. The Vassar graduate who has failed to make a name for herself, to "keep up," extend her interests, is because of her training, more poignantly conscious of backsliding than her contemporary at Barnard or Holyoke. And unlike the progressive-college graduate, on the other hand, who has been catered to and conciliated by her instructors, the Vassar girl who drifts into matronhood or office work is more inclined to blame herself than society for what has happened, and to feel that she has let the college down by not becoming famous or "interesting." The alumnae records are full of housewives, doctors, teachers, educators, social workers, child-welfare specialists, public-health consultants. But the Vassar dream obdurately prefers such figures at Inez Milholland, '09, who rode a white horse down Fifth Avenue campaigning for woman suffrage; Edna St. Vincent Millay, '17, the *révoltée* girl-poet who made herself a byword of sexual love and disenchanted lyricism; Elizabeth Hawes, '25, iconoclastic dress designer and author of *Fashion Is Spinach.* The Vassar romanticism will pass over a college president in favor of an author or journalist—Constance Rourke, '07, pioneer folklorist and author of *American Humor;* Muriel Rukeyser, ex-'34, Eleanor Clark, Elizabeth Bishop, '34, poets and writers, Jean Poletti, '25, Lois ("Lipstick" of *The New Yorker*) Long, '22, Beatrice Berle, '23, noted for her opinions on marriage and for the twin bathtubs she and her husband, Adolf A. Berle, Jr., shared in their Washington house—and it will recognize as its own even such antipodal curiosities as Elizabeth Bentley, '30, the ex-Communist spy queen, and Major Julia Hamblet, '37, the first woman to enlist in the Marines.

The incongruities on this list are suggestive. An *arresting performance* in politics, fashion, or art is often taken by the Vassar mind to be synonymous with true accomplishment. The Vassar dynamism drives toward money and success and the limelight in a truly Roman fashion, when it is not yoked to their opposite—service. With its alertness, its eagerness to *do* things, it tends, once the academic restraints are removed, to succumb to a rather journalistic notion of what constitutes value.

In the arts, after the first few intransigent gestures, Vassar talent streams into commercial side lines—advertising, fashion writing, publicity, promotion—and here assurance and energy case the Vassar success woman in an elephant-hide of certainties—a sort of proud flesh. This older Vassar career woman is nearly as familiar to American folklore as the intrepid young Portia or Rosalind she may at one time have passed for. Conscious of being set apart by a superior education, confident of her powers in her own field of enterprise, she is impervious to the universe, which she dominates, both mentally and materially. On the campus, she is found at vocational conferences, panel discussions, committee meetings—she is one of those women who are always dominating, in an advisory capacity. In the world, she is met in political-action groups, consumers' leagues, on school boards and in charitable drives, at forums and round-tables. Married, almost professionally so, the mother of children, she is regarded as a force in her community or business, is respected and not always liked. Vassar, of course, has no patent on this model of the American woman, but there is a challenge in the Vassar atmosphere that makes her graduates feel that they owe it as a positive duty to the college and to the human community to be outstanding, aggressive, and secure.

## WRITE BETWEEN READINGS

1. You have now a sketch of Vassar life from the first half of this century. In the next essay, William Zinsser will be offering his view of college life in the 1970s. Before you read his essay, make your own observations. Address an audience of your peers, your fellow college students, as if in a school newspaper. Drawing on McCarthy's piece and any other information you have, try to describe what makes college life in your particular decade or year different from that of years gone by. Your purpose should be mostly persuasive: try to get your audience to agree with you that your class has particularly ripe opportunities or faces particularly severe challenges.

## DISCUSS BETWEEN READINGS

1. Mary McCarthy writes about college life as it was for her around 1930, but she does so from her position in the 1940s. Her comments on the "new" Vassar girl, then, are already thirty-five years old. From what she writes, what can you tell about the audience she was addressing? Are their educational values similar to yours? Was a college education then—for women or men—what it is now?
2. What kind of expectations about Vassar are produced in the reader by the description in the first paragraph? Is this first impression later confirmed or modified? How does this description contribute to McCarthy's larger purpose?

*William Zinsser*

# "COLLEGE PRESSURES"

Dear Carlos: I desperately need a dean's excuse for my chem midterm which will begin in about 1 hour. All I can say is that I totally blew it this week. I've fallen incredibly, inconceivably behind.

Carlos: Help! I'm anxious to hear from you. I'll be in my room and won't leave it until I hear from you. Tomorrow is the last day for . . .

Carlos: I left town because I started bugging out again. I stayed up all night to finish a take-home make-up exam & am typing it to hand in on the 10th. It was due on the 5th. P.S. I'm going to the dentist. Pain is pretty bad.

Carlos: Probably by Friday I'll be able to get back to my studies. Right now I'm going to take a long walk. This whole thing has taken a lot out of me.

Carlos: I'm really up the proverbial creek. The problem is I really *bombed* the history final. Since I need that course for my major . . .

Carlos: Here follows a tale of woe. I went home this weekend, had to help my Mom, & caught a fever so didn't have much time to study. My professor . . .

Carlos: Aargh! Trouble. Nothing original but everything's piling up at once. To be brief, my job interview . . .

Hey Carlos, good news! I've got mononucleosis.

Who are these wretched supplicants, scribbling notes so laden with anxiety, seeking such miracles of postponement and balm? They are men and women who belong to Branford College, one of the twelve residential colleges at Yale University, and the messages are just a few of the hundreds that they left for their dean, Carlos Hortas—often slipped under his door at 4 A.M.—last year.

But students like the ones who wrote those notes can also be found on campuses from coast to coast—especially in New England and at many other private colleges across the country that have high academic standards and highly motivated students.

Nobody could doubt that the notes are real. In their urgency and their gallows humor they are authentic voices of a generation that is panicky to succeed.

My own connection with the message writers is that I am master of Branford College. I live in its Gothic quadrangle and know the students well. (We have 485 of them.) I am privy to their hopes and fears—and also to their stereo music and their piercing cries in the dead of night ("Does anybody *ca-a-are*?"). If they went to Carlos to ask how to get through tomorrow, they come to me to ask how to get through the rest of their lives.

Mainly I try to remind them that the road ahead is a long one and that it will have more unexpected turns than they think. There will be plenty of time to change jobs, change careers, change whole attitudes and approaches. They don't want to hear such liberating news. They want a map—right now—that they can follow unswervingly to career security, financial security. Social Security and, presumably, a prepaid grave.

What I wish for all students is some release from the clammy grip of the future. I wish them a chance to savor each segment of their education as an experience in itself and not as a grim preparation for the next step. I wish them the right to experiment, to trip and fall, to learn that defeat is as instructive as victory and is not the end of the world.

My wish, of course, is naive. One of the few rights that America does not proclaim is the right to fail. Achievement is the national god, venerated in our media—the million-dollar athlete, the wealthy executive—and glorified in our praise of possessions. In the presence of such a potent state religion, the young are growing up old.

I see four kinds of pressure working on college students today: economic pressure, parental pressure, peer pressure, and self-induced pressure. It is easy to look around for villains—to blame the colleges for charging too much money, the professors for assigning too much work, the parents for pushing their children too far, the students for driving themselves too hard. But there are no villains; only victims.

"In the late 1960s," one dean told me, "the typical question that I got from students was 'Why is there so much suffering in the world?' or 'How can I make a contribution?' Today it's 'Do you think it would look better for getting into law school if I did a double major in history and political science, or just majored in one of them?'" Many other deans confirmed this pattern. One said: "They're trying to find an edge—the intangible something that will look better on paper if two students are about equal."

Note the emphasis on looking better. The transcript has become a sacred document, the passport to security. How one appears on paper is more important than how one appears in person. *A* is for Admirable and *B* is for Borderline, even though, in Yale's official system of grading, *A* means "excellent" and *B* means "very good." Today, looking very good is no longer good enough, especially for students who hope to go on to law school or medical school. They know that entrance into the better schools will be an entrance into the better law firms and better medical practices where they will make a lot of money. They also know that the odds are harsh. Yale

Law School, for instance, matriculates 170 students from an applicant pool of 3,700; Harvard enrolls 550 from a pool of 7,000.

It's all very well for those of us who write letters of recommendation for our students to stress the qualities of humanity that will make them good lawyers or doctors. And it's nice to think that admission officers are really reading our letters and looking for the extra dimension of commitment or concern. Still, it would be hard for a student not to visualize these officers shuffling so many transcripts studded with *A*s that they regard a *B* as positively shameful.

The pressure is almost as heavy on students who just want to graduate and get a job. Long gone are the days of the "gentleman's C," when students journeyed through college with a certain relaxation, sampling a wide variety of courses—music, art, philosophy, classics, anthropology, poetry, religion—that would send them out as liberally educated men and women. If I were an employer I would rather employ graduates who have this range and curiosity than those who narrowly pursued safe subjects and high grades. I know countless students whose inquiring minds exhilarate me. I like to hear the play of their ideas. I don't know if they are getting *A*s or *C*s, and I don't care. I also like them as people. The country needs them, and they will find satisfying jobs. I tell them to relax. They can't.

Nor can I blame them. They live in a brutal economy. Tuition, room, and board at most private colleges now comes to at least $7,000, not counting books and fees. This might seem to suggest that the colleges are getting rich. But they are equally battered by inflation. Tuition covers only 60 percent of what it costs to educate a student, and ordinarily the remainder comes from what colleges receive in endowments, grants, and gifts. Now the remainder keeps being swallowed by the cruel costs—higher ever year—of just opening the doors. Heating oil is up. Insurance is up. Postage is up. Health-premium costs are up. Everything is up. Deficits are up. We are witnessing in America the creation of a brotherhood of paupers—colleges, parents, and students, joined by the common bond of debt.

Today it is not unusual for a student, even if he works part time at college and full time during the summer, to accrue $5,000 in loans after four years—loans that he must start to repay within one year after graduation. Exhorted at commencement to go forth into the world, he is already behind as he goes forth. How could he not feel under pressure throughout college to prepare for this day of reckoning? I have used "he," incidentally, only for brevity. Women at Yale are under no less pressure to justify their expensive education to themselves, their parents, and society. In fact, they are probably under more pressure. For although they leave college superbly equipped to bring fresh leadership to traditionally male jobs, society hasn't yet caught up with this fact.

Along with economic pressure goes parental pressure. Inevitably, the two are deeply intertwined.

I see many students taking pre-medical courses with joyless tenacity. They go off to their labs as if they were going to the dentist. It saddens me because I know them in other corners of their life as cheerful people.

"Do you want to go to medical school?" I ask them.

"I guess so," they say, without conviction, or "Not really."

"Then why are you going?"

"Well, my parents want me to be a doctor. They're paying all this money and..."

Poor students, poor parents. They are caught in one of the oldest webs of love and duty and guilt. The parents mean well; they are trying to steer their sons and daughters toward a secure future. But the sons and daughters want to major in history or classics or philosophy—subjects with no "practical" value. Where's the payoff on the humanities? It's not easy to persuade such loving parents that the humanities do indeed pay off. The intellectual faculties developed by studying subjects like history and classics—an ability to synthesize and relate, to weigh cause and effect, to see events in perspective—are just the faculties that make creative leaders in business or almost any general field. Still, many fathers would rather put their money on courses that point toward a specific profession—courses that are pre-law, pre-medical, pre-business, or, as I sometimes heard it put, "pre-rich."

But the pressure on students is severe. They are truly torn. One part of them feels obligated to fulfill their parents' expectations; after all, their parents are older and presumably wiser. Another part tells them that the expectations that are right for their parents are not right for them.

I know a student who wants to be an artist. She is very obviously an artist and will be a good one—she has already had several modest local exhibits. Meanwhile she is growing as a well-rounded person and taking humanistic subjects that will enrich the inner resources out of which her art will grow. But her father is strongly opposed. He thinks that an artist is a "dumb" thing to be. The student vacillates and tries to please everybody. She keeps up with her art somewhat furtively and takes some of the "dumb" courses her father wants her to take—at least they are dumb courses for her. She is a free spirit on a campus of tense students—no small achievement in itself—and she deserves to follow her muse.

Peer pressure and self-induced pressure are also intertwined, and they begin almost at the beginning of freshman year.

"I had a freshman student I'll call Linda," one dean told me, "who came in and said she was under terrible pressure because her roommate, Barbara, was much brighter and studied all the time. I couldn't tell her that Barbara had come in two hours earlier to say the same thing about Linda."

The story is almost funny—except that it's not. It's symptomatic of all the pressures put together. When every student thinks every other student is working harder and doing better, the only solution is to study harder still. I see students going off to the library every night after dinner and coming back when it closes at midnight. I wish they would sometimes forget about their peers and go to a movie. I hear the clacking of typewriters in the hours before dawn. I see the tension in their eyes when exams are approaching and papers are due: "*Will I get everything done?*"

Probably they won't. They will get sick. They will get "blocked." They will sleep. They will oversleep. They will bug out. *Hey Carlos, help!*

Part of the problem is that they do more than they are expected to do. A professor will assign five-page papers. Several students will start writing ten-page papers to impress him. Then more students will write ten-page papers, and a few will raise the ante to fifteen. Pity the poor student who is still just doing the assignment.

"Once you have twenty or thirty percent of the student population deliberately overexerting," one dean points out, "it's bad for everybody. When a teacher gets more and more effort from his class, the student who is doing normal work can be perceived as not doing well. The tactic works, psychologically."

Why can't the professor just cut back and not accept longer papers? He can, and he probably will. But by then the term will be half over and the damage done. Grade fever is highly contagious and not easily reversed. Besides, the professor's main concern is with his course. He knows his students only in relation to the course and doesn't know that they are also overexerting in their other courses. Nor is it really his business. He didn't sign up for dealing with the student as a whole person and with all the emotional baggage the student brought along from home. That's what deans, masters, chaplains, and psychiatrists are for.

To some extent this is nothing new: a certain number of professors have always been self-contained islands of scholarship and shyness, more comfortable with books than with people. But the new pauperism has widened the gap still further, for professors who actually like to spend time with students don't have as much time to spend. They also are overexerting. If they are young, they are busy trying to publish in order not to perish, hanging by their finger nails onto a shrinking profession. If they are old and tenured, they are buried under the duties of administering departments—as departmental chairmen or members of committees—that have been thinned out by the budgetary axe.

Ultimately it will be the students' own business to break the circles in which they are trapped. They are too young to be prisoners of their parents' dreams and their classmates' fears. They must be jolted into believing in themselves as unique men and women who have the power to shape their own future.

"Violence is being done to the undergraduate experience," says Carlos Hortas. "College should be open-ended: at the end it should open many, many roads. Instead, students are choosing their goal in advance, and their choices narrow as they go along. It's almost as if they think that the country has been codified in the type of jobs that exist—that they've got to fit into certain slots. Therefore, fit into the best-paying slot.

"They ought to take chances. Not taking chances will lead to a life of colorless mediocrity. They'll be comfortable. But something in the spirit will be missing."

I have painted too drab a portrait of today's students, making them seem a solemn lot. That is only half of their story; if they were so dreary I wouldn't so thoroughly enjoy their company. The other half is that they are easy to like. They are quick to laugh and to offer friendship. They are not introverts. They are usually kind and are more considerate of one another than any student generation I have known.

Nor are they so obsessed with their studies that they avoid sports and extracurricular activities. On the contrary, they juggle their crowded hours to play on a variety of teams, perform with musical and dramatic groups, and write for campus publications. But this in turn is one more cause of anxiety. There are too many choices. Academically, they have 1,300 courses to select from; outside class they have to decide how much spare time they can spare and how to spend it.

This means that they engage in fewer extracurricular pursuits than their predecessors did. If they want to row on the crew and play in the symphony they will eliminate one; in the '60s they would have done both. They also tend to choose activities that are self-limiting. Drama, for instance, is flourishing in all twelve of Yale's residential colleges as it never has before. Students hurl themselves into these productions—as actors, directors, carpenters, and technicians—with a dedication to create the best possible play, knowing that the day will come when the run will end and they can get back to their studies.

They also can't afford to be the willing slave of organizations like the *Yale Daily News*. Last spring at the one-hundredth anniversary banquet of that paper—whose past chairmen include such once and future kings as Potter Stewart, Kingman Brewster, and William F. Buckley, Jr.—much was made of the fact that the editorial staff used to be small and totally committed and that "newsies" routinely worked fifty hours a week. In effect they belonged to a club; Newsies is how they defined themselves at Yale. Today's student will write one or two articles a week, when he can, and he defines himself as a student. I've never heard the word Newsie except at the banquet.

If I have described the modern undergraduate primarily as a driven creature who is largely ignoring the blithe spirit inside who keeps trying to come out and play, it's because that's where the crunch is, not only at Yale but throughout American education. It's why I think we should all be worried about the values that are nurturing a generation so fearful of risk and so goal-obsessed at such an early age.

I tell students that there is no one "right" way to get ahead—that each of them is a different person, starting from a different point and bound for a different destination. I tell them that change is a tonic and that all the slots are not codified nor the frontiers closed. One of my ways of telling them is to invite men and women who have achieved success outside the academic world to come and talk informally with my students during the year. They are heads of companies or ad agencies, editors of magazines, politicians, public officials, television magnates, labor leaders, business executives, Broadway producers, artists, writers, economists, photographers, scientists, historians—a mixed bag of achievers.

I ask them to say a few words about how they got started. The students assume that they started in their present profession and knew all along that it was what they wanted to do. Luckily for me, most of them got into their field by a circuitous route, to their surprise, after many detours. The students are startled. They can hardly conceive of a career that was not pre-planned. They can hardly imagine allowing the hand of God or chance to nudge them down some unforeseen trail.

## SUGGESTIONS FOR DISCUSSION

1. Having read McCarthy and perhaps written an essay of your own, what do you think Zinsser's purpose is here? How does his purpose differ from McCarthy's

purpose in the previous essay?

2. McCarthy, writing about college life as it was fifty years ago, describes the atmosphere as leisurely and reflective. Zinsser contends that today the atmosphere is altogether different. How do the goals of present-day students differ from those of the Vassar students that McCarthy knew? Would you say that the college atmosphere has changed for the better or worse?
3. In order to give his musings coherence, Zinsser uses a device familiar to good essay exam writers. He begins by announcing that he sees "four kinds of pressures working on college students today." The essay that follows then comes in four rough sections, ordered according to the list he gives. Does Zinsser's scheme hold together? Are the four pressures roughly equal and parallel? Does he move smoothly from one to the next? Would some other organizational scheme have been as good or better?

## SUGGESTIONS FOR WRITING

1. One of Zinsser's tactics in this essay is to present himself as a highly qualified commentator on his subject—and he does so in such a way that we have only his word for it. It is a tactic we all end up using some time or another. Indeed, almost any time we ask for something—grant money, a job, a promotion, admission to graduate school—we end up needing to create a highly qualified *persona.* For this assignment, write three versions of a letter to a prospective employer. (You may pick the job.) In the first version, give as inflated a version of your abilities as you can manage without outright lying. For instance, the paper route you had at age ten becomes "Sales Experience" or "Ran my own business." In version two, try a very humble approach, emphasizing your willingness to learn, trying to flatter your reader. In the third version, write what you would call an ordinary letter of application.

# 13

# Ultimate Goals

*William G. Perry, Jr.*

"EXAMSMANSHIP AND THE LIBERAL ARTS: A STUDY IN EDUCATIONAL EPISTEMOLOGY"

*Adrienne Rich*

"TAKING WOMEN STUDENTS SERIOUSLY"

The last two essays in this part address the question of the ultimate goals of education. William Perry discusses two types of learning, one that involves understanding and relating concepts and one that is limited to the rote memorizing of facts. He argues that the ultimate goals of education have little to do with how much knowledge a student accumulates and much more to do with what kind of thinker that student becomes. Adrienne Rich criticizes the passivity and complacency that she sees permeating most colleges and universities. She calls for articulate, assertive students who engage in independent thinking and creative criticism. Her major concern is developing the student's sense of self, rather than developing the traditional analytical abilities that Perry describes.

## *William G. Perry, Jr.*

## "EXAMSMANSHIP AND THE LIBERAL ARTS: A STUDY IN EDUCATIONAL EPISTEMOLOGY"

"But sir, I don't think I really deserve it, it was mostly bull, really." This disclaimer from a student whose examination we have awarded a straight "A" is wondrously depressing. Alfred North Whitehead invented its only possible rejoinder: "Yes sir, what you wrote is nonsense, utter nonsense. But ah! Sir! It's the right *kind* of nonsense!"

Bull, in this university,* is customarily a source of laughter, or a problem in ethics. I shall step a little out of fashion to use the subject as a take-off point for a study in comparative epistemology. The phenomenon of bull, in all the honor and opprobrium with which it is regarded by students and faculty, says something, I think, about our theories of knowledge. So too, the grades which we assign on examinations communicate to students what these theories may be.

We do not have to be out-and-out logical-positivists to suppose that we have something to learn about "what we think knowledge is" by having a good look at "what we do when we go about measuring it." We know the straight "A" examination when we see it, of course, and we have reason to hope that the student will understand why his work receives our recognition. He doesn't always. And those who receive lesser honor? Perhaps an understanding of certain anomalies in our customs of grading good bull will explain the students' confusion.

I must beg patience, then, both of the reader's humor and of his morals. Not that I ask him to suspend his sense of humor but that I shall ask him to go beyond it. In a great university the picture of a bright student attempting to outwit his professor while his professor takes pride in not being outwitted is certainly ridiculous. I shall report just such a scene, for its implications bear upon my point. Its comedy need not present a serious obstacle to thought.

As for the ethics of bull, I must ask for a suspension of judgment. I wish that students could suspend theirs. Unlike humor, moral commitment is hard to think beyond. Too early a moral judgment is precisely what stands between many able students and a liberal education. The stunning realization that the Harvard Faculty will often accept, as evidence of knowledge, the cerebrations of a student who has little data at his disposal, confronts every student with an ethical dilemma. For some it forms an academic focus for what used to be thought of as "adolescent disillusion." It is irrelevant that rumor inflates the phenomenon to mythical proportions. The students know that beneath the myth there remains a solid and haunting reality. The moral "bind" consequent on this awareness appears most poignantly in serious students who are reluctant to concede the competitive advantage to the bullster and who yet feel a deep personal shame when, having succumbed to "temptation," they themselves receive a high grade for work they consider "dishonest."

I have spent many hours with students caught in this unwelcome bitterness. These hours lend an urgency to my theme. I have found that students have been able to come to terms with the ethical problem, to the extent that it is real, only after a refined study of the true nature of bull and its relation to "knowledge." I shall submit grounds for my suspicion that we can be found guilty of sharing the students' confusion of moral and epistemological issues.

* Harvard.—Eds.

## I

I present as my "premise," then, an amoral *fabliau.* Its hero-villain is the Abominable Mr. Metzger '47. Since I celebrate his virtuosity, I regret giving him a pseudonym, but the peculiar style of his bravado requires me to honor also his modesty. Bull in pure form is rare; there is usually some contamination by data. The community has reason to be grateful to Mr. Metzger for having created an instance of laboratory purity, free from any adulteration by matter. The more credit is due him, I think, because his act was free from premeditation, deliberation, or hope of personal gain.

Mr. Metzger stood one rainy November day in the lobby of Memorial Hall. A junior, concentrating in mathematics, he was fond of diverting himself by taking part in the drama, a penchant which may have had some influence on the events of the next hour. He was waiting to take part in a rehearsal in Sanders Theatre, but, as sometimes happens, no other players appeared. Perhaps the rehearsal had been canceled without his knowledge? He decided to wait another five minutes.

Students, meanwhile, were filing into the Great Hall opposite, and taking seats at the testing tables. Spying a friend crossing the lobby toward the Great Hall's door, Metzger greeted him and extended appropriate condolences. He inquired, too, what course his friend was being tested in. "Oh, Soc. Sci. something-or-other." "What's it all about?" asked Metzger, and this, as Homer remarked of Patroclus, was the beginning of evil for him.

"It's about Modern Perspectives on Man and Society and All That," said his friend. "Pretty interesting, really."

"Always wanted to take a course like that," said Metzger. "Any good reading?"

"Yeah, great. There's this book"—his friend did not have time to finish.

"Take your seats please" said a stern voice beside them. The idle conversation had somehow taken the two friends to one of the tables in the Great Hall. Both students automatically obeyed; the proctor put blue-books before them; another proctor presented them with copies of the printed hour-test.

Mr. Metzger remembered afterwards a brief misgiving that was suddenly overwhelmed by a surge of curiosity and puckish glee. He wrote "George Smith" on the blue book, opened it, and addressed the first question.

I must pause to exonerate the Management. The Faculty has a rule that no student may attend an examination in a course in which he is not enrolled. To the wisdom of this rule the outcome of this deplorable story stands witness. The Registrar, charged with the enforcement of the rule, has developed an organization with procedures which are certainly the finest to be devised. In November, however, class rosters are still shaky, and on this particular day another student, named Smith, was absent. As for the culprit, we can reduce his guilt no further than to suppose that he was ignorant of the rule, or, in the face of the momentous challenge before him, forgetful.

We need not be distracted by Metzger's performance on the "objective" or "spot" questions on the test. His D on these sections can be explained by those versed in the theory of probability. Our interest focuses on the quality of his essay. It appears that when Metzger's friend picked up his own blue book a few days later, he found himself in company with a large proportion of his section in having received on the essay a C+. When he quietly picked up "George Smith's" blue book to return it to Metzger, he observed that the grade for the essay was A–. In the margin was a note in the section man's hand. It read "Excellent work. Could you have pinned these observations down a bit more closely? Compare. . . in . . . pp. . . ."

Such news could hardly be kept quiet. There was a leak, and the whole scandal broke on the front page of Tuesday's *Crimson.* With the press Metzger was modest, as becomes a hero. He said that there had been nothing to it at all, really. The essay question had offered a choice of two books, Margaret Mead's *And Keep Your Powder Dry* or Geoffrey Gorer's *The American People.* Metzger reported that having read neither of them, he had chosen the second "because the title gave me some notion as to what the book might be about." On the test, two critical comments were offered on each book, one favorable, one unfavorable. The students were asked to "discuss." Metzger conceded that he had played safe in throwing his lot with the more laudatory of the two comments, "but I did not forget to be balanced."

I do not have Mr. Metzger's essay before me except in vivid memory. As I recall, he took his first cue from the name Geoffrey, and committed his strategy to the premise that Gorer was born into an "Anglo-Saxon" culture, probably English, but certainly "English speaking." Having heard that Margaret Mead was a social anthropologist, he inferred that Gorer was the same. He then entered upon his essay, centering his inquiry upon what he supposed might be the problems inherent in an anthropologist's observation of a culture which was his own, or nearly his own. Drawing in part from memories of table-talk on cultural relativity* and in part from creative logic, he rang changes on the relation of observer to observed, and assessed the kind and degree of objectivity which might accrue to an observer through training as an anthropologist. He concluded that the book in question did in fact contribute a considerable range of "'objective', and even 'fresh'," insights into the nature of our culture. "At the same time," he warned, "these observations must be understood within the context of their generation by a person only partly freed from his embeddedness in the culture he is observing, and limited in his capacity to transcend those particular tendencies and biases which he has himself developed as a personality in his interaction with this culture since his birth. In this sense the book portrays as much the character of Geoffrey Gorer as it analyzes that of the American people." It is my regrettable duty to report that at this moment of triumph Mr. Metzger was carried away by the temptations of parody and added, "We are thus much the richer."

In any case, this was the essay for which Metzger received his honor grade and his public acclaim. He was now, of course, in serious trouble with the authorities.

I shall leave him for the moment to the mercy of the Administrative Board of Harvard College and turn the reader's attention to the section man who ascribed the

* "An important part of Harvard's education takes place during meals in the Houses." An Official Publication.—Au.

grade. He was in much worse trouble. All the consternation in his immediate area of the Faculty and all the glee in other areas fell upon his unprotected head. I shall now undertake his defense.

I do so not simply because I was acquainted with him and feel a respect for his intelligence; I believe in the justice of his grade! Well, perhaps "justice" is the wrong word in a situation so manifestly absurd. This is more a case in "equity." That is, the grade is equitable if we accept other aspects of the situation which are equally absurd. My proposition is this: if we accept as valid those C grades which were accorded students who, like Metzger's friend, demonstrated a thorough familiarity with the details of the book without relating their critique to the methodological problems of social anthropology, then "George Smith" deserved not only the same, but better.

The reader may protest that the C's given to students who showed evidence only of diligence were indeed not valid and that both these students and "George Smith" should have received E's. To give the diligent E is of course not in accord with custom. I shall take up this matter later. For now, were I to allow the protest, I could only restate my thesis: that "George Smith's" E would, in a college of liberal arts, be properly a "better" E.

At this point I need a short-hand. It is a curious fact that there is no academic slang for the presentation of evidence of diligence alone. "Parroting" won't do; it is possible to "parrot" bull. I must beg the reader's pardon, and, for reasons almost too obvious to bear, suggest "cow."

Stated as nouns, the concepts look simple enough:

cow (pure): data, however relevant, without relevancies.
bull (pure): relevancies, however relevant, without data.

The reader can see all too clearly where this simplicity would lead. I can assure him that I would not have imposed on him this way were I aiming to say that knowledge in this university is definable as some neuter compromise between cow and bull, some infertile hermaphrodite. This is precisely what many diligent students seem to believe: that what they must learn to do is to "find the right mean" between "amounts" of detail and "amounts" of generalities. Of course this is not the point at all. The problem is not quantitative, nor does its solution lie on a continuum between the particular and the general. Cow and bull are not poles of a single dimension. A clear notion of what they really are is essential to my inquiry, and for heuristic purposes I wish to observe them further in the celibate state.

When the pure concepts are translated into verbs, their complexities become apparent in the assumptions and purposes of the students as they write:

To cow (*v. intrans.*) or the act of cowing:

To list data (or perform operations) without awareness of, or comment upon, the contexts, frames of reference, or points of observation which determine the origin, nature, and meaning of the data (or procedures). To write on the assumption that "a fact is a fact." To present evidence of hard work as a substitute for understanding, without any intent to deceive.

To bull (*v. intrans.*) or the act of bulling:

To discourse upon the contexts, frames of reference and points of observation which would determine the origin, nature, and meaning of data if one had any. To present evidence of an understanding of form in the hope that the reader may be deceived into supposing a familiarity with content.

At the level of conscious intent, it is evident that cowing is more moral, or less immoral, than bulling. To speculate about unconscious intent would be either an injustice or a needless elaboration of my theme. It is enough that the impression left by cow is one of earnestness, diligence, and painful naiveté. The grader may feel disappointment or even irritation, but these feelings are usually balanced by pity, compassion, and a reluctance to hit a man when he's both down and moral. We may feel some challenge to his teaching, but none whatever to his one-ups-manship. He writes in the margin: "See me."

We are now in a position to understand the anomaly of custom: As instructors, we always assign bull an E, *when we detect it;* whereas we usually give cow a C, *even though it is always obvious.*

After all, we did not ask to be confronted with a choice between morals and understanding (or did we?). We evince a charming humanity, I think, in our decision to grade in favor of morals and pathos. "I simply *can't* give this student an E after he has *worked* so hard." At the same time we tacitly express our respect for the bullster's strength. We recognize a colleague. If he knows so well how to dish it out, we can be sure that he can also take it.

Of course, it is just possible that we carry with us, perhaps from our own school-days, an assumption that if a student is willing to work hard and collect "good hard facts" he can always be taught to understand their relevance, whereas a student who has caught onto the forms of relevance without working at all is a lost scholar.

But this is not in accord with our experience.

It is not in accord either, as far as I can see, with the stated values of a liberal education. If a liberal education should teach students "how to think," not only in their own fields but in fields outside their own—that is, to understand "how the other fellow orders knowledge," then bulling, even in its purest form, expresses an important part of what a pluralist university holds dear, surely a more important part than the collecting of "facts that are facts" which schoolboys learn to do. Here then, good bull appears not as ignorance at all but as an aspect of knowledge. It is both relevant and "true." In a university setting good bull is therefore of more value than "facts," which, without a frame of reference, are not even "true" at all.

Perhaps this value accounts for the final anomaly: as instructors, we are inclined to reward bull highly, *where we do not detect its intent,* to the consternation of the bullster's acquaintances. And often we do not examine the matter too closely. After a long evening of reading blue books full of cow, the sudden meeting with a student who at least understands the problems of one's field provides a lift like a draught of refreshing wine, and a strong disposition toward trust.

This was, then, the sense of confidence that came to our unfortunate section man as he read "George Smith's" sympathetic considerations.

## II

In my own years of watching over students' shoulders as they work, I have come to believe that this feeling of trust has a firmer basis than the confidence generated by evidence of diligence alone. I believe that the theory of a liberal education holds. Students who have dared to understand man's real relation to his knowledge have shown themselves to be in a strong position to learn content rapidly and meaningfully, and to retain it. I have learned to be less concerned about the education of a student who has come to understand the nature of man's knowledge, even though he has not yet committed himself to hard work, than I am about the education of the student who, after one or two terms at Harvard is working desperately hard and still believes that collected "facts" constitute knowledge. The latter, when I try to explain to him, too often understands me to be saying that he "doesn't *put in enough generalities.*" Surely he has "put in *enough* facts."

I have come to see such quantitative statements as expressions of an entire, coherent epistemology. In grammar school the student is taught that Columbus discovered America in 1492.The *more* such items he gets "right" on a given test the more he is credited with "knowing." From years of this sort of thing it is not unnatural to develop the conviction that knowledge consists of the accretion of hard facts by hard work.

The student learns that the more facts and procedures he can get "right" in a given course, the better will be his grade. The more courses he takes, the more subjects he has "had," the more credits he accumulates, the more diplomas he will get, until, after graduate school, he will emerge with his doctorate, a member of the community of scholars.

The foundation of this entire life is the proposition that a fact is a fact. The necessary correlate of this proposition is that a fact is either right or wrong. This implies that the standard against which the rightness or wrongness of a fact may be judged exists *someplace* —perhaps graven upon a tablet in a Platonic world outside and above *this* cave of tears. In grammar school it is evident that the tablets which enshrine the spelling of a word or the answer to an arithmetic problem are visible to my teacher who need only compare my offerings to it. In high school I observe that my English teachers disagree. This can only mean that the tablets in such matters as the goodness of a poem are distant and obscured by clouds. They surely exist. The pleasing of befuddled English teachers degenerates into assessing their prejudices, a game in which I have no protection against my competitors more glib of tongue. I respect only my science teachers, authorities who *really know.* Later I learn from them that "this is only what we think *now.*" But eventually, surely. . . . Into this epistemology of education, apparently shared by teachers in such terms as "credits," "semester hours" and "years of French" the student may invest his ideals, his drive, his competitiveness, his safety, his self-esteem, and even his love.

College raises other questions: by whose calendar is it proper to say that Columbus discovered America in 1492? How, when and by whom was the year 1 established in this calendar? What of other calendars? In view of the evidence for Leif

Ericson's previous visit (and the American Indians), what historical ethnocentrism is suggested by the use of the word "discover" in this sentence? As for Leif Ericson, in accord with what assumptions do you order the evidence?

These questions and their answers are not "more" knowledge. They are devastation. I do not need to elaborate upon the epistemology, or rather epistemologies, they imply. A fact has become at last "an observation or an operation performed in a frame of reference." A liberal education is founded in an awareness of frame of reference even in the most immediate and empirical examination of data. Its acquirement involves relinquishing hope of absolutes and of the protection they afford against doubt and the glib-tongued competitor. It demands an ever widening sophistication about systems of thought and observation. It leads, not away from, but *through* the arts of gamesmanship to a new trust.

This trust is in the value and integrity of systems, their varied character, and the way their apparently incompatible metaphors enlighten, from complementary facets, the particulars of human experience. As one student said to me: "I used to be cynical about intellectual games. Now I want to know them thoroughly. You see I came to realize that it was only when I knew the rules of the game cold that I could tell whether what I was saying was tripe."

We too often think of the bullster as cynical. He can be, and not always in a light-hearted way. We have failed to observe that there can lie behind cow the potential of a deeper and more dangerous despair. The moralism of sheer work and obedience can be an ethic that, unwilling to face a despair of its ends, glorifies its means. The implicit refusal to consider the relativity of both ends and means leaves the operator in an unconsidered proprietary absolutism. History bears witness that in the pinches this moral superiority has no recourse to negotiation, only to force.

A liberal education proposes that man's hope lies elsewhere: in the negotiability that can arise from an understanding of the integrity of systems and of their origins in man's address to his universe. The prerequisite is the courage to accept such a definition of knowledge. From then on, of course, there is nothing incompatible between such an epistemology and hard work. Rather the contrary.

I can now at last let bull and cow get together. The reader knows best how a productive wedding is arranged in his own field. This is the nuptial he celebrates with a straight A on examinations. The masculine context must embrace the feminine particular, though itself "born of woman." Such a union is knowledge itself, and it alone can generate new contexts and new data which can unite in their turn to form new knowledge.

In this happy setting we can congratulate in particular the Natural Sciences, long thought to be barren ground to the bullster. I have indeed drawn my examples of bull from the Social Sciences, and by analogy from the Humanities. Essay-writing in these fields has long been thought to nurture the art of bull to its prime. I feel, however, that the Natural Sciences have no reason to feel slighted. It is perhaps no accident that Metzger was a mathematician. As part of my researches for this paper, furthermore, a student of considerable talent has recently honored me with an impressive analysis of the art of amassing "partial credits" on examinations in advanced physics. Though beyond me in some respects, his presentation confirmed my impression that instructors of Physics frequently honor on examinations operations structurally similar to those requisite in a good essay.

The very qualities that make the Natural Sciences fields of delight for the eager gamesman have been essential to their marvelous fertility.

## III

As priests of these mysteries, how can we make our rites more precisely expressive? The student who merely cows robs himself, without knowing it, of his education and his soul. The student who only bulls robs himself, as he knows full well, of the joys of inductive discovery—that is, of engagement. The introduction of frames of reference in the new curricula of Mathematics and Physics in the schools is a hopeful experiment. We do not know yet how much of these potent revelations the very young can stand, but I suspect they may rejoice in them more than we have supposed. I can't believe they have never wondered about Leif Ericson and that word "discovered," or even about 1492. They have simply been too wise to inquire.

Increasingly in recent years better students in the better high schools and preparatory schools *are* being allowed to inquire. In fact they appear to be receiving both encouragement and training in their inquiry. I have the evidence before me.

Each year for the past five years all freshmen entering Harvard and Radcliffe have been asked in freshman week to "grade" two essays answering an examination question in History. They are then asked to give their reasons for their grades. One essay, filled with dates, is 99% cow. The other, with hardly a date in it, is a good essay, easily mistaken for bull. The "official" grades of these essays are, for the first (alas!) C + "because he has worked so hard," and for the second (soundly, I think) B +. Each year a larger majority of freshmen evalute these essays as would the majority of the faculty, and for the faculty's reasons, and each year a smaller minority give the higher honor to the essay offering data alone. Most interesting, a larger number of students each year, while not overrating the second essay, award the first the straight E appropriate to it in a college of liberal arts.

For us who must grade such students in a university, these developments imply a new urgency, did we not feel it already. Through our grades we describe for the students, in the showdown, what we believe about the nature of knowledge. The subtleties of bull are not peripheral to our academic concerns. That they penetrate to the center of our care is evident in our feelings when a student whose good work we have awarded a high grade reveals to us that he does not feel he deserves it. Whether he disqualifies himself because "there's too much bull in it," or worse because "I really don't think I've worked that hard," he presents a serious educational problem. Many students feel this sleaziness; only a few reveal it to us.

We can hardly allow a mistaken sense of fraudulence to undermine our students' achievements. We must lead students beyond their concept of bull so that they may honor relevancies that are really relevant. We can willingly acknowledge that, in lieu of the date 1492, a consideration of calendars and of the word "discovered," may well be offered with intent to deceive. We must insist that this does not make such considerations intrinsically immoral, and that, contrariwise, the date 1492 may be no substitute for them. Most of all, we must convey the impression that we grade understanding qua understanding. To be convincing, I suppose we must concede to ourselves in advance that a bright student's understanding is understanding even if he achieved it by osmosis rather than by hard work in our course.

These are delicate matters. As for cow, its complexities are not what need concern us. Unlike good bull, it does not represent partial knowledge at all. It belongs to a different theory of knowledge entirely. In our theories of knowledge it represents total ignorance, or worse yet, a knowledge downright inimical to understanding. I even go so far as to propose that we award no more C's for cow. To do so is rarely, I feel, the act of mercy it seems. Mercy lies in clarity.

The reader may be afflicted by a lingering curiosity about the fate of Mr. Metzger. I hasten to reassure him. The Administrative Board of Harvard College, whatever its satanic reputations, is a benign body. Its members, to be sure, were on the spot. They delighted in Metzger's exploit, but they were responsible to the Faculty's rule. The hero stood in danger of probation. The debate was painful. Suddenly one member, of a refined legalistic sensibility, observed that the rule applied specifically to "examinations" and that the occasion had been simply an hour-test. Mr. Metzger was merely "admonished."

## *Adrienne Rich*
## "TAKING WOMEN STUDENTS SERIOUSLY"

I see my function here today as one of trying to create a context, delineate a background, against which we might talk about women as students and students as women. I would like to speak for awhile about this background, and then I hope that we can have, not so much a question period, as a raising of concerns, a sharing of questions for which we as yet may have no answers, an opening of conversations which will go on and on.

When I went to teach at Douglass, a women's college, it was with a particular background which I would like briefly to describe to you. I had graduated from an all-girls' school in the 1940s, where the head and the majority of the faculty were independent, unmarried women. One or two held doctorates, but had been forced by the Depression (and by the fact that they were women) to take secondary school teaching jobs. These women cared a great deal about the life of the mind, and they gave a great deal of time and energy—beyond any limit of teaching hours—to those of us who showed special intellectual interest or ability. We were taken to libraries, art museums, lectures at neighboring colleges, set to work on extra research projects, given extra French or Latin reading. Although we sometimes felt "pushed" by them, we held those women in a kind of respect which even then we dimly perceived was not generally accorded to women in the world at large. They were vital individuals, defined not by their relationships but by their personalities; and although under the pressure of the culture we were all certain we wanted to get married, their lives did not appear empty or dreary to us. In a kind of cognitive dissonance, we knew they were "old maids" and therefore supposed to be bitter and lonely; yet we saw them vigorously involved with life. But despite their existence as alternate models of women, the *content* of the education they gave us in no way prepared us to survive as women in a world organized by and for men.

From that school, I went on to Radcliffe, congratulating myself that now I would have great men as my teachers. From 1947 to 1951, when I graduated, I never saw a single woman on a lecture platform, or in front of a class, except when a woman graduate student gave a paper on a special topic. The "great men" talked of other "great men," of the nature of Man, the history of Mankind, the future of Man; and never again was I to experience, from a teacher, the kind of prodding, the insistence that my best could be even better, that I had known in high school. Women students were simply not taken very seriously. Harvard's message to women was an elite mystification: we were, of course, part of Mankind; we were special, achieving women, or we would not have been there; but of course our real goal was to marry—if possible, a Harvard graduate.

In the late sixties, I began teaching at the City College of New York—a crowded, public, urban, multiracial institution as far removed from Harvard as possible. I went there to teach writing in the SEEK Program, which predated Open Admissions and which was then a kind of model for programs designed to open up higher education to poor, black, and Third World students. Although during the next few years we were to see the original concept of SEEK diluted, then violently attacked and betrayed, it was for a short time an extraordinary and intense teaching and learning environment. The characteristics of this environment were a deep commitment on the part of teachers to the minds of their students; a constant, active effort to create or discover the conditions for learning, and to educate ourselves to meet the needs of the new college population; a philosophical attitude based on open discussion of racism, oppression, and the politics of literature and language; and a belief that learning in the classroom could not be isolated from the student's experience as a member of an urban minority group in white America. Here are some of the kinds of questions we, as teachers of writing, found ourselves asking:

(1) What has been the student's experience of education in the inadequate, often abusively racist public school system, which rewards passivity and treats a questioning attitude or independent mind as a behavior problem? What has been her or his experience in a society that consistently undermines the selfhood of the poor and the nonwhite? How can such a student gain that sense of self which is necessary for active participation in education? What does all this mean for us as teachers?

(2) How do we go about teaching a canon of literature which has consistently excluded or depreciated nonwhite experience?

(3) How can we connect the process of learning to write well with the student's own reality, and not simply teach her/him how to write acceptable lies in standard English?

When I went to teach at Douglass College in 1976, and in teaching women's writing workshops elsewhere, I came to perceive stunning parallels to the questions I had first encountered in teaching the so-called disadvantaged students at City. But in this instance, and against the specific background of the women's movement, the questions framed themselves like this:

(1) What has been the student's experience of education in schools which reward female passivity, indoctrinate girls and boys in stereotypic sex roles, and do not take the female mind seriously? How does a woman gain a sense of her *self* in a system—in this case, patriarchal capitalism—which devalues work done by women, denies the importance and uniqueness of female experience, and is physically violent toward women? What does this mean for a woman teacher?

(2) How do we, as women, teach women students a canon of literature which has consistently excluded or depreciated female experience, and which often expresses hostility to women and validates violence against us?

(3) How can we teach women to move beyond the desire for male approval and getting "good grades" and seek and write their own truths that the culture has distorted or made taboo? (For women, of course, language itself is exclusive: I want to say more about this further on.)

In teaching women, we have two choices: to lend our weight to the forces that indoctrinate women to passivity, self-depreciation, and a sense of powerlessness, in which case the issue of "taking women students seriously" is a moot one; or to consider what we have to work against, as well as with, in ourselves, in our students, in the content of the curriculum, in the structure of the institution, in the society at large. And this means, first of all, taking ourselves seriously: Recognizing that central responsibility of a woman to herself, without which we remain always the Other, the defined, the object, the victim; believing that there is a unique quality of validation, affirmation, challenge, support, that one woman can offer another. Believing in the value and significance of women's experience, traditions, perceptions. Thinking of ourselves seriously, not as one of the boys, not as neuters, or androgynes, but *as women.*

Suppose we were to ask ourselves, simply: What does a woman need to know? Does she not, as a self-conscious, self-defining human being, need a knowledge of her own history, her much-politicized biology, an awareness of the creative work of women of the past, the skills and crafts and techniques and powers exercised by women in different times and cultures, a knowledge of women's rebellions and organized movements against our oppression and how they have been routed or diminished? Without such knowledge women live and have lived without context, vulnerable to the projections of male fantasy, male prescriptions for us, estranged from our own experience because our education has not reflected or echoed it. I would suggest that not biology, but ignorance of our selves, has been the key to our powerlessness.

But the university curriculum, the high-school curriculum, do not provide this kind of knowledge for women, the knowledge of Womankind, whose experience has been so profoundly different from that of Mankind. Only in the precariously budgeted, much-condescended-to area of women's studies is such knowledge available to women students. Only there can they learn about the lives and work of women other than the few select women who are included in the "mainstream" texts, usually misrepresented even when they do appear. Some students, at some institutions, manage to take a majority of courses in women's studies, but the message from on high is that this is self-indulgence, soft-core education: the "real" learning is the study of Mankind.

If there is any misleading concept, it is that of "coeducation": that because women and men are sitting in the same classrooms, hearing the same lectures, reading the same books, performing the same laboratory experiments, they are receiving an equal education. They are not, first because the content of education itself validates men even as it invalidates women. Its very message is that men have been the shapers and thinkers of the world, and that this is only natural. The bias of higher education, including the so-called sciences, is white and male, racist and sexist; and this bias is expressed in both subtle and blatant ways. I have mentioned already the exlusiveness of grammar itself: "The student should test himself on the above questions"; "The poet is representative. He stands among partial men for the complete man." Despite a few half-hearted departures from custom, what the linguist Wendy Martyna has named "He-Man" grammar prevails throughout the culture. The efforts of feminists to reveal the profound ontological implications of sexist grammar are routinely ridiculed by academicians and journalists, including the professedly liberal *Times* columnist, Tom Wicker, and the professed humanist, Jacques Barzun. Sexist grammar burns into the brains of little girls and young women a message that the male is the norm, the standard, the central figure besides which we are the deviants, the marginal, the dependent variables. It lays the foundation for androcentric thinking, and leaves men safe in their solipsistic tunnel-vision.

Women and men do not receive an equal education because outside the classroom women are perceived not as sovereign beings but as prey. The growing incidence of rape on and off the campus may or may not be fed by the proliferations of pornographic magazines and X-rated films available to young males in fraternities and student unions; but it is certainly occurring in a context of widespread images of sexual violence against women, on billboards and in so-called high art. More subtle, more daily than rape is the verbal abuse experienced by the woman student on many campuses—Rutgers for example—where, traversing a street lined with fraternity houses, she must run a guantlet of male commentary and verbal assault. The undermining of self, of a woman's sense of her right to occupy space and walk freely in the world, is deeply relevant to education. The capacity to think independently, to take intellectual risks, to assert ourselves mentally, is inseparable from our physical way of being in the world, our feelings of personal integrity. If it is dangerous for me to walk home late of an evening from the library, *because I am a woman and can be raped,* how self-possessed, how exuberant can I feel as I sit working in that library? how much of my working energy is drained by the subliminal knowledge that, as a woman, I test my physical right to exist each time I go out alone? Of this knowledge, Susan Griffin has written:

> . . . more than rape itself, the fear of rape permeates our lives. And what does one do from day to day, with *this* experience, which says, without words and directly to the heart, *your existence, your experience, may end at any moment.* Your experience may end, and the best defense against this is not to be, to deny being in the body, as a self, to . . . avert your gaze, make yourself, as a presence in the world, less felt.*

Finally, rape of the mind. Women students are more and more often now reporting sexual overtures by male professors—one part of our overall growing consciousness of sexual harassment in the workplace. At Yale a legal suit has been brought against the university by a group of women demanding an explicit policy against sexual advances toward female students by male professors. Most young women experience a profound mixture of humiliation and intellectual self-doubt over seductive gestures by men who have the power to award grades, open doors to grants and graduate school, or extend special knowledge and training. Even if turned aside, such gestures constitute mental rape, destructive to a woman's ego. They are acts of domination, as despicable as the molestation of the daughter by the father.

But long before entering college the woman student has experienced her alien identity in a world which misnames her, turns her to its own uses, denying her the resources she needs to become self-affirming, self-defined. The nuclear family teaches her that relationships are more important than selfhood or work; that "whether the phone rings for you, and how often," having the right clothes, doing the dishes, take precedence over study or solitude; that too much intelligence or intensity may make her unmarriageable; that marriage and children—service to others—are, finally, the points on which her life will be judged a success or a failure. In high school, the polarization between feminine attractiveness and independent intelligence comes to an absolute. Meanwhile the culture resounds with messages. During Solar Energy Week in New York I saw young women wearing "ecology" T-shirts with the legend: CLEAN, CHEAP AND AVAILABLE; a reminder of the 1960s antiwar button which read: CHICKS SAY YES TO MEN WHO SAY NO. Department store windows feature female mannequins in chains, pinned to the wall with legs spread, smiling in positions of torture. Feminists are depicted in the media as "shrill," "strident," "puritanical," or "humorless," and the lesbian choice—the choice of the woman-identified woman—as pathological or sinister. The young woman sitting in the philosophy classroom, the political science lecture, is already gripped by tensions between her nascent sense of self-worth, and the battering force of messages like these.

Look at a classroom: look at the many kinds of women's faces, postures, expressions. Listen to the women's voices. Listen to the silences, the unasked questions, the blanks. Listen to the small, soft voices, often courageously trying to speak up, voices of women taught early that tones of confidence, challenge, anger, or assertiveness, are strident and unfeminine. Listen to the voices of the women and the voices of the men; observe the space men allow themselves, physically and verbally, the male

* Quoted from her book, *Rape: The Power of Consciousness;* published in 1979 by Harper & Row.—Au.

assumption that people will listen, even when the majority of the group is female. Look at the faces of the silent, and of those who speak. Listen to a woman groping for language in which to express what is on her mind, sensing that the terms of academic discourse are not her language, trying to cut down her thought to the dimensions of a discourse not intended for her (*for it is not fitting that a woman speak in public*); or reading her paper aloud at breakneck speed, throwing her words away, deprecating her own work by a reflex prejudgment: *I do not deserve to take up time and space.*

As women teachers, we can either deny the importance of this context in which women students think, write, read, study, project their own futures; or try to work with it. We can either teach passively, accepting these conditions, or actively, helping our students identify and resist them.

One important thing we can do is *discuss* the context. And this need not happen only in a women's studies course; it can happen anywhere. We can refuse to accept passive, obedient learning and insist upon critical thinking. We can become harder on our women students, giving them the kinds of "cultural prodding" that men receive, but on different terms and in a different style. Most young women need to have their intellectual lives, their work, legitimized against the claims of family, relationships, the old message that a woman is always available for service to others. We need to keep our standards very high, not to accept a woman's preconceived sense of her limitations; we need to be hard to please, while supportive of risk-taking, because self-respect often comes only when exacting standards have been met. At a time when adult literacy is generally low, we need to demand more, not less, of women, both for the sake of their futures as thinking beings, and because historically women have always had to be better than men to do half as well. A romantic sloppiness, an inspired lack of rigor, a self-indulgent incoherence, are symptoms of female self-depreciation. We should help our women students to look very critically at such symptoms, and to understand where they are rooted.

Nor does this mean we should be training women students to "think like men." Men in general think badly: in disjuncture from their personal lives, claiming objectivity where the most irrational passions seethe, losing, as Virginia Woolf observed, their senses in the pursuit of professionalism. It is not easy to think like a woman in a man's world, in the world of the professions; yet the capacity to do that is a strength which we can try to help our students develop. To think like a woman in a man's world means thinking critically, refusing to accept the givens, making connections between facts and ideas which men have left unconnected. It means remembering that every mind resides in a body; remaining accountable to the female bodies in which we live; constantly retesting given hypotheses against lived experience. It means a constant critique of language, for as Wittgenstein (no feminist) observed, "The limits of my language are the limits of my world." And it means that most difficult thing of all: listening and watching in art and literature, in the social sciences, in all the descriptions we are given of the world, for the silences, the absences, the nameless, the unspoken, the encoded—for there we will find the true knowledge of women. And in breaking those silences, naming our selves, uncovering the hidden, making ourselves present, we begin to define a reality which resonates to *us,* which affirms *our* being, which allows the woman teacher and the woman student alike to take ourselves, and each other, seriously: meaning, to begin taking charge of our lives.

## SUGGESTIONS FOR DISCUSSION

1. Think about the audiences these two writers address: Perry has an Ivy League, academic crowd; Rich has an audience of teachers at a conference on Women's Education. How closely do they identify with those audiences? What do they see as their role with regard to them? Do they seem to think the audience is hostile or sympathetic? When they make arguments, what kinds of evidence do they muster? Do they appeal to their audience's reason or emotions? How do such arguments affect your sense of their *persona*?
2. Both these people can be considered successful writers. Their styles, though, are strikingly different. Take Perry's fifth paragraph ("As for the ethics of bull. . .") and Rich's sixth ("In teaching women, we have two choices. . ."). Using whatever skills you have, compare the styles. Look at the length and type of sentences, the way one sentence connects to the next, and the way sentences are extended or interrupted. Examine the choice of words. Try to see how the paragraph holds together internally, how it reflects what has come before and anticipates what comes next. What can you say about their styles?
3. Perry's essay is one of his many writings about Harvard education, some of which have already become classics of a kind. What would Adrienne Rich say about his writing or his thinking? How does her attack on the notion of "coeducation" compare with what Perry is writing?

## SUGGESTIONS FOR WRITING

1. Here is a question you probably know enough about to answer without research: What were the causes of the American revolution? Assuming that you do know enough (if not, make up another question), write two answers. Make the first entirely what Perry calls "cow"; make the second what he calls "bull." Which is harder? Which feels more "correct"?
2. Near the end of her essay Adrienne Rich writes that men "in general think badly." In the context of your class, or outside it if necessary, find several people of the opposite sex and interview them about the way they think. Ask them, for example, what part of school they like best, and get them to tell you why. Ask them about hobbies, about favorite books or authors, about household chores they prefer; in all cases, lead them to tell what they like about the mental processes involved. When you've written these down, share them in class. Does there seem to be a distinctly gender-based kind of thinking? What are its characteristics, if any?

# *Part Four*

# FREEDOM AND INDIVIDUALITY

*For what it cost me to be free*
*I might have bought an anchor.*
—WITTER BYNNER

In *The Scarlet Letter,* Hester Prynne struggles to maintain her sense of integrity and individuality against the rigid moral code of Puritan New England. In Twain's novel, Huck Finn wages a similar battle against racism and conformity. In Kesey's *One Flew Over the Cuckoo's Nest,* Patrick McMurphy is defeated in his confrontation with Big Nurse and the institutions that she represents. These novels and many other great works of literature powerfully dramatize and partially define the perennial struggle between the individual and society. Many of these works exalt individuality and place its value above that of social conventions. Most people, however, need a sense of community as well as a sense of individuality. Almost all of us would like to feel that we belong to something larger, that we are useful members of society, and that we are capable of cooperation. But when does cooperation become a sacrifice of individuality? How can we preserve our integrity and personal identity and still be contributing members of a community? Can we be genuine individuals without paying the price of loneliness and isolation?

The eight essays in this part examine these questions from a variety of perspectives. Some writers emphasize individual freedom and warn against what John Stuart Mill terms "collective mediocrity." Others affirm the fulfillment and security which can be gained from living within the roles and limits prescribed by society. The relative importance placed on freedom not only varies from person to person but also fluctuates with changing times. The emphasis on personal liberty and experimentation that characterized the sixties and seventies, for example, has gradually engendered a fear of disorder and selfishness. A new respect for social responsibility and custom is becoming increasingly apparent in the eighties.

# 14

# Society and the Individual

*John Stuart Mill*

"OF INDIVIDUALITY, AS ONE OF THE ELEMENTS OF WELL-BEING"

*Ilse Aichinger*

"THE BOUND MAN"

For one of the most impressive defenses of individual freedom, we must go back to the previous century. John Stuart Mill, in his essay "On Individuality," warns that society itself will become stagnant and dull unless individuals, even eccentrics, are encouraged to develop and express themselves. Mill sees the forces of repression, whether they take the form of custom, authority, or conformity, as a dangerous threat to human dignity. Ilse Aichinger's "The Bound Man," on the other hand, suggests that restrictions are not only necessary to society, but also helpful to the individual. The main character in her story does his best work only when he submits to the ropes which bind him.

## *John Stuart Mill*
## "OF INDIVIDUALITY, AS ONE OF THE ELEMENTS OF WELL-BEING"

Let us. . .examine whether. . .men should be free to act upon their opinions—to carry these out in their lives, without hindrance, either physical or moral, from their fellow-men, so long as it is at their own risk and peril. This last proviso is of course indispensable. No one pretends that actions should be as free as opinions. On the contrary, even opinions lose their immunity, when the circumstances in which they are expressed are such as to constitute their expression a positive instigation to some mischievous act. An opinion that corn-dealers are starvers of the poor, or that private property is robbery, ought to be unmolested when simply circulated through the press, but may justly incur punishment when delivered orally to an excited mob assembled before the house of a corn-dealer, or when handed about among the same mob in the form of a placard. Acts, of whatever kind, which, without justifiable cause, do harm to others, may be, and in the more important cases absolutely require to be, controlled by the unfavourable sentiments, and, when needful, by the active interference of mankind. The liberty of the individual must be thus far limited; he must not make himself a nuisance to other people. But if he refrains from molesting others in what concerns them, and merely acts according to his own inclination and judgment in things which concern himself, the same reasons which show that opinion should be free, prove also that he should be allowed, without molestation, to carry his opinions into practice at his own cost. That mankind are not infallible; that their truths, for the most part, are only half-truths; that unity of opinion, unless resulting from the fullest and freest comparison of opposite opinions, is not desirable, and diversity not an evil, but a good, until mankind are much more capable than at present of recognising all sides of the truth, are principles applicable to men's modes of action, not less than to their opinions. As it is useful that while mankind are imperfect there should be different opinions, so is it that there should be different experiments of living; that free scope should be given to varieties of character, short of injury to others; and that the worth of different modes of life should be proved practically, when any one thinks fit to try them. It is desirable, in short, that in things which do not primarily concern others, individuality should assert itself. Where, not the person's own character, but the traditions or customs of other people are the rule of conduct, there is wanting one of the principal ingredients of human happiness, and quite the chief ingredient of individual and social progress.

In maintaining this principle, the greatest difficulty to be encountered does not lie in the appreciation of means towards an acknowledged end, but in the indifference of persons in general to the end itself. If it were felt that the free development of individuality is one of the leading essentials of well-being; that it is not only a coordinate element with all that is designated by the terms civilization, instruction, education, culture, but is itself a necessary part and condition of all those things; there would be no danger that liberty should be undervalued, and the adjustment of the boundaries between it and social control would present no extraordinary difficulty. But the evil is, that individual spontaneity is hardly recognized by the common modes of thinking, as having any intrinsic worth, or deserving any regard on its own account. The majority, being satisfied with the ways of mankind as they now are (for it is they who make them what they are), cannot comprehend why those ways should not be good enough for everybody; and what is more, spontaneity forms no part of the ideal of the majority of moral and social reformers, but is rather looked on with jealousy, as a troublesome and perhaps rebellious obstruction to the general acceptance of what these reformers, in their own judgment, think would be best for mankind. Few persons, out of Germany, even comprehend the meaning of the doctrine which Wilhelm von Humboldt, so eminent both as a *savant* and as a politician, made the text of a treatise—that "the end of man, or that which is prescribed by the eternal or immutable dictates of reason, and not suggested by vague and transient desires, is the highest and most harmonious development of his powers to a complete and consistent whole"; that, therefore, the object "towards which every human being must ceaselessly direct his efforts, and on which especially those who design to influence their fellow-men must ever keep their eyes, is the individuality of power and development"; that for this there are two requisites, "freedom, and a variety of situations"; and that from the union of these arise "individual vigour and manifold diversity," which combine themselves in "originality."*

Little, however, as people are accustomed to a doctrine like that of von Humboldt, and surprising as it may be to them to find so high a value attached to individuality, the question, one must nevertheless think, can only be one of degree. No one's idea of excellence in conduct is that people should do absolutely nothing but copy one another. No one would assert that people ought not to put into their mode of life, and into the conduct of their concerns, any impress whatever of their own judgment, or of their own individual character. On the other hand, it would be absurd to pretend that people ought to live as if nothing whatever had been known in the world before they came into it; as if experience had as yet done nothing towards showing that one mode of existence, or of conduct, is preferable to another. Nobody denies that people should be so taught and trained in youth, as to know and benefit by the ascertained results of human experience. But it is the privilege and proper condition of a human being, arrived at the maturity of his faculties, to use and interpret experience in his own way. It is for him to find out what part of recorded experience is properly applicable to his own circumstances and character. The traditions and customs of other people are, to a certain extent, evidence of what their experience has taught *them*; presumptive evidence, and as such, have a claim to his deference: but, in the first place, their experience may be too narrow; or they may not have interpreted it rightly. Secondly, their interpretation of experience may be correct, but unsuitable to him. Customs are made for customary circumstances, and customary characters: and his circumstances or his character may be uncustomary. Thirdly, though the customs be both good as customs, and suitable to him, yet to conform to custom, merely *as* custom, does not educate or develop in him any of the qualities which are the distinctive endowment of a human being. The human faculties of perception, judgment, discriminative feeling, mental activity, and even moral preference, are exercised only in making a choice. He who does anything because it is the custom, makes no choice. He gains no practice either in discerning or in desiring what is best. The mental and moral, like the muscular powers, are improved only by being used. The faculties are called into no exercise by doing a thing merely because others do it, no more than by believing a thing only because others believe it. If the grounds of an opinion are not conclusive to the person's own reason, his reason cannot be strengthened, but is likely to be weakened by his adopting it: and if the inducements to an act are not such as are consentaneous to his own feelings and character (where affection, or the rights of others, are not concerned) it is so much done towards rendering his feelings and character inert and torpid, instead of active and energetic.

* *The Sphere and Duties of Government,* from the German of Baron Wilhelm von Humboldt, pp. 11-13.—Au.

He who lets the world, or his own portion of it, choose his plan of life for him, has no need of any other faculty than the ape-like one of imitation. He who chooses his plan for himself, employs all his faculties. He must use observation to see, reasoning and judgment to foresee, activity to gather materials for decision, discrimination to decide, and when he has decided, firmness and self-control to hold to his deliberate decision. And these qualities he requires and exercises exactly in proportion as the part of his conduct which he determines according to his own judgment and feelings is a large one. It is possible that he might be guided in some good path, and kept out of harm's way, without any of these things. But what will be his comparative worth as a human being? It really is of importance, not only what men do, but also what manner of men they are that do it. Among the works of man, which human life is rightly employed in perfecting and beautifying, the first in importance surely is man himself. Supposing it were possible to get houses built, corn grown, battles fought, causes tried, and even churches erected and prayers said, by machinery—by automatons in human form—it would be a considerable loss to exchange for these automatons even the men and women who at present inhabit the more civilized parts of the world, and who assuredly are but starved specimens of what nature can and will produce. Human nature is not a machine to be built after a model, and set to do exactly the work prescribed for it, but a tree, which requires to grow and develop itself on all sides, according to the tendency of the inward forces which make it a living thing.

It will probably be conceded that it is desirable people should exercise their understandings, and that an intelligent following of custom, or even occasionally an intelligent deviation from custom, is better than a blind and simply mechanical adhesion to it. To a certain extent it is admitted, that our understanding should be our own: but there is not the same willingness to admit that our desires and impulses should be our own likewise; or that to possess impulses of our own, and of any strength, is anything but a peril and a snare. Yet desires and impulses are as much a part of a perfect human being, as beliefs and restraints: and strong impulses are only perilous when not properly balanced; when one set of aims and inclinations is developed into strength, while others, which ought to co-exist with them, remain weak and inactive. It is not because men's desires are strong that they act ill; it is because their consciences are weak. There is no natural connexion between strong impulses and a weak conscience. The natural connexion is the other way. To say that one person's desires and feelings are stronger and more various than those of another, is merely to say that he has more of the raw material of human nature, and is therefore capable, perhaps of more evil, but certainly of more good. Strong impulses are but another name for energy. Energy may be turned to bad uses; but more good may always be made of an energetic nature, than of an indolent and impassive one. Those who have most natural feeling, are always those whose cultivated feelings may be made the strongest. The same strong susceptibilities which make the personal impulses vivid and powerful, are also the source from whence are generated the most passionate love of virtue, and the sternest self-control. It is through the cultivation of these, that society both does its duty and protects its interests: not by rejecting the stuff of which heroes are made, because it knows not how to make them. A person whose desires and impulses are his own—are the expression of his own nature, as it has been developed and modified by his own culture—is said to have a character. One whose desires and impulses are not his own, has no character, no more than a steam-engine has a character. If, in addition to being his own, his impulses are strong, and are under the government of a strong will, he has an energetic character. Whoever thinks that individuality of desires and impulses should not be encouraged to unfold itself, must maintain that society has no need of strong natures—is not the better for containing many persons who have much character—and that a high general average of energy is not desirable.

In some early states of society, these forces might be, and were, too much ahead of the power which society then possessed of disciplining and controlling them. There has been a time when the element of spontaneity and individuality was in excess, and the social principle had a hard struggle with it. The difficulty then was, to induce men of strong bodies or minds to pay obedience to any rules which required them to control their impulses. To overcome this difficulty, law and discipline, like the Popes struggling against the Emperors, asserted a power over the whole man, claiming to control all his life in order to control his character—which society had not found any other sufficient means of binding. But society has now fairly got the better of individuality; and the danger which threatens human nature is not the excess, but the deficiency, of personal impulses and preferences. Things are vastly changed, since the passions of those who were strong by station or by personal endowment were in a state of habitual rebellion against laws and ordinances, and required to be rigorously chained up to enable the persons within their reach to enjoy any particle of security. In our times, from the highest class of society down to the lowest, every one lives as under the eye of a hostile and dreaded censorship. Not only in what concerns others, but in what concerns only themselves, the individual, or the family, do not ask themselves—what do I prefer? or, what would suit my character and disposition? or, what would allow the best and highest in me to have fair play, and enable it to grow and thrive? They ask themselves, what is suitable to my position? what is usually done by persons of my station and pecuniary circumstances? or (worse still) what is usually done by persons of a station and circumstances superior to mine? I do not mean that they choose what is customary, in preference to what suits their own inclination. It does not occur to them to have any inclination, except for what is customary. Thus the mind itself is bowed to the yoke: even in what people do for pleasure, conformity is the first thing thought of; they like in crowds; they exercise choice only among things commonly done: peculiarity of taste, eccentricity of conduct, are shunned equally with crimes: until by dint of not following their own nature, they have no nature to follow: their human capacities are withered and starved: they become incapable of any strong wishes or native pleasures, and are generally without either opinions or feelings of home growth, or properly their own. Now is this, or is it not, the desirable condition of human nature? . . .

In some such insidious form there is at present a strong tendency to this narrow theory of life, and to the pinched and hidebound type of human character which it patronizes. Many persons, no doubt, sincerely think that human beings thus cramped and dwarfed, are as their Maker designed them to be; just as many have thought that trees are a much finer thing when clipped into pollards, or cut out into figures of animals, than as nature made them. But if it be any part of religion to believe that man was made by a good being, it is more consistent with that faith to believe, that this Being gave all human faculties that they might be cultivated and unfolded, not rooted out and consumed, and that he takes delight in every nearer approach made by his creatures to the ideal conception embodied in them, every increase in any of their capabilities of comprehension, of action, or of enjoyment. There is a different type of human excellence from the Calvinistic; a conception of humanity as having its nature bestowed on it for other purposes than merely to be abnegated. "Pagan self-assertion" is one of the elements of human worth, as well as "Christian self-denial."* There is a Greek ideal of self-development, which the Platonic and Christian ideal of self-government blends with, but does not supersede. It may be better to be a John Knox than an Alcibiades, but it is better to be a Pericles than either; nor would a Pericles, if we had one in these days, be without anything good which belonged to John Knox.

It is not by wearing down into uniformity all that is individual in themselves, but by cultivating it and calling it forth, within the limits imposed by the rights and interests of others, that human beings become a noble and beautiful object of contemplation; and as the works partake the character of those who do them, by the same process human life also becomes rich, diversified, and animating, furnishing more abundant aliment to high thoughts and elevating feelings, and strengthening the tie which binds every individual to the race, by making the race infinitely better worth belonging to. In proportion to the development of his individuality, each person becomes more valuable to himself, and is therefore capable of being more valuable to others. There is a greater fulness of life about his own existence, and when there is more life in the units there is more in the mass which is composed of them. As much compression as is necessary to prevent the stronger specimens of human nature from encroaching on the rights of others, cannot be dispensed with; but for this there is ample compensation even in the point of view of human development. The means of development which the individual loses by being prevented from gratifying his inclinations to the injury of others, are chiefly obtained at the expense of the development of other people. And even to himself there is a full equivalent in the better development of the social part of his nature, rendered possible by the restraint put upon the selfish part. To be held to rigid rules of justice for the sake of others, develops the feelings and capacities which have the good of others for their object. But to be restrained in things not affecting their good, by their mere displeasure, develops nothing valuable, except such force of character as may unfold itself in resisting the restraint. If acquiesced in, it dulls and blunts the whole nature. To give any fair play to the nature of each, it is essential that different persons should be allowed to lead different lives. In proportion as this latitude has been exercised in any age, has that age been noteworthy to posterity. Even despotism does not produce its worst effects, so long as Individuality exists under it; and whatever crushes individu-

* These phrases are from John Sterling's *Essays and Tales,* ed. J. C. Hare [1848], I, 190.—Eds.

ality is despotism, by whatever name it may be called, and whether it professes to be enforcing the will of God or the injunctions of men.

Having said that Individuality is the same thing with development, and that it is only the cultivation of individuality which produces, or can produce, well-developed human beings, I might here close the argument: for what more or better can be said of any condition of human affairs, than that it brings human beings themselves nearer to the best thing they can be? or what worse can be said of any obstruction to good, than that it prevents this? Doubtless, however, these considerations will not suffice to convince those who most need convincing; and it is necessary further to show, that these developed human beings are of some use to the undeveloped—to point out to those who do not desire liberty, and would not avail themselves of it, that they may be in some intelligible manner rewarded for allowing other people to make use of it without hindrance.

In the first place, then, I would suggest that they might possibly learn something from them. It will not be denied by anybody, that originality is a valuable element in human affairs. There is always need of persons not only to discover new truths, and point out when what were once truths are true no longer, but also to commence new practices, and set the example of more enlightened conduct, and better taste and sense in human life. This cannot well be gainsaid by anybody who does not believe that the world has already attained perfection in all its ways and practices. It is true that this benefit is not capable of being rendered by everybody alike: there are but few persons, in comparison with the whole of mankind, whose experiments, if adopted by others, would be likely to be any improvement on established practice. But these few are the salt of the earth; without them, human life would become a stagnant pool. Not only is it they who introduce good things which did not before exist; it is they who keep the life in those which already existed. If there were nothing new to be done, would human intellect cease to be necessary? Would it be a reason why those who do the old things should forget why they are done, and do them like cattle, not like human beings? There is only too great a tendency in the best beliefs and practices to degenerate into the mechanical; and unless there were a succession of persons whose ever-recurring originality prevents the grounds of those beliefs and practices from becoming merely traditional, such dead matter would not resist the smallest shock from anything really alive, and there would be no reason why civilization should not die out, as in the Byzantine Empire. Persons of genius, it is true, are, and are always likely to be, a small minority; but in order to have them, it is necessary to preserve the soil in which they grow. Genius can only breathe freely in an *atmosphere* of freedom. Persons of genius are, *ex vi termini,* * *more* individual than any other people—less capable, consequently, of fitting themselves, without hurtful compression, into any of the small number of moulds which society provides in order to save its members the trouble of forming their own character. If from timidity they consent to be forced into one of these moulds, and to let all that part of themselves which cannot expand under the pressure remain unexpanded, society will be little

* *ex vi termini*—by definition.—Eds.

the better for their genius. If they are of a strong character, and break their fetters, they become a mark for the society which has not succeeded in reducing them to commonplace, to point at with solemn warning as "wild," "erratic," and the like; much as if one should complain of the Niagara river for not flowing smoothly between its banks like a Dutch canal.

I insist thus emphatically on the importance of genius, and the necessity of allowing it to unfold itself freely both in thought and in practice, being well aware that no one will deny the position in theory, but knowing also that almost every one, in reality, is totally indifferent to it. People think genius a fine thing if it enables a man to write an exciting poem, or paint a picture. But in its true sense, that of originality in thought and action, though no one says that it is not a thing to be admired, nearly all, at heart, think that they can do very well without it. Unhappily this is too natural to be wondered at. Originality is the one thing which unoriginal minds cannot feel the use of. They cannot see what it is to do for them: how should they? If they could see what it would do for them, it would not be originality. The first service which originality has to render them, is that of opening their eyes: which being once fully done, they would have a chance of being themselves original. Meanwhile, recollecting that nothing was ever yet done which some one was not the first to do, and that all good things which exist are the fruits of originality, let them be modest enough to believe that there is something still left for it to accomplish, and assure themselves that they are more in need of originality, the less they are conscious of the want.

In sober truth, whatever homage may be professed, or even paid, to real or supposed mental superiority, the general tendency of things throughout the world is to render mediocrity the ascendant power among mankind. In ancient history, in the middle ages, and in a diminishing degree through the long transition from feudality to the present time, the individual was a power in himself; and if he had either great talents or a high social position, he was a considerable power. At present individuals are lost in the crowd. In politics it is almost a triviality to say that public opinion now rules the world. The only power deserving the name is that of masses, and of governments while they make themselves the organ of the tendencies and instincts of masses. This is as true in the moral and social relations of private life as in public transactions. Those whose opinions go by the name of public opinion, are not always the same sort of public: in America they are the whole white population; in England, chiefly the middle class. But they are always a mass, that is to say, collective mediocrity. And what is a still greater novelty, the mass do not now take their opinions from dignitaries in Church or State, from ostensible leaders, or from books. Their thinking is done for them by men much like themselves, addressing them or speaking in their name, on the spur of the moment, through the newspapers. I am not complaining of all this. I do not assert that anything better is compatible, as a general rule, with the present low state of the human mind. But that does not hinder the government of mediocrity from being mediocre government. No government by a democracy or a numerous aristocracy, either in its political acts or in the opinions, qualities, and tone of mind which it fosters, ever did or could rise above mediocrity, except in so far as the sovereign Many have let themselves be guided (which in their best times they always have done) by the counsels and influence of a more highly gifted and instructed One or Few. The initiation of all wise or noble things, comes and must come from individuals; generally at first from some one individual. The honour and glory of the average man is that he is capable of following that initiative; that he can respond internally to wise and noble things, and be led to them with his eyes open. I am not countenancing the sort of "hero-worship" which applauds the strong man of genius for forcibly seizing on the government of the world and making it do his bidding in spite of itself. All he can claim is, freedom to point out the way. The power of compelling others into it, is not only inconsistent with the freedom and development of all the rest, but corrupting to the strong man himself. It does seem, however, that when the opinions of masses of merely average men are everywhere become or becoming the dominant power, the counterpoise and corrective to that tendency would be, the more and more pronounced individuality of those who stand on the higher eminences of thought. It is in these circumstances most especially, that exceptional individuals, instead of being deterred, should be encouraged in acting differently from the mass. In other times there was no advantage in their doing so, unless they acted not only differently, but better. In this age the mere example of non-conformity, the mere refusal to bend the knee to custom, is itself a service. Precisely because the tyranny of opinion is such as to make eccentricity a reproach, it is desirable, in order to break through that tyranny, that people should be eccentric. Eccentricity has always abounded when and where strength of character has abounded; and the amount of eccentricity in a society has generally been proportional to the amount of genius, mental vigour, and moral courage which it contained. That so few now dare to be eccentric, marks the chief danger of the time.

I have said that it is important to give the freest scope possible to uncustomary things, in order that it may in time appear which of these are fit to be converted into customs. But independence of action, and disregard of custom are not solely deserving of encouragement for the chance they afford that better modes of action, and customs more worthy of general adoption, may be struck out; nor is it only persons of decided mental superiority who have a just claim to carry on their lives in their own way. There is no reason that all human existence should be constructed on some one, or some small number of patterns. If a person possesses any tolerable amount of common sense and experience, his own mode of laying out his existence is the best, not because it is the best in itself, but because it is his own mode. Human beings are not like sheep; and even sheep are not undistinguishably alike. A man cannot get a coat or a pair of boots to fit him, unless they are either made to his measure, or he has a whole warehouseful to choose from: and is it easier to fit him with a life than with a coat, or are human beings more like one another in their whole physical and spiritual conformation than in the shape of their feet? If it were only that people have diversities of taste, that is reason enough for not attempting to shape them all after one model. But different persons also require different conditions for their spiritual development; and can no more exist healthily in the same moral, than all the variety of plants can in the same physical, atmosphere and climate. The same things which are helps to one person towards the cultivation of his higher nature, are hindrances to another. The same mode of life is a healthy excitement to one, keeping all his faculties of action and enjoyment in their best order, while to another it is a distracting burthen, which suspends or crushes all internal life. Such are the differences among human beings in their sources of pleasure, their susceptibilities of pain, and the operation on them of different physical and moral agencies, that unless there is a corresponding diversity in their modes of life, they neither obtain their fair share of happiness, nor grow up to the mental, moral, and aesthetic stature of which their nature is capable. Why then should tolerance, as far as the public sentiment is concerned, extend only to tastes and modes of life which extort acquiescence by the multitude of their adherents? Nowhere (except in some monastic institutions) is diversity of taste entirely unrecognised; a person may, without blame, either like or dislike rowing, or smoking, or music, or athletic exercises, or chess, or cards, or study, because both those who like each of these things, and those who dislike them, are too numerous to be put down. But the man, and still more the woman, who can be accused either of doing "what nobody does," or of not doing "what everybody does," is the subject of as much depreciatory remark as if he or she had committed some grave moral delinquency. Persons require to possess a title, or some other badge of rank, or of the consideration of people of rank, to be able to indulge somewhat in the luxury of doing as they like without detriment to their estimation. To indulge somewhat, I repeat: for whoever allow themselves much of that indulgence, incur the risk of something worse than disparaging speeches—they are in peril of a commission *de lunatico,* * and of having their property taken from them and given to their relations.

There is one characteristic of the present direction of public opinion, peculiarly calculated to make it intolerant of any marked demonstration of individuality. The general average of mankind are not only moderate in intellect, but also moderate in inclinations; they have no tastes or wishes strong enough to incline them to do anything unusual, and they consequently do not understand those who have, and class all such with the wild and intemperate whom they are accustomed to look down upon. Now, in addition to this fact which is general, we have only to suppose that a strong movement has set in towards the improvement of morals, and it is evident what we have to expect. In these days such a movement has set in; much has actually been effected in the way of increased regularity of conduct, and discouragement of excesses; and there is a philanthropic spirit abroad, for the exercise of which there is no more inviting field than the moral and prudential improvement of our fellow-creatures. These tendencies of the times cause the public to be more disposed than at most former periods to prescribe general rules of conduct, and endeavour to make every one conform to the approved standard. And that standard, express or tacit, is to desire nothing strongly. Its ideal of character is to be without any marked character; to maim by compression, like a Chinese lady's foot, every part of human nature which stands out prominently, and tends to make the person markedly dissimilar in outline to commonplace humanity.

As is usually the case with ideals which exclude one-half of what is desirable, the present standard of approbation produces only an inferior imitation of the other half.

* A "commission *de lunatico*" is a court authorization to inquire into the sanity of an individual.—Eds.

Instead of great energies guided by vigorous reason, and strong feelings strongly controlled by a conscientious will, its result is weak feelings and weak energies, which therefore can be kept in outward conformity to rule without any strength either of will or of reason. Already energetic characters on any large scale are becoming merely traditional. There is now scarcely any outlet for energy in this country except business. The energy expended in that may still be regarded as considerable. What little is left from that employment, is expended on some hobby; which may be a useful, even a philanthropic hobby, but is always some one thing, and generally a thing of small dimensions. The greatness of England is now all collective: individually small, we only appear capable of anything great by our habit of combining; and with this our moral and religious philanthropists are perfectly contented. But it was men of another stamp than this that made England what it has been; and men of another stamp will be needed to prevent its decline.

The despotism of custom is everywhere the standing hindrance to human advancement, being in unceasing antagonism to that disposition to aim at something better than customary, which is called, according to circumstances, the spirit of liberty, or that of progress or improvement. The spirit of improvement is not always a spirit of liberty, for it may aim at forcing improvements on an unwilling people; and the spirit of liberty, in so far as it resists such attempts, may ally itself locally and temporarily with the opponents of improvement; but the only unfailing and permanent source of improvement is liberty, since by it there are as many possible independent centres of improvement as there are individuals. The progressive principle, however, in either shape, whether as the love of liberty or of improvement, is antagonistic to the sway of Custom, involving at least emancipation from that yoke; and the contest between the two constitutes the chief interest of the history of mankind. The greater part of the world has, properly speaking, no history, because the despotism of Custom is complete . . .

What is it that has hitherto preserved Europe from this lot? What has made the European family of nations an improving, instead of a stationary portion of mankind? Not any superior excellence in them, which, when it exists, exists as the effect, not as the cause; but their remarkable diversity of character and culture. Individuals, classes, nations, have been extremely unlike one another: they have struck out a great variety of paths, each leading to something valuable; and although at every period those who travelled in different paths have been intolerant of one another, and each would have thought it an excellent thing if all the rest could have been compelled to travel his road, their attempts to thwart each other's development have rarely had any permanent success, and each has in time endured to receive the good which the others have offered. Europe is, in my judgment, wholly indebted to this plurality of paths for its progressive and many-sided development. But it already begins to possess this benefit in a considerably less degree. It is decidedly advancing towards the Chinese ideal of making all people alike. M. de Tocqueville, in his last important work, remarks how much more the Frenchmen of the present day resemble one another, than did those even of the last generation.* The same remark might be made

* *L'ancien régime et la revolution* (1856), ch. VIII.—Au.

of Englishmen in a far greater degree. In a passage already quoted from Wilhelm von Humboldt, he points out two things as necessary conditions of human development, because necessary to render people unlike one another; namely, freedom, and variety of situations. The second of these two conditions is in this country every day diminishing. The circumstances which surround different classes and individuals, and shape their characters, are daily becoming more assimilated. Formerly, different ranks, different neighbourhoods, different trades and professions, lived in what might be called different worlds; at present, to a great degree in the same. Comparatively speaking, they now read the same things, listen to the same things, see the same things, go to the same places, have their hopes and fears directed to the same objects, have the same rights and liberties, and the same means of asserting them. Great as are the differences of position which remain, they are nothing to those which have ceased. And the assimilation is still proceeding. All the political changes of the age promote it, since they all tend to raise the low and to lower the high. Every extension of education promotes it, because education brings people under common influences, and gives them access to the general stock of facts and sentiments. Improvements in the means of communication promote it, by bringing the inhabitants of distant places into personal contact, and keeping up a rapid flow of changes of residence between one place and another. The increase of commerce and manufactures promotes it, by diffusing more widely the advantages of easy circumstances, and opening all objects of ambition, even the highest, to general competition, whereby the desire of rising becomes no longer the character of a particular class, but of all classes. A more powerful agency than even all these, in bringing about a general similarity among mankind, is the complete establishment, in this and other free countries, of the ascendancy of public opinion in the State. As the various social eminences which enabled persons entrenched on them to disregard the opinion of the multitude, gradually become levelled; as the very idea of resisting the will of the public, when it is positively known that they have a will, disappears more and more from the minds of practical politicians; there ceases to be any social support for non-conformity—any substantive power in society, which, itself opposed to the ascendancy of numbers, is interested in taking under its protection opinions and tendencies at variance with those of the public.

The combination of all these causes forms so great a mass of influences hostile to Individuality, that it is not easy to see how it can stand its ground. It will do so with increasing difficulty, unless the intelligent part of the public can be made to feel its value—to see that it is good there should be differences, even though not for the better, even though, as it may appear to them, some should be for the worse. If the claims of Individuality are ever to be asserted, the time is now, while much is still wanting to complete the enforced assimilation. It is only in the earlier stages that any stand can be successfully made against the encroachment. The demand that all other people shall resemble ourselves, grows by what it feeds on. If resistance waits till life is reduced *nearly* to one uniform type, all deviations from that type will come to be considered impious, immoral, even monstrous and contrary to nature. Mankind speedily become unable to conceive diversity, when they have been for some time unaccustomed to see it.

# *Ilse Aichinger*
# "THE BOUND MAN"

Sunlight on his face woke him, but made him shut his eyes again; it streamed unhindered down the slope, collected itself into rivulets, attracted swarms of flies, which flew low over his forehead, circled, sought to land, and were overtaken by fresh swarms. When he tried to whisk them away he discovered that he was bound. A thin rope cut into his arms. He dropped them, opened his eyes again, and looked down at himself. His legs were tied all the way up to his thighs; a single length of rope was tied round his ankles, criss-crossed all the way up his legs, and encircled his hips, his chest, and his arms. He could not see where it was knotted. He showed no sign of fear or hurry, though he thought he was unable to move, until he discovered that the rope allowed his legs some free play, and that round his body it was almost loose. His arms were tied to each other but not to his body, and had some free play too. This made him smile, and it occurred to him that perhaps children had been playing a practical joke on him.

He tried to feel for his knife, but again the rope cut softly into his flesh. He tried again, more cautiously this time, but his pocket was empty. Not only his knife, but the little money that he had on him, as well as his coat, were missing. His shoes had been pulled from his feet and taken too. When he moistened his lips he tasted blood, which had flowed from his temples down his cheeks, his chin, his neck, and under his shirt. His eyes were painful; if he kept them open for long he saw reddish stripes in the sky.

He decided to stand up. He drew his knees up as far as he could, rested his hands on the fresh grass and jerked himself to his feet. An elder-branch stroked his cheek, the sun dazzled him, and the rope cut into his flesh. He collapsed to the ground again, half out of his mind with pain, and then tried again. He went on trying until the blood started flowing from his hidden weals. Then he lay still again for a long while, and let the sun and the flies do what they liked.

When he awoke for the second time the elder-bush had cast its shadow over him, and the coolness stored in it was pouring from between its branches. He must have been hit on the head. Then they must have laid him down carefully, just as a mother lays here baby behind a bush when she goes to work in the fields.

His chances all lay in the amount of free play allowed him by the rope. He dug his elbows into the ground and tested it. As soon as the rope tautened he stopped, and tried again more cautiously. If he had been able to reach the branch over his head he could have used it to drag himself to his feet, but he could not reach it. He laid his head back on the grass, rolled over, and struggled to his knees. He tested the ground with his toes, and then managed to stand up almost without effort.

A few paces away lay the path across the plateau, and among the grass were wild pinks and thistles in bloom. He tried to lift his foot to avoid trampling on them, but the rope round his ankles prevented him. He looked down at himself.

The rope was knotted at his ankles, and ran round his legs in a kind of playful pattern. He carefully bent and tried to loosen it, but, loose though it seemed to be, he could not make it any looser. To avoid treading on the thistles with his bare feet he hopped over them like a bird.

The cracking of a twig made him stop. People in this district were very prone to laughter. He was alarmed by the thought that he was in no position to defend himself. He hopped on until he reached the path. Bright fields stretched far below. He could see no sign of the nearest village, and, if he could move no faster than this, night would fall before he reached it.

He tried walking, and discovered that he could put one foot before another if he lifted each foot a definite distance from the ground and then put it down again before the rope tautened. In the same way he could actually swing his arms a little.

After the first step he fell. He fell right across the path, and made the dust fly. He expected this to be a sign for the long-suppressed laughter to break out, but all remained quiet. He was alone. As soon as the dust had settled he got up and went on. He looked down and watched the rope slacken, grow taut, and then slacken again.

When the first glow-worms appeared he managed to look up. He felt in control of himself again, and his impatience to reach the nearest village faded.

Hunger made him light-headed, and he seemed to be going so fast that not even a motor-cycle could have overtaken him; alternatively he felt as if he were standing still and that the earth was rushing past him, like a river flowing past a man swimming against the stream. The stream carried branches which had been bent southwards by the north wind, stunted young trees, and patches of grass with bright, long-stalked flowers. It ended by submerging the bushes and the young trees, leaving only the sky and the man above water-level. The moon had risen, and illuminated the bare, curved summit of the plateau, the path, which was overgrown with young grass, the bound man making his way along it with quick, measured steps, and two hares, which ran across the hill just in front of him and vanished down the slope. Though the nights were still cool at this time of the year, before midnight the bound man lay down at the edge of the escarpment and went to sleep.

In the light of morning the animal-tamer who was camping with his circus in the field outside the village saw the bound man coming down the path, gazing thoughtfully at the ground. The bound man stopped and bent down. He held out one arm to help keep his balance and with the other picked up an empty wine-bottle. Then he straightened himself and stood erect again. He moved slowly, to avoid being cut by the rope, but to the circus proprietor what he did suggested the voluntary limitation of an enormous swiftness of movement. He was enchanted by its extraordinary gracefulness, and while the bound man looked about for a stone on which to break the bottle, so that he could use the splintered neck to cut the rope, the animal-tamer walked across the field and approached him. The first leaps of a young panther had never filled him with such delight.

"Ladies and gentlemen, the bound man!" His very first movements let loose a storm of applause, which out of sheer excitement caused the blood to rush to the cheeks of the animal-tamer standing at the edge of the arena. The bound man rose to his feet. His surprise whenever he did this was like that of a four-footed animal which has managed to stand on its hind-legs. He knelt, stood up, jumped, and turned cart-wheels. The spectators found it as astonishing as if they had seen a bird which voluntarily remained earth-bound, and confined itself to hopping. The bound man became an enormous draw. His absurd steps and little jumps, his elementary exercises in movement, made the rope-dancer superfluous. His fame grew from village to village, but the motions he went through were few and always the same; they were really quite ordinary motions, which he had continually to practise in the day-time in the half-dark tent in order to retain his shackled freedom. In that he remained entirely within the limits set by his rope he was free of it, it did not confine him, but gave him wings and endowed his leaps and jumps with purpose; just as the flights of birds of passage have purpose when they take wing in the warmth of summer and hesitantly make small circles in the sky.

All the children of the neighbourhood started playing the game of "bound man". They formed rival gangs, and one day the circus people found a little girl lying bound in a ditch, with a cord tied round her neck so that she could hardly breathe. They released her, and at the end of the performance that night the bound man made a speech. He announced briefly that there was no sense in being tied up in such a way that you could not jump. After that he was regarded as a comedian.

Grass and sunlight, tent-pegs driven into the ground and then pulled up again, and on to the next village. "Ladies and gentlemen, the bound man!" The summer mounted towards its climax. It bent its face deeper over the fish-ponds in the hollows, taking delight in its dark reflection, skimmed the surface of the rivers, and made the plain into what it was. Everyone who could walk went to see the bound man.

Many wanted a close-up view of how he was bound. So the circus proprietor announced after each peformance that anyone who wanted to satisfy himself that the knots were real and the rope not made of rubber was at liberty to do so. The bound man generally waited for the crowd in the area outside the tent. He laughed or remained serious, and held out his arms for inspection. Many took the opportunity to look him in the face, others gravely tested the rope, tried the knots on his ankles, and wanted to know exactly how the lengths compared with the length of his limbs. They asked him how he had come to be tied up like that, and he answered patiently, always saying the same thing. Yes, he had been tied up, he said, and when he awoke he found that he had been robbed as well. Those who had done it must have been pressed for time, because they had tied him up somewhat too loosely for someone who was not supposed to be able to move and somewhat too tightly for some who was expected to be able to move. But he did move, people pointed out. Yes, he replied, what else could he do?

Before he went to bed he always sat for a time in front of the fire. When the circus proprietor asked him why he didn't make up a better story, he always answered that he hadn't made up that one, and blushed. He preferred staying in the shade.

The difference between him and the other performers was that when the show was over he did not take off his rope. The result was that every movement that he made was worth seeing, and the villagers used to hang about the camp for hours, just for the sake of seeing him get up from in front of the fire and roll himself in his blanket. Sometimes the sky was beginning to lighten when he saw their shadows disappear.

The circus proprietor often remarked that there was no reason why he should not be untied after the evening performance and tied up again next day. He pointed out that the rope-dancers, for instance, did not stay on their rope over night. But no-one took the idea of untying him seriously.

For the bound man's fame rested on the fact that he was always bound, that whenever he washed himself he had to wash his clothes too and *vice versa,* and that his only way of doing so was to jump in the river just as he was every morning when the sun came out, and that he had to be careful not to go too far for fear of being carried away by the stream.

The proprietor was well aware that what in the last resort protected the bound man from the jealousy of the other performers was his helplessness; he deliberately left them the pleasure of watching him groping painfully from stone to stone on the river bank every morning with his wet clothes clinging to him. When his wife pointed out that even the best clothes would not stand up indefinitely to such treatment (and the bound man's clothes were by no means of the best) he replied curtly that it was not going to last for ever. That was his answer to all objections—it was for the summer season only. But when he said this he was not being serious; he was talking like a gambler who has no intention of giving up his vice. In reality he would have been prepared cheerfully to sacrifice his lions and his rope-dancers for the bound man.

He proved this on the night when the rope-dancers jumped over the fire. Afterwards he was convinced that they did it, not because it was midsummer's day, but because of the bound man, who as usual was lying and watching them, with that peculiar smile that might have been real or might have been only the effect of the glow on his face. In any case no-one knew anything about him, because he never talked about anything that had happened to him before he emerged from the wood that day.

But that evening two of the performers suddenly picked him up by the arms and legs, carried him to the edge of the fire and started playfully swinging him to and fro, while two others held out their arms to catch him on the other side. In the end they threw him, but too short. The two men on the other side drew back—they explained afterwards that they did so the better to take the shock. The result was that the bound man landed at the very edge of the flames and would have been burned if the circus proprietor had not seized his arms and quickly dragged him away to save the rope which was starting to get singed. He was certain that the object had been to burn the rope. He sacked the four men on the spot.

A few nights later the proprietor's wife was awakened by the sound of footsteps on the grass, and went outside just in time to prevent the clown from playing his last practical joke. He was carrying a pair of scissors. When he was asked for an explanation he insisted that he had had no intention of taking the bound man's life, but only wanted to cut his rope, because he felt sorry for him. But he was sacked too.

These antics amused the bound man, because he could have freed himself if he had wanted to whenever he liked, but perhaps he wanted to learn a few new jumps first. The children's rhyme: "We travel with the circus, we travel with the circus" sometimes occurred to him while he lay awake at night. He could hear the voices of spectators on the opposite bank who had been driven too far downstream on the way

home. He could see the river gleaming in the moonlight, and the young shoots growing out of the thick tops of the willow trees, and did not think about autumn yet.

The circus proprietor dreaded the danger involved for the bound man by sleep. Attempts were continually made to release him while he slept. The chief culprits were sacked rope-dancers, or children who were bribed for the purpose. But measures could be taken to safeguard against these. A much bigger danger was that which he represented to himself. In his dreams he forgot his rope, and was surprised by it when he woke in the darkness of morning. He would angrily try to get up, but lose his balance and fall back again. The previous evening's applause was forgotten, sleep was still too near, his head and neck too free. He was just the opposite of a hanged man—his neck was the only part of him that was free. You had to make sure that at such moments no knife was within his reach. In the early hours of the morning the circus proprietor sometimes sent his wife to see whether the bound man was all right. If he was asleep she would bend over him and feel the rope. It had grown hard from dirt and damp. She would test the amount of free play it allowed him, and touch his tender wrists and ankles.

The most varied rumours circulated about the bound man. Some said he had tied himself up and invented the story of having been robbed, and towards the end of the summer that was the general opinion. Others maintained that he had been tied up at his own request, perhaps in league with the circus proprietor. The hesitant way in which he told of his story, his habit of breaking off when the talk got round to the attack on him, contributed greatly to these rumours. Those who still believed in the robbery-with-violence story were laughed at. Nobody knew what difficulties the circus proprietor had in keeping the bound man, and how often he said he had had enough and wanted to clear off, for too much of the summer had passed.

Later, however, he stopped talking about clearing off. When the proprietor's wife brought him his food by the river and asked him how long he proposed to stay with them, he did not answer. She thought he had got used, not to being tied up, but to not forgetting for a moment that he was tied up—the only thing that anyone in his position could get used to. She asked him whether he did not think it ridiculous to be tied up all the time, but he answered that he did not. Such a variety of people—clowns, freaks, and comics, to say nothing of elephants and tigers—travelled with circuses that he did not see why a bound man should not travel with a circus too. He told her about the movements he was practising, the new ones he had discovered, and about a new trick that had occurred to him while he was whisking flies from the animals' eyes. He described to her how he always anticipated the effect of the rope and always restrained his movements in such a way as to prevent it from ever tautening; and she knew that there were days when he was hardly aware of the rope when he jumped down from the wagon and slapped the flanks of the horses in the morning, as if he were moving in a dream. She watched him vault over the bars almost without touching them, and saw the sun on his face, and he told her that sometimes he felt as if he were not tied up at all. She answered that if he were prepared to be untied there would never be any need for him to feel tied up. He agreed that he could be untied whenever he felt like it.

The woman ended by not knowing whether she were more concerned with the man or with the rope that tied him. She told him that he could go on travelling with the circus without his rope, but he did not believe it. For what would be the point of his antics without his rope, and what would he amount to without it? Without his rope he would leave them, and the happy days would be over. She would no longer be able to sit beside him on the stones by the river without rousing suspicion, and she knew that his continued presence, and her conversations with him, of which the rope was the only subject, depended on it. Whenever she agreed that the rope had its advantages he would start talking about how troublesome it was, and whenever he started talking about its advantages she would urge him to get rid of it. All this seemed as endless as the summer itself.

At other times she was worried at the thought that she was herself hastening the end by her talk. Sometimes she would get up in the middle of the night and run across the grass to where he slept. She wanted to shake him, wake him up and ask him to keep the rope. But then she would see him lying there; he had thrown off his blanket, and there he lay like a corpse, with his legs outstretched and his arms close together, with the rope tied round them. His clothes had suffered from the heat and the water, but the rope had grown no thinner. She felt that he would go on travelling with the circus until the flesh fell from him and exposed the joints. Next morning she would plead with him more ardently than ever to get rid of his rope.

The increasing coolness of the weather gave her hope. Autumn was coming, and he would not be able to go on jumping into the river with his clothes on much longer. But the thought of losing his rope, about which he had felt indifferent earlier in the season, now depressed him.

The songs of the harvesters filled him with foreboding. "Summer has gone, summer has gone." But he realized that soon he would have to change his clothes, and he was certain that when he had been untied it would be impossible to tie him up again in exactly the same way. About this time the proprietor started talking about travelling south that year.

The heat changed without transition into quiet, dry cold, and the fire was kept in all day long. When the bound man jumped down from the wagon he felt the coldness of the grass under his feet. The stalks were bent with ripeness. The horses dreamed on their feet and the wild animals, crouching to leap even in their sleep, seemed to be collecting gloom under their skins which would break out later.

On one of these days a young wolf escaped. The circus proprietor kept quiet about it, to avoid spreading alarm, but the wolf soon started raiding cattle in the neighbourhood. People at first believed that the wolf had been driven to these parts by the prospect of a severe winter, but the circus soon became suspect. The proprietor could not conceal the loss of the animal from his own employees, so the truth was bound to come out before long. The circus people offered their aid in tracking down the beast to the burgomasters of the neighbouring villages, but all their efforts were vain. Eventually the circus was openly blamed for the damage and the danger, and spectators stayed away.

The bound man went on performing before half-empty seats without losing anything of his amazing freedom of movement. During the day he wandered among the surrounding hills under the thin-beaten silver of the autumn sky, and, whenever he could, lay down where the sun shone longest. Soon he found a place which the twilight reached last of all, and when at last it reached him he got up most unwillingly from the withered grass. In coming down the hill he had to pass through a little wood on its southern slope, and one evening he saw the gleam of two little green lights. He knew that they came from no church window, and was not for a moment under any illusion about what they were.

He stopped. The animal came towards him through the thinning foliage. He could make out its shape, the slant of its neck, its tail which swept the ground, and its receding head. If he had not been bound, perhaps he would have tried to run away, but as it was he did not even feel fear. He stood calmly with dangling arms and looked down at the wolf's bristling coat, under which the muscles played like his own underneath the rope. He thought the evening wind was still between him and the wolf when the beast sprang. The man took care to obey his rope.

Moving with the deliberate care that he had so often put to the test, he seized the wolf by the throat. Tenderness for a fellow-creature arose in him, tenderness for the upright being concealed in the four-footed. In a movement that resembled the drive of a great bird—he felt a sudden awareness that flying would be possible only if one were tied up in a special way—he flung himself at the animal and brought it to the ground. He felt a slight elation at having lost the fatal advantage of free limbs which causes men to be worsted.

The freedom he enjoyed in this struggle was having to adapt every movement of his limbs to the rope that tied him—the freedom of panthers, wolves, and the wild flowers that sway in the evening breeze. He ended up lying obliquely down the slope, clasping the animal's hind-legs between his own bare feet and its head between his hands. He felt the gentleness of the faded foliage stroking the back of his hands, and he felt his own grip almost effortlessly reaching its maximum, and he felt too how he was in no way hampered by the rope.

As he left the wood light rain began to fall and obscured the setting sun. He stopped for a while under the trees at the edge of the wood. Beyond the camp and the river he saw the fields where the cattle grazed, and the places where they crossed. Perhaps he would travel south with the circus after all. He laughed softly. It was against all reason. Even if he went on putting up with his joints' being covered with sores, which opened and bled when he made certain movements, his clothes would not stand up much longer to the friction of the rope.

The circus proprietor's wife tried to persuade her husband to announce the death of the wolf without mentioning that it had been killed by the bound man. She said that even at the time of his greatest popularity people would have refused to believe him capable of it, and in their present angry mood, with the nights getting cooler, they would be more incredulous than ever. The wolf had attacked a group of children at play that day, and nobody would believe that it had really been killed; for the circus proprietor had many wolves, and it was easy enough for him to hang a skin on the rail and allow free entry. But he was not to be dissuaded. He thought that the announcement of the bound man's act would revive the triumphs of the summer.

That evening the bound man's movements were uncertain. He stumbled in one of his jumps, and fell. Before he managed to get up he heard some low whistles and catcalls, rather like birds calling at dawn. He tried to get up too quickly, as he had done once or twice during the summer, with the result that he tautened the rope and fell back again. He lay still to regain his calm, and listened to the boos and catcalls growing into an uproar. "Well, bound man, and how did you kill the wolf?" they shouted, and: "Are you the man who killed the wolf?" If he had been one of them he would not have believed it himself. He thought they had a perfect right to be angry: a circus at this time of year, a bound man, an escaped wolf, and all ending up with this. Some groups of spectators started arguing with others, but the greater part of the audience thought the whole thing a bad joke. By the time he had got to his feet there was such a hubbub that he was barely able to make out individual words.

He saw people surging up all around him, like faded leaves raised by a whirlwind in a circular valley at the centre of which all was yet still. He thought of the golden sunsets of the last few days; and the cemetery light which lay over the blight of all that he had built up during so many nights, the gold frame which the pious hang round dark, old pictures, this sudden collapse of everything, filled him with anger.

They wanted him to repeat his battle with the wolf. He said that such a thing had no place in a circus performance, and the proprietor declared that he did not keep animals to have them slaughtered in front of an audience. But the mob stormed the ring and forced them towards the cages. The proprietor's wife made her way between the seats to the exit and managed to get round to the cages from the other side. She pushed aside the attendant whom the crowd had forced to open a cage door, but the spectators dragged her back and prevented the door from being shut.

"Aren't you the woman who used to lie with him by the river in the summer?" they called out. "How does he hold you in his arms?" She shouted back at them that they needn't believe in the bound man if they didn't want to, [that] they had never deserved him—painted clowns were good enough for them.

The bound man felt as if the bursts of laughter were what he had been expecting ever since early May. What had smelt so sweet all through the summer now stank. But, if they insisted, he was ready to take on all the animals in the circus. He had never felt so much at one with his rope.

Gently he pushed the woman aside. Perhaps he would travel south with them after all. He stood in the open doorway of the cage, and he saw the wolf, a strong young animal, rise to its feet, and he heard the proprietor grumbling again about the loss of his exhibits. He clapped his hands to attract the animal's attention, and when it was near enough he turned to slam the cage door. He looked the woman in the face. Suddenly he remembered the proprietor's warning to suspect of murderous intentions anyone near him who had a sharp instrument in his hand. At the same moment he felt the blade on his wrists, as cool as the water of the river in autumn, which during the last few weeks he had been barely able to stand. The rope curled up in a tangle beside him while he struggled free. He pushed the woman back, but there was no point in anything he did now. Had he been insufficiently on his guard against those who wanted to release him, against the sympathy in which they wanted to lull him? Had he lain too long on the river bank? If she had cut the cord at any other moment it would have been better than this.

He stood in the middle of the cage, and rid himself of the rope like a snake discarding its skin. It amused him to see the spectators shrinking back. Did they realise that he had no choice now? Or that fighting the wolf now would prove nothing whatever? At the same time he felt all his blood rush to his feet. He felt suddenly weak.

The rope, which fell at its feet like a snare, angered the wolf more than the entry of a stranger into its cage. It crouched to spring. The man reeled, and grabbed the pistol that hung ready at the side of the cage. Then, before anyone could stop him, he shot the wolf between the eyes. The animal reared, and touched him in falling.

On the way to the river he heard the footsteps of his pursuers—spectators, the rope-dancers, the circus proprietor, and the proprietor's wife, who persisted in the chase longer than anyone else. He hid in a clump of bushes and listened to them hurrying past, and later on streaming in the opposite direction back to the camp. The moon shone on the meadow; in that light its colour was that of both growth and death.

When he came to the river his anger died away. At dawn it seemed to him as if lumps of ice were floating in the water, and as if snow had fallen, obliterating memory.

## SUGGESTIONS FOR DISCUSSION

1. Both Mill's essay and Aichinger's short story treat, in some sense, the concept of individual freedom. Mill addresses the issue head-on, in a tradition that might be called philosophic or academic. Aichinger's treatment is far more oblique and might be called allegorical. What differences do the genres make in the treatment of the concept? What different demands do they make on readers? Do you think that Aichinger was trying to "make a point," just like Mill, only the long way around? What, in short, are the writers' respective purposes?
2. Mill's prose style is dense and complex. In addition, he writes with many general statements and few specific examples. Read aloud the last paragraph of the essay. How is this paragraph organized? What are the strengths of Mill's language and sentence structure?
3. "The Bound Man" is probably, in your experience, a rather strange and strangely told story. Where does it take place? When? Why are we given no names? Why is there almost no dialogue? Who is the narrator, and why has Aichinger chosen him or her to tell the tale instead of the bound man or the circus owner's wife?

   Let's assume that the story is at least in some sense allegorical, a kind of extended metaphor in which the events and characters convey meanings outside of the story. Did you, as you read it the first time, make guesses about those meanings? How about on second reading, or on reflection? For instance, what might the rope represent? Or the circus?
4. Mill writes that "society has now fairly got the better of individuality; and the danger which threatens human nature is not the excess, but the deficiency, of personal impulses and preferences." This statement was written in England in 1854–55. Is American society today one which accepts individuality? Give evidence for your answer.

## SUGGESTIONS FOR WRITING

1. The most difficult thing to control in first-time allegory writing may be the tendency to simply "mask" an argument in a transparent fictional guise: writing a story about a real family, for example, simply by turning all the people into birds. To avoid that trap, try this assignment: Create for yourself a character like Aichinger's Bound Man. He or she can be any age, from any place, have any name, or have no name. But give this character some extraordinary quality or restriction that no other character will have. Put the character in a box, for example, or make him or her mute, or invisible. Then write that character into a situation that you know well enough to write about: playing basketball in a gym, having a beer, attending a wake. See where your exploration leads.
2. Mill is very critical of custom in this essay. What kind of customs are destructive? Can custom ever be a positive influence? Some people say that traditions or customs are "group efforts to keep the unexpected from happening." Write an essay in which you defend or refute this statement. Be sure to supply illustrations of specific customs.

# 15

# Minority Rights

*Martin Luther King, Jr.*

"LETTER FROM BIRMINGHAM JAIL"

*Maya Angelou*

"MAMA AND THE DENTIST"

In contrast to the more general discussion of freedom in Mill and Aichinger, Martin Luther King examines the specific issues of minority rights and racial oppression in "Letter from Birmingham Jail." After defining unjust laws, he defends civil disobedience in the face of injustice and asserts that individual conscience and higher moral laws should dictate one's course of action. He views resistance to unjust laws not only as a human right but also as a moral responsibility. Maya Angelou dramatizes the problem on a more personal level. In "Mama and the Dentist" she presents alternating feelings of pride, shame, and bitterness as she struggles against racial discrimination.

## *Martin Luther King, Jr.*
## "LETTER FROM BIRMINGHAM JAIL"

April 16, 1963

*My Dear Fellow Clergymen:*

While confined here in the Birmingham city jail, I came across your recent statement calling my present activities "unwise and untimely." Seldom do I pause to answer criticism of my work and ideas. If I sought to answer all the criticisms that cross my desk, my secretaries would have little time for anything other than such correspondence in the course of the day, and I would have no time for constructive work. But since I feel that you are men of genuine good will and that your criticisms are sincerely set forth, I want to try to answer your statement in what I hope will be patient and reasonable terms.

I think I should indicate why I am here in Birmingham, since you have been influenced by the view which argues against "outsiders coming in." I have the honor of serving as president of the Southern Christian Leadership Conference, an organization operating in every southern state, with headquarters in Atlanta, Georgia. We have some eighty-five affiliated organizations across the South, and one of them is the Alabama Christian Movement for Human Rights. Frequently we share staff, educational and financial resources with our affiliates. Several months ago the affiliate here in Birmingham asked us to be on call to engage in a nonviolent direct-action program if such were deemed necessary. We readily consented, and when the hour came we lived up to our promise. So I, along with several members of my staff, am here because I was invited here. I am here because I have organizational ties here.

But more basically, I am in Birmingham because injustice is here. Just as the prophets of the eighth century B.C. left their villages and carried their "thus saith the Lord" far beyond the boundaries of their home towns, and just as the Apostle Paul left his village of Tarsus and carried the gospel of Jesus Christ to the far corners of the Greco-Roman world, so am I compelled to carry the gospel of freedom beyond my own home town. Like Paul, I must constantly respond to the Macedonian call for aid.

Moreover, I am cognizant of the interrelatedness of all communities and states. I cannot sit idly by in Atlanta and not be concerned about what happens in Birmingham. Injustice anywhere is a threat to justice everywhere. We are caught in an inescapable network of mutuality, tied in a single garment of destiny. Whatever affects one directly, affects all indirectly. Never again can we afford to live with the narrow, provincial "outside agitator" idea. Anyone who lives inside the United States can never be considered an outsider anywhere within its bounds.

You deplore the demonstrations taking place in Birmingham. But your statement, I am sorry to say, fails to express a similar concern for the conditions that brought about the demonstrations. I am sure that none of you would want to rest content with the superficial kind of social analysis that deals merely with effects and does not grapple with underlying causes. It is unfortunate that demonstrations are taking place in Birmingham, but it is even more unfortunate that the city's white power structure left the Negro community with no alternative.

In any nonviolent campaign there are four basic steps: collection of the facts to determine whether injustices exist; negotiation; self-purification; and direct action. We have gone through all these steps in Birmingham. There can be no gainsaying the fact that racial injustice engulfs this community. Birmingham is probably the most thoroughly segregated city in the United States. Its ugly record of brutality is widely known. Negroes have experienced grossly unjust treatment in the courts. There have been more unsolved bombings of Negro homes and churches in Birmingham than in any other city in the nation. These are the hard, brutal facts of the case. On the basis of these conditions, Negro leaders sought to negotiate with the city fathers. But the latter consistently refused to engage in good-faith negotiation.

Then, last September, came the opportunity to talk with leaders of Birmingham's economic community. In the course of the negotiations, certain promises were made by the merchants—for example, to remove the stores' humiliating racial signs. On the basis of these promises, the Reverend Fred Shuttlesworth and the leaders of the Alabama Christian Movement for Human Rights agreed to a moratorium on all demonstrations. As the weeks and months went by, we realized that we were the victims of a broken promise. A few signs, briefly removed, returned; the others remained.

As in so many past experiences, our hopes had been blasted, and the shadow of deep disappointment settled upon us. We had no alternative except to prepare for direct action, whereby we would present our very bodies as a means of laying our case before the conscience of the local and the national community. Mindful of the difficulties involved, we decided to undertake a process of self-purification. We began a series of workshops on nonviolence, and we repeatedly asked ourselves: "Are you able to accept blows without retaliating?" "Are you able to endure the ordeal of jail?" We decided to schedule our direct-action program for the Easter season, realizing that except for Christmas, this is the main shopping period of the year. Knowing that a strong economic-withdrawal program would be the byproduct of direct action, we felt that this would be the best time to bring pressure to bear on the merchants for the needed change.

Then it occurred to us that Birmingham's mayoralty election was coming up in March, and we speedily decided to postpone action until after election day. When we discovered that the Commissioner of Public Safety, Eugene "Bull" Connor, had piled up enough votes to be in the run-off; we decided again to postpone action until the day after the run-off so that the demonstrations could not be used to cloud the issues. Like many others, we waited to see Mr. Connor defeated, and to this end we endured postponement after postponement. Having aided in this community need, we felt that our direct-action program could be delayed no longer.

You may well ask: "Why direct action? Why sit-ins, marches and so forth? Isn't negotiation a better path?" You are quite right in calling for negotiation. Indeed, this is the very purpose of direct action. Nonviolent direct action seeks to create such a crisis and foster such a tension that a community which has constantly refused to negotiate is forced to confront the issue. It seeks so to dramatize the issue that it can no longer be ignored. My citing the creation of tension as part of the work of the nonviolent-resister may sound rather shocking. But I must confess that I am not afraid of the word "tension." I have earnestly opposed violent tension, but there is a type of constructive, nonviolent tension which is necessary for growth. Just as Socrates felt that it was necessary to create a tension in the mind so that individuals could rise from the bondage of myths and half-truths to the unfettered realm of creative analysis and objective appraisal, so must we see the need for nonviolent gadflies to create the kind of tension in society that will help men rise from the dark depths of prejudice and racism to the majestic heights of understanding and brotherhood.

The purpose of our direct-action program is to create a situation so crisis-packed that it will inevitably open the door to negotiation. I therefore concur with you in your call for negotiation. Too long has our beloved Southland been bogged down in a tragic effort to live in monologue rather than dialogue.

One of the basic points in your statement is that the action that I and my associates have taken in Birmingham is untimely. Some have asked: "Why didn't you give the new city administration time to act?" The only answer that I can give to this query is that the new Birmingham administration must be prodded about as much as the outgoing one, before it will act. We are sadly mistaken if we feel that the election of Albert Boutwell as mayor will bring the millennium to Birmingham. While Mr. Boutwell is a much more gentle person than Mr. Connor, they are both segregationists, dedicated to maintenance of the status quo. I have hope that Mr. Boutwell will be reasonable enough to see the futility of massive resistance to desegregation. But he will not see this without pressure from devotees of civil rights. My friends, I must say to you that we have not made a single gain in civil rights without determined legal and nonviolent pressure. Lamentably, it is an historical fact that privileged groups seldom give up their privileges voluntarily. Individuals may see the moral light and voluntarily give up their unjust posture; but, as Reinhold Niebuhr has reminded us, groups tend to be more immoral than individuals.

We know through painful experience that freedom is never voluntarily given by the oppressor; it must be demanded by the oppressed. Frankly, I have yet to engage in a direct-action campaign that was "well timed" in the view of those who have not suffered unduly from the disease of segregation. For years now I have heard the word "Wait!" It rings in the ear of every Negro with piercing familiarity. This "Wait" has almost always meant "Never." We must come to see, with one of our distinguished jurists, that "justice too long delayed is justice denied."

We have waited for more than 340 years for our constitutional and God-given rights. The nations of Asia and Africa are moving with jetlike speed toward gaining political independence, but we still creep at horse-and-buggy pace toward gaining a cup of coffee at a lunch counter. Perhaps it is easy for those who have never felt the stinging darts of segregation to say, "Wait." But when you have seen vicious mobs lynch your mothers and fathers at will and drown your sisters and brothers at whim; when you have seen hate-filled policemen curse, kick and even kill your black brothers and sisters; when you see the vast majority of your twenty million Negro brothers smothering in an airtight cage of poverty in the midst of an affluent society; when you suddenly find your tongue twisted and your speech stammering as you seek to explain to your six-year-old daughter why she can't go to the public amusement park that has just been advertised on television, and see tears welling up in her eyes when she is told that Funtown is closed to colored children, and see ominous clouds of inferiority beginning to form in her little mental sky, and see her beginning to distort her personality by developing an unconscious bitterness toward white people; when you have to concoct an answer for a five-year-old son who is asking: "Daddy, why do white people treat colored people so mean?"; when you take a cross-country drive and find it necessary to sleep night after night in the uncomfortable corners of your automobile because no motel will accept you; when you are humiliated day in and day out by nagging signs reading "white" and "colored"; when your first name becomes "nigger," your middle name becomes "boy" (however old you are) and your last name becomes "John," and your wife and mother are never given the respected title "Mrs."; when you are harried by day and haunted by night by the fact that you are a Negro, living constantly at tiptoe stance, never quite knowing what to expect next, and are plagued with inner fears and outer resentments; when you are forever fighting a degenerating sense of "nobodiness"—then you will understand why we find it difficult to wait. There comes a time when the cup of endurance runs over, and men are no longer willing to be plunged into the abyss of despair. I hope, sirs, you can understand our legitimate and unavoidable impatience.

You express a great deal of anxiety over our willingness to break laws. This is certainly a legitimate concern. Since we so diligently urge people to obey the Supreme Court's decision of 1954 outlawing segregation in the public schools, at first glance it may seem rather paradoxical for us consciously to break laws. One may well ask: "How can you advocate breaking some laws and obeying others?" The answer lies in the fact that there are two types of laws: just and unjust. I would be the first to advocate obeying just laws. One has not only a legal but a moral responsibility to obey just laws. Conversely, one has a moral responsibility to disobey unjust laws. I would agree with St. Augustine that "an unjust law is no law at all."

Now, what is the difference between the two? How does one determine whether a law is just or unjust? A just law is a man-made code that squares with the moral law or the law of God. An unjust law is a code that is out of harmony with the moral law. To put it in the terms of St. Thomas Aquinas: An unjust law is a human law that is not rooted in eternal law and natural law. Any law that uplifts human personality is just. Any law that degrades human personality is unjust. All segregation statutes are unjust because segregation distorts the soul and damages the personality. It gives the segregator a false sense of superiority and the segregated a false sense of inferiority. Segregation, to use the terminology of the Jewish philosopher Martin Buber, substitutes an "I-it" relationship for an "I-thou" relationship and ends up relegating persons to the status of things. Hence segregation is not only politically, economically and sociologically unsound, it is morally wrong and sinful. Paul Tillich has said that sin is separation. Is not segregation an existential expression of man's tragic separation, his awful estrangement, his terrible sinfulness? Thus it is that I can urge men to obey the 1954 decision of the Supreme Court, for it is morally right; and I can urge them to disobey segregation ordinances, for they are morally wrong.

Let us consider a more concrete example of just and unjust laws. An unjust law is a code that a numerical or power majority group compels a minority group to obey but does not make binding on itself. This is *difference* made legal. By the same token, a just law is a code that a majority compels a minority to follow and that it is willing to follow itself. This is *sameness* made legal.

Let me give another explanation. A law is unjust if it is inflicted on a minority that, as a result of being denied the right to vote, had no part in enacting or devising the law. Who can say that the legislature of Alabama which set up that state's segregation laws was democratically elected? Throughout Alabama all sorts of devious methods are used to prevent Negroes from becoming registered voters, and there are some counties in which, even though Negroes constitute a majority of the population, not a single Negro is registered. Can any law enacted under such circumstances be considered democratically structured?

Sometimes a law is just on its face and unjust in its application. For instance, I have been arrested on a charge of parading without a permit. Now, there is nothing wrong in having an ordinance which requires a permit for a parade. But such an ordinance becomes unjust when it is used to maintain segregation and to deny citizens the First-Amendment privilege of peaceful assembly and protest.

I hope you are able to see the distinction I am trying to point out. In no sense do I advocate evading or defying the law, as would the rabid segregationist. That would lead to anarchy. One who breaks an unjust law must do so openly, lovingly, and with a willingness to accept the penalty. I submit that an individual who breaks a law that conscience tells him is unjust, and who willingly accepts the penalty of imprisonment in order to arouse the conscience of the community over its injustice, is in reality expressing the highest respect for law.

Of course, there is nothing new about this kind of civil disobedience. It was evidenced sublimely in the refusal of Shadrach, Meshach and Abednego to obey the laws of Nebuchadnezzar, on the ground that a higher moral law was at stake. It was practiced superbly by the early Christians, who were willing to face hungry lions and the excruciating pain of chopping blocks rather than submit to certain unjust laws of the Roman Empire. To a degree, academic freedom is a reality today because Socrates practiced civil disobedience. In our own nation, the Boston Tea Party represented a massive act of civil disobedience.

We should never forget that everything Adolf Hitler did in Germany was "legal" and everything the Hungarian freedom fighters did in Hungary was "illegal." It was "illegal" to aid and comfort a Jew in Hitler's Germany. Even so, I am sure that, had I lived in Germany at the time, I would have aided and comforted my Jewish brothers. If today I lived in a Communist country where certain principles dear to the Christian faith are suppressed, I would openly advocate disobeying that country's antireligious laws.

I must make two honest confessions to you, my Christian and Jewish brothers. First, I must confess that over the past few years I have been gravely disappointed with the white moderate. I have almost reached the regrettable conclusion that the Negro's great stumbling block in his stride toward freedom is not the White Citizen's Counciler or the Ku Klux Klanner, but the white moderate, who is more devoted to "order" than to justice; who prefers a negative peace which is the absence of tension to a positive peace which is the presence of justice; who constantly says: "I agree with you in the goal you seek, but I cannot agree with your methods of direct action"; who paternalistically believes he can set the timetable for another man's freedom; who lives by a mythical concept of time and who constantly advises the Negro to wait for a "more convenient season." Shallow understanding from people of good will is more frustrating than absolute misunderstanding from people of ill will. Lukewarm acceptance is much more bewildering than outright rejection.

I had hoped that the white moderate would understand that law and order exist for the purpose of establishing justice and that when they fail in this purpose they become the dangerously structured dams that block the flow of social progress. I had hoped that the white moderate would understand that the present tension in the South is a necessary phase of the transition from an obnoxious negative peace, in which the Negro passively accepted his unjust plight, to a substantive and positive peace, in which all men will respect the dignity and worth of human personality. Actually, we who engage in nonviolent direct action are not the creators of tension. We merely bring to the surface the hidden tension that is already alive. We bring it out in the open, where it can be seen and dealt with. Like a boil that can never be cured so long as it is covered up but must be opened with all its ugliness to the natural medicines of air and light, injustice must be exposed, with all the tension its exposure creates, to the light of human conscience and the air of national opinion before it can be cured.

In your statement you assert that our actions, even though peaceful, must be condemned because they precipitate violence. But is this a logical assertion? Isn't this like condemning a robbed man because his possession of money precipitated the evil act of robbery? Isn't this like condemning Socrates because his unswerving commitment to truth and his philosophical inquiries precipitated the act by the misguided populace in which they made him drink hemlock? Isn't this like condemning Jesus because his unique God-consciousness and never-ceasing devotion to God's will precipitated the evil act of crucifixion? We must come to see that, as the federal courts have consistently affirmed, it is wrong to urge an individual to cease his efforts to gain his basic constitutional rights because the quest may precipitate violence. Society must protect the robbed and punish the robber.

I had also hoped that the white moderate would reject the myth concerning time in relation to the struggle for freedom. I have just received a letter from a white brother in Texas. He writes: "All Christians know that the colored people will receive equal rights eventually, but it is possible that you are in too great a religious hurry. It has taken Christianity almost two thousand years to accomplish what it has. The teachings of Christ take time to come to earth." Such an attitude stems from a tragic misconception of time, from the strangely irrational notion that there is something in the very flow of time that will inevitably cure all ills. Actually, time itself is neutral; it can be used either destructively or constructively. More and more I feel that the people of ill will have used time much more effectively than have the people of good will. We will have to repent in this generation not merely for the hateful words and actions of the bad people but for the appalling silence of the good people. Human progress never rolls in on wheels of inevitability; it comes through the tireless efforts of men willing to be co-workers with God, and without this hard work, time itself becomes an ally of the forces of social stagnation. We must use time creatively, in the knowledge that the time is always ripe to do right. Now is the time to make real the promise of democracy and transform our pending national elegy into a creative psalm of brotherhood. Now is the time to lift our national policy from the quicksand of racial injustice to the solid rock of human dignity.

You speak of our activity in Birmingham as extreme. At first I was rather disappointed that fellow clergymen would see my nonviolent efforts as those of an extremist. I began thinking about the fact that I stand in the middle of two opposing forces in the Negro community. One is a force of complacency, made up in part of Negroes who, as a result of long years of oppression, are so drained of self-respect and a sense of "somebodiness" that they have adjusted to segregation; and in part of a few middle-class Negroes who, because of a degree of academic and economic security and because in some ways they profit by segregation, have become insensitive to the problems of the masses. The other force is one of bitterness and hatred, and it comes perilously close to advocating violence. It is expressed in the various black nationalist groups that are springing up across the nation, the largest and best-known being Elijah Muhammad's Muslim movement. Nourished by the Negro's frustration over the continued existence of racial discrimination, this movement is made up of people who have lost faith in America, who have absolutely repudiated Christianity, and who have concluded that the white man is an incorrigible "devil."

I have tried to stand between these two forces, saying that we need emulate neither the "do-nothingism" of the complacent nor the hatred and despair of the black nationalist. For there is the more excellent way of love and nonviolent protest. I am grateful to God that, through the influence of the Negro church, the way of nonviolence became an integral part of our struggle.

If this philosophy had not emerged, by now many streets of the South would, I am convinced, be flowing with blood. And I am further convinced that if our white brothers dismiss as "rabble-rousers" and "outside agitators" those of us who employ nonviolent direct action, and if they refuse to support our nonviolent efforts, millions of Negroes will, out of frustration and despair, seek solace and security in black-nationalist ideologies—a development that would inevitably lead to a frightening racial nightmare.

Oppressed people cannot remain oppressed forever. The yearning for freedom eventually manifests itself, and that is what has happened to the American Negro. Something within has reminded him of his birthright of freedom, and something without has reminded him that it can be gained. Consciously or unconsciously, he has been caught up by the *Zeitgeist,* * and with his black brothers of Africa and his brown and yellow brothers of Asia, South America and the Caribbean, the United States Negro is moving with a sense of great urgency toward the promised land of racial justice. If one recognizes this vital urge that has engulfed the Negro community, one should readily understand why public demonstrations are taking place. The Negro has many pent-up resentments and latent frustrations, and he must release them. So let him march; let him make prayer pilgrimages to the city hall; let him go on freedom rides—and try to understand why he must do so. If his repressed emotions are not released in nonviolent ways, they will seek expression through violence; this is not a threat but a fact of history. So I have not said to my people: "Get rid of your discontent." Rather, I have tried to say that this normal and healthy discontent can be channeled into the creative outlet of nonviolent direct action. And now this approach is being termed extremist.

But though I was initially disappointed at being categorized as an extremist, as I continued to think about the matter I gradually gained a measure of satisfaction from the label. Was not Jesus an extremist for love: "Love your enemies, bless them that curse you, do good to them that hate you, and pray for them which despitefully use you, and persecute you." Was not Amos an extremist for justice: "Let justice roll down like waters and righteousness like an ever-flowing stream." Was not Paul an

* *Zeitgeist*—spirit of the times—Eds.

extremist for the Christian gospel: "I bear in my body the marks of the Lord Jesus." Was not Martin Luther an extremist: "Here I stand; I cannot do otherwise, so help me God." And John Bunyan: "I will stay in jail to the end of my days before I make a butchery of my conscience." And Abraham Lincoln: "This nation cannot survive half slave and half free." And Thomas Jefferson: "We hold these truths to be self-evident, that all men are created equal . . ." So the question is not whether we will be extremists but what kind of extremists we will be. Will we be extremists for hate or for love? Will we be extremists for the preservation of injustice or for the extension of justice? In that dramatic scene on Calvary's hill three men were crucified. We must never forget that all three were crucified for the same crime—the crime of extremism. Two were extremists for immorality, and thus fell below their environment. The other Jesus Christ, was an extremist for love, truth and goodness, and thereby rose above his environment. Perhaps the South, the nation and the world are in dire need of creative extremists.

I had hoped that the white moderate would see this need. Perhaps I was too optimistic; perhaps I expected too much. I suppose I should have realized that few members of the oppressor race can understand the deep groans and passionate yearnings of the oppressed race, and still fewer have the vision to see that injustice must be rooted out by strong, persistent and determined action. I am thankful, however, that some of our white brothers in the South have grasped the meaning of this social revolution and committed themselves to it. They are still all too few in quantity, but they are big in quality. Some—such as Ralph McGill, Lillian Smith, Harry Golden, James McBride Dabbs, Ann Braden and Sarah Patton Boyle—have written about our struggle in eloquent and prophetic terms. Others have marched with us down nameless streets of the South. They have languished in filthy, roach-infested jails, suffering the abuse and brutality of policemen who view them as "dirty nigger-lovers." Unlike so many of their moderate brothers and sisters, they have recognized the urgency of the moment and sensed the need for powerful "action" antidotes to combat the disease of segregation.

Let me take note of my other major disappointment. I have been so greatly disappointed with the white church and its leadership. Of course, there are some notable exceptions. I am not unmindful of the fact that each of you has taken some significant stands on this issue. I commend you, Reverend Stallings, for your Christian stand on this past Sunday, in welcoming Negroes to your worship service on a nonsegregated basis. I commend the Catholic leaders of this state for integrating Spring Hill College several years ago.

But despite these notable exceptions, I must honestly reiterate that I have been disappointed with the Church. I do not say this as one of those negative critics who can always find something wrong with the church. I say this as a minister of the gospel, who loves the church; who was nurtured in its bosom; who has been sustained by its spiritual blessings and who will remain true to it as long as the cord of life shall lengthen.

When I was suddenly catapulted into the leadership of the bus protest in Montgomery, Alabama, a few years ago, I felt we would be supported by the white church. I felt that the white ministers, priests and rabbis of the South would be among our strongest allies. Instead, some have been outright opponents, refusing to understand the freedom movement and misrepresenting its leaders; all too many others have been more cautious than courageous and have remained silent behind the anesthetizing security of stained-glass windows.

In spite of my shattered dreams, I came to Birmingham with the hope that the white religious leadership of this community would see the justice of our cause and, with deep moral concern, would serve as the channel through which our just grievances could reach the power structure. I had hoped that each of you would understand. But again I have been disappointed.

I have heard numerous southern religious leaders admonish their worshippers to comply with a desegregation decision because it is the law, but I have longed to hear white ministers declare: "Follow this decree because integration is morally right and because the Negro is your brother." In the midst of blatant injustices inflicted upon the Negro, I have watched white churchmen stand on the sideline and mouth pious irrelevancies and sanctimonious trivialities. In the midst of a mighty struggle to rid our nation of racial and economic injustice, I have heard many ministers say: "Those are social issues, with which the gospel has no real concern." And I have watched many churches commit themselves to a completely other-worldly religion which makes a strange, un-Biblical distinction between body and soul, between the sacred and the secular.

I have traveled the length and breadth of Alabama, Mississippi and all the other southern states. On sweltering summer days and crisp autumn mornings I have looked at the South's beautiful churches with their lofty spires pointing heavenward. I have beheld the impressive outlines of her massive religious-education buildings. Over and over I have found myself saying: "What kind of people worship here? Who is their God? Where were their voices when the lips of Governor Barnett dripped with words of interposition and nullification? Where were they when Governor Wallace gave a clarion call for defiance and hatred? Where were their voices of support when bruised and weary Negro men and women decided to rise from the dungeons of complacency to the bright hills of creative protest?"

Yes, these questions are still in my mind. In deep disappointment I have wept over the laxity of the church. But be assured that my tears have been tears of love. There can be no deep disappointment where there is not deep love. Yes, I love the church. How could I do otherwise? I am in the rather unique position of being the son, the grandson and the great-grandson of preachers. Yes, I see the church as the body of Christ. But, oh! How we have blemished and scarred that body through social neglect and through fear of being nonconformists.

There was a time when the church was very powerful—in the time when the early Christians rejoiced at being deemed worthy to suffer for what they believed. In those days the church was not merely a thermometer that recorded the ideas and principles of popular opinion; it was a thermostat that transformed the mores of society. Whenever the early Christians enterd a town, the people in power became disturbed and immediately sought to convict the Christians for being "disturbers of the peace" and "outside agitators." But the Christians pressed on, in the conviction that they were "a colony of heaven," called to obey God rather than man. Small in number, they were big in commitment. They were too God-intoxicated to be "astronomically intimidated." By their effort and example they brought an end to such ancient evils as infanticide and gladiatorial contests.

Things are different now. So often the contemporary church is a weak, ineffectual voice with an uncertain sound. So often it is an archdefender of the status quo. Far from being disturbed by the presence of the church, the power structure of the average community is consoled by the church's silent—and often even vocal—sanction of things as they are.

But the judgment of God is upon the church as never before. If today's church does not recapture the sacrificial spirit of the early church, it will lose its authenticity, forfeit the loyalty of millions, and be dismissed as an irrelevant social club with no meaning for the twentieth century. Every day I meet young people whose disappointment with the church has turned into outright disgust.

Perhaps I have once again been too optimistic. Is organized religion too inextricably bound to the status quo to save our nation and the world? Perhaps I must turn my faith to the inner spiritual church, the church within the church, as the true *ekklesia** and the hope of the world. But again I am thankful to God that some noble souls from the ranks of organized religion have broken loose from the paralyzing chains of conformity and joined us as active partners in the struggle for freedom. They have left their secure congregations and walked the streets of Albany, Georgia, with us. They have gone down the highways of the South on tortuous rides for freedom. Yes, they have gone to jail with us. Some have been dismissed from their churches, have lost the support of their bishops and fellow ministers. But they have acted in the faith that right defeated is stronger than evil triumphant. Their witness has been the spiritual salt that has preserved the true meaning of the gospel in these troubled times. They have carved a tunnel of hope through the dark mountain of disappointment.

I hope the church as a whole will meet the challenge of this decisive hour. But even if the church does not come to the aid of justice, I have no despair about the future. I have no fear about the outcome of our struggle in Birmingham, even if our motives are at present misunderstood. We will reach the goal of freedom in Birmingham and all over the nation, because the goal of America is freedom. Abused and scorned though we may be, our destiny is tied up with America's destiny. Before the pilgrims landed at Plymouth, we were here. Before the pen of Jefferson etched the majestic words of the Declaration of Independence across the pages of history, we were here. For more than two centuries our forebears labored in this country without wages; they made cotton king; they built the homes of their masters while suffering gross injustice and shameful humiliation—and yet out of bottomless vitality they continued to thrive and develop. If the inexpressible cruelties of slavery could not stop us, the opposition we now face will surely fail. We will win our freedom because the sacred heritage of our nation and the eternal will of God are embodied in our echoing demands.

Before closing I feel impelled to mention one other point in your statement that

* *ekklesia*—Greek word for the early church. (By extension, the original spirit of Christianity.)—Eds.

has troubled me profoundly. You warmly commended the Birmingham police force for keeping "order" and "preventing violence." I doubt that you would have so warmly commended the police force if you had seen its dogs sinking their teeth into unarmed, nonviolent Negroes. I doubt that you would so quickly commend the policemen if you were to observe their ugly and inhumane treatment of Negroes here in the city jail; if you were to watch them push and curse old Negro women and young Negro girls; if you were to see them slap and kick old Negro men and young boys; if you were to observe them, as they did on two occasions, refuse to give us food because we wanted to sing our grace together. I cannot join you in your praise of the Birmingham police department.

It is true that the police have exercised a degree of discipline in handling the demonstrators. In this sense they have conducted themselves rather "nonviolently" in public. But for what purpose? To preserve the evil system of segregation. Over the past few years I have consistently preached that nonviolence demands that the means we use must be as pure as the ends we seek. I have tried to make clear that it is wrong to use immoral means to attain moral ends. But now I must affirm that it is just as wrong, or perhaps even more so, to use moral means to preserve immoral ends. Perhaps Mr. Connor and his policemen have been rather nonviolent in public, as was Chief Pritchett in Albany, Georgia, but they have used the moral means of nonviolence to maintain the immoral end of racial injustice. As T. S. Eliot has said: "The last temptation is the greatest treason: To do the right deed for the wrong reason."

I wish you had commended the Negro sit-inners and demonstrators of Birmingham for their sublime courage, their willingness to suffer and their amazing discipline in the midst of great provocation. One day the South will recognize its real heroes. They will be the James Merediths, with the noble sense of purpose that enables them to face jeering and hostile mobs, and with the agonizing loneliness that characterizes the life of the pioneer. They will be old, oppressed, battered Negro women, symbolized in a seventy-two-year-old woman in Montgomery, Alabama, who rose up with a sense of dignity and with her people decided not to ride segregated buses, and who responded with ungrammatical profundity to one who inquired about her weariness: "My feets is tired, but my soul is at rest." They will be the young high school and college students, the young ministers of the gospel and a host of their elders, courageously and nonviolently sitting in at lunch counters and willingly going to jail for conscience' sake. One day the South will know that when these disinherited children of God sat down at lunch counters, they were in reality standing up for what is best in the American dream and for the most sacred values in our Judaeo-Christian heritage, thereby bringing our nation back to those great wells of democracy which were dug deep by the founding fathers in their formulation of the Constitution and the Declaration of Independence.

Never before have I written so long a letter. I'm afraid it is much too long to take your precious time. I can assure you that it would have been much shorter if I had been writing from a comfortable desk, but what else can one do when he is alone in a narrow jail cell, other than write long letters, think long thoughts and pray long prayers?

If I have said anything in this letter that overstates the truth and indicates an unreasonable impatience, I beg you to forgive me. If I have said anything that understates the truth and indicates my having a patience that allows me to settle for anything less than brotherhood, I beg God to forgive me.

I hope this letter finds you strong in the faith. I also hope that circumstances will soon make it possible for me to meet each of you, not as an integrationist or a civil-rights leader but as a fellow clergyman and a Christian brother. Let us all hope that the dark clouds of racial prejudice will soon pass away and the deep fog of misunderstanding will be lifted from our fear-drenched communities, and in some not too distant tomorrow the radiant stars of love and brotherhood will shine over our great nation with all their scintillating beauty.

Yours for the cause of Peace and Brotherhood,

*Martin Luther King, Jr.*

## *Maya Angelou*
## "MAMA AND THE DENTIST"

The angel of the candy counter had found me out at last, and was exacting excruciating penance for all the stolen Milky Ways, Mounds, Mr. Goodbars and Hersheys with Almonds. I had two cavities that were rotten to the gums. The pain was beyond the bailiwick of crushed aspirins or oil of cloves. Only one thing could help me, so I prayed earnestly that I'd be allowed to sit under the house and have the building collapse on my left jaw. Since there was no Negro dentist in Stamps, nor doctor either, for that matter, Momma had dealt with previous toothaches by pulling them out (a string tied to the tooth with the other end looped over her fist), pain killers and prayer. In this particular instance the medicine had proved ineffective; there wasn't enough enamel left to hook a string on, and the prayers were being ignored because the Balancing Angel was blocking their passage.

I lived a few days and nights in blinding pain, not so much toying with as seriously considering the idea of jumping in the well, and Momma decided I had to be taken to a dentist. The nearest Negro dentist was in Texarkana, twenty-five miles away, and I was certain that I'd be dead long before we reached half the distance. Momma said we'd go to Dr. Lincoln, right in Stamps, and he'd take care of me. She said he owed her a favor.

I knew that there were a number of whitefolks in town that owed her favors. Bailey and I had seen the books which showed how she had lent money to Blacks and whites alike during the Depression, and most still owed her. But I couldn't aptly remember seeing Dr. Lincoln's name, nor had I ever heard of a Negro's going to him as a patient. However, Momma said we were going, and put water on the stove for our baths. I had never been to a doctor, so she told me that after the bath (which would make my mouth feel better) I had to put on freshly starched and ironed underclothes from inside out. The ache failed to respond to the bath, and I knew then that the pain was more serious than that which anyone had ever suffered.

Before we left the Store, she ordered me to brush my teeth and then wash my mouth with Listerine. The idea of even opening my clamped jaws increased the pain, but upon her explanation that when you go to a doctor you have to clean yourself all over, but most especially the part that's to be examined, I screwed up my courage and unlocked my teeth. The cool air in my mouth and the jarring of my molars dislodged what little remained of my reason. I had frozen to the pain, my family nearly had to tie me down to take the toothbrush away. It was no small effort to get me started on the road to the dentist. Momma spoke to all the passers-by, but didn't stop to chat. She explained over her shoulder that we were going to the doctor and she'd "pass the time of day" on our way home.

Until we reached the pond the pain was my world, an aura that haloed me for three feet around. Crossing the bridge into whitefolks' country, pieces of sanity pushed themselves forward. I had to stop moaning and start walking straight. The white towel, which was drawn under my chin and tied over my head, had to be arranged. If one was dying, it had to be done in style if the dying took place in whitefolk's part of town.

On the other side of the bridge the ache seemed to lessen as if a whitebreeze blew off the whitefolks and cushioned everything in their neighborhood—including my jaw. The gravel road was smoother, the stones smaller and the tree branches hung down around the path and nearly covered us. If the pain didn't diminish then, the familiar yet strange sights hypnotized me into believing that it had.

But my head continued to throb with the measured insistence of a bass drum, and how could a toothache pass the calaboose, hear the songs of the prisoners, their blues and laughter, and not be changed? How could one or two or even a mouthful of angry tooth roots meet a wagonload of powhitetrash children, endure their idiotic snobbery and not feel less important?

Behind the building which housed the dentist's office ran a small path used by servants and those tradespeople who catered to the butcher and Stamps' one restaurant. Momma and I followed that lane to the backstairs of Dentist Lincoln's office. The sun was bright and gave the day a hard reality as we climbed up the steps to the second floor.

Momma knocked on the back door and a young white girl opened it to show surprise at seeing us there. Momma said she wanted to see Dentist Lincoln and to tell him Annie was there. The girl closed the door firmly. Now the humiliation of hearing Momma describe herself as if she had no last name to the young white girl was equal to the physical pain. It seemed terribly unfair to have a toothache and a headache and have to bear at the same time the heavy burden of Blackness.

It was always possible that the teeth would quiet down and maybe drop out of their own accord. Momma said we would wait. We leaned in the harsh sunlight on the shaky railings of the dentist's back porch for over an hour.

He opened the door and looked at Momma. "Well, Annie, what can I do for you?"

He didn't see the towel around my jaw or notice my swollen face.

Momma said, "Dentist Lincoln. It's my grandbaby here. She got two rotten teeth that's giving her a fit."

She waited for him to acknowledge the truth of her statement. He made no comment, orally or facially.

"She had this toothache purt' near four days now, and today I said, 'Young lady, you going to the Dentist.'"

"Annie?"

"Yes, sir, Dentist Lincoln."

He was choosing words the way people hunt for shells. "Annie, you know I don't treat nigra, colored people."

"I know, Dentist Lincoln. But this here is just my little grandbaby, and she ain't gone be no trouble to you . . ."

"Annie, everybody has a policy. In this world you have to have a policy. Now, my policy is I don't treat colored people."

The sun had baked the oil out of Momma's skin and melted the Vaseline in her hair. She shone greasily as she leaned out of the dentist's shadow.

"Seem like to me, Dentist Lincoln, you might look after her, she ain't nothing but a little mite. And seems like maybe you owe me a favor or two."

He reddened slightly. "Favor or no favor. The money has all been repaid to you and that's the end of it. Sorry, Annie." He had his hand on the doorknob. "Sorry." His voice was a bit kinder on the second "Sorry," as if he really was.

Momma said, "I wouldn't press on you like this for myself but I can't take No. Not for my grandbaby. When you come to borrow my money you didn't have to beg. You asked me, and I lent it. Now, it wasn't my policy. I ain't no moneylender, but you stood to lose this building and I tried to help you out."

"It's been paid, and raising your voice won't make me change my mind. My policy . . ." He let go of the door and stepped nearer Momma. The three of us were crowded on the small landing. "Annie, my policy is I'd rather stick my hand in a dog's mouth than in a nigger's."

He had never once looked at me. He turned his back and went through the door into the cool beyond. Momma backed up inside herself for a few minutes. I forgot everything except her face which was almost a new one to me. She leaned over and took the doorknob, and in her everyday soft voice she said, "Sister, go on downstairs. Wait for me. I'll be there directly."

Under the most common of circumstances I knew it did no good to argue with Momma. So I walked down the steep stairs, afraid to look back and afraid not to do so. I turned as the door slammed, and she was gone.

*Momma walked in that room as if she owned it. She shoved that silly nurse aside with one hand and strode into the dentist's office. He was sitting in his chair, sharpening his mean instruments and putting extra sting into his medicines. Her eyes were blazing like live coals and her arms had doubled themselves in length. He looked up at her just before she caught him by the collar of his white jacket.*

*"Stand up when you see a lady, you contemptuous scoundrel." Her tongue had thinned out and the words rolled off well enunciated. Enunciated and sharp like little claps of thunder.*

*The dentist had no choice but to stand at R. O. T. C. attention. His head dropped after a minute and his voice was humble. "Yes, ma'am, Mrs. Henderson."*

*"You knave, do you think you acted like a gentleman, speaking to me like that in front of my*

*granddaughter?" She didn't shake him, although she had the power. She simply held him upright.*

*"No, ma'am, Mrs. Henderson."*

*"No, ma'am, Mrs. Henderson, what?" Then she did give him the tiniest of shakes, but because of her strength the action set his head and arms to shaking loose on the ends of his body. He stuttered much worse than Uncle Willie. "No, ma'am. Mrs. Henderson, I'm sorry."*

*With just an edge of her disgust showing, Momma slung him back in his dentist's chair. "Sorry is as sorry does, and you're about the sorriest dentist I ever laid my eyes on." (She could afford to slip into the vernacular because she had such eloquent command of English.)*

*"I didn't ask you to apologize in front of Marguerite, because I don't want her to know my power, but I order you, now and herewith. Leave Stamps by sundown."*

*"Mrs. Henderson, I can't get my equipment. . ." He was shaking terribly now.*

*"Now, that brings me to my second order. You will never again practice dentistry. Never! When you get settled in your next place, you will be a vegetarian caring for dogs with the mange, cats with the cholera and cows with the epizootic. Is that clear?"*

*The saliva ran down his chin and his eyes filled with tears. "Yes, ma'am. Thank you for not killing me. Thank you, Mrs. Henderson."*

*Momma pulled herself back from being ten feet tall with eight-foot arms and said, "You're welcome for nothing, you varlet, I wouldn't waste a killing on the likes of you."*

*On her way out she waved her handkerchief at the nurse and turned her into a crocus sack of chicken feed.*

Momma looked tired when she came down the stairs, but who wouldn't be tired if they had gone through what she had. She came close to me and adjusted the towel under my jaw (I had forgotten the toothache; I only knew that she made her hands gentle in order not to awaken the pain). She took my hand. Her voice never changed. "Come on, Sister."

I reckoned we were going home where she would concoct a brew to eliminate the pain and maybe give me new teeth too. New teeth that would grow overnight out of my gums. She led me toward the drugstore, which was in the opposite direction from the Store. "I'm taking you to Dentist Baker in Texarkana."

I was glad after all that I had bathed and put on Mum and Cashmere Bouquet talcum powder. It was a wonderful surprise. My toothache had quieted to solemn pain, Momma had obliterated the evil white man, and we were going on a trip to Texarkana, just the two of us.

On the Greyhound she took an inside seat in the back, and I sat beside her. I was so proud of being her granddaughter and sure that some of her magic must have come down to me. She asked if I was scared. I only shook my head and leaned over on her cool brown upper arm. There was no chance that a dentist, especially a Negro dentist, would dare hurt me then. Not with Momma there. The trip was uneventful, except that she put her arm around me, which was very unusual for Momma to do.

The dentist showed me the medicine and the needle before he deadened my gums, but if he hadn't I wouldn't have worried. Momma stood right behind him. Her arms were folded and she checked on everything he did. The teeth were extracted and she bought me an ice cream cone from the side window of a drug counter. The trip back to Stamps was quiet, except that I had to spit into a very small empty snuff can which she had gotten for me and it was difficult with the bus humping and jerking on our country roads.

At home, I was given a warm salt solution, and when I washed out my mouth I showed Bailey the empty holes, where the clotted blood sat like filling in a pie crust. He said I was quite brave, and that was my cue to reveal our confrontation with the peckerwood dentist and Momma's incredible powers.

I had to admit that I didn't hear the conversation, but what else could she have said than what I said she said? What else done? He agreed with my analysis in a lukewarm way, and I happily (after all, I'd been sick) flounced into the Store. Momma was preparing our evening meal and Uncle Willie leaned on the door sill. She gave her version.

"Dentist Lincoln got right uppity. Said he'd rather put his hand in a dog's mouth. And when I reminded him of the favor, he brushed it off like a piece of lint. Well, I sent Sister downstairs and went inside. I hadn't never been in his office before, but I found the door to where he takes out teeth, and him and the nurse was in there thick as thieves. I just stood there till he caught sight of me." Crash bang the pots on the stove. "He jumped just like he was sitting on a pin. He said, 'Annie, I done tole you, I ain't gonna mess around in no niggah's mouth.' I said, 'Somebody's got to do it then,' and he said, 'Take her to Texarkana to the colored dentist' and that's when I said, 'If you paid me my money I could afford to take her.' He said, 'It's all been paid.' I tole him everything but the interest had been paid. He said, 'Twasn't no interest.' I said, 'Tis now. I'll take ten dollars as payment in full.' You know, Willie, it wasn't no right thing to do, 'cause I lent that money without thinking about it."

"He tole that little snippity nurse of his'n to give me ten dollars and make me sign a 'paid in full' receipt. She gave it to me and I signed the papers. Even though by rights he was paid up before, I figger, he gonna be that kind of nasty, he gonna have to pay for it."

Momma and her son laughed and laughed over the white man's evilness and her retributive sin.

I preferred, much preferred, my version.

## SUGGESTIONS FOR DISCUSSION

1. One of King's main concerns is a definition of a "just law." How does he define the term? Why is this definition central to his argument? Do you think this is an adequate definition?
2. At one point Maya Angelou asks herself if it is possible to "meet a wagonload of powhitetrash children, endure their idiotic snobbery and not feel less important." How would you answer this question? Is it possible to maintain one's self-respect without having the respect of others?
3. The writers of both pieces do more than present the difficulties of their time and place; they offer, inevitably, strategies for handling those difficulties, ways of dealing with racism. What are those strategies? How are they different? Remember that King is writing as an adult, and as the leader of a nonviolent movement, while

Angelou is writing as an adult looking back through her own childhood eyes. How different are their purposes in writing? Which of the characters in Angelou's story would most likely meet with King's approval?

## SUGGESTIONS FOR WRITING

1. Martin Luther King is attacking a serious form of injustice, but all of us, in some ways, are aware of lesser kinds of injustice in our society. Choose an ethical issue on which you hold the minority opinion. You might consider subjects such as draft registration, the fraternity/sorority system, drinking laws, or graduation requirements.
   **a.** Identify specifically the "hostile audience"—that group with whom you disagree.
   **b.** Write a letter to that group defending your point of view. Be sure to argue logically and to include specific examples.
2. Whether by choice or by chance, all of us belong to groups that are stereotyped. Think about stereotyped groups you are part of, select one, and then write a persuasive essay showing that the generalizations often made about the group don't apply to you. You can probably begin the essay with a brief description of the stereotype; make sure you highlight the qualities that you can use yourself to refute. The rest of your argument would then demonstrate how, for the two or three qualities you highlighted, you are an exception that invalidates the rule and breaks the stereotype.

# 16

# Prescribed Roles

*Brigid Brophy*
"WOMEN: INVISIBLE CAGES"

*D. Keith Mano*
"CRUEL LIB"

Complementing King and Angelou's discussions of society's attitudes toward race, the essays by Brigid Brophy and D. Keith Mano examine society's view of gender and its prescribed roles. Brophy analyzes the subtle forces, the cages without bars, that keep individuals confined to traditional spheres. She argues that society should "set both sexes free to make a free choice." Mano reacts to libertarian views such as Brophy's with a plea to recognize the essential mediocrity of most people. He concludes that conventional roles protect individuals and that, for most people, so-called liberation only leads to confusion and unhappiness.

## *Brigid Brophy*
## "WOMEN: INVISIBLE CAGES"

All right, nobody's disputing it. Women are free. At least, they *look* free. They even feel free. But in reality women in the western, industrialised world today are like the animals in a modern zoo. There are no bars. It appears that cages have been abolished. Yet in practice women are still kept in their place just as firmly as the animals are kept in their enclosures. The barriers which keep them in now are invisible.

It is about forty years since the pioneer feminists, several of whom were men, raised such a rumpus by rattling the cage bars—or created such a conspicuous nuisance by chaining themselves to them—that society was at last obliged to pay attention. The result was that the bars were uprooted, the cage thrown open: whereupon the majority of the women who had been held captive decided they would rather stay inside anyway.

To be more precise, they *thought* they decided; and society, which can with perfect truth point out "Look, no bars," *thought* it was giving them the choice. There are no laws and very little discrimination to prevent western, industrialised women from voting, being voted for or entering the professions. If there are still comparatively few women lawyers and engineers, let alone women presidents of the United States, what are women to conclude except that this is the result either of their own free choice or of something inherent in female nature?

Many of them do draw just this conclusion. They have come back to the old argument of the anti-feminists, many of whom were women, that women are unfit by nature for life outside the cage. And in letting this old wheel come full cycle women have fallen victim to one of the most insidious and ingenious confidence tricks ever perpetrated.

In point of fact, neither female nature nor women's individual free choice has been put to the test. As American Negroes have discovered, to be officially free is by no means the same as being actually and psychologically free. A society as adept as ours has become at propaganda—whether political or commercial—should know that "persuasion," which means the art of launching myths and artificially inducing inhibitions, is every bit as effective as force of law. No doubt the reason society eventually agreed to abolish its anti-women laws was that it had become confident of commanding a battery of hidden dissuaders which would do the job just as well. Cage bars are clumsy methods of control, which excite the more rebellious personalities inside to rattle them. Modern society, like the modern zoo, has contrived to get rid of the bars without altering the fact of imprisonment. All the zoo architect needs to do is run a zone of hot or cold air, whichever the animal concerned cannot tolerate, round the cage where the bars used to be. Human animals are not less sensitive to social climate.

The ingenious point about the new-model zoo is that it deceives both sides of the invisible barrier. Not only can the animal not see how it is imprisoned; the visitor's conscience is relieved of the unkindness of keeping animals shut up. He can say "Look, no bars round the animals," just as society can say "Look, no laws restricting women" even while it keeps women rigidly in place by zones of fierce social pressure.

There is, however, one great difference. A woman, being a thinking animal, may actually be more distressed because the bars of her cage cannot be seen. What relieves society's conscience may afflict hers. Unable to perceive what is holding her back, she may accuse herself and her whole sex of craven timidity because women have not jumped at what has the appearance of an offer of freedom. Evidently quite a lot of women have succumbed to guilt of this sort, since in recent years quite an industry has arisen to assuage it. Comforting voices make the air as thick and reassuring as cotton wool while they explain that there is nothing shameful in not wanting a career, that to be intellectually unadventurous is no sin, that taking care of home and family may be personally "fulfilling" and socially valuable.

This is an argument without a flaw: except that it is addressed exclusively to women. Address it to both sexes and instantly it becomes progressive and humane. As it stands, it is merely antiwoman prejudice revamped.

That many women would be happier not pursuing careers or intellectual adventures is only part of the truth. The whole truth is that many *people* would be. If society had the clear sight to assure men as well as women that there is no shame in preferring to stay non-competitively and non-aggressively at home, many masculine neuroses and ulcers would be avoided, and many children would enjoy the benefit of being brought up by a father with a talent for the job instead of by a mother with no talent for it but a sense of guilt about the lack.

But society does nothing so sensible. Blindly it goes on insisting on the tradition that men are the ones who go out to work and adventure—an arrangement which simply throws talent away. All the home-making talent which happens to be born inside male bodies is wasted; and our businesses and governments are staffed quite largely by people whose aptitude for the work consists solely of their being what is, by tradition, the right sex for it.

The pressures society exerts to drive men out of the house are very nearly as irrational and unjust as those by which it keeps women in. The mistake of the early reformers was to assume that men were emancipated already and that therefore reform need ask only for the emancipation of women. What we ought to do now is go right back to scratch and demand the emancipation of both sexes. It is only because men are not free themselves that they have found it necessary to cheat women by the deception which makes them appear free when they are not.

The zones of hot and cold air which society uses to perpetuate its uneconomic and unreasonable state of affairs are the simplest and most effective conceivable. Society is playing on our sexual vanity. Just as the sexual regions are the most vulnerable part of the body, sexuality is the most vulnerable part of the Ego. Tell a man that he is not a real man, or a woman that she is not one hundred per cent woman and you are threatening both with not being attractive to the opposite sex. No one can bear not to be attractive to the opposite sex. That is the climate which the human animal cannot tolerate.

So society has us all at its mercy. It has only to murmur to the man that staying at home is a feminine characteristic, and he will be out of the house like a bullet. It has only to suggest to the woman that logic and reason are the province of the masculine mind, whereas "intuition" and "feeling" are the female *forte,* and she will throw her physics textbooks out of the window, barricade herself into the house and give herself up to having wishy-washy poetical feelings while she arranges the flowers.

She will, incidentally, take care that her feelings *are* wishy-washy. She has been persuaded that to have cogent feelings, of the kind which really do go into great poems (most of which are by men), would make her an unfeminine woman, a woman who imitates men. In point of fact, she would not be imitating men as such, most of whom have never written a line of great poetry, but poets, most of whom so far happen to be men. But the bad logic passes muster with her because part of the mythology she has swallowed ingeniously informs her that logic is not her *forte.*

Should a woman's talent or intelligence be so irrepressible that she insists on producing cogent works of art or watertight meshes of argument, she will be said to have "a mind like a man's." This is simply current idiom; translated, it means "a good mind." The use of the idiom contributes to an apparently watertight proof that all good minds are masculine, since whenever they occur in women they are described as "like a man's."

What is more, this habit of thought actually contributes to perpetuating a state of affairs where most good minds really do belong to men. It is difficult for a woman to *want* to be intelligent when she has been told that to be so will make her like a man. She inclines to think an intelligence would be as unbecoming to her as a moustache; and many women have tried in furtive privacy to disembarrass themselves of intellect as though it were facial hair.

Discouraged from growing "a mind like a man's," women are encouraged to have thoughts and feelings of a specifically feminine tone. For society is cunning enough not to place its whole reliance on threatening women with blasts of icy air. It also flatters them with a zone of hot air. The most deceptive and cynical of its blandishments is the notion that women have some specifically feminine contribution to make to culture. Unfortunately, as culture had already been shaped and largely built up by men before the invitation was issued, this leaves women little to do. Culture consists of reasoned thought and works of art composed of cogent feeling and imagination. There is only one way to be reasonable, and that is to reason correctly; and the only kind of art which is any good is good art. If women are to eschew reason and artistic imagination in favour of "intuition" and "feeling," it is pretty clear what is meant. "Intuition" is just a polite name for bad reasoning, and "feeling" for bad art.

In reality, the whole idea of a specifically feminine—or, for the matter of that, masculine—contribution to culture is a contradiction of culture. A contribution to culture is not something which could not have been made by the other sex—it is something which could not have been made by any other *person*. Equally, the notion that anyone, of either sex, can create good art out of simple feeling, untempered by discipline, is a philistine one. The arts are a sphere where women seem to have done well; but really they have done *too* well—too well for the good of the arts. Instead of women sharing the esteem which ought to belong to artists, art is becoming smeared with femininity. We are approaching a philistine state of affairs where the arts are something which it is nice for women to take up in their spare time—men having slammed out of the house to get on with society's "serious" business, like making money, administering the country and running the professions.

In that "serious" sphere it is still rare to encounter a woman. A man sentenced to prison would probably feel his punishment was redoubled by indignity if he were to be sentenced by a woman judge under a law drafted by a woman legislator—and if, on admission, he were to be examined by a woman prison doctor. If such a thing happened every day, it would be no indignity but the natural course of events. It has never been given the chance to become the natural course of events and never will be so long as women remain persuaded it would be unnatural of them to want it.

So brilliantly has society contrived to terrorise women with this threat that certain behaviour is unnatural and unwomanly that it has left them no time to consider—or even sheerly observe—what womanly nature really is. For centuries arrant superstitions were accepted as natural law. The physiological fact that only women can secrete milk for feeding babies was extended into the pure myth that it was women's business to cook for and wait on the entire family. The kitchen became woman's "natural" place because, for the first few months of her baby's life, the nursery really was. To this day a woman may suspect that she is unfeminine if she can discover in herself no aptitude or liking for cooking. Fright has thrown her into such a muddle that she confuses having no taste for cookery with having no breasts, and conversely assumes that nature has endowed the human female with a special handiness with frying pans.

Even psycho-analysis, which in general has been the greatest benefactor of civilisation since the wheel, has unwittingly reinforced the terrorisation campaign. The trouble was that it brought with it from its origin in medical therapy a criterion of normality instead of rationality. On sheer statistics every pioneer, genius and social reformer, including the first woman who demanded to be let out of the kitchen and into the polling booth, is abnormal, along with every lunatic and eccentric. What distinguishes the genius from the lunatic is that the genius's abnormality is justifiable by reason or aesthetics. If a woman who is irked by confinement to the kitchen merely looks round to see what other women are doing and finds they are accepting their kitchens, she may well conclude that she is abnormal and had better enlist her psycho-analyst's help towards "living with" her kitchen. What she ought to ask is whether it is rational for women to be kept to the kitchen, and whether nature really does insist on that in the way it insists women have breasts. And in a far-reaching sense to ask that question is much more normal and natural than learning to "live with" the handicap of women's inferior social status. The normal and natural thing for human beings is not to tolerate handicaps but to reform society and to circumvent or supplement nature. We don't learn to live minus a leg; we devise an artificial limb.

That, indeed, is the crux of the matter. Not only are the distinctions we draw between male nature and female nature largely arbitrary and often pure superstition: they are completely beside the point. They ignore the essence of *human* nature. The important question is not whether women are or are not less logical by nature than men, but whether education, effort and the abolition of our illogical social pressures can improve on nature and make them (and, incidentally, men as well) *more* logical. What distinguishes human from any other animal nature is its ability to be unnatural. Logic and art are not natural or instinctive activities; but our nature includes a propensity to acquire them. It is not natural for the human body to orbit the earth; but the human mind has a natural adventurousness which enables it to invent machines whereby the body can do so. There is, in sober fact, no such creature as a natural man. Go as far back as they will, the archaeologists cannot come on a wild man in his natural habitat. At his most primitive, he has already constructed himself an artificial habitat, and decorated it not by a standardised instinctual method, as birds build nests, but by individualised—that is, abnormal—works of art or magic. And in doing so he is not limited by the fingers nature gave him; he has extended their versatility by making tools.

Civilisation consists not necessarily in defying nature but in making it possible for us to do so if we judge it desirable. The higher we can lift our noses from the grindstone of nature, the wider the area we have of choice; and the more choices we have freely made, the more individualised we are. We are at our most civilised when nature does not dictate to us, as it does to animals and peasants, but when we can opt to fall in with it or better it. If modern civilisation has invented methods of education which make it possible for men to feed babies and for women to think logically, we are betraying civilisation itself if we do not set both sexes free to make a free choice.

## WRITE BETWEEN READINGS

1. You have just read Brigid Brophy's "Women: Invisible Cages," a rather theoretical article making the argument that "women in the western, industrialized world today are . . . kept in their place just as firmly as the animals are kept in their enclosures." It is a good argument, and you might want to reread it to see just how it works. For this writing assignment what is most important is that you understand the level on which it works; that is, it operates in the realm of ideas, of abstractions, not in the realm of particulars or concrete things. She doesn't write about any one *woman,* but about *women.* Your object is to do the same thing, to write on an abstract plane as effectively as she does. It might help if you pick a topic similar to hers, one that deals with the differences between appearance and reality. (Consider, for example: "American schools offer free, public education. Perhaps it is public, but is it free and educational?")

# *D. Keith Mano*
# "CRUEL LIB"

Let's call him Fred. I met Fred during his junior year at college. All Fred wanted was love and a rewarding sexual relationship—is that not an inalienable right by now? Fred was purposelessly big, overweight. His arm flesh hung down, white as a brandy Alexander, full of stretch marks. His face, in contrast, was bluish: acne scars that might have been haphazard tattooing. A nice guy, intelligent enough, but the coeds were put off. Fred wooed them at mixers with his face half-averted, as if it were an illicit act.

Fred was without sexual prejudice: as they say, he could go both ways. There was a militant gay-lib branch on campus. For months, struck out at mixers, he had considered joining. It was a painful decision: if he came out of the closet, Fred knew, his mother and father would probably go in—hidden there for shame. Yet mimeo sheets from gay lib offered a tacit, thrilling promise: new life, freedom. I remember the day Fred told me he had come out: he was relieved, optimistic. But being gay and free didn't cosmetize his face. When Fred let it all hang out, it just dangled there. After a while he noticed the good-looking gays dated the good-looking gays, as a first-string quarterback goes out with a home-coming queen. Fred had caused his family anguish for small compensation: he was now a wallflower in both sexes. Liberation. The tacit promise had been empty, and it had cracked his fragile spirit. Three months later Fred committed suicide.

Let's call her Gwen. The usual: $40,000 bilevel house, three kids, married to a good provider. Her unwed sister-in-law, however, ran the local women's-lib cell. Gwen's sister-in-law made fun of the drudgery: dishes; that unending double-play combo, hamper to washer to dryer; the vacuum she used and the one she lived in. It seemed so *uncreative.* Creativity, you know, is another inalienable American right. Gwen was 34 and, good grief, only a housewife. There were wonderful, though unspecified, resources inside her. After some time, marriage, in Gwen's mind, became a kind of moth closet.

Ms. Gwen is divorced now. Mr. Gwen still loves her; he has taken the children. Gwen enrolled in a community college, but she didn't do well. Term papers were drudgery. For some time she made lopsided ashtrays at a Wednesday-night ceramics class. She was free and bored to death with herself. Now Gwen drinks a lot; she has some talent in that direction. Her children, well. . . all three understand, of course, that they were exploiting Gwen for twelve and nine and seven years respectively.

It's an unattractive human truth, but every now and then someone should put it on record: most people—Christians used to acknowledge this fact without embarrassment—most people are not particularly talented or beautiful or charismatic. Set free to discover "the true self," very often they find nothing there at all. Men and women who determine "to do their own thing" commonly learn that they have little of note to do. Yet these people are harassed, shamed by the Zeitgeist* and its glib armies into disparaging their conventional roles. The bubble-gum tune goes like this: American civilization, through some spiteful, stupid conspiracy, means to thwart self-expression. We are all frustrated painters, explorers, starlets, senators. But there are times when it's more healthful to be frustrated than to have one's mediocrity confirmed in the light of common day.

Roles don't limit people; roles protect them. And, yes, most people need protection: deserve it. Not so long ago our society honored the husband and the wife, the mother and the father. These were titles that carried merit enough to justify a full human life. Remember the phrase? "It's like attacking motherhood." Times have changed. On the lecture circuit today, you can pull down a nice income plus expenses attacking motherhood.

Yet probably the cruelest of libs is education lib. Ed lib hasn't been formally incorporated, but it's very well sustained by an immense bureaucracy of teachers, professors, administrators, foundations, Federal agencies. Strike a match and you learn inside the pad how John earned respect from his bowling team as a correspondence-school computer executive. And on the crosstown bus they tell you DON'T PREPARE FOR TOMORROW WITH YESTERDAY'S SKILLS (picture of a wheelbarrow). Or, A MIND IS A TERRIBLE THING TO WASTE. Sure. But what about a pair of hands, damn it? Even at fifteen bucks per hour, we humiliate our labor force in a programmatic way. The elitism of it all is pernicious and disgusting.

Some few centuries ago another kind of lib prevailed. Christianity, they called it. Christian lib isn't a "now" item; it comes due in another life. Prerequisites are faith, works, humility: children are raised, things are made, to God's glory. Christians

* Zeitgeist—spirit of the times.—Eds.

know personal gratification for what it is: a brummagem trinket. And this has been the shrewd beauty of Communism. Lenin cribbed his tactics from the New Testament. Liberation is promised through an arduous class struggle—but not in anyone's lifetime. This lib movement, moreover, functions within a powerfully structured, oppressive social system. Not only do totalitarian governments curtail personal liberty, but they are downright prissy when it comes to permissive sex. Yet people, in general, accept. Their roles are clear, and those roles are esteemed.

In this country, circa 1975, lib has become a growth industry. Many who are otherwise talentless have made it their profession. But what Ralph Nader will hold them accountable for the Freds and the Gwens, for those who have been dispirited by a society that no longer prized sexual restraint or menial labor or the nuclear family? We have, I hold it self-evident, an inalienable right to be unliberated. This nation—another unattractive truth—doesn't need more personal freedom. The human spirit can be an unruly beast; a little restraint is wholesome. Let people be cherished for what they are, not for ambiguous thwarted gifts, or for the social responsibilities they default on. The men and women of Middle America have earned that small consideration. Really "creative" people will surface anyway. They usually do. And they will have their great rewards.

## SUGGESTIONS FOR DISCUSSION

1. Brophy and Mano make an interesting pair. Brophy, writing in 1963 about the Women's Movement, is arguing that people are trapped by forces they really cannot see, "invisible barriers." Mano, writing twelve years later, argues against what he sees as the indiscriminate destruction of what he might call constructive barriers, people's roles. And so, at first glance, they seem to be opposed. But are they? Precisely what is Brophy's argument? Mano's? How would Brophy explain Fred or Gwen's tragedies?
2. Both Mano and Brophy write with persuasive purposes. Aristotle distinguished three kinds of appeals in persuasion: the logical appeal, based on reason; the ethical appeal, based on an audience's perception of the speaker (for which we'll substitute writer); and the "pathetic" appeal, based on the emotions of the audience. Which of the three does Brophy rely on most? Mano? Can you find examples of other kinds of appeals in both essays?
3. Sometimes the opening lines of an essay, especially those in the popular press, can be crucial. Along with the title, they go a long way toward establishing our expectations about the author's *persona*. (Try flipping back through this collection looking at openings like Alda's, Parker's, Mencken's, and so on.) Reread the two openings here. What are Brophy and Mano trying to do? (Note: Many writers—novice and experienced—report that the most difficult part of writing for them is coming up with that first line or two; once they have that, they say, the rest seems to "flow." Are these lines equally important for readers? Can an essay recover from a weak opening?)
4. At one point Mano asserts: "It's an unattractive human truth, . . . most people are not particularly talented or beautiful or charismatic." How do his assumptions about human beings differ from those of Mill? From those of Brophy?

## SUGGESTIONS FOR WRITING

1. If you have written the assignment given between these two essays, you will have tried writing an essay like Brophy's, one that operates at a fairly high level of abstraction, that presents sound arguments without ever working from specific, individual cases. Now that you have read Mano, though, you can see that there is another way to argue: you can begin with specifics—in this case, almost case studies—and then move to the more general level. Using the same topic you used for your Brophy analogue, write an argument constructed more like Mano's. What are the differences between the two? Which was easier?

# 17

# Self-Assertion

*Manuel J. Smith*

"ASSERTIVE RIGHTS"

*Margaret Halsey*

"WHAT'S WRONG WITH 'ME, ME, ME' "

In recent times the subject of self-assertion has become a much-discussed topic, at times even superseding the more classic concerns relating to individual freedom. Supporters of self-assertion, such as Manuel J. Smith, regard traditional politeness as harmful to individual development. In his popular list of "Assertive Rights," he gives readers a precise bill of rights to protect their identity, along with an explanation of the dangers of placing the needs of others higher than the needs of the self. Margaret Halsey responds to such ideas with skepticism and claims that they produce self-centeredness. She gently ridicules the notion that individual identity can be established without social responsibility and contends that there is more virtue in self-forgetfulness than in assertive individuality.

## *Manuel J. Smith*
## "ASSERTIVE RIGHTS"

**ASSERTIVE RIGHT I: YOU HAVE THE RIGHT TO OFFER NO REASON OR EXCUSES TO JUSTIFY YOUR BEHAVIOR.**

. . . The right not to give reasons for what you do is derived from your prime assertive right to be the ultimate judge of all you are and do. If you are your own ultimate judge, you do not need to explain your behavior to someone else for them to decide if it is right, wrong, correct, incorrect, or whatever tag they want to use. Of course, other people always have the assertive option to tell you they do not like what you are doing. You then have the option to disregard their preferences, or work out a compromise, or respect their preferences and change your behavior completely. But if you are your own ultimate judge, other people do not have the right to manipulate your behavior and feelings by demanding reasons from you in order to convince you that you are wrong. The childish belief that underlies this type of manipulation goes something like this: *You should explain your reasons for your behavior to other people since you are responsible to them for your actions. You should justify your actions to them.* An everyday use of this manipulative belief is seen, for example, when a salesclerk asks a customer who is returning a pair of shoes: "Why don't you like these shoes?" (Unspoken: it seems unusual for someone not to like these shoes.) With this question the salesclerk is making a judgment for the customer that she should have a reason for not liking the shoes that is satisfactory to him. If the customer lets the salesclerk decide that there must be some reason for not liking the shoes, she will feel ignorant. Feeling ignorant, the customer will likely feel compelled to explain why she doesn't like the shoes. If she does give reasons, she allows the salesclerk to give her equally valid reasons why she should like them. Depending upon who can think up the most reasons, she or the salesclerk, she will probably finish by keeping a pair of shoes she doesn't like, as the following manipulative dialogue points out:

SALESCLERK: Why don't you like these shoes?

CUSTOMER: They're the wrong shade of magenta.

SALESCLERK: Nonsense, dear! This is just the color you need to match your toenail polish!

CUSTOMER: But they are too loose and the heel straps keep falling down.

SALESCLERK: We can fix that by putting in arch pads. They are only $3.95.

CUSTOMER: But they are too tight in the instep.

SALESCLERK: Simple to fix! I'll take them in the back right now and stretch them a little.

If the customer makes her own decision on whether or not she requires an answer to the "why" question, she is more likely to respond simply by stating the facts of the situation: "No reason, I just don't like the shoes."

People whom I teach to be assertive, invariably ask, "How can I refuse to give reasons to a friend when he asks for them? He won't like that." My answer is a series of provocative questions in reply: "How come your friend is requiring you to give reasons to explain your behavior?" "Is that a condition of his friendship, that you allow him to make decisions about the appropriateness of your behavior?" "If you don't give him a reason for not lending him your car, is that all that is required to end your friendship?" "How valuable is such a fragile friendship?" If some of your friends refuse to acknowledge your assertive right to halt manipulation by being your own judge, perhaps these friends are incapable of dealing with you on any other basis but manipulation. Your choice in friends, like anything else, is entirely up to you.

## ASSERTIVE RIGHT II: YOU HAVE THE RIGHT TO JUDGE WHETHER YOU ARE RESPONSIBLE FOR FINDING SOLUTIONS TO OTHER PEOPLE'S PROBLEMS.

Each of us is ultimately responsible for our own psychological well-being, happiness, and success in life. As much as we might wish good things for one another, we really do not have the ability to create mental stability, well-being, or happiness for someone else.

You have the ability to please someone temporarily by doing what he or she wants, but that person has to go through all the work, sweat, pain, and fear of failure to arrange his own life in a way that makes him healthy and happy. In spite of your compassion for the troubles of others, the reality of the human condition is that each of us must come to terms with the problems of living by learning to cope on our own. This reality is expressed in one of the first principles of modern psychotherapy. Practitioners of this healing art have learned that the process of therapy does not solve problems for the patient, but helps the patient gain the ability to solve his own problems. Any of us can help temporarily by giving advice or counsel, but the person with the problem has the responsibility to solve it himself. Your own actions may even have been directly or indirectly the cause for their problems. Nevertheless, other people have the ultimate responsibility to solve their own problems, no matter who or what the cause may be. If you do not recognize your assertive right to choose to be responsible only for yourself, other people can and will manipulate you into doing what they want by presenting their own problems to you as if they were your problems. The childish belief underlying this type of manipulation goes something like this: *You have an obligation to things and institutions greater than yourself which groups of other people have set up to conduct the business of living. You should sacrifice your own values to keep these systems from falling apart. If these systems do not always work effectively, you should bend or change, not the system. If any problems occur in dealing with the system, they are your problems and not the responsibility of the system.* Examples of manipulative behavior produced by this childish belief abound in our common dealings with people. You may see wives or husbands manipulate each other by saying: "If you don't stop irritating me, we are going to have to get a divorce." Statements like this induce guilty feelings by implying that the marriage contract and relationship are more important than the individual desires and happiness of either partner. If their mates also have this childish belief, they have the option (1) to do what they want individually and feel guilty for placing their own wants above the marriage relationship, or (2) to do what their spouses want and be frustrated, angry, aggressively cause more friction, or get depressed and withdrawn. If the marriage partner threatened with divorce nonassertively responds with a defensive posture that divorce is not a possible alternative solution to their problems, he or she may be manipulated into doing what the spouse wants, as pointed out in the following dialogue:

MATE ONE: If you don't stop irritating me with all your excuses for not doing anything around here, we might as well get a divorce!

MATE TWO: (in frustrated anger) Don't be silly. You don't really want a divorce!

MATE ONE: I do! Don't you care about our marriage and what I'll have to go through being single again?

MATE TWO: (feeling guilty) Of course I care! What kind of person do you think I am? I do a lot of things for us!

MATE ONE: You only do things that *you* care about. Why are you so stubborn? If you really cared about our marriage, you would try to make things a bit easier for me! I do all these things and what do you do?

If, on the other hand, the spouse threatened with the prospect of divorce assertively makes his or her own judgment on where the problem and responsibility for solving it lies (on the spouse threatened with divorce or on the marriage relationship), he or she is likely to reply: "If you truly feel that you can't cope with the way I am, perhaps you're right. If we can't work it out, maybe we should consider a divorce."

In commercial dealings you can see other everyday examples of people manipulatively trying to get you to place the well-being of ineffective systems of doing things above your own well-being. Salesclerks may often try to get a determined customer (you) to stop complaining about defective merchandise by saying: "You are holding up the line. All these other people want to be served too." In making this statement, the clerk is manipulatively inducing guilt in you by implying that you have some responsibility to see that the store is able to serve other people without making them wait. The judgment made by the salesclerk *for you* is that if the store's system of processing complaints does not work well in processing your complaint, the responsibility for solving the problem lies with you and not with the store. But if you were to make your own decision on where the responsibility lies, you would simply state the facts of the situation; for example: "That's true, I am holding up the line. I suggest you satisfy my complaint quickly or they will have to wait even longer."

When you try to get adequate repairs on defective merchandise, or a refund, you will often observe salesclerks and managers saying things like: "Your problem is not with us. You have a problem with the manufacturer (or the body shop, or the factory, or the main office, or the importer, or the shipping line, or the insurance company, etc.). The manufacturer won't give us a refund for defective merchandise, so we can't give you one." This type of statement is a manipulative evasion of responsibility. If you allow the clerk or manager to make the decision for you that you must provide a solution to the store's problem of staying in business and not losing money on defective merchandise, you are forced into the ludicrous position of: (1) ceasing to press your claim of value for money paid; (2) accepting the childish notion that you should not cause problems for the employees or the company; and (3) having the frustration of not knowing how to get what you want without causing problems for others. If, on the other hand, you make your own decisions on whether or not you need to be responsible for finding a solution to the store's problems with the manufacturer, you can assertively reply: "I am not interested in your problems with the manufacturer (or the radiator shop, etc.). I am only interested in getting acceptable repairs (or a refund for defective merchandise)."

My favorite summary of the concept of defining your own responsibility for the problems of others was given in a joke, current several years ago. After being surrounded by 10,000 hostile Indians, the Lone Ranger turned to Tonto and remarked, "I guess this is it, Kimo Sabe. It looks like we have had it," whereupon Tonto, surveying the impending disaster, turned and replied, "What do you mean *we, white man?*"

## *Margaret Halsey*
## "WHAT'S WRONG WITH 'ME, ME, ME' "

Tom Wolfe has christened today's young adults the "me" generation, and the 1970s—obsessed with things like consciousness expansion and self-awareness—have been described as the decade of the new narcissism. The cult of "I," in fact, has taken hold with the strength and impetus of a new religion. But the joker in the pack is that it is all based on a false idea.

The false idea is that inside every human being, however unprepossessing, there is a glorious, talented and overwhelmingly attractive personality. This personality—so runs the erroneous belief—will be revealed in all its splendor if the individual just forgets about courtesy, cooperativeness and consideration for others and proceeds to do exactly what he or she feels like doing.

Nonsense.

Inside each of us is a mess of unruly primitive impulses, and these can sometimes, under the strenuous self-discipline and dedication of art, result in notable creativity. But there is no such thing as a pure, crystalline and well-organized "native" personality, though a host of trendy human-potential groups trade on the mistaken assumption that there is. And backing up the human-potential industry is the advertising profession, which also encourages the idea of an Inner Wonderfulness that will be unveiled to a suddenly respectful world upon the purchase of this or that commodity.

However, an individual does not exist in a vacuum. A human being is not an isolated, independent thing-in-itself, but inevitably reflects the existence of others. The young adults of the "me" generation would never have lived to grow up if a great many parents, doctors, nurses, farmers, factory workers, teachers, policemen, firemen and legions of others had not ignored their human potential and made themselves do jobs they did not perhaps feel like doing in order to support the health and growth of children.

And yet, despite the indulgence of uninhibited expression, the "self" in self-awareness seems to cause many new narcissists and members of the "me" generation a lot of trouble. This trouble emerges in talk about "identity." We hear about the search for identity and a kind of distress called an identity crisis.

"I don't know who I am." How many bartenders and psychiatrists have stifled yawns on hearing that popular threnody for the thousandth time!

But this sentence has no meaning unless spoken by an amnesia victim, because many of the people who say they do not know who they are, actually *do* know. What such people really mean is that they are not satisfied with who they are. They feel themselves to be timid and colorless or to be in some way or other fault-ridden, but they have soaked up enough advertising and enough catch-penny ideas of self-improvement to believe in universal Inner Wonderfulness. So they turn their backs on their honest knowledge of themselves—which with patience and courage could start them on the road to genuine development—and embark on a quest for a will-o'-the-wisp called "identity."

But a *search* for identity is predestined to fail. Identity is not found, the way Pharaoh's daughter found Moses in the bulrushes. Identity is built. It is built every day and every minute throughout the day. The myraid choices, small and large, that human beings make all the time determine identity. The fatal weakness of the currently fashionable approach to personality is that the "self" of the self-awareness addicts, the self of Inner Wonderfulness, is static. Being perfect, it does not need to change. But genuine identity changes as one matures. If it does not, if the 40-year-old has an identity that was set in concrete at the age of 18, he or she is in trouble. The idea of a universal Inner Wonderfulness that will be apparent to all beholders after a six-week course in self-expression is fantasy.

But how did this fantasy gain wide popular acceptance as a realizable fact?

Every society tries to produce a prevalent psychological type that will best serve its ends, and that type is always prone to certain emotional malfunctions. In early capitalism, which was a producing society, the ideal type was acquisitive, fanatically devoted to hard work and fiercely repressive of sex. The emotional malfunctions to which this type was liable were hysteria and obsession. Later capitalism, today's capitalism, is a consuming society, and the psychological type it strives to create, in order to build up the largest possible markets, is shallow, easily swayed and characterized much more by self-infatuation than self-respect. The emotional malfunction of this type is narcissism.

It will be argued that the cult of "I" has done some individuals a lot of good. But at whose expense? What about the people to whom these "healthy" egotists are rude or even abusive? What about the people over whom they ride roughshod? What about the people they manipulate and exploit? And—the most important question of all—how good a preparation for inevitable old age and death is a deliberately cultivated self-love? The psychologists say that the full-blown classic narcissists lose all dignity and go mad with fright as they approach their final dissolution. Ten or fifteen years from now—when the young adults of the "me" generation hit middle age—will be the time to ask whether "self-awareness" really does people any good.

A long time ago, in a book called "Civilization and Its Discontents," Freud pointed out that there is an unresolvable conflict between the human being's selfish, primitive, infantile impulses and the restraint he or she must impose on those impulses if a stable society is to be maintained. The "self" is not a handsome god or goddess waiting coyly to be revealed. On the contrary, its complexity, confusion and mystery have proved so difficult that throughout the ages men and women have talked gratefully about *losing* themselves. They *lose* the self in contemplating a great work of art, or in nature, or in scientific research, or in writing poetry, or in fashioning things with their hands or in projects that will benefit others rather than themselves.

The current glorification of self-love will turn out in the end to be a no-win proposition, because in questions of personality or "identity," what counts is not who you are, but what you do. "By their fruits, ye shall know them." And by their fruits, they shall know themselves.

## SUGGESTIONS FOR DISCUSSION

1. As is often the case, this pair of readings seems to represent opposing viewpoints. Smith seems to encourage people to "look out for Number One," while Halsey denigrates the "Me, Me, Me" generation. But read closely. What would Smith say about Halsey's assertion that "Identity is built"? How would Halsey react to Smith's saying that we ought to be our own ultimate judges, that we don't need to explain our behavior to anyone to find out how they will label it? Does Smith's assertiveness turn out to be the same thing as what Halsey labels "self-love?"
2. Halsey writes that the statement "I don't know who I am" has "no meaning unless spoken by an amnesia victim." Why does she find this statement so offensive? What would Smith say about it?
3. Halsey argues that inside each of us is "a mess of unruly, primitive impulses," not "Inner Wonderfulness." What is the effect of her shift from rather objective language ("primitive impulses") to emotive diction ("Inner Wonderfulness")?
4. In the Appendix to this collection there is an essay by Walker Gibson called "Hearing Voices: Tough Talk, Sweet Talk, Stuffy Talk." According to this essay, which category does Manuel Smith belong to? Margaret Halsey? Can you identify the features of their writing that make them candidates for the category you have chosen?

## SUGGESTIONS FOR WRITING

1. Assertive Right I states, "You have the right to offer no reasons or excuses to justify your behavior." Write two dialogues modeled after the one Smith writes in his first paragraph. In one, show a situation that would seem to warrant Smith's approach. In the second, show a situation where such an approach is not justified.
2. We don't often expect our writing to change the way people behave, to change what they really do. More often—as the readings in this book demonstrate—we want to change what people think or believe, sometimes in the hope that such internal changes will lead to changes in behavior. Manuel Smith, though, has written a self-improvement book. It tells us how to change our beliefs *and* how to act accordingly. It probably isn't as easy as it may seem. Pick a situation in which you know your fellow college students could stand some behavioral reform: standing in lines at the cafeteria; pacing their studying; taking what you consider to be unwarranted abuse from faculty or administration. Come up with an assessment of the rules involved—call them rights, if the term fits—and write them out, with examples, following Smith's lead.

# *Part Five*

# SUCCESS AND FAILURE

*Success is counted sweetest*
*By those who ne'er succeed.*
—EMILY DICKINSON

Dreams of fame, wealth, and happiness are probably universal, but the American preoccupation with success is especially intense. Our emphasis on productivity and achievement contributes to an atmosphere in which ambition receives a high degree of respect. This is not to say that ambition in any form is considered acceptable. Americans have always viewed the hustler and the "workaholic" with suspicion, especially when their goals seemed to be entirely materialistic. Furthermore, there have been periods in history, such as the time of the Watergate scandals, when mistrust of ambition became widespread. On the whole, however, Americans enthusiastically endorse the pursuit of success. Joseph Epstein has said that "the real question posed by ambition is whether or not each of us has a true hand in shaping his own destiny." Long regarded by other nations as the most optimistic (or most naive) of people, Americans seem to persist in the belief that people can shape their own destinies. These essays examine some of the rewards and pitfalls of different kinds of ambition.

This part is divided into three categories. In the first category the writers present both skeptical and affirmative attitudes toward success. In the next category, the essayists examine specific goals, such as wealth, fame, and self-fulfillment. They disagree about either the wisdom or the method of pursuing these goals. Finally, Loren Eiseley and Virginia Woolf discuss some common barriers to success, and Eiseley, especially, questions the value of winning in the traditional way.

Concepts of success vary as much as attitudes toward ambition. Some see it as a massive accumulation of wealth, while others see it as a spiritual journey toward simplicity and quietness. Some associate it with freedom, while others associate it with commitment. Some sacrifice everything for it, some willingly give it up, and some refuse to pursue it at all. Most people want some kind of success; however, some individuals claim that it is, in certain situations, better to fail.

# 18

# Ambition: A Skeptical View

*Ecclesiastes*

## (CHAPTERS 1-3), THE KING JAMES VERSION AND THE LIVING BIBLE TRANSLATION

*Suzanne Britt Jordan*

## "THAT LEAN AND HUNGRY LOOK"

The Old Testament book of Ecclesiastes expresses the most famous and most skeptical view of ambition. The world-weary writer of this piece presents a majestic and despairing account of his disenchantment, observing that the distribution of earthly rewards has nothing to do with actual merit. Suzanne Britt Jordan is also suspicious of human ambition, but not because of the arbitrary results. In "That Lean and Hungry Look," a whimsical comparison of achievers and nonachievers, she demonstrates that the unambitious are warmer people and better companions.

### WRITE BEFORE READING

1. All the essays in this part, including these first two, deal directly or indirectly with success: what it is, who attains it, what it costs. You almost certainly have your own opinions about what constitutes success, even if you've never thought very consciously about them. Imagine yourself, then, in a career-planning seminar. Your assignment for the first meeting is to *define* success. You can do it in any way that makes you comfortable: describe people you think are successful and say why you think so; outline your own dreams and tell why you've chosen those over others; or even give an abstract, more theoretical definition, one that could cover any number of particular paths to success. Your purpose is partly expressive and partly persuasive; you will be sharing this essay with your seminar colleagues, all of whom will have their own ideas of what success is.

# *Ecclesiastes*
# (CHAPTERS 1-3)

## THE KING JAMES VERSION

660 CHAPTER 1

THE words of the Preacher, the son of David, king in Jerusalem.

2 Vanity of vanities, saith the Preacher, vanity of vanities; all *is* vanity.

3 What profit hath a man of all his labour which he taketh under the sun?

4 *One* generation passeth away, and *another* generation cometh: but the earth abideth for ever.

5 The sun also ariseth, and the sun goeth down, and hasteth to his place where he arose.

6 The wind goeth toward the south, and turneth about unto the north; it whirleth about continually, and the wind returneth again according to his circuits.

7 All the rivers run into the sea; yet the sea *is* not full; unto the place from whence the rivers come, thither they return again.

8 All things *are* full of labour; man cannot utter *it:* the eye is not satisfied with seeing, nor the ear filled with hearing.

9 The thing that hath been, it *is that* which shall be; and that which is done *is* that which shall be done: and *there is* no new *thing* under the sun.

10 Is there *any* thing whereof it may be said, See, this *is* new? it hath been already of old time, which was before us.

11 *There is* no remembrance of former *things;* neither shall there be *any* remembrance of *things* that are to come with *those* that shall come after.

12 ¶ I the Preacher was king over Israel in Jerusalem.

13 And I gave my heart to seek and search out by wisdom concerning all *things* that are done under heaven: this sore travail hath God given to the sons of man to be exercised therewith.

## THE LIVING BIBLE TRANSLATION

1 THE AUTHOR: SOLOMON of Jerusalem, King David's son, "The Preacher."

[2]In my opinion, nothing is worthwhile; everything is futile. [3-7]For what does a man get for all his hard work?

Generations come and go but it makes no difference. The sun rises and sets and hurries around to rise again. The wind blows south and north, here and there, twisting back and forth, getting nowhere. The rivers run into the sea but the sea is never full, and the water returns again to the rivers, and flows again to the sea... [8-11]everything is unutterably weary and tiresome. No matter how much we see, we are never satisfied; no matter how much we hear, we are not content.

History merely repeats itself. Nothing is truly new; it has all been done or said before. What can you point to that is new? How do you know it didn't exist long ages ago? We don't remember what happened in those former times, and in the future generations no one will remember what we have done back here.

[12-15]I, the Preacher, was king of Israel, living in Jerusalem. And I applied myself to search for understanding about everything in the universe. I discovered that the lot of man, which God has dealt to him, is not a happy one. It is all foolishness, chasing the wind. What is wrong cannot be righted; it is water over the dam; and there is no use thinking of what might have been.

[16-18]I said to myself, "Look, I am better educated than any of the kings before me in Jerusalem. I have greater wisdom and knowledge." So I worked hard to be wise instead of foolish—but now I realize that

14 I have seen all the works that are done under the sun; and, behold, all *is* vanity and vexation of spirit.

15 *That which is* crooked cannot be made straight: and that which is wanting cannot be numbered.

16 I communed with mine own heart, saying, Lo, I am come to great estate, and have gotten more wisdom than all *they* that have been before me in Jerusalem: yea, my heart had great experience of wisdom and knowledge.

17 And I gave my heart to know wisdom, and to know madness and folly: I perceived that this also is vexation of spirit.

18 For in much wisdom *is* much grief: and he that increaseth knowledge increaseth sorrow.

even this was like chasing the wind. For the more my wisdom, the more my grief; to increase knowledge only increases distress.

661 CHAPTER 2

I SAID in mine heart, Go to now, I will prove thee with mirth, therefore enjoy pleasure: and, behold, this also *is* vanity.

2 I said of laughter, *It is* mad: and of mirth, What doeth it?

3 I sought in mine heart to give myself unto wine, yet acquainting mine heart with wisdom; and to lay hold on folly, till I might see what *was* that good for the sons of men, which they should do under the heaven all the days of their life.

4 I made me great works; I builded me houses; I planted me vineyards:

5 I made me gardens and orchards, and I planted trees in them of all *kinds of* fruits:

6 I made me pools of water, to water therewith the wood that bringeth forth trees:

7 I got *me* servants and maidens, and had servants born in my house; also I had great possessions of great and small cattle above all that were in Jerusalem before me:

8 I gathered me also silver and gold, and the peculiar treasure of kings and of the provinces: I gat me men singers and women singers, and the delights of the sons of men, *as* musical instruments, and that of all sorts.

9 So I was great, and increased more than all that were before me in Jerusalem: also my wisdom remained with me.

2 I SAID TO myself, "Come now, be merry; enjoy yourself to the full." But I found that this, too, was futile. For it is silly to be laughing all the time; what good does it do?

[3]So, after a lot of thinking, I decided to try the road of drink, while still holding steadily to my course of seeking wisdom.

Next I changed my course again and followed the path of folly, so that I could experience the only happiness most men have throughout their lives.

[4,5,6]Then I tried to find fulfillment by inaugurating a great public works program: homes, vineyards, gardens, parks and orchards for myself, and reservoirs to hold the water to irrigate my plantations.

[7,8]Next I bought slaves, both men and women, and others were born within my household. I also bred great herds and flocks, more than any of the kings before me. I collected silver and gold as taxes from many kings and provinces.

In the cultural arts, I organized men's and women's choirs and orchestras.

And then there were my many beautiful concubines.

[9]So I became greater than any of the kings in Jerusalem before me, and with it all

10 And whatsoever mine eyes desired I kept not from them, I withheld not my heart from any joy; for my heart rejoiced in all my labour: and this was my portion of all my labour.

11 Then I looked on all the works that my hands had wrought, and on the labour that I had laboured to do: and, behold, all *was* vanity and vexation of spirit, and *there was* no profit under the sun.

12 ¶ And I turned myself to behold wisdom, and madness, and folly: for what *can* the man *do* that cometh after the king? *even* that which hath been already done.

13 Then I saw that wisdom excelleth folly, as far as light excelleth darkness.

14 The wise man's eyes *are* in his head; but the fool walketh in darkness; and I myself perceived also that one event happeneth to them all.

15 Then said I in my heart, As it happeneth to the fool, so it happeneth even to me; and why was I then more wise? Then I said in my heart, that this also *is* vanity.

16 For *there is* no remembrance of the wise more than of the fool for ever; seeing that which now *is* in the days to come shall all be forgotten. And how dieth the wise *man?* as the fool.

17 Therefore I hated life; because the work that is wrought under the sun *is* grievous unto me: for all *is* vanity and vexation of spirit.

18 ¶ Yea, I hated all my labour which I had taken under the sun: because I should leave it unto the man that shall be after me.

19 And who knoweth whether he shall be a wise *man* or a fool? yet shall he have rule over all my labour wherein I have laboured, and wherein I have shewed myself wise under the sun. This *is* also vanity.

20 Therefore I went about to cause my heart to despair of all the labour which I took under the sun.

21 For there is a man whose labour *is* in wisdom, and in knowledge, and in equity; yet to a man that hath not laboured therein shall he leave it *for* his portion. This also *is* vanity and a great evil.

I remained clear-eyed, so that I could evaluate all these things. [10]Anything I wanted, I took, and did not restrain myself from any joy. I even found great pleasure in hard work. This pleasure was, indeed, my only reward for all my labors.

[11]But as I looked at everything I had tried, it was all so useless, a chasing of the wind, and there was nothing really worthwhile anywhere. [12]Now I began a study of the comparative virtues of wisdom and folly, and anyone else would come to the same conclusion I did— [13,14]that wisdom is of more value than foolishness, just as light is better than darkness; for the wise man sees, while the fool is blind. And yet I noticed that there was one thing that happened to wise and foolish alike— [15]just as the fool will die, so will I. So of what value is all my wisdom? Then I realized that even wisdom is futile. [16]For the wise and fool both die, and in the days to come both will be long forgotten. [17]So now I hate life because it is all so irrational; all is foolishness, chasing the wind.

[18]And I am disgusted about this, that I must leave the fruits of all my hard work to others. [19]And who can tell whether my son will be a wise man or a fool? And yet all I have will be given to him—how discouraging!

[20-23]So I turned in despair from hard work as the answer to my search for satisfaction. For though I spend my life searching for wisdom, knowledge, and skill, I must leave all of it to someone who hasn't done a day's work in his life; he inherits all my efforts, free of charge. This is not only foolish, but unfair. So what does a man get for all his hard work? Days full of sorrow and grief, and restless, bitter nights. It is all utterly ridiculous.

[24-26]So I decided that there was nothing better for a man to do than to enjoy his food and drink, and his job. Then I realized that even this pleasure is from the hand of God. For who can eat or enjoy apart from him? For God gives those who please him wisdom, knowledge, and joy; but if a sinner becomes wealthy, God takes the wealth away

22 For what hath man of all his labour, and of the vexation of his heart, wherein he hath laboured under the sun?

23 For all his days *are* sorrows, and his travail grief; yea, his heart taketh not rest in the night. This is also vanity.

24 ¶*There is* nothing better for a man, *than* that he should eat and drink, and *that* he should make his soul enjoy good in his labour. This also I saw, that it *was* from the hand of God.

25 For who can eat, or who else can hasten *hereunto,* more than I?

26 For *God* giveth to a man that *is* good in his sight wisdom, and knowledge, and joy: but to the sinner he giveth travail, to gather and to heap up, that he may give to *him that is* good before God. This also *is* vanity and vexation of spirit.

from him and gives it to those who please him. So here, too, we see an example of foolishly chasing the wind.

662 CHAPTER 3

TO every *thing there is* a season, and a time to every purpose under the heaven:

2 A time to be born, and a time to die; a time to plant, and a time to pluck up *that which is* planted;

3 A time to kill, and a time to heal; a time to break down, and a time to build up;

4 A time to weep, and a time to laugh; a time to mourn, and a time to dance;

5 A time to cast away stones, and a time to gather stones together; a time to embrace, and a time to refrain from embracing;

6 A time to get, and a time to lose; a time to keep, and a time to cast away;

7 A time to rend, and a time to sew; a time to keep silence, and a time to speak;

8 A time to love, and a time to hate; a time of war, and a time of peace.

9 What profit hath he that worketh in that wherein he laboureth?

10 I have seen the travail, which God hath given to the sons of men to be exercised in it.

11 He hath made every *thing* beautiful in his time: also he hath set the world in their heart, so that no man can find out the work that God maketh from the beginning to the end.

3 THERE IS A right time for everything:
2 A time to be born, a time to die;
A time to plant;
A time to harvest;
3 A time to kill;
A time to heal;
A time to destroy;
A time to rebuild;
4 A time to cry;
A time to laugh;
A time to grieve;
A time to dance;
5 A time for scattering stones;
A time for gathering stones;
A time to hug;
A time not to hug;
6 A time to find;
A time to lose;
A time for keeping;
A time for throwing away;
7 A time to tear;
A time to repair;
A time to be quiet;
A time to speak up;
8 A time for loving;
A time for hating;
A time for war;
A time for peace.

12 I know that *there is* no good in them, but for *a man* to rejoice, and to do good in his life.

13 And also that every man should eat and drink, and enjoy the good of all his labour, it *is* the gift of God.

14 I know that, whatsoever God doeth, it shall be for ever: nothing can be put to it, nor any thing taken from it: and God doeth *it,* that *men* should fear before him.

15 That which hath been is now; and that which is to be hath already been; and God requireth that which is past.

16 ¶ And moreover I saw under the sun the place of judgment, *that* wickedness *was* there; and the place of righteousness, *that* iniquity *was* there.

17 I said in mine heart, God shall judge the righteous and the wicked: for *there is* a time there for every purpose and for every work.

18 I said in mine heart concerning the estate of the sons of men, that God might manifest them, and that they might see that they themselves are beasts.

19 For that which befalleth the sons of men befalleth beasts; even one thing befalleth them: as the one dieth, so dieth the other; yea, they have all one breath; so that a man hath no preeminence above a beast: for all *is* vanity.

20 All go unto one place; all are of the dust, and all turn to dust again.

21 Who knoweth the spirit of man that goeth upward, and the spirit of the beast that goeth downward to the earth?

22 Wherefore I perceive that *there is* nothing better, than that a man should rejoice in his own works; for that *is* his portion: for who shall bring him to see what shall be after him?

9What does one really get from hard
work? 10I have thought about this in connection with all the various kinds of work God
has given to mankind. 11Everything is appropriate in its own time. But though God
has planted eternity in the hearts of men,
even so, man cannot see the whole scope of
God's work from beginning to end. 12So I
conclude that, first, there is nothing better
for a man than to be happy and to enjoy
himself as long as he can; 13and second, that
he should eat and drink and enjoy the fruits
of his labors, for these are gifts from God.

14And I know this, that whatever God
does is final—nothing can be added or taken
from it; God's purpose in this is that man
should fear the all-powerful God.

15Whatever is, has been long ago; and
whatever is going to be has been before;
God brings to pass again what was in the
distant past and disappeared.

16Moreover, I notice that throughout
the earth justice is giving way to crime and
even the police courts are corrupt. 17I said to
myself, "In due season God will judge
everything man does, both good and bad."

18And then I realized that God is letting
the world go on its sinful way so that he can
test mankind, and so that men themselves
will see that they are no better than beasts.
19For men and animals both breathe the
same air, and both die. So mankind has no
real advantage over the beasts; what an ab-
surdity! 20All go to one place—the dust from
which they came and to which they must return. 21For who can prove that the spirit of
man goes upward and the spirit of animals
goes downward into dust? 22So I saw that
there is nothing better for men than that
they should be happy in their work, for that
is what they are here for, and no one can
bring them back to life to enjoy what will be
in the future, so let them enjoy it now.

## *Suzanne Britt Jordan*
# "THAT LEAN AND HUNGRY LOOK"

Caesar was right. Thin people need watching. I've been watching them for most of my adult life, and I don't like what I see. When these narrow fellows spring at me, I quiver to my toes. Thin people come in all personalities, most of them menacing. You've got your "together" thin person, your mechanical thin person, your condescending thin person, your tsk-tsk thin person, your efficiency-expert thin person. All of them are dangerous.

In the first place, thin people aren't fun. They don't know how to goof off, at least in the best, fat sense of the word. They've always got to be adoing. Give them a coffee break, and they'll jog around the block. Supply them with a quiet evening at home, and they'll fix the screen door and lick S&H green stamps. They say things like "there aren't enough hours in the day." Fat people never say that. Fat people think the day is too damn long already.

Thin people make me tired. They've got speedy little metabolisms that cause them to bustle briskly. They're forever rubbing their bony hands together and eying new problems to "tackle." I like to surround myself with sluggish, inert, easygoing fat people, the kind who believe that if you clean it up today, it'll just get dirty again tomorrow.

Some people say the business about the jolly fat person is a myth, that all of us chubbies are neurotic, sick, sad people. I disagree. Fat people may not be chortling all day long, but they're a hell of a lot *nicer* than the wizened and shriveled. Thin people turn surly, mean and hard at a young age because they never learn the value of a hot-fudge sundae for easing tension. Thin people don't like gooey soft things because they themselves are neither gooey nor soft. They are crunchy and dull, like carrots. They go straight to the heart of the matter while fat people let things stay all blurry and hazy and vague, the way things actually are. Thin people want to face the truth. Fat people know there is no truth. One of my thin friends is always staring at complex, unsolvable problems and saying, "The key thing is . . ." Fat people never say that. They know there isn't any such thing as the key thing about anything. Thin people believe in logic. Fat people see all sides. The sides fat people see are rounded blobs, usually gray, always nebulous and truly not worth worrying about. But the thin person persists. "If you consume more calories than you burn," says one of my thin friends, "you will gain weight. It's that simple." Fat people always grin when they hear statements like that. They know better.

Fat people realize that life is illogical and unfair. They know very well that God is not in his heaven and all is not right with the world. If God was up there, fat people could have two doughnuts and a big orange drink anytime they wanted it.

Thin people have a long list of logical things they are always spouting off to me. They hold up one finger at a time as they reel off these things, so I won't lose track. They speak slowly as if to a young child. The list is long and full of holes. It contains tidbits like "get a grip on yourself," "cigarettes kill," "cholesterol clogs," "fit as a fiddle," "ducks in a row," "organize" and "sound fiscal management." Phrases like that.

They think these 2,000-point plans lead to happiness. Fat people know happiness is elusive at best and even if they could get the kind thin people talk about, they wouldn't want it. Wisely, fat people see that such programs are too dull, too hard, too off the mark. They are never better than a whole cheesecake.

Fat people know all about the mystery of life. They are the ones acquainted with the night, with luck, with fate, with playing it by ear. One thin person I know once suggested that we arrange all the parts of a jigsaw puzzle into groups according to size, shape and color. He figured this would cut the time needed to complete the puzzle by at least 50 per cent. I said I wouldn't do it. One, I like to muddle through. Two, what good would it do to finish early? Three, the jigsaw puzzle isn't the important thing. The important thing is the fun of four people (one thin person included) sitting around a card table, working a jigsaw puzzle. My thin friend had no use for my list. Instead of joining us, he went outside and mulched the boxwoods. The three remaining fat people finished the puzzle and made chocolate, double-fudged brownies to celebrate.

The main problem with thin people is they oppress. Their good intentions, bony torsos, tight ships, neat corners, cerebral machinations and pat solutions loom like dark clouds over the loose, comfortable, spread-out, soft world of the fat. Long after fat people have removed their coats and shoes and put their feet up on the coffee table, thin people are still sitting on the edge of the sofa, looking neat as a pin, discussing rutabagas. Fat people are heavily into fits of laughter, slapping their thighs and whooping it up, while thin people are still politely waiting for the punch line. Thin people are downers. They like math and morality and reasoned evaluation of the limitations of human beings. They have their skinny little acts together. They expound, prognose, probe and prick.

Fat people are convivial. They will like you even if you're irregular and have acne. They will come up with a good reason why you never wrote the great American novel. They will cry in your beer with you. They will put your name in the pot. They will let you off the hook. Fat people will gab, giggle, guffaw, gallumph, gyrate and gossip. They are generous, giving and gallant. They are gluttonous and goodly and great. What you want when you're down is soft and jiggly, not muscled and stable. Fat people know this. Fat people have plenty of room. Fat people will take you in.

## SUGGESTIONS FOR DISCUSSION

1. What attitude toward success does the passage from Ecclesiastes reveal? How does this attitude compare to that expressed by Suzanne Britt Jordan?
2. Jordan does not attempt to present a closely reasoned argument. Instead, she enlists our sympathy for easygoing people and our dislike for ambitious individuals through images and associations. What concrete images does she use? What associations do these images have? How do they affect our responses?
3. Translations are not, of course, the simple trading of words in one language for words in another. The object is much more like trying to render a *meaning* presented in one language in another. Compare the following three translations of Ecclesiastes, Chapter 3, verse 1:

   a. King James Version: "To every thing there is a season and a time to every purpose under heaven."

**b.** New English Bible: "For everything its season, and for every activity under heaven its time."

**c.** Living Bible: "There is a right time for everything."

Discuss the differences in meaning and tone.

**4.** Suzanne Britt Jordan's essay is what is usually called a comparison-and-contrast essay. The name doesn't imply anything rhetorical — nothing to do with audience or purpose—but it does suggest a pattern of thinking that is probably fundamental. That is, in order to deal with the world we constantly divide things into groups and compare them. In an essay, this comparing can be done in any number of ways. In this essay, for example, Jordan could have divided the essay in half: first half about thin people, second half about fat people. Or she could have compared by paragraphs: one paragraph thin, one fat, one thin, and so on. As it turns out, she has her own rhythm for moving back and forth between the compared groups. What is that rhythm? What effect does it produce? How would the essay have been different if she had done the comparing and contrasting in other ways?

**5.** One striking difference in the modern translation is the use of the phrase "chasing the wind" for the King James phrase "vexation of spirit" (see 1:17 and 2:26). A similar difference in translation appears in Chapter 11, verse 4. The King James translators write, "He that observeth the wind shall not sow, and he that regardeth the clouds shall not reap." In the Living Bible the passage reads, "If you wait for perfect conditions, you will never get anything done." What is the effect of the change from metaphor to abstract statement?

## SUGGESTIONS FOR WRITING

**1.** It is quite clear that Jordan's fat and thin are not merely physical characteristics, but values and personality traits as well. Using her definitions as a guide, try writing an Aichinger-like allegory about a fat person in a world of thin people, or a thin person in a world of fat people. It would probably be easiest if you focused on one or two manageable situations: a family quarrel, a job interview, a trial scene.

**2.** Very few people are as disillusioned about life as the writer of Ecclesiastes, but almost everyone has experienced minor episodes of disenchantment. Narrate an incident which caused you to become disillusioned about yourself or someone else. You might wish to consider one of the following subjects:

**a.** Your realization that you had misjudged someone

**b.** Your hero or idol who was human after all

**c.** Your discovery that you had a mean or cowardly streak

# 19

# Ambition: An Affirmative View

*Muriel James and Dorothy Jongeward*
"WINNERS AND LOSERS"

*Joseph Epstein*
"THE VIRTUES OF AMBITION: SOME KIND WORDS FOR MONEY, FAME, AND POWER"

In marked contrast to the skepticism expressed in the two previous essays, the essay by Muriel James and Dorothy Jongeward provides a wholehearted endorsement of ambition. These authors contend that individuals can take charge of their lives if they are sincere and confident. Unlike the writer of Ecclesiastes, who attributes overwhelming powers to "time and chance," these two writers suggest that human beings create their own successes and failures. Joseph Epstein presents a more complex assessment of the subject in "The Virtues of Ambition." He observes that one's position in life is an unpredictable mixture of conscious choices and chance factors, but he still maintains a positive view of ambition. For Epstein, ambition represents an assertion of individual responsibility in a world where it is all too easy to retreat into fatalism.

## *Muriel James and Dorothy Jongeward* "WINNERS AND LOSERS"

Each human being is born as something new, something that never existed before. Each is born with the capacity to win at life. Each person has a unique way of seeing, hearing, touching, tasting, and thinking. Each has his or her own unique potentials—capabilities and limitations. Each can be a significant, thinking, aware, and creative being—a productive person, a winner.

The words "winner" and "loser" have many meanings. When we refer to a person as a winner, we do not mean one who makes someone else lose. To us, a winner is one who responds authentically by being credible, trustworthy, responsive, and genuine, both as an individual and as a member of society. A loser is one who fails to respond authentically. Martin Buber makes this distinction as he retells the old story of the rabbi who, on his deathbed, is asked if he is ready for the world to come. The rabbi says yes. After all, he will not be asked, "Why were you not Moses?" He will only be asked, "Why were you not yourself. . . ."

Winners have different potentials. Achievement is not the most important thing. Authenticity is. The authentic person experiences self-reality by knowing, being, and becoming a credible, responsive person. Authentic people actualize their own unprecedented uniqueness and appreciate the uniqueness of others.

Authentic persons—winners—do not dedicate their lives to a concept of what they imagine they *should* be; rather, they are themselves and as such do not use their energy putting on a performance, maintaining pretence, and manipulating others. Winners can reveal themselves instead of projecting images that please, provoke, or entice others. They are aware that there is a difference between being loving and acting loving, between being stupid and acting stupid, between being knowledgeable and acting knowledgeable. Winners do not need to hide behind a mask. They throw off unrealistic self-images of inferiority or superiority. Autonomy does not frighten winners.

All people have moments of autonomy, if only fleeting. However, winners are able to sustain their autonomy over ever-increasing periods of time. Winners may lose ground occasionally and may even fail. Yet, in spite of setbacks winners maintain a basic self-confidence.

Winners are not afraid to do their own thinking and to use their own knowledge. They can separate facts from opinion and don't pretend to have all the answers. They listen to others, evaluate what they say, but come to their own conclusions. Although winners can admire and respect other people, they are not totally defined, demolished, bound, or awed by them.

Winners do not play "helpless," nor do they play the blaming game. Instead, they assume responsibility for their own lives. They do not give others a false authority over them. Winners are their own bosses and know it.

A winner's timing is right. Winners respond appropriately to the situation. Their responses are related to the message sent and preserve the significance, worth, well-being, and dignity of the people involved. Winners know that for everything there is a season and for every activity a time.

*A time to be aggressive and a time to be passive,*
*A time to be together and a time to be alone,*
*A time to fight and a time to love,*
*A time to work and a time to play,*
*A time to cry and a time to laugh.*
*A time to confront and a time to withdraw,*
*A time to speak and a time to be silent,*
*A time to hurry and a time to wait.*

To winners, time is precious. Winners don't kill it, but live it here and now. Living in the now does not mean that winners foolishly ignore their own past history or fail to prepare for the future. Rather, winners know their past, are aware and alive in the present, and look forward to the future.

Winners learn to know their feelings and limitations and to be unafraid of them. Winners are not stopped by their own contradictions and ambivalences. Being authentic, they know when they are angry and can listen when others are angry with them. Winners can give and receive affection. Winners are able to love and be loved.

Winners can be spontaneous. They do not have to respond in predetermined, rigid ways, but can change their plans when the situation calls for it. Winners have a zest for life, enjoying work, play, food, other people, sex, and the world of nature. Without guilt they enjoy their own accomplishments. Without envy they enjoy the accomplishments of others.

Although winners can freely enjoy themselves, they can also postpone enjoyment, can discipline themselves in the present to enhance their enjoyment in the future. Winners are not afraid to go after what they want, but they do so in appropriate ways. Winners do not get their security by controlling others. They do not set themselves up to lose.

A winner cares about the world and its peoples. A winner is not isolated from the general problems of society, but is concerned, compassionate, and committed to improving the quality of life. Even in the face of national and international adversity, a winner's self-image is not one of a powerless individual. A winner works to make the world a better place.

Although people are born to win, they are also born helpless and totally dependent on their environment. Winners successfully make the transition from total helplessness to independence, and then to interdependence. Losers do not. Somewhere along the line they begin to avoid becoming responsible for their own lives. . . .

A lack of response to dependency needs, poor nutrition, brutality, unhappy relationships, disease, continuing disappointments, inadequate physical care, and traumatic events are among the many experiences that contribute to making people losers. Such experiences interrupt, deter, or prevent the normal progress toward autonomy and self-actualization. To cope with negative experiences, children learn to manipulate themselves and others. These manipulative techniques are hard to give up later in life and often become set patterns. Winners work to shed them. Losers hang on to them.

Some losers speak of themselves as successful but anxious, successful but trapped, or successful but unhappy. Others speak of themselves as totally beaten, without purpose, unable to move, half dead, or bored to death. Losers may not recognize that, for the most part, they have been building their own cages, digging their own graves, and boring themselves.

A loser seldom lives in the present, but instead destroys the present by focusing on past memories or future expectations. The loser who lives in the past dwells on the good old days or on past personal misfortunes. Nostalgically, the loser either clings to the way things "used to be" or bemoans his or her bad luck. The loser is self-pitying and shifts the responsibility for an unsatisfactory life onto others. Blaming others and excusing oneself are often part of the loser's game. A loser who lives in the past may lament *if only:*

"If only I had married someone else . . ."
"If only I had a different job . . ."
"If only I had finished school . . ."
"If only I had been handsome (beautiful) . . ."
"If only my spouse had stopped drinking . . ."
"If only I had been born rich . . ."
"If only I had had better parents . . ."

People who live in the future may dream of some miracle after which they can "live happily ever after." Rather than pursuing their own lives, losers wait—wait for the magical rescue. How wonderful life will be *when:*

"When Prince Charming or the ideal woman finally comes . . ."
"When school is over . . ."
"When the kids grow up . . ."
"When the new job opens . . ."
"When the boss dies . . ."
"When my ship comes in . . ."

In contrast to those who live with the delusion of a magical rescue, some losers live constantly under the dread of future catastrophe. They conjure up expectations of *what if:*

"What if I lose my job . . ."
"What if I lose my mind . . ."
"What if something falls on me . . ."
"What if I break my leg . . ."
"What if they don't like me . . ."
"What if I make a mistake . . ."

By continually focusing on the future, these losers experience anxiety in the present. They are anxious over what they anticipate—either real or imagined—tests, bill paying, a love affair, crisis, illness, retirement, the weather, and so forth. Persons overly involved with imaginings let the actual possibilities of the moment pass them by. They occupy their minds with material that is irrelevant to the current situation. Anxiety tunes out current reality. Consequently, these people are unable to see for themselves, hear for themselves, feel for themselves, or taste, touch, or think for themselves.

Unable to bring the full potential of their senses into the immediate situation, losers' perceptions are incorrect or incomplete. They see themselves and others through a prismlike distortion. Their ability to deal effectively with the real world is hampered.

Losers spend much of their time play-acting, pretending, manipulating, and perpetuating old roles from childhood. Losers invest their energy in maintaining masks, often projecting a phony front. Karen Horney writes, "The fostering of the phony self is always at the expense of the real self, the latter being treated with disdain, at best like a poor relative." To the play-acting loser, performance is often more important than reality.

Losers repress their capacities to express spontaneously and appropriately the full range of possible behavior. They may be unaware of other options for a more productive, self-fulfilling life path. Losers are afraid to try new things and instead maintain their own status quo. Losers are repeaters, repeating not only their own mistakes, but often those of their families and culture as well.

A loser has difficulty giving and receiving affection and does not enter into intimate, honest, direct relationships with others. Instead, a loser tries to manipulate them into living up to his or her expectations. Losers' energies are often channeled into living up to the expectations of others.

People who are losers are not using their intellect appropriately, but instead are misusing it to rationalize and intellectualize. When rationalizing, losers give excuses to make their actions seem plausible. When intellectualizing, they try to snow others with verbiage. Consequently, much of their potential remains dormant, unrealized, and unrecognized. Like the frog prince in the fairy tale, losers are spellbound and live their lives being something they aren't meant to be.

Few people are one hundred percent winners or one hundred percent losers. It's a matter of degree. Most people are winners in some areas of their lives and losers in others. Their winning or losing is influenced by what happens to them in childhood. However, once a person is on the road to being a winner, his or her chances are greater for becoming even more so.

*Joseph Epstein*

# "THE VIRTUES OF AMBITION: SOME KIND WORDS FOR MONEY, FAME, AND POWER"

Ambition is one of those Rorschach words: define it and you instantly reveal a great deal about yourself. Even that most neutral of works, *Webster's,* in its Seventh New Collegiate Edition, gives itself away, defining ambition first and foremost as "an ardent desire for rank, fame, or power." Ardent immediately assumes a heat incommensurate with good sense and stability, and rank, fame, and power have come under fairly heavy attack for at least a century. One can, after all, be ambitious for the public good, for the alleviation of suffering, for the enlightenment of mankind, though there are some who say that these are precisely the ambitious people most to be distrusted.

Surely ambition is behind dreams of glory, of wealth, of love, of distinction, of accomplishment, of pleasure, of goodness. What life does with our dreams and expectations cannot, of course, be predicted. Some dreams, begun in selflessness, end in rancor; other dreams, begun in selfishness, end in large-heartedness. The unpredictability of the outcome of dreams is no reason to cease dreaming.

To be sure, ambition, the sheer thing unalloyed by some larger purpose than merely clambering up, is never a pretty prospect to ponder. The single-mindedly ambitious is an old human type—"Cromwell, I charge thee, fling away Ambition," wrote Shakespeare in *Henry VIII.* "By that sinne fell the Angels"—and scarcely a type that has gone out of style, or soon figures to. As drunks have done to alcohol, the single-minded have done to ambition—given it a bad name. Like a taste for alcohol, too, ambition does not always allow for easy satiation. Some people cannot handle it; it has brought grief to others, and not merely the ambitious alone. Still, none of this seems sufficient cause for driving ambition under the counter, in an undeclared Volstead Act.

By this I do not mean to say that ambition has gone or been driven out of style. It hasn't. Or at least not completely. In our day many people, goaded by ambition, go in for self-improvement programs of one kind or another: speed reading, assertiveness training, the study of books calling for looking out for number one and other forms of aggressiveness. But such activities have always seemed déclassé, and the sort of person who goes to est today thirty or forty years ago might have enrolled in a Dale Carnegie course. In most respects, it appears that the more educated a person is, the more hopeless life seems to him. This being so, ambition, to the educated class, has come to seem pointless at best, vicious at worst. Ambition connotes a certain Rotarian optimism, a thing unseemly, in very poor taste, rather like a raging sexual appetite in someone quite elderly. None of this, of course, has stopped the educated classes from attempting to get their own out of the world—lots of the best of everything, as a famous epicure once put it—which they continue to do very effectively. To renunciation is thus added more than a piquant touch of hypocrisy.

If the above assertions seem overstated, consider what seems to me the unarguableness of the following assertions. If one feels the stirrings of ambition, it is on the whole best to keep them hidden. To say of a young man or woman that he or she is ambitious is no longer, as it once was, a clear compliment. Rather the reverse. A person called ambitious is likely to arouse anxiety, for in our day anyone so called is thought to be threatening, possibly a trifle neurotic. Energy is still valued, so too is competence, but ambition is in bad repute. And perhaps nowhere more than in America. . . .

What is the worst that can be said— that has been said—about ambition? Here is a (surely) partial list:

To begin with, it, ambition, is often antisocial, and indeed is now outmoded, belonging to an age when individualism was more valued and useful than it is today. The person strongly imbued with ambition ignores the collectivity; socially detached, he is on his own and out for his own. Individuality and ambition are firmly linked. The ambitious individual, far from identifying himself and his fortunes with the group, wishes to rise above it. The ambitious man or woman sees the world as a battle; rivalrousness is his or her principal emotion: the world has limited prizes to offer, and he or she is determined to get his or hers. Ambition is, moreover, jesuitical; it can argue those possessed by it into believing that what they want for themselves is good for everyone—that the satisfaction of their own desire is best for the commonweal. At bottom the truly ambitious believe that it is a dog-eat-dog world, and they are distinguished by wanting to be the dogs that do the eating.

But the ambitious pay a steep price, it is felt, for harboring their antisocial and outmoded view of the world. To be ambitious is, by definition, to be driven. Balzac, in his novel *Lost Illusions,* speaks of a character who, having ambition roused in him, has been "imprudently doomed . . . to great suffering." In the same novel he speaks about another character, "A saintly creature," who "little knew that when ambition comes it puts an end to natural feeling." To be ambitious is not thus only to be driven but to be a bit inhuman into the bargain. The great men and women in history have always been able to flout the small but crucially important human emotions. Great figures may even despise mankind a little.

Ambition, it has been further if not argued at least implied, is inherently tragic in its consequences. If the ambitious, in their varying ways, strive after human grandeur, such striving does not come cheaply. In the *Antigone,* Sophocles wrote: "That greatness never/Shall touch the life of man without destruction." What is, or can be, inherently tragic about ambition is that it is often insatiable. Ambition, deep-down ambition, can finally know no satisfaction. Ambition works on a person, eats away at him, grinds him down. So, at any rate, it is said.

Ambition is also, in the ordinary way of the world, it is argued, likely to corrupt those touched by it. Antisocial in its impulse, gnawing in its emotional effects, ambition let loose works its way into, and figures ultimately to rot, character. Macbeth, Lear's two disloyal daughters, Mark Antony, Coriolanus—it sometimes seems as if Shakespeare's plays are scarcely about anything other than corruption by way of ambition. Once a man is roused by ambition, the standard argument has it, his conscience goes into retreat. To be ambitious is to be, if not outside the bounds of morality, then to feel less constrained by those bounds. Absolute power corrupts absolutely, said Lord Acton in a famous *mot,* but merely a touch of ambition can achieve the same end.

From here it is but a short hop to believe that those who have achieved the common goals of ambition—money, fame, power— have achieved them through corruption of a greater or lesser degree, mostly a greater. Thus all politicians in high places, thought to be ambitious, are understood to be, ipso facto, without moral scruples. How could they have such scruples—a weighty burden in a high climb—and still have risen as they have?

Behind ambition—and none too far behind—are commmonly understood to lie vanity, greed, the will to power. Ambition, when given free rein, is certain to bring out the worst in people. The greatest victims of ambition, however, are those who achieve their goals. (Whom the gods would make mad, they first allow their dreams to come true . . . and so forth.) But of course those who do achieve the goals of their ambition are not the only victims of ambition. The field is liberally strewn with other casualties. Those, to name one category, whose lives have been poisoned by feverish but ill-defined ambition; those, to name another, who have felt the endless discouragement of living without the distinction they crave; and those, to name a third, paralyzed by fear of entering the battle to begin with.

What is the worst that can be said about ambition? In sum, that it is antisocial; that it is insatiable; that it is corrupting; that it leaves only victims, rendering men mad (like Macbeth) or insensately vulgar (like Sammy Glick) or pathetically broken (like Arthur Miller's Willy Loman). Of great men of ambition, Hegel, in his *Lectures* on *The Philosophy of History,* said: "Their whole life is labor and trouble. . . . They die early, like Alexander; they are murdered, like Caesar, transported to St. Helena, like Napoleon." Theodore Dreiser spoke about "the virus of success," but the virus starts earlier—it enters the bloodstream with ambition. The ambitious view of life is forbidding and unforgiving. Its price is too high. It is inhuman in its demands; it is inhumane in its toll. If life is to be lived differently, if life is to be more spiritual, more tender minded and large hearted, ambition, clearly, must go. Or so it is said.

The worst that *can* be said about ambition is what frequently *is* said about ambition. How did this come about? How did "the tradition of ambition," once so firm and strong, become so wobbly and weak? Ambition itself is an ideal, something passed on from generation to generation, a quality that, like love or truthfulness or courage, it was once felt ought to be inculcated in the young. Ambition is an ideal to which one must aspire. But if ambition is to endure as an ideal, it must command wide respect. Ample is the evidence that this respect has begun to wear away.

. . . . . . . . . . . . . . . . . . . . . . . . . .

The attacks on ambition are many and come from various angles; its public defenders are few and unimpressive, where they are not extremely unattractive. As a result, the support for ambition as a healthy impulse, a quality to be admired and inculcated in the young, is probably lower than it has ever been in the United States. This does not mean that ambition is at an end, that people no longer feel its stirrings and promptings, but only that, no longer openly honored, it is less often openly professed. Consequences follow from this, of course, some of which are that ambition is driven underground, or made sly, or perverse. It can also be forced into vulgarity, as witness the blatant pratings of its contemporary promoters. Such, then, is the way things stand: on the left angry critics, on the right obtuse supporters, and in the middle, as usual, the majority of earnest people trying to get on in life.

Many people are naturally distrustful of ambition, feeling that it represents something intractable in human nature. Thus John Dean entitled his book about his involvement in the Watergate affair during the Nixon administration *Blind Ambition,* as if ambition were to blame for his ignoble actions, and not the constellation of qualities that make up his rather shabby character. Ambition, it must once again be underscored, is morally a two-sided street. Place next to John Dean Andrew Carnegie, who, among other philanthropic acts, bought the library of Lord Acton, at a time when Acton was in financial distress, and assigned its custodianship to Acton, who never was told who his benefactor was. Need much more be said on the subject than that, important though ambition is, there are some things that one must not sacrifice to it?

But going at things the other way, sacrificing ambition so as to guard against its potential excesses, is to go at things wrongly. To discourage ambition is to discourage dreams of grandeur and greatness. All men and women are born, live, suffer, and die; what distinguishes us one from another is our dreams, whether they be dreams about worldly or unworldy things, and what we do to make them come about. "To fulfill the dreams of one's youth," says Father Vaillant, in Willa Cather's *Death Comes for the Archbishop,* "this is the best that can happen to a man."

The quality of an age's ambitions distinguishes it from other ages. An age's ambitions, similarly, mark the quality of its human energy. Sometimes great causes will loose this energy—the founding of new religions, great new movements in the arts, wars and revolutions; sometimes inventions and radical technological advances will spring this energy forward—steam power, air travel, space exploration; sometimes there is a concentration of great men; and sometimes all these forces come together—as the Industrial Revolution, the quest for empire, and an efflorescence of statesmen, artists, and intellectuals did in Victorian England. Yet our own age, whose chief accomplishments are likely to be considered by history as scientific and technological appears otherwise strangely enervated, oddly shorn of human energy. "Moderation," says La Rochefoucauld, "is languor and idleness of the soul, ambition is its activity and energy." But neither, it must be added, is ours an age noted for moderation.

The current age is beginning to seem an age of social insecurity, whose leading belief is in the inability of individuals to change the drift of things. A dash of Marxism, a touch of Freudianism, a vague groaning about something called "the system," a distrust of action, a denigration of success—such appear to constitute the chief strands of social thought of the day. None of this allows much leeway for the use of intelligence, courage, and resolution on the part of individuals. It is almost as if we subscribed to a form of social determinism that has no name and whose causes and effects we haven't quite managed to formulate, but to which we feel ourselves helplessly hostage.

The discouragement of ambition is partly—even greatly—responsible for this feeling of helplessness. It may seem an exaggeration to say that ambition is the linchpin of society, holding many of its disparate elements together, but it is not an exaggeration by much. Remove ambition and the essential elements of society seem to fly apart. Ambition, as opposed to mere fantasizing about desires, implies work and discipline to achieve goals, personal and social, of a kind society cannot survive without. Ambition is intimately connected with family, for men and women not only work partly for their families; husbands and wives are often ambitious for each other, but harbor some of their most ardent ambitions for their children; yet to have a family nowadays—with birth control readily available, and inflation a good economic argument against having children—is nearly an expression of ambition in itself. Finally, though ambition was once the domain chiefly of monarchs and aristocrats, it has, in more recent times, increasingly become the domain of the middle classes. Ambition and futurity—a sense of building for tomorrow—are inextricable. Working, saving, planning, these, the daily aspects of ambition, have always been the distinguishing marks of a rising middle class. The attack against ambition is not incidentally an attack on the middle class and what it stands for. Like it or not, the middle class has done much of society's work in America; and it, the middle class, has from the beginning run on ambition.

Of longer standing is the argument against ambition holding that, in the long view, it is finally worthless. Recall Dr. Johnson's "The Vanity of Human Wishes," with its view that all but the most serious religious faith is vanity. Dr. Johnson is of course correct—again in the long view. But George Santayana's riposte, in a poem of his young manhood, seems closer to the mark for most of mankind, who must, after all, take the short view and live in the world as we find it:

*That all is vanity is undeniable,*
*But joy is no less joy for being vain*
*And evils to which everything is liable*
*Are evils of which nothing should complain.*
*The facts are fixed, our mood alone is pliable*
*And call it dew or drizzle, rain is rain,*
*And by the proof that life is an inanity*
*We cannot change the fortune of humanity.*

It is not difficult to imagine a world shorn of ambition. It would probably be a kinder world: without demands, without abrasions, without disappointments. People would have time for reflection. Such work as they did would not be for themselves but for the collectivity. Competition would never enter in. Flutes and oboes would play. Conflict would be eliminated, tension become a thing of the past. The stress of creation would be at an end. Art would no longer be troubling, but purely celebratory in its functions. Flowers and vegetables would be grown. Children, necessary to the preservation of the species, would be raised in common. The family would become superfluous as a social unit, with all its former power for bringing about neurosis drained away. Longevity would be increased, for fewer people would die of heart attack or stroke caused by tumultuous endeavor. Anxiety would be extinct. Time would stretch on and on, with ambition long departed from the human heart.

Ah, how unrelievedly boring life would be!

Although people will always argue about the ends to which ambition is put, the real question posed by ambiton is whether or not each of us has a true hand in shaping his own destiny. People who believe that our control over our own destinies is slight, if not nonexistent, will not think very well of ambition: it may even seem rather comical to them. For such people forces, not individual will, are what count; history, not biography, is decisive. One would be foolish not to grant historical forces their due; nor should the importance of accident be overlooked. But give forces too much due, allow too much importance to accident, and the significance of our actions become nil. "No," Alexander Solzhenitsyn wrote, "we must not hide behind fate's petticoats; the most important decisions in our lives, when all is said, we make for ourselves." To the extent that one believes that each of us is largely responsible for his own fate, to that extent will one believe in the importance of ambition, which, in one of its many aspects, is the expression of the desire to shape one's own fate.

Ideas have consequences, bad ideas fully as much consequence as good ones. Some people hold that we are, essentially, what we keep hidden about ourselves, our fears and secrets. Other people hold that, whatever our personal secrets and fears, we are what we do. There is often a conflict among men and women of good heart between those who believe that it is what one achieves that matters and those who believe that what one is and how one lives matters more. Some of us are Hamlets in our outlook, some Don Quixotes. In many the two types are combined in unending battle. But at the moment, among the best educated, Hamlet's view seems to predominate. Oddly—and ironically—the loss of confidence in ambition comes at a time when the gates of opportunity have never been thrown so wide open. Until fairly recently, for example, women were discouraged from harboring large ambitions, and only truly exceptional women had a chance to make their mark. The same can be said for minority groups. Ambition has never seemed a possibility for so many. Equality of opportunity has grown greater and greater. Yet neither hope nor ambition has kept pace.

There is a strong view that holds that success is a myth, and ambition therefore a sham. Does this mean that success does not really exist? That achievement is at bottom empty? That the efforts of men and women are of no significance alongside the force of movements and events? Now not all success, obviously, is worth esteeming, nor all ambition worth cultivating. Which are and which are not is something one soon enough learns on one's own. But even the most cynical secretly admit that success exists; that achievement counts for a great deal; and that the true myth is that the actions of men and women are useless. To believe otherwise is to take on a point of view that is likely to be deranging. It is in its implications, to remove all motive for competence, interest in attainment, and regard for posterity.

We do not choose to be born. We do not choose our parents. We do not choose our historical epoch, or the country of our birth, or the immediate circumstances of our upbringing. We do not, most of us, choose to die; nor do we choose the time or conditions of our death. But within all this realm of choicelessness, we do choose how we shall live: courageously or in cowardice, honorably or dishonorably, with purpose or in drift. We decide what is important and what is trivial in life. We decide that what makes us significant is either what we do or what we refuse to do. But no matter how indifferent the universe may be to our choices and decisions, these choices and decisions are ours to make. We decide. We choose. And as we decide and choose, so are our lives formed. In the end, forming our own destiny is what ambition is about.

## SUGGESTIONS FOR DISCUSSION

1. Style, to oversimplify a bit, might be described as certain words in a certain order. The writers of both "Winners and Losers" and "The Virtues of Ambition" view success in positive ways, but stylistically these essays are radically different. For example, James and Jongeward have the rather startling habit of beginning nearly every sentence with a noun or pronoun, and usually the same noun or pronoun for four or five sentences in a row. As a result, their sentences never refer back to anything (so they seldom write "on the other hand," "still," or "however"). Epstein, on the other hand, begins his sentences in many different ways, and constantly relates one sentence to the others: "after all," "to be sure," "still." Why does Epstein write in such a complex way while James and Jongeward write simple straightforward prose? Remember that a writer's style often reflects his view of the world as much as his content does.
2. The words that we use may be roughly divided into two categories: those that appeal to the intellect (e.g., idea, conclusion, quality, goal) and those that appeal to

the senses (e.g., juicy, silky, crushing, sour). What kind of words do James and Jongeward rely on in this essay? Do you think their word choice is effective?

If you have read Jordan's essay, "That Lean and Hungry Look," analyze her choice of words in terms of these two categories.

3. Epstein says that "the real question posed by ambition is whether or not each of us has a true hand in shaping his own destiny." Examine the other essays in this section that deal with ambition: Does the author of Ecclesiastes feel that individuals shape their own destinies? What does Suzanne Britt Jordan think? James and Jongeward? In the essay you wrote before beginning this section, how did you deal with ambition? Are ambition and success separable?
4. The James and Jongeward reading is taken from their book *Born to Win: Transactional Analysis with Gestalt Experiments,* while Epstein's essay, which first appeared in *Harper's,* is from his book called *Ambition: The Secret Passion.* Compare the audiences you think the two texts might be aimed at. Who would buy a book called *Born to Win*? How much would potential buyers be attracted or put off by the subtitle? Who might read *Harper's,* see Epstein's essay, and read his book? To what extent do the authors' purposes define the membership of their audiences?
5. Jargon is not a language problem that appears very often in the readings of this collection. James and Jongeward, though, present us with some examples: "Authentic people actualize their own unprecedented uniqueness and appreciate the uniqueness in others." What does that mean? How does reading a sentence like that make you feel? Look through this pair of readings and see if you can locate any other examples of jargon.

## SUGGESTIONS FOR WRITING

1. Writers seem to like to divide things into twos: Epstein says "some of us are Hamlets in our outlook, some Don Quixotes." James and Jongeward divide us into "winners" and "losers." Both essays make allowance for a mixture—Epstein says the two can "struggle," James and Jongeward that we all have some of both—but the polarizing is still there. For this assignment, try to move beyond either/or thinking. In a letter addressed to someone younger than yourself—a brother or sister, for example—explain ambition by creating at least four categories. Your purpose is to persuade, and in some sense to confuse: such an audience would *prefer* you tell them that life is simple, black and white. You must convince them that it is not, that it is much more complicated. Be aware of what it feels like to write in an authoritative voice.

# 20

# Wealth and Acquisition

*Andrew Carnegie*
"THE GOSPEL OF WEALTH"

*Anne Morrow Lindbergh*
"CHANNELLED WHELK"

Andrew Carnegie and Anne Morrow Lindbergh present contrasting perspectives on the pursuit of wealth. Carnegie explains his views on wealth and acquisition in a well-known essay, "The Gospel of Wealth." His tough-minded argument presents competition for material goods as a worthy occupation that benefits the poor as well as the rich. In dramatic contrast to Carnegie's wide-ranging conclusions are Lindbergh's personal reflections in "Channelled Whelk." She regards material possessions as barriers to the life of simplicity and contemplation that she seeks, and this essay describes her attempts to shed these burdens.

## *Andrew Carnegie*
## "THE GOSPEL OF WEALTH"

The problem of our age is the proper administration of wealth, that the ties of brotherhood may still bind together the rich and poor in harmonious relationship. The conditions of human life have not only been changed, but revolutionized, within the past few hundred years. In former days there was little difference between the dwelling, dress, food, and environment of the chief and those of his retainers. The Indians are to-day where civilized man then was. When visiting the Sioux, I was led to the wigwam of the chief. It was like the others in external appearance, and even within the difference was trifling between it and those of the poorest of his braves. The contrast between the palace of the millionaire and the cottage of the laborer with us to-day measures the change which has come with civilization. This change, however, is not to be deplored, but welcomed as highly beneficial. It is well, nay, essential, for the progress of the race that the houses of some should be homes for all that is highest and best in literature and the arts, and for all the refinements of civilization, rather than that none should be so. Much better this great irregularity than universal squalor. Without wealth there can be no Maecenas.* The "good old times" were not good old times. Neither master nor servant was as well situated then as to-day. A relapse to old conditions would be disastrous to both—not the least so to him who serves—and would sweep away civilization with it. But whether the change be for good or ill, it is upon us, beyond our power to alter, and, therefore, to be accepted and made the best of. It is a waste of time to criticize the inevitable. . . .

The price we pay for this salutary change is, no doubt, great. We assemble thousands of operatives in the factory, and in the mine, of whom the employer can know little or nothing, and to whom he is little better than a myth. All intercourse between them is at an end. Rigid castes are formed, and, as usual, mutual ignorance breeds mutual distrust. Each caste is without sympathy with the other, and ready to credit anything disparaging in regard to it. Under the law of competition, the employer of thousands is forced into the strictest economies, among which the rates paid to labor figure prominently, and often there is friction betwen the employer and the employed, between capital and labor, between rich and poor. Human society loses homogeneity.

The price which society pays for the law of competition, like the price it pays for cheap comforts and luxuries, is also great; but the advantages of this law are also greater still than its cost—for it is to this law that we owe our wonderful material development, which brings improved conditions in its train. But, whether the law be benign or not, we must say of it, as we say of the change in the conditions of men to which we have referred: It is here; we cannot evade it; no substitutes for it have been found; and while the law may be sometimes hard for the individual, it is best for the race, because it insures the survival of the fittest in every department. We accept and welcome, therefore, as conditions to which we must accommodate ourselves, great inequality of environment; the concentration of business, industrial and commercial, in the hands of a few; and the law of competition between these, as being not only beneficial, but essential to the future progress of the race. Having accepted these, it follows that there must be great scope for the exercise of special ability in the merchant and in the manufacturer who has to conduct affairs upon a great scale. That this talent for organization and management is rare among men is proved by the fact that it invariably secures enormous rewards for its possessor, no matter where or under what laws or conditions. The experienced in affairs always rate the MAN whose services can be obtained as a partner as not only the first consideration, but such as render the question of his capital scarcely worth considering: for able men soon create capital; in the hands of those without the special talent required, capital soon takes wings. Such men become interested in firms or corporations using mil-

* Maecenas—ancient Roman aristocrat who used his extensive wealth to promote the arts.—Eds.

lions; and, estimating only simple interest to be made upon the capital invested, it is inevitable that their income must exceed their expenditure and that they must, therefore, accumulate wealth. Nor is there any middle ground which such men can occupy, because the great manufacturing or commercial concern which does not earn at least interest upon its capital soon becomes bankrupt. It must either go forward or fall behind; to stand still is impossible. It is a condition essential to its successful operation that it should be thus far profitable, and even that, in addition to interest on capital, it should make profit. It is a law, as certain as any of the others named, that men possessed of this peculiar talent for affairs, under the free play of economic forces must, of necessity, soon be in receipt of more revenue than can be judiciously expended upon themselves; and this law is as beneficial for the race as the others.

Objections to the foundations upon which society is based are not in order, because the condition of the race is better with these than it has been with any other which has been tried. Of the effect of any new substitutes proposed we cannot be sure. The Socialist or Anarchist who seeks to overturn present conditions is to be regarded as attacking the foundation upon which civilization itself rests, for civilization took its start from the day when the capable, industrious workman said to his incompetent and lazy fellow, "If thou dost not sow, thou shalt not reap," and thus ended primitive Communism by separating the drones from the bees. One who studies this subject will soon be brought face to face with the conclusion that upon the sacredness of property civilization itself depends—the right of the laborer to his hundred dollars in the savings-bank, and equally the legal right of the millionaire to his millions. Every man must be allowed "to sit under his own vine and fig-tree, with none to make afraid," if human society is to advance, or even to remain so far advanced as it is. To those who propose to substitute Communism for this intense Individualism, the answer therefore is: The race has tried that. All progress from that barbarous day to the present time has resulted from its displacement. Not evil, but good, has come to the race from the accumulation of wealth by those who have had the ability and energy to produce it. But even if we admit for a moment that it might be better for the race to discard its present foundation, Individualism,—that it is a nobler ideal that man should labor, not for himself alone, but in and for a brotherhood of his fellows, and share with them all in common, realizing Swedenborg's idea of heaven,* where, as he says, the angels derive their happiness, not from laboring for self, but for each other,—even admit all this, and a sufficient answer is, This is not evolution, but revolution. It necessitates the changing of human nature itself—a work of eons, even if it were good to change it, which we cannot know.

It is not practicable in our day or in our age. Even if desirable theoretically, it belongs to another and long-succeeding sociological stratum. Our duty is with what is practicable now—with the next step possible in our day and generation. It is criminal to waste our energies in endeavoring to uproot, when all we can profitably accomplish is to bend the universal tree of humanity a little in the direction most favorable to the production of good fruit under existing circumstances. We might as

* Carnegie is referring to Emanuel Swedenborg's (1688-1771) mystical theology expressed in his work *Heaven and Hell.*—Eds.

well urge the destruction of the highest existing type of man because he failed to reach our ideal as to favor the destruction of Individualism, Private Property, the Law of Accumulation of Wealth, and the Law of Competition; for these are the highest result of human experience, the soil in which society, so far, has produced the best fruit. Unequally or unjustly, perhaps, as these laws sometimes operate, and imperfect as they appear to the Idealist, they are, nevertheless, like the highest type of man, the best and most valuable of all that humanity has yet accomplished.

We start, then, with a condition of affairs under which the best interests of the race are promoted, but which inevitably gives wealth to the few. Thus far, accepting conditions as they exist, the situation can be surveyed and pronounced good. The question then arises,—and if the foregoing be correct, it is the only question with which we have to deal,—What is the proper mode of administering wealth after the laws upon which civilization is founded have thrown it into the hands of the few? And it is of this great question that I believe I offer the true solution. It will be understood that fortunes are here spoken of, not moderate sums saved by many years of effort, the returns from which are required for the comfortable maintenance and education of families. This is not wealth, but only competence, which it should be the aim of all to acquire, and which it is for the best interests of society should be acquired.

There are but three modes in which surplus wealth can be disposed of. It can be left to the families of the decedents; or it can be bequeathed for public purposes; or, finally, it can be administered by its possessors during their lives. Under the first and second modes most of the wealth of the world that has reached the few has hitherto been applied. Let us in turn consider each of these modes. The first is the most injudicious. In monarchical countries, the estates and the greatest portion of the wealth are left to the first son, that the vanity of the parent may be gratified by the thought that his name and title are to descend unimpaired to succeeding generations. The condition of this class in Europe to-day teaches the failure of such hopes or ambitions. The successors have become impoverished through their follies, or from the fall in the value of land. Even in Great Britain the strict law of entail has been found inadequate to maintain an hereditary class. Its soil is rapidly passing into the hands of the stranger. Under republican institutions the division of property among the children is much fairer; but the question which forces itself upon thoughtful men in all lands is, Why should men leave great fortunes to their children? If this is done from affection, is it not misguided affection? Observation teaches that, generally speaking, it is not well for the children that they should be so burdened. Neither is it well for the State. Beyond providing for the wife and daughters moderate sources of income, and very moderate allowances indeed, if any, for the sons, men may well hesitate; for it is no longer questionable that great sums bequeathed often work more for the injury than for the good of the recipients. Wise men will soon conclude that, for the best interests of the members of their families, and of the State, such bequests are an improper use of their means.

It is not suggested that men who have failed to educate their sons to earn a livelihood shall cast them adrift in poverty. If any man has seen fit to rear his sons with a view to their living idle lives, or, what is highly commendable, has instilled in them the sentiment that they are in a position to labor for public ends without reference to pecuniary considerations, then, of course, the duty of the parent is to see that such are provided for in moderation. There are instances of millionaires' sons unspoiled by wealth, who, being rich, still perform great services to the community. Such are the very salt of the earth, as valuable as, unfortunately, they are rare. It is not the exception, however, but the rule, that men must regard; and, looking at the usual result of enormous sums conferred upon legatees, the thoughtful man must shortly say, "I would as soon leave to my son a curse as the almighty dollar," and admit to himself that it is not the welfare of the children, but family pride, which inspires these legacies.

As to the second mode, that of leaving wealth at death for public uses, it may be said that this is only a means for the disposal of wealth, provided a man is content to wait until he is dead before he becomes of much good in the world. Knowledge of the results of legacies bequeathed is not calculated to inspire the brightest hopes of much posthumous good being accomplished by them. The cases are not few in which the real object sought by the testator is not attained, nor are they few in which his real wishes are thwarted. In many cases the bequests are so used as to become only monuments of his folly. It is well to remember that it requires the exercise of not less ability than that which acquires it, to use wealth so as to be really beneficial to the community. Besides this, it may fairly be said that no man is to be extolled for doing what he cannot help doing, nor is he to be thanked by the community to which he only leaves wealth at death. Men who leave vast sums in this way may fairly be thought men who would not have left it at all had they been able to take it with them. The memories of such cannot be held in grateful remembrance, for there is no grace in their gifts. It is not to be wondered at that such bequests seem so generally to lack the blessing. . . .

There remains, then, only one mode of using great fortunes; but in this we have the true antidote for the temporary unequal distribution of wealth, the reconciliation of the rich and the poor—a reign of harmony, another ideal, differing, indeed, from that of the Communist in requiring only the further evolution of existing conditions, not the total overthrow of our civilization. It is founded upon the present most intense Individualism, and the race is prepared to put it in practice by degrees whenever it pleases. Under its sway we shall have an ideal State, in which the surplus wealth of the few will become, in the best sense, the property of the many, because administered for the common good; and this wealth, passing through the hands of the few, can be made a much more potent force for the elevation of our race than if distributed in small sums to the people themselves. Even the poorest can be made to see this, and to agree that great sums gathered by some of their fellow-citizens and spent for public purposes, from which the masses reap the principal benefit, are more valuable to them than if scattered among themselves in trifling amounts through the course of many years.

If we consider the results which flow from the Cooper Institute,* for instance, to the best portion of the race in New York not possessed of means, and compare these with those which would have ensued for the good of the masses from an equal sum

* Cooper Institute—a philanthropic organization dedicated to adult education.—Eds.

distributed by Mr. Cooper in his lifetime in the form of wages, which is the highest form of distribution, being for work done and not for charity, we can form some estimate of the possibilities for the improvement of the race which lie embedded in the present law of the accumulation of wealth. Much of this sum, if distributed in small quantities among the people, would have been wasted in the indulgence of appetite, some of it in excess, and it may be doubted whether even the part put to the best use, that of adding to the comforts of the home, would have yielded results for the race, as a race, at all comparable to those which are flowing and are to flow from the Cooper Institute from generation to generation. Let the advocate of violent or radical change ponder well this thought. . . .

This, then, is held to be the duty of the man of wealth: To set an example of modest, unostentatious living, shunning display or extravagance; to provide moderately for the legitimate wants of those dependent upon him; and, after doing so, to consider all surplus revenues which come to him simply as trust funds, which he is called upon to administer, and strictly bound as a matter of duty to administer in the manner which, in his judgment, is best calculated to produce the most beneficial results for the community—the man of wealth thus becoming the mere trustee and agent for his poorer brethren, bringing to their service his superior wisdom, experience, and ability to administer, doing for them better than they would or could do for themselves.

We are met here with the difficulty of determining what are moderate sums to leave to members of the family; what is modest, unostentatious living; what is the test of extravagance. There must be different standards for different conditions. The answer is that it is as impossible to name exact amounts or actions as it is to define good manners, good taste, or the rules of propriety; but, nevertheless, these are verities, well known, although indefinable. Public sentiment is quick to know and to feel what offends these. So in the case of wealth. The rule in regard to good taste in dress of men or women applies here. Whatever makes one conspicuous offends the canon. If any family be chiefly known for display, for extravagance in home, table, or equipage, for enormous sums ostentatiously spent in any form upon itself—if these be its chief distinctions, we have no difficulty in estimating its nature or culture. So likewise in regard to the use or abuse of its surplus wealth, or to generous, freehanded cooperation in good public uses, or to unabated efforts to accumulate and hoard to the last, or whether they administer or bequeath. The verdict rests with the best and most enlightened public sentiment. The community will surely judge, and its judgments will not often be wrong.

The best uses to which surplus wealth can be put have already been indicated. Those who would administer wisely must, indeed, be wise; for one of the serious obstacles to the improvement of our race is indiscriminate charity. It were better for mankind that the millions of the rich were thrown into the sea than so spent as to encourage the slothful, the drunken, the unworthy. Of every thousand dollars spent in so-called charity to-day, it is probable that nine hundred and fifty dollars is unwisely spent—so spent, indeed, as to produce the very evils which it hopes to mitigate or cure. A well-known writer of philosophic books admitted the other day that he had given a quarter of a dollar to a man who approached him as he was coming to visit the house of his friend. He knew nothing of the habits of this beggar, knew not the use that would be made of this money, although he had every reason to suspect that it would be spent improperly. This man professed to be a disciple of Herbert Spencer; yet the quarter-dollar given that night will probably work more injury than all the money will do good which its thoughtless donor will ever be able to give in true charity. He only gratified his own feelings, saved himself from annoyance—and this was probably one of the most selfish and very worst actions of his life, for in all respects he is most worthy.

In bestowing charity, the main consideration should be to help those who will help themselves; to provide part of the means by which those who desire to improve may do so; to give those who desire to rise the aids by which they may rise; to assist, but rarely or never to do all. Neither the individual nor the race is improved by almsgiving. Those worthy of assistance, except in rare cases, seldom require assistance. The really valuable men of the race never do, except in case of accident or sudden change. Every one has, of course, cases of individuals brought to his own knowledge where temporary assistance can do genuine good, and these he will not overlook. But the amount which can be wisely given by the individual for individuals is necessarily limited by his lack of knowledge of the circumstances connected with each. He is the only true reformer who is as careful and as anxious not to aid the unworthy as he is to aid the worthy, and, perhaps, even more so, for in almsgiving more injury is probably done by rewarding vice than by relieving virtue.

The rich man is thus almost restricted to following the examples of Peter Cooper, Enoch Pratt of Baltimore, Mr. Pratt of Brooklyn, Senator Stanford,* and others, who know that the best means of benefiting the community is to place within its reach the ladders upon which the aspiring can rise—free libraries, parks, and means of recreation, by which men are helped in body and mind; works of art, certain to give pleasure and improve the public taste; and public institutions of various kinds, which will improve the general condition of the people; in this manner returning their surplus wealth to the mass of their fellows in the forms best calculated to do them lasting good.

Thus is the problem of rich and poor to be solved. The laws of accumulation will be left free, the laws of distribution free. Individualism will continue, but the millionaire will be but a trustee for the poor, intrusted for a season with a great part of the increased wealth of the community, but administering it for the community far better than it could or would have done for itself. The best minds will thus have reached a stage in the development of the race in which it is clearly seen that there is no mode of disposing of surplus wealth creditable to thoughtful and earnest men into whose hands it flows, save by using it year by year for the general good. This day already dawns. Men may die without incurring the pity of their fellows, still sharers in great business enterprises from which their capital cannot be or has not been withdrawn, and which is left chiefly at death for public uses; yet the day is not far distant when the man who dies leaving behind him millions of available wealth, which was free to him to administer during life, will pass away "unwept, unhonored, and unsung," no

* American philanthropists.—Eds.

matter to what uses he leaves the dross which he cannot take with him. Of such as these the public verdict will then be: "The man who dies thus rich dies disgraced."

Such, in my opinion is the true gospel concerning wealth, obedience to which is destined some day to solve the problem of the rich and the poor, and to bring "Peace on earth, among men good will."

. . . . . . . . . . . . . . . . . . . . . . . . . .

Time was when the words concerning the rich man entering the kingdom of heaven were regarded as a hard saying. To-day, when all questions are probed to the bottom and the standards of faith receive the most liberal interpretations, the startling verse has been relegated to the rear, to await the next kindly revision as one of those things which cannot be quite understood, but which, meanwhile, it is carefully to be noted, are not to be understood literally. But is it so very improbable that the next stage of thought is to restore the doctrine in all its pristine purity and force, as being in perfect harmony with sound ideas upon the subject of wealth and poverty, the rich and the poor, and the contrasts everywhere seen and deplored? In Christ's day, it is evident, reformers were against the wealthy. It is none the less evident that we are fast recurring to that position to-day; and there will be nothing to surprise the student of sociological development if society should soon approve the text which has caused so much anxiety: "It is easier for a camel to enter the eye of a needle than for a rich man to enter the kingdom of heaven." Even if the needle were the small casement at the gates, the words betoken serious difficulty for the rich. It will be but a step for the theologian from the doctrine that he who dies rich dies disgraced, to that which brings upon the man punishment or deprivation hereafter.

The gospel of wealth but echoes Christ's words. It calls upon the millionaire to sell all that he hath and give it in the highest and best form to the poor by administering his estate himself for the good of his fellows, before he is called upon to lie down and rest upon the bosom of Mother Earth. So doing, he will approach his end no longer the ignoble hoarder of useless millions; poor, very poor indeed, in money, but rich, very rich, twenty times a millionaire still, in the affection, gratitude, and admiration of his fellow-men, and—sweeter far—soothed and sustained by the still, small voice within, which, whispering, tells him that, because he has lived, perhaps one small part of the great world has been bettered just a little. This much is sure: against such riches as these no bar will be found at the gates of Paradise.

## *Anne Morrow Lindbergh*
## "CHANNELLED WHELK"

The shell in my hand is deserted. It once housed a whelk, a snail-like creature, and then temporarily, after the death of the first occupant, a little hermit crab, who has run away, leaving his tracks behind him like a delicate vine on the sand. He ran away, and left me his shell. It was once a protection to him. I turn the shell in my hand, gazing into the wide open door from which he made his exit. Had it become an encumbrance? Why did he run away? Did he hope to find a better home, a better mode of living? I too have run away, I realize, I have shed the shell of my life, for these few weeks of vacation.

But his shell—it is simple; it is bare, it is beautiful. Small, only the size of my thumb, its architecture is perfect, down to the finest detail. Its shape, swelling like a pear in the center, winds in a gentle spiral to the pointed apex. Its color, dull gold, is whitened by a wash of salt from the sea. Each whorl, each faint knob, each criss-cross vein in its egg-shell texture, is as clearly defined as on the day of creation. My eye follows with delight the outer circumference of that diminutive winding staircase up which this tenant used to travel.

My shell is not like this, I think. How untidy it has become! Blurred with moss, knobby with barnacles, its shape is hardly recognizable any more. Surely, it had a shape once. It has a shape still in my mind. What is the shape of my life?

The shape of my life today starts with a family. I have a husband, five children and a home just beyond the suburbs of New York. I have also a craft, writing, and therefore work I want to pursue. The shape of my life is, of course, determined by many other things; my background and childhood, my mind and its education, my conscience and its pressures, my heart and its desires. I want to give and take from my children and husband, to share with friends and community, to carry out my obligations to man and to the world as a woman, as an artist, as a citizen.

But I want first of all—in fact, as an end to these other desires—to be at peace with myself. I want a singleness of eye, a purity of intention, a central core to my life that will enable me to carry out these obligations and activities as well as I can. I want, in fact—to borrow from the language of the saints—to live "in grace" as much of the time as possible. I am not using this term in a strictly theological sense. By grace I mean an inner harmony, essentially spiritual, which can be translated into outward harmony. I am seeking perhaps what Socrates asked for in the prayer from the *Phaedrus* when he said, "May the outward and inward man be at one." I would like to achieve a state of inner spiritual grace from which I could function and give as I was meant to in the eye of God.

Vague as this definition may be, I believe most people are aware of periods in their lives when they seem to be "in grace" and other periods when they feel "out of grace," even though they may use different words to describe these states. In the first happy condition, one seems to carry all one's tasks before one lightly, as if borne alone on a great tide; and in the opposite state one can hardly tie a shoe-string. It is true that a large part of life consists in learning a technique of tying the shoe-string, whether one is in grace or not. But there are techniques of living too; there are even techniques in the search for grace. And techniques can be cultivated. I have learned by some experience, by many examples, and by the writings of countless others before me, also occupied in the search, that certain environments, certain modes of life, certain rules of conduct are more conducive to inner and outer harmony than others. There are, in fact, certain roads that one may follow. Simplification of life is one of them.

I mean to lead a simple life, to choose a simple shell I can carry easily—like a hermit crab. But I do not, I find that my frame of life does not foster simplicity. My husband and five children must make their way in the world. The life I have chosen as wife and mother entrains a whole caravan of complications. It involves a house in the suburbs and either household drudgery or household help which wavers between scarcity and non-existence for most of us. It involves food and shelter; meals, planning, marketing, bills, and making the ends meet in a thousand ways. It involves not only the butcher, the baker, the candlestickmaker but countless other experts to keep my modern house with its modern "simplifications" (electricity, plumbing, refrigerator, gas-stove, oil-burner, dish-washer, radios, car, and numerous other labor-saving devices) functioning properly. It involves health; doctors, dentists, appointments, medicine, cod-liver oil, vitamins, trips to the drugstore. It involves education, spiritual, intellectual, physical; schools, school conferences, carpools, extra trips for basket-ball or orchestra practice; tutoring; camps, camp equipment and transportation. It involves clothes, shopping, laundry, cleaning, mending, letting skirts down and sewing buttons on, or finding someone else to do it. It involves friends, my husband's, my children's, my own, and endless arrangements to get together; letters, invitations, telephone calls and transportation hither and yon.

For life today in America is based on the premise of ever-widening circles of contact and communication. It involves not only family demands, but community demands, national demands, international demands on the good citizen, through social and cultural pressures, through newspapers, magazines, radio programs, political drives, charitable appeals, and so on. My mind reels with it. What a circus act we women perform every day of our lives. It puts the trapeze artist to shame. Look at us. We run a tight rope daily, balancing a pile of books on the head. Baby-carriage, parasol, kitchen chair, still under control. Steady now!

This is not the life of simplicity but the life of multiplicity that the wise men warn us of. It leads not to unification but to fragmentation. It does not bring grace; it destroys the soul. And this is not only true of my life, I am forced to conclude; it is the life of millions of women in America. I stress America, because today, the American women more than any other has the privilege of choosing such a life. Woman in large parts of the civilized world has been forced back by war, by poverty, by collapse, by the sheer struggle to survive, into a smaller circle of immediate time and space, immediate family life, immediate problems of existence. The American woman is still relatively free to choose the wider life. How long she will hold this enviable and precarious position no one knows. But her particular situation has a significance far above its apparent economic, national or even sex limitations.

For the problem of the multiplicity of life not only confronts the American woman, but also the American man. And it is not merely the concern of the American as such, but of our whole modern civilization, since life in America today is held up as the ideal of a large part of the rest of the world. And finally, it is not limited to our present civilization, though we are faced with it now in an exaggerated form. It has always been one of the pitfalls of mankind. Plotinus was preaching the dangers of multiplicity of the world back in the third century. Yet, the problem is particularly and essentially woman's. Distraction is, always has been, and probably will be, inherent in woman's life.

For to be a woman is to have interests and duties, raying out in all directions from the central mother-core, like spokes from the hub of a wheel. The pattern of our lives is essentially circular. We must be open to all points of the compass; husband, children, friends, home, community; stretched out, exposed, sensitive like a spider's web to each breeze that blows, to each call that comes. How difficult for us, then, to achieve a balance in the midst of these contradictory tensions, and yet how necessary for the proper functioning of our lives. How much we need, and how arduous of attainment is that steadiness preached in all rules for holy living. How desirable and how distant is the ideal of the contemplative, artist, or saint—the inner inviolable core, the single eye.

With a new awareness, both painful and humorous, I begin to understand why the saints were rarely married women. I am convinced it has nothing inherently to do, as I once supposed, with chastity or children. It has to do primarily with distractions. The bearing, rearing, feeding and educating of children; the running of a house with its thousand details; human relationships with their myriad pulls—woman's normal occupations in general run counter to creative life, or contemplative life, or saintly life. The problem is not merely one of *Woman and Career, Woman and the Home, Woman and Independence.* It is more basically: how to remain whole in the midst of the distractions of life; how to remain balanced, no matter what centrifugal forces tend to pull one off center; how to remain strong, no matter what shocks come in at the periphery and tend to crack the hub of the wheel.

What is the answer? There is no easy answer, no complete answer. I have only clues, shells from the sea. The bare beauty of the channelled whelk tells me that one answer, and perhaps a first step, is in simplification of life, in cutting out some of the distractions. But how? Total retirement is not possible. I cannot shed my responsibilities. I cannot permanently inhabit a desert island. I cannot be a nun in the midst of family life. I would not want to be. The solution for me, surely, is neither in total renunciation of the world, nor in total acceptance of it. I must find a balance somewhere, or an alternating rhythm between these two extremes; a swinging of the pendulum between solitude and communication, between retreat and return. In my periods of retreat, perhaps I can learn something to carry back into my worldly life. I can at least practice for these two weeks the simplification of outward life, as a beginning. I can follow this superficial clue, and see where it leads. Here, in beach living, I can try.

One learns first of all in beach living the art of shedding; how little one can get along with, not how much. Physical shedding to begin with, which then mysteriously spreads into other fields. Clothes, first. Of course, one needs less in the sun. But one needs less anyway, one finds suddenly. One does not need a closet-full, only a small suitcase-full. And what a relief it is! Less taking up and down of hems, less mending and—best of all—less worry about what to wear. One finds one is shedding not only clothes—but vanity.

Next, shelter. One does not need the airtight shelter one has in winter in the North. Here I live in a bare sea-shell of a cottage. No heat, no telephone, no plumbing to speak of, no hot water, a two-burner oil stove, no gadgets to go wrong. No rugs. There were some, but I rolled them up the first day; it is easier to sweep the sand off a bare floor. But I find I don't bustle about with unnecessary sweeping and cleaning here. I am no longer aware of the dust. I have shed my Puritan conscience about absolute tidiness and cleanliness. Is it possible that, too, is a material burden? No curtains. I do not need them for privacy; the pines around my house are enough protection. I want the windows open all the time, and I don't want to worry about rain. I begin to shed my Martha-like anxiety about many things. Washable slip-covers, faded and old—I hardly see them; I don't worry about the impression they make on other people. I am shedding pride. As little furniture as possible; I shall not need much. I shall ask into my shell only those friends with whom I can be completely honest. I find I am shedding hypocrisy in human relationships. What a rest that will be! The most exhausting thing in life, I have discovered, is being insincere. That is why so much of social life is exhausting; one is wearing a mask. I have shed my mask.

I find I live quite happily without those things I think necessary in winter in the North. And as I write these words, I remember, with some shock at the disparity in our lives, a similar statement made by a friend of mine in France who spent three years in a German prison camp. Of course, he said, qualifying his remark, they did not get enough to eat, they were sometimes atrociously treated, they had little physical freedom. And yet, prison life taught him how little one can get along with, and what extraordinary spiritual freedom and peace such simplification can bring. I remember again, ironically, that today more of us in America than anywhere else in the world have the luxury of choice between simplicity and complication of life. And for the most part, we, who could choose simplicity, choose complication. War, prison, survival periods, enforce a form of simplicity on man. The monk and the nun choose it of their own free will. But if one accidentally finds it, as I have for a few days, one finds also the serenity it brings.

Is it not rather ugly, one may ask? One collects material possessions not only for security, comfort or vanity, but for beauty as well. Is your sea-shell house not ugly and bare? No, it is beautiful, my house. It is bare, of course, but the wind, the sun, the smell of the pines blow through its bareness. The unfinished beams in the roof are veiled by cobwebs. They are lovely, I think, gazing up at them with new eyes; they soften the hard lines of the rafters as grey hairs soften the lines on a middle-aged face. I no longer pull out grey hairs or sweep down cobwebs. As for the walls, it is true they looked forbidding at first. I felt cramped and enclosed by their blank faces. I wanted to knock holes in them, to give them another dimension with pictures or windows. So I dragged home from the beach grey arms of driftwood, worn satin-smooth by wind and sand. I gathered trailing green vines with floppy red-tipped leaves. I picked up the whitened skeletons of conchshells, their curious hollowed-out shapes faintly reminiscent of abstract sculpture. With these tacked to walls and propped up in corners, I am satisfied. I have a periscope out to the world. I have a window, a view, a point of flight from my sedentary base.

I am content. I sit down at my desk, a bare kitchen table with a blotter, a bottle of ink, a sand dollar to weight down one corner, a clam shell for a pen tray, the broken tip of a conch, pink-tinged, to finger, and a row of shells to set my thoughts spinning.

I love my sea-shell of a house. I wish I could live in it always. I wish I could transport it home. But I cannot. It will not hold a husband, five children and the necessities and trappings of daily life. I can only carry back my little channelled whelk. It will sit on my desk in Connecticut, to remind me of the ideal of a simplified life, to encourage me in the game I played on the beach. To ask how little, not how much, can I get along with. To say—is it necessary?—when I am tempted to add one more accumulation to my life, when I am pulled toward one more centifugal activity.

Simplification of outward life is not enough. It is merely the outside. But I am starting with the outside. I am looking at the outside of a shell, the outside of my life—the shell. The complete answer is not to be found on the outside, in an outward mode of living. This is only a technique, a road to grace. The final answer, I know, is always inside. But the outside can give a clue, can help one to find the inside answer. One is free, like the hermit crab, to change one's shell.

Channelled whelk, I put you down again, but you have set my mind on a journey, up an inwardly winding spiral staircase of thought.

## SUGGESTIONS FOR DISCUSSION

1. One kind of evidence that a writer can offer is the appeal to authority, or an attempt to win the reader's assent by invoking a respected thinker or document. Which authorities does Carnegie make use use of in his presentation? Are his appeals to authority fair and convincing?
2. It is clear that Lindbergh's values are different from Carnegie's, a difference reflected in the language they use. For example, Carnegie writes of "material development" while Lindbergh writes of "material burdens." Carnegie sees "progress" where Lindbergh sees "complications."

   Make a list of Carnegie's favorite words and phrases and try to determine what words Lindbergh would use for the same phenomena. Then make a list of Lindbergh's favorite words and speculate on how Carnegie would respond.
3. Consider the following statement by Abraham Lincoln: "That some should be rich, shows that others may become rich, and hence is just encouragement to industry and enterprise. Let not him who is houseless pull down the house of another; but let him labor diligently and build one for himself." Do Carnegie and Lincoln justify wealth for the same reasons? Do you see any difference in their attitudes? Does Lincoln seem to agree with Carnegie's assertion that wealth will inevitably fall into "the hands of the few"?

## SUGGESTIONS FOR WRITING

1. Anne Morrow Lindbergh's essay might be called a meditation: her thinking is inspired by and builds upon the shell of the channelled whelk in a kind of extended metaphor. For this assignment, try a meditation yourself. Find an object or a living creature that you like, that fascinates you. Write more or less freely about it, and about what it tells you about yourself—either in ways you are alike or unlike.
2. Everyone has beliefs which seem so self-evident that they require no explanation or support. These beliefs are called assumptions, and they are often unstated. A careful reader can often ascertain a writer's assumptions even when they are not expressed.

   What assumptions does Carnegie seem to hold about the nature and ability of the average person? Write an essay describing Carnegie's assumptions and analyzing the strengths and weaknesses of his argument.

# 21

# Fame and Recognition

*Daniel J. Boorstin*

## "FROM HERO TO CELEBRITY"

*Diana Trilling*

## "THE DEATH OF MARILYN MONROE"

The next pair of essays analyzes the quest for fame and recognition. Daniel Boorstin works out a thorough and careful definition of modern celebrities by contasting them to traditonal heroes. Boorstin suggests that fame has become an empty distinction created entirely by the media, and that our present celebrities are merely "receptables into which we pour our own purposelessness." In "The Death of Marilyn Monroe," Diana Trilling demonstrates the potentially destructive impact of fame on the vulnerable psyche of one particular individual. Trilling sympathetically describes Monroe's sense of alienation and the special burden she felt in maintaining the image of a sex object.

### WRITE BEFORE READING

1. The next two essays deal with success of a special kind, the success that is created and controlled by the media. It is a subject on which most Americans are minor authorities, as evidenced by the talk shows, sports, *Us* and *People* magazines, and so on. Before you read on, then, try this writing assignment. Imagine yourself to be a visitor to America from some other planet, one where there are no such things as celebrities. As part of a series of reports to your people, you write one on this phenomenon that consumes so much time and energy for this strange people. Remember that your purpose is to inform an audience that knows nothing about the subject; it will help if the *persona* you use has considerable innocence too.

*Daniel J. Boorstin*

# "FROM HERO TO CELEBRITY"

## I

Our age has produced a new kind of eminence. This is as characteristic of our culture and our century as was the divinity of Greek gods in the sixth century B.C. or the chivalry of knights and courtly lovers in the middle ages. It has not yet driven heroism, sainthood, or martyrdom completely out of our consciousness. But with every decade it overshadows them more. All older forms of greatness now survive only in the shadow of this new form. This new kind of eminence is "celebrity."

The word "celebrity" (from the Latin *celebritas* for "multitude" or "fame" and *celeber* meaning "frequented," "populous," or "famous") originally meant not a person but a condition—as the Oxford English Dictionary says, "the condition of being much talked about; famousness, notoriety." In this sense its use dates from at least the early seventeenth century. Even then it had a weaker meaning than "fame" or "renown." Matthew Arnold, for example, remarked in the nineteenth century that while the philosopher Spinoza's followers had "celebrity," Spinoza himself had "fame."

For us, however, "celebrity" means primarily a person—"a person of celebrity." This usage of the word significantly dates from the early years of the Graphic Revolution, the first example being about 1850. Emerson spoke of "the celebrities of wealth and fashion" (1848). Now American dictionaries define a celebrity as "a famous or well-publicized person."

The celebrity in the distinctive modern sense could not have existed in any earlier age, or in America before the Graphic Revolution. *The celebrity is a person who is known for his well-knownness.*

His qualities—or rather his lack of qualities—illustrate our peculiar problems. He is neither good nor bad, great nor petty. He is the human pseudo-event. He has been fabricated on purpose to satisfy our exaggerated expectations of human greatness. He is morally neutral. The product of no conspiracy, of no group promoting vice or emptiness, he is made by honest, industrious men of high professional ethics doing their job, "informing" and educating us. He is made by all of us who willingly read about him, who like to see him on television, who buy recordings of his voice, and talk about him to our friends. His relation to morality and even to reality is highly ambiguous. He is like the woman *in* an Elinor Glyn novel who describes another by saying "She is like a figure in an Elinor Glyn novel."

The massive *Celebrity Register* (1959), compiled by Earl Blackwell and Cleveland Amory, now gives us a well-documented definition of the word, illustrated by over 2,200 biographies. "We think we have a better yardstick than the *Social Register,* or *Who's Who,* or any such book," they explain. "Our point is that it is impossible to be accurate in listing a man's social standing—even if anyone cared; and it's impossible to list accurately the success or value of men; but you *can* judge a man as a celebrity—

all you have to do is weigh his press clippings." The *Celebrity Register's* alphabetical order shows Mortimer Adler followed by Polly Adler, the Dalai Lama listed beside TV comedienne Dagmar, Dwight Eisenhower preceding Anita Ekberg, ex-President Herbert Hoover following ex-torch singer Libby Holman, Pope John XXIII coming after Mr. John the hat designer, and Bertrand Russell followed by Jane Russell. They are all celebrities. The well-knownness which they have in common overshadows everything else.

The advertising world has proved the market appeal of celebrities. In trade jargon celebrities are "big names." Endorsement advertising not only uses celebrities; it helps make them. Anything that makes a well-known name still better known automatically raises its status as a celebrity. The old practice, well established before the nineteenth century, of declaring the prestige of a product by the phrase "By Appointment to His Majesty" was, of course, a kind of use of the testimonial endorsement. But the King was in fact a great person, one of illustrious lineage and with impressive actual and symbolic powers. The King was not a venal endorser, and he was likely to use only superior products. He was not a mere celebrity. For the test of celebrity is nothing more than well-knownness.

Studies of biographies in popular magazines suggest that editors, and supposedly also readers, of such magazines not long ago shifted their attention away from the old-fashioned hero. From the person known for some serious achievement, they have turned their biographical interests to the new-fashioned celebrity. Of the subjects of biographical articles appearing in the *Saturday Evening Post* and the now-defunct *Collier's* in five sample years between 1901 and 1914, 74 per cent came from politics, business, and the professions. But after about 1922 well over half of them came from the world of entertainment. Even among the entertainers an ever decreasing proportion has come from the serious arts—literature, fine arts, music, dance, and theater. An ever increasing proportion (in recent years nearly all) comes from the fields of light entertainment, sports, and the night club circuit. In the earlier period, say before World War I, the larger group included figures like the President of the United States, a Senator, a State Governor, the Secretary of the Treasury, the banker J. P. Morgan, the railroad magnate James J. Hill, a pioneer in aviation, the inventor of the torpedo, a Negro educator, an immigrant scientist, an opera singer, a famous poet, and a popular fiction writer. By the 1940's the larger group included figures like the boxer Jack Johnson, Clark Gable, Bobby Jones, the movie actresses Brenda Joyce and Brenda Marshall, William Powell, the woman matador Conchita Cintron, the night club entertainer Adelaide Moffett, and the gorilla Toto. Some analysts say the shift is primarily the sign of a new focus of popular attention away from production and toward consumption. But this is oversubtle.

A simpler explanation is that the machinery of information has brought into being a new substitute for the hero, who is the celebrity, and whose main characteristic is his well-knownness. In the democracy of pseudo-events, anyone can become a celebrity, if only he can get into the news and stay there. Figures from the world of entertainment and sports are most apt to be well known. If they are successful enough, they actually overshadow the real figures they portray. George Arliss overshadowed Disraeli, Vivian Leigh overshadowed Scarlett O'Hara, Fess Parker overshadowed Davy Crockett. Since their stock in trade is their well-knownness, they are most apt to have energetic press agents keeping them in the public eye.

It is hardly surprising then that magazine and newspaper readers no longer find the lives of their heroes instructive. Popular biographies can offer very little in the way of solid information. For the subjects are themselves mere figments of the media. If their lives are empty of drama or achievement, it is only as we might have expected, for they are not known for drama or achievement. They are celebrities. Their chief claim to fame is their fame itself. They are notorious for their notoriety. If this is puzzling or fantastic, if it is mere tautology, it is no more puzzling or fantastic or tautologous than much of the rest of our experience. Our experience tends more and more to become tautology—needless repetition of the same in different words and images. Perhaps what ails us is not so much a vice as a "nothingness." The vacuum of our experience is actually made emptier by our anxious straining with mechanical devices to fill it artificially. What is remarkable is not only that we manage to fill experience with so much emptiness, but that we manage to give the emptiness such appealing variety.

We can hear ourselves straining. "He's the greatest!" Our descriptions of celebrities overflow with superlatives. In popular magazine biographies we learn that a Dr. Brinkley is the "best-advertised doctor in the United States"; an actor is the "luckiest man in the movies today"; a Ringling is "not only the greatest, but the first real showman in the Ringling family"; a general is "one of the best mathematicians this side of Einstein"; a columnist has "one of the strangest of courtships"; a statesman has "the world's most exciting job"; a sportsman is "the loudest and by all odds the most abusive"; a newsman is "one of the most consistently resentful men in the country"; a certain ex-King's mistress is "one of the unhappiest women that ever lived." But, despite the "supercolossal" on the label, the contents are very ordinary. The lives of celebrities which we like to read, as Leo Lowenthal remarks, are a mere catalog of "hardships" and "breaks." These men and women are "the proved specimens of the average."

No longer external sources which fill us with purpose, these new-model "heroes" are receptacles into which we pour our own purposelessness. They are nothing but ourselves seen in a magnifying mirror. Therefore the lives of entertainer-celebrities cannot extend our horizon. Celebrities populate our horizon with men and women we already know. Or, as an advertisement for the *Celebrity Register* cogently puts it, celebrities are "the 'names' who, once made by news, now make news by themselves." Celebrity is made by simple familiarity, induced and re-enforced by public means. The celebrity therefore is the perfect embodiment of tautology: the most familiar is the most familiar.

## II

The hero was distinguished by his achievement; the celebrity by his image or trademark. The hero created himself; the celebrity is created by the media. The hero was a big man; the celebrity is a big name.

Formerly a public man needed a *private* secretary for a barrier between himself and the public. Nowadays he has a *press* secretary, to keep him properly in the public eye. Before the Graphic Revolution (and still in countries which have not undergone that revolution) it was a mark of solid distinction in a man or a family to keep out of the news. A lady of aristocratic pretensions was supposed to get her name in the papers only three times: when she was born, when she married, and when she died. Now the families who are Society are by definition those always appearing in the papers. The man of truly heroic stature was once supposed to be marked by scorn for publicity. He quietly relied on the power of his character or his achievement.

In the South, where the media developed more slowly than elsewhere in the country, where cities appeared later, and where life was dominated by rural ways, the celebrity grew more slowly. The old-fashioned hero was romanticized. In this as in many other ways, the Confederate General Robert E. Lee was one of the last surviving American models of the older type. Among his many admirable qualities, Southern compatriots admired none more than his retirement from public view. He had the reputation for never having given a newspaper interview. He steadfastly refused to write his memoirs. "I should be trading on the blood of my men," he said. General George C. Marshall (1880–1959) is a more recent and more anachronistic example. He, too, shunned publicity and refused to write his memoirs, even while other generals were serializing theirs in the newspapers. But by this time, few people any longer considered this reticence a virtue. His old-fashioned unwillingness to enter the publicity arena finally left him a victim of the slanders of Senator Joseph McCarthy and others.

The hero was born of time: his gestation required at least a generation. As the saying went, he had "stood the test of time." A maker of tradition, he was himself made by tradition. He grew over the generations as people found new virtues in him and attributed to him new exploits. Receding into the misty past he became more, and not less, heroic. It was not necessary that his face or figure have a sharp, well-delineated outline, nor that his life be footnoted. Of course there could not have been any photographs of him, and often there was not even a likeness. Men of the last century were more heroic than those of today; men of antiquity were still more heroic; and those of pre-history became demigods. The hero was always somehow ranked among the ancients.

The celebrity, on the contrary, is always a contemporary. The hero is made by folklore, sacred texts, and history books, but the celebrity is the creature of gossip, of public opinion, of magazines, newspapers, and the ephemeral images of movie and television screen. The passage of time, which creates and establishes the hero, destroys the celebrity. One is made, the other unmade, by repetition. The celebrity is born in the daily papers and never loses the mark of his fleeting origin.

The very agency which first makes the celebrity in the long run inevitably destroys him. He will be destroyed, as he was made, by publicity. The newspapers make him, and they unmake him—not by murder but by suffocation or starvation. No one is more forgotten than the last generation's celebrity. This fact explains the newspaper feature "Whatever Became Of. . .?" which amuses us by accounts of the present obscurity of former celebrities. One can always get a laugh by referring knowingly to the once-household names which have lost their celebrity in the last few decades: Mae Bush, William S. Hart, Clara Bow. A woman reveals her age by the celebrities she knows.

There is not even any tragedy in the celebrity's fall, for he is a man returned to his proper anonymous station. The tragic hero, in Aristotle's familiar definition, was a man fallen from great estate, a great man with a tragic flaw. He had somehow become the victim of his own greatness. Yesterday's celebrity, however, is a commonplace man who has been fitted back into his proper commonplaceness not by any fault of his own, but by time itself.

The dead hero becomes immortal. He becomes more vital with the passage of time. The celebrity even in his lifetime becomes passé: he passes out of the picture. The white glare of publicity, which first gave him his specious brilliance, soon melts him away. This was so even when the only vehicles of publicity were the magazine and the newspaper. Still more now with our vivid round-the-clock media, with radio and television. Now when it is possible, by bringing their voices and images daily into our living rooms, to make celebrities more quickly than ever before, they die more quickly than ever. This has been widely recognized by entertainment celebrities and politicians. President Franklin Delano Roosevelt was careful to space out his fireside chats so the citizenry would not tire of him. Some comedians (for example, Jackie Gleason in the mid-1950's) have found that when they have weekly programs they reap quick and remunerative notoriety, but that they soon wear out their images. To extend their celebrity-lives, they offer their images more sparingly—once a month or once every two months instead of once a week.

There is a subtler difference between the personality of the hero and that of the celebrity. The figures in each of the two classes become assimilated to one another, but in two rather different ways. Heroes standing for greatness in the traditional mold tend to become colorless and cliché. The greatest heroes have the least distinctiveness of face or figure. We may show our reverence for them, as we do for God, by giving them beards. Yet we find it hard to imagine that Moses or Jesus could have had other special facial characteristics. The hero while being thus idealized and generalized loses his individuality. The fact that George Washington is not a vivid personality actually helps him serve as the heroic Father of Our Country. Perhaps Emerson meant just this when he said that finally every great hero becomes a great bore. To be a great hero is actually to become lifeless; to become a face on a coin or a postage stamp. It is to become a Gilbert Stuart's Washington. Contemporaries, however, and the celebrities made of them, suffer from idiosyncrasy. They are too vivid, too individual to be polished into a symmetrical Greek statue. The Graphic Revolution, with its klieg lights on face and figure, makes the images of different men more distinctive. This itself disqualifies them from becoming heroes or demigods.

While heroes are assimilated to one another by the great simple virtues of their character, celebrities are differentiated mainly by trivia of personality. To be known for your personality actually proves you a celebrity. Thus a synonym for "a celebrity" is "a personality." Entertainers, then, are best qualified to become celebrities because they are skilled in the marginal differentiation of their personalities. They succeed by skillfully distinguishing themselves from others essentially like them.

They do this by minutiae of grimace, gesture, language, and voice. We identify Jimmy ("Schnozzola") Durante by his nose, Bob Hope by his fixed smile, Jack Benny by his stinginess, Jack Paar by his rudeness, Jackie Gleason by his waddle, Imogene Coca by her bangs.

With the mushroom-fertility of all pseudo-events, celebrities tend to breed more celebrities. They help make and celebrate and publicize one another. Being known primarily for their well-knownness, celebrities intensify their celebrity images simply by becoming widely known for relations among themselves. By a kind of symbiosis, celebrities live off one another. One becomes better known by being the habitual butt of another's jokes, by being another's paramour or ex-wife, by being the subject of another's gossip, or even by being ignored by another celebrity. Elizabeth Taylor's celebrity appeal has consisted less perhaps in her own talents as an actress than in her connections with other celebrities—Nick Hilton, Mike Todd, and Eddie Fisher. Arthur Miller, the playwright, became a "real" celebrity by his marriage to Marilyn Monroe. When we talk or read or write about celebrities, our emphasis on their marital relations and sexual habits, on their tastes in smoking, drinking, dress, sports cars, and interior decoration is our desperate effort to distinguish among the indistinguishable. How can those commonplace people like us (who, by the grace of the media, happened to become celebrities) be made to seem more interesting or bolder than we are?

## III

As other pseudo-events in our day tend to overshadow spontaneous events, so celebrities (who are human pseudo-events) tend to overshadow heroes. They are more up-to-date, more nationally advertised, and more apt to have press agents. And there are far more of them. Celebrities die quickly but they are still more quickly replaced. Every year we experience a larger number than the year before.

Just as real events tend to be cast in the mold of pseudo-events, so in our society heroes survive by acquiring the qualities of celebrities. The best-publicized seems the most authentic experience. If someone does a heroic deed in our time, all the machinery of public information—press, pulpit, radio, and television—soon transform him into a celebrity. If they cannot succeed in this, the would-be hero disappears from public view.

A dramatic, a tragic, example is the career of Charles A. Lindbergh. He performed singlehanded one of the heroic deeds of this century. His deed was heroic in the best epic mold. But he became degraded into a celebrity. He then ceased to symbolize the virtues to which his heroic deed gave him a proper claim. He became filled with emptiness; then he disappeared from view. How did this happen?

On May 21, 1927, Charles A. Lindbergh made the first nonstop solo flight from Roosevelt Field, New York, to Le Bourget Air Field, Paris, in a monoplane, "The Spirit of St. Louis." This was plainly a heroic deed in the classic sense; it was a deed of valor—alone against the elements. In a dreary, unheroic decade Lindbergh's flight was a lightning flash of individual courage. Except for the fact of his flight, Lindberg was a commonplace person. Twenty-five years old at the time, he had been born in Detroit and raised in Minnesota. He was not a great inventor or a leader of men. He was not extraordinarily intelligent, eloquent, or ingenious. Like many another young man in those years, he had a fanatical love of flying. The air was his element. There he showed superlative skill and extraordinary courage—even to foolhardiness.

He was an authentic hero. Yet this was not enough. Or perhaps it was too much. For he was destined to be made into a mere celebrity; and he was to be the American celebrity par excellence. His rise and fall as a hero, his tribulations, his transformation, and his rise and decline as a celebrity are beautifully told in Kenneth S. Davis' biography.

Lindbergh himself had not failed to predict that his exploit would put him in the news. Before leaving New York he had sold to *The New York Times* the exclusive story of his flight. A supposedly naive and diffident boy, on his arrival in Paris he was confronted by a crowd of newspaper reporters at a press conference in Ambassador Myron T. Herrick's residence. But he would not give out any statement until he had clearance from the *Times* representative. He had actually subscribed to a newspaper clipping service, the clippings to be sent to his mother, who was then teaching school in Minnesota. With uncanny foresight, however, he had limited his subscriptions to clippings to the value of $50. (This did not prevent the company, doubtless seeking publicity as well as money, from suing him for not paying them for clippings beyond the specified amount.) Otherwise he might have had to spend the rest of his life earning the money to pay for clippings about himself.

Lindbergh's newspaper success was unprecedented. The morning after his flight *The New York Times,* a model of journalistic sobriety, gave him the whole of its first five pages, except for a few ads on page five. Other papers gave as much or more. Radio commentators talked of him by the hour. But there was not much hard news available. The flight was a relatively simple operation, lasting only thirty-three and a half hours. Lindbergh had told reporters in Paris just about all there was to tell. During his twenty-five years he had led a relatively uneventful life. He had few quirks of face, of figure, or of personality; little was known about his character. Some young women called him "tall and handsome," but his physical averageness was striking. He was the boy next door. To tell about this young man on the day after his flight, the nation's newspapers used 25,000 tons of newsprint more than usual. In many places sales were two to five times normal, and might have been higher if the presses could have turned out more papers.

When Lindbergh returned to New York on June 13, 1927, *The New York Times* gave its first sixteen pages the next morning almost exclusively to news about him. At the testimonial dinner in Lindbergh's honor at the Hotel Commodore (reputed to be the largest for an individual "in modern history") Charles Evans Hughes, former Secretary of State, and about to become Chief Justice of the United States, delivered an extravagant eulogy. With unwitting precision he characterized the American hero-turned-celebrity: "We measure heroes as we do ships, by their displacement. Colonel Lindbergh has displaced everything."

Lindbergh was by now the biggest human pseudo-event of modern times. His achievement, actually because it had been accomplished so neatly and with such spectacular simplicity, offered little spontaneous news. The biggest news about Lindbergh was that he was such big news. Pseudo-events multiplied in more than the usual geometric progression, for Lindbergh's well-knownness was so sudden and so overwhelming. It was easy to make stories about what a big celebrity he was; how this youth, unknown a few days before, was now a household word; how he was received by Presidents and Kings and Bishops. There was little else one could say about him. Lindbergh's singularly impressive heroic deed was soon far overshadowed by his even more impressive publicity. If well-knownness made a celebrity, here was the greatest. Of course it was remarkable to fly the ocean by oneself, but far more remarkable thus to dominate the news. His stature as hero was nothing compared with his stature as celebrity. All the more because it had happened, literally, overnight.

A large proportion of the news soon consisted of stories of how Lindbergh reacted to the "news" and to the publicity about himself. People focused their admiration on how admirably Lindbergh responded to publicity, how gracefully he accepted his role of celebrity. "Quickie" biographies appeared. These were little more than digests of newspaper accounts of the publicity jags during Lindbergh's ceremonial visits to the capitals of Europe and the United States. This was the celebrity after-life of the heroic Lindbergh. This was the tautology of celebrity.

During the next few years Lindbergh stayed in the public eye and remained a celebrity primarily because of two events. One was his marriage on May 27, 1929, to the cultivated and pretty Anne Morrow, daughter of Dwight Morrow, a Morgan partner, then Ambassador to Mexico. Now it was "The Lone Eagle and His Mate." As a newlywed he was more than ever attractive raw material for news. The maudlin pseudo-events of romance were added to all the rest. His newsworthiness was revived. There was no escape. Undaunted newsmen, thwarted in efforts to secure interviews and lacking solid facts, now made columns of copy from Lindbergh's efforts to keep out of the news! Some newspapermen, lacking other material for speculation, cynically suggested that Lindbergh's attempts to dodge reporters were motivated by a devious plan to increase his news-interest. When Lindbergh said he would co-operate with sober, respectable papers, but not with others, those left out pyramided his rebuffs into more news than his own statements would have made.

The second event which kept Lindbergh alive as a celebrity was the kidnaping of his infant son. This occurred at his new country house at Hopewell, New Jersey, on the night of March 1, 1932. For almost five years "Lindbergh" had been an empty receptacle into which news makers had poured their concoctions—saccharine, maudlin, legendary, slanderous, adulatory, or only fantastic. Now, when all other news-making possibilities seemed exhausted, his family was physically consumed. There was a good story in it. Here was "blood sacrifice," as Kenneth S. Davis calls it, to the gods of publicity. Since the case was never fully solved, despite the execution of the supposed kidnaper, no one can know whether the child would have been returned unharmed if the press and the public had behaved differently. But the press (with the collaboration of the bungling police) who had unwittingly destroyed real clues, then garnered and publicized innumerable false clues, and did nothing solid to help. They exploited Lindbergh's personal catastrophe with more than their usual energy.

In its way the kidnaping of Lindbergh's son was as spectacular as Lindbergh's transatlantic flight. In neither case was there much hard news, but this did not prevent the filling of newspaper columns. City editors now gave orders for no space limit on the kidnaping story. "I can't think of any story that would compare with it," observed the general news manager of the United Press, "unless America should enter a war." Hearst's INS photo service assigned its whole staff. They chartered two ambulances which, with sirens screaming, shuttled between Hopewell and New York City carrying photographic equipment out to the Lindbergh estate, and on the way back to the city served as mobile darkrooms in which pictures were developed and printed for delivery on arrival. For on-the-spot reporting at Hopewell, INS had an additional five men with three automobiles. United Press had six men and three cars; the Associated Press had four men, two women, and four cars. By midnight of March 1 the New York *Daily News* had nine reporters at Hopewell, and three more arrived the next day; the New York *American* had a dozen (including William Randolph Hearst, Jr., the paper's president); the New York *Herald Tribune,* four; the New York *World-Telegram, The New York Times,* and the Philadelphia *Ledger,* each about ten. This was only a beginning.

The next day the press agreed to Lindbergh's request to stay off the Hopewell grounds in order to encourage the kidnaper to return the child. The torrent of news did not stop. Within twenty-four hours INS sent over its wires 50,000 words (enough to fill a small volume) about the crime, 30,000 words the following day, and for some time thereafter 10,000 or more words a day. The Associated Press and United Press served their subscribers just as well. Many papers gave the story the whole of the front page, plus inside carry-overs, for a full week. There were virtually no new facts available. Still the news poured forth—pseudo events by the score—clues, rumors, local color features, and what the trade calls "think" pieces.

Soon there was almost nothing more to be done journalistically with the crime itself. There was little more to be reported, invented, or conjectured. Interest then focused on a number of sub-dramas created largely by newsmen themselves. These were stories about how the original event was being reported, about the mix-up among the different police that had entered the case, and about who would or should be Lindbergh's spokesman to the press world and his go-between with the kidnaper. Much news interest still centered on what a big story all the news added up to, and on how Mr. and Mrs. Lindbergh reacted to the publicity.

At this point the prohibition era crime celebrities came into the picture. "Salvy" Spitale and Irving Bitz, New York speakeasy owners, briefly held the spotlight. They had been suggested by Morris Rosner, who, because he had underworld connections, soon became a kind of personal secretary to the Lindberghs. Spitale and Bitz earned headlines for their effort to make contact with the kidnapers, then suspected to be either the notorious Purple Gang of Detroit or Al Capone's mob in Chicago. The two go-betweens became big names, until Spitale bowed out, appropriately enough, at a press conference. There he explained: "If it was someone I knew, I'll be God-damned if I wouldn't name him. I been in touch all around, and I come to the conclusion that this one was pulled by an independent." Al Capone himself, more a celebrity than ever, since he was about to begin a Federal prison term for income-tax evasion, increased his own newsworthiness by trying to lend a hand. In an interview with the "serious" columnist Arthur Brisbane of the Hearst papers, Capone offered $10,000 for information leading to the recovery of the child unharmed and to the capture of the kidnapers. It was even hinted that to free Capone might help recover the child.

The case itself produced a spate of new celebrities, whose significance no one quite understood but whose newsworthiness itself made them important. These included Colonel H. Norman Schwarzkopf, commander of the New Jersey State Police; Harry Wolf, Chief of Police in Hopewell; Betty Gow, the baby's nurse; Colonel Breckenridge, Lindbergh's personal counsel; Dr. J. F. ("Jafsie") Condon, a retired Bronx schoolteacher who was a volunteer go-between (he offered to add to the ransom money his own $1,000 life savings "so a loving mother may again have her child and Colonel Lindbergh may know that the American people are grateful for the honor bestowed on them by his pluck and daring"); John Hughes Curtis, a half-demented Norfolk, Virginia, boat-builder who pretended to reach the kidnapers; Gaston B. Means (author of *The Strange Death of President Harding*), later convicted of swindling Mrs. Evalyn Walsh McLean out of $104,000 by posing as a negotiator with the kidnapers; Violet Sharpe, a waitress in the Morrow home, who married the Morrow butler and who had had a date with a young man not her husband on the night of the kidnaping (she committed suicide on threat of being questioned by the police); and countless others.

Only a few years later the spotlight was turned off Lindbergh as suddenly as it had been turned on him. *The New York Times Index*—a thick volume published yearly which lists all references to a given subject in the pages of the newspaper during the previous twelve months—records this fact with statistical precision. Each volume of the index for the years 1927 to 1940 contains several columns of fine print merely itemizing the different news stories which referred to Lindbergh. The 1941 volume shows over three columns of such listings. Then suddenly the news stream dries up, first to a mere trickle, then to nothing at all. The total listings for all seventeen years from 1942 through 1958 amount to less than two columns—only about half that found in the single year 1941. In 1951 and 1958 there was not even a single mention of Lindbergh. In 1957 when the movie *The Spirit of St. Louis,* starring James Stewart, was released, it did poorly at the box office. A poll of the preview audiences showed that few viewers under forty years of age knew about Lindbergh.

A *New Yorker* cartoon gave the gist of the matter. A father and his young son are leaving a movie house where they have just seen *The Spirit of St. Louis.* "If everyone thought what he did was so marvelous," the boy asks his father, "how come he never got famous?"

The hero thus died a celebrity's sudden death. In his fourteen years he had already long outlasted the celebrity's usual life span. An incidental explanation of this quick demise of Charles A. Lindbergh was his response to the pressure to be "all-around." Democratic faith was not satisfied that its hero be only a dauntless flier. He had to become a scientist, an outspoken citizen, and a leader of men. His celebrity status unfortunately had persuaded him to become a public spokesman. When Lindbergh gave in to these temptations, he offended. But his offenses (unlike those, for example, of Al Capone and his henchmen, who used to be applauded when they took their seats in a ball park) were not in themselves dramatic or newsworthy enough to create a new notoriety. His pronouncements were dull, petulant, and vicious. He acquired a reputation as a pro-Nazi and a crude racist; he accepted a decoration from Hitler. Very soon the celebrity was being uncelebrated. The "Lindbergh Beacon" atop a Chicago skyscraper was renamed the "Palmolive Beacon," and high in the Colorado Rockies "Lindbergh Peak" was rechristened the noncommital, "Lone Eagle Peak."

## *Diana Trilling*
## "THE DEATH OF MARILYN MONROE"

On a Sunday morning in August 1962, Marilyn Monroe, aged thirty-six, was found dead in the bedroom of her home in Los Angeles, her hand on the telephone as if she had just received or, far more likely, been about to make a call. On the night table next to her bed stood a formidable array of medicines, among them a bottle that had held twenty-five Nembutal pills, now empty. Two weeks later a team of psychiatrists, appointed by the state in conformity with California law, brought in its report on the background and circumstances of her death, declaring it a suicide. There had of course never been any suggestion of foul play. The death was clearly self-inflicted, a climax of extended mental suffering. In fact, it was soon revealed that on Saturday evening Marilyn Monroe had made an emergency call to the psychoanalyst who had been treating her for her acute sleeplessness, her anxieties and depression, and that he had paid her a visit. But the formal psychiatric verdict had to do with the highly technical question of whether the overdose of barbiturates was purposeful or accidental: had Marilyn Monroe *intended* to kill herself when she took the twenty-five sleeping pills? The jury of experts now ruled it was purposeful: she had wanted to die.

It is an opinion, or at least a formulation, that can bear, I believe, a certain amount of modification. Obviously, I'm not proposing that Marilyn Monroe's death was accidental in the sense that she took too large a dose of pills with no knowledge of their lethal properties. But I think it would be more precise to call this kind of death incidental rather than purposeful—incidental to the desire to escape the pain of living. I am not a psychiatrist and I never knew Marilyn Monroe, but it seems to me that a person can want to be released from consciousness without seeking actual death; that someone can want to stop living without wishing to die. And this is my feeling about Marilyn Monroe, that even when she had spoken of "wanting to die" she really meant that she wanted to end her suffering, not her life. She wanted to destroy consciousness rather than herself. Then, having taken the pills, she realized she might never return from the sleep she craved so passionately and reached for the phone for help.

But this is of course only speculation, and more appropriately engaged in by the medical profession than by the layman. For the rest of us, the motives surrounding Marilyn Monroe's suicide fade in importance before the all-encompassing reality of the act itself: Marilyn Monroe terminated her life. While the medical experts pondered the delicate difference between accident and suicide, the public recognized that the inevitable had at last occurred: Marilyn Monroe had killed herself. Shocked and grieved as everyone was, no one was at all surprised that she had died by her own hand, because for some years now the world had been prepared for just some such tragic outcome to one of the extraordinary careers of our time.

The potentiality of suicide or, at any rate, the threat of extreme mental breakdown had been, after all, conveyed to us by virtually every news story about Marilyn Monroe of recent years. I don't mean that it had been spelled out that she would one day take her life or otherwise go off the deep psychic end. But no one seemed able to write about her without reassuring us that despite her instability and the graveness of her emotional problems, she was still vital and eager, still, however, precariously, a going concern. Marilyn Monroe was an earnest, ambitious actress, determined to improve her skill; Marilyn Monroe had failed in several marriages but she was still in pursuit of fulfillment in love; Marilyn Monroe had several times miscarried but she still looked forward to having children; Marilyn Monroe was seriously engaged in psychoanalysis; Marilyn Monroe's figure was better than ever; she was learning to be prompter; she was coping, or was struggling to cope, with whatever it was that had intervened in the making of her last picture—so, on the well-worn track, ran all the news stories. Even what may have been her last interview to appear in print (by the time it came out, she was already dead) sounded the same dominant chord of hopefulness, telling us of a Marilyn Monroe full of confidence that she would improve her acting and find her roles, and that between the two therapies, hard work and psychoanalysis, she would achieve the peace of mind that had for so long eluded her.

Where there is this much need for optimism, surely there is great peril, and the public got the message. But what is striking is the fact that throughout this period of her mounting difficulties, with which we were made so familiar, the popular image remained intact. Whatever we were told of her weak hold on life, we retained our image of Marilyn Monroe as the very embodiment of life energy. I think my response to her death was the common one: it came to me with the impact of a personal deprivation but I also felt it as I might a catastrophe in history or in nature; there was less in life, there was less of life, because she had ceased to exist. In her loss life itself had been injured.

In my own instance, it happens that she was already an established star before I knew her as anything except the latest pin-up girl. There is always this shield of irony some of us raise between ourselves and any object of popular adulation, and I had made my dull point of snubbing her pictures. Then one evening I chanced on a television trailer for *Bus Stop,* and there she was. I'm not even sure I knew whom I was seeing on the screen, but a light had gone on in the room. Where everything had been gray there was all at once an illumination, a glow of something beyond the ordinarily human. It was a remarkable moment, of a kind I don't recall having had with any other actress, and it has its place with certain rare, cherished experiences of art such as my youthful remembrance of Pavlova, the most perfect of performing artists, whose control of her body was like a radiance, or even the quite recent experience of seeing some photographs of Nijinsky in motion. Marilyn Monroe was in motion, too, which is important, since no still picture could quite catch her electric quality; in posed pictures the redundancy of flesh was what first imposed itself, dimming one's perception of its peculiar aliveness, of the translucence that infused body with spirit. In a moment's flash of light, the ironies with which I had resisted this sex idol, this object of an undifferentiating public taste, dropped from me never to be restored.

But mine was a minority problem; the world had long since recognized Marilyn Monroe's unique gift of physical being and responded to it as any such gift of life demands. From the start of her public career it had acknowledged the genius of biology or chemistry or whatever it was that set this young woman apart from the general kind. And once it had admitted her magic, nothing it was to learn of her "morbidity" could weigh against the conviction that she was alive in a way not granted the rest of us, or, more accurately, that she communicated such a charge of vitality as altered our imagination of life, which is of course the whole job and wonder of art.

Since her death it has occurred to me that perhaps the reason we were able to keep these two aspects in which we knew Marilyn Monroe—her life affirmation and her impulse to death—in such discreet balance was that they never presented themselves to us as mutually exclusive but, on the contrary, as two intimately related, even expectable, facets of her extraordinary endowment. It is as if the world that loved Marilyn Monroe understood that her superabundant biology had necessarily to provoke its own restraint, that this is the cruel law by which nature, or at least nature within civilization, punishes those of us who ask too much of life or bring too much to life. We are told that when one of the senses is defective, nature frequently provides a compensation in another of the senses; the blind often hear better than the seeing, or have a sharper sense of touch. What we are not told but perhaps understand nonetheless is the working of nature's system of negative compensation—the price we pay for gift, the revenge that life seems so regularly to take upon distinction. Certainly our awareness of the more, the plus, in Marilyn Monroe prepared us for some sort of minus. The fact that this young woman whose biological gift was so out of the ordinary was in mental pain seemed to balance the ledger. And one can speculate that had we not known of her emotional suffering, we would have been prepared for some other awful fate for her—an airplane disaster, maybe, or a deforming illness. So superstition may be thought of as an accurate reading of the harder rules of life.

And yet it is difficult to suppose the gods could be all that jealous. Had Marilyn Monroe not been enough punished in childhood to ensure her against further misfortune? Once this poor forlorn girl had been so magically brought into her own, the most superstitious of us had the right to ask happiness for her ever after. It is impossible to think of Marilyn Monroe except as Cinderella. The strange power of her physical being seemed best explained and justified by the extreme circumstances of her early life—the illegitimate birth, the mad mother, the orphanage and near-mad foster homes, the rape by one of her early guardians. If there was no good fairy in Marilyn Monroe's life and no Prince Charming, unless Hollywood, this didn't rob her story of its fairy-book miraculousness; it merely assimilated to the old tale our newer legend of the self-made hero or heroine. Grace Kelly had had her good Philadelphia family to pave her path and validate her right to a crown. But Marilyn Monroe reigned only by virtue of her beauty and her determination to be raised out of the squalor and darkness, and to shine in the full, the fullest, light. It is scarcely a surprise that the brighter her radiance, the more we listened for the stroke of midnight that would put a limit on such transcendence.

But it was not only the distance Marilyn Monroe had traveled from her unhappy beginnings that represented for us a challenge of reality, to be punished by reality. If her gift is to be regarded not as that of the stage or screen, which I think it primarily was not, but as the gift of biology, she was among those who are greatly touched with power; she was of the true company of artists. And her talent was so out of the range of the usual that we were bound to feel of it that it was not to be contained in society as we know it; therefore it proposed its own dissolution. Like any great artistic gift, Marilyn Monroe's power of biology was explosive, a primitive and savage force. It had, therefore and inevitably, to be a danger both to herself and to the world in which it did its work. All art is fierce in the measure that it matters, finally, and in its savagery it chooses either to push against society, against the restrictions that hedge it in, or against the artist himself. And no doubt it is the incapacity of most human beings to sustain this inordinate pressure that accounts for the fact that the artist is an exception in any civilized population. To mediate between the assault upon oneself and upon society, to keep alive in the battle and come out more or less intact, is a giant undertaking in which the native endowment of what we call talent is probably but a small element.

Among the very few weapons available to the artist in this monstrous struggle, naiveté can be the most useful. But it is not at all my impression that Marilyn Monroe was a naive person. I think she was innocent, which is very different. To be naive is to be simple or stupid on the basis of experience, and Marilyn Monroe was far from stupid; no one who was stupid could have been so quick to turn her wit against herself, or to manage the ruefulness with which she habitually replied to awkward questioning. To be innocent is to suffer one's experience without being able to learn self-protection from it; as if will-lessly, innocence is at the mercy of experience, unable to mobilize counterforces to fortune.

Of Ernest Hemingway, for example, I feel much as I do of Marilyn Monroe, that he was unable to marshal any adequate defense against the painful events of his childhood, and this despite his famous toughness and the courage he could call upon in war, in hunting, in all the dangerous enterprises that seduced him. He was an innocent man, not a naive man, though not always intelligent. Marilyn Monroe offers us a similar paradox. Even while she symbolized an extreme of experience, of sexual knowingness, she took each new circumstance of life, as it came to her or as she sought it, like a newborn babe. And yet this was what made her luminous—her innocence. The glow was not rubbed off her by her experience of the ugliness of life because finally, in some vital depth, she had been untouched by it.

From the psychiatrist's point of view, too much innocence, a radical disproportion between what has happened to a person and what he has absorbed from his experience, is a symptom, and alarming. It can indicate a rude break in his connection with himself, and if he is in treatment, it suggests a difficult cure, since, in emotional logic, he will probably be as impervious to the therapy as to the events through which he has passed, and yet without any mitigation of suffering. In the creative spheres, an excess of innocence unquestionably exercises an enormous fascination on us; it produces the purity of expression which leads us to say of an artistic creation or performance that it is "out of this world." But the psychiatric judgment has to pick its way on tiptoe between the gift and the pathology. What constitutes a person's art may eventually spell his emotional undoing.

I can suppose of Marilyn Monroe that she was peculiarly elusive to the psychiatrists or analysts who tried to help her, that emotionally speaking she presented herself to them as a kind of blank page on which nothing had been written, failing to make the connection between herself and them even as she pleaded for it. And yet disconnection was at the heart of her gift, it defined her charm for the world, much as Hemingway's dissociation from his own experience was determinative of his gift.

For several decades, scores of writers have tried to imitate Hemingway's style: the flexibility and purity of his prose, the bright, cogent distance he was able to put between himself and the object under examination. But none has succeeded. And I believe this is because his prose was, among many other things, a direct report of the unbridgeable distance between external reality and his emotions. Just so, Marilyn Monroe was inimitable. Hollywood, Broadway, the night clubs: they all regularly produce their quota of sex queens, but the public takes them and leaves them, or doesn't really take them: the world is not enslaved as it was by Marilyn Monroe because none but Marilyn Monroe could suggest such a purity of sexual delight. The boldness with which she could parade herself and yet never be gross, her sexual flamboyance and bravado which yet breathed an air of mystery and even reticence, her voice which carried such ripe overtones of erotic excitement and yet was the voice of a shy child—these complications were integral to her gift. And they described a young woman trapped in some never-never land of unawareness.

What I imply here, of course, is a considerable factitiousness in Marilyn Monroe as a sexual figure. Certainly the two or three men I've known who met her in "real life" were agreed on her lack of direct sexual impact; she was sweet and beautiful and lovely, yes, but somehow not at all the arousing woman they had expected. The nature of true sexuality is most difficult to define, so much of what we find sexually compelling has its source in phantasies that have little to do with the primary sexual instinct. Especially in the case of a movie star we enter a realm where dream and biology make their easiest merger. The art of acting is the art of *performing as if,* and the success of this feat of suggestion depends upon the degree to which it speaks to some phantasy of the onlookers.

Marilyn Monroe spoke to our dreams as much as to our animal nature, but in a most unusual way. For what she appealed to was our determination to be rid of phantasy and to get down to the rock-bottom actuality. She gratified our wish to confront our erotic desires without romance, without diversion. And working within a civilization like ours, in which sexuality is so surrounded with restraints and fears and prohibitions, she perhaps came as close as possible to giving us the real thing. But she didn't give us the real thing; she merely acted as if she were giving it to us.

She glamorized sexuality to the point at which it lost its terrors for us; and maybe it was this veil that she raised to sexual reality that permitted women, no less than men, to respond to her so generously. Instinctively, I think, women understood that this seemingly most sexual of female creatures was no threat to them.

The myth of Marilyn Monroe was thus even more of a myth than we realized, for this girl who was supposed to release us from our dreams into sexual actuality was in all probability not actual even to herself. Least of all could she have been sexually actual to herself and at the same time such a marvelous public performer of sex, such a conscious artist of sex. And we can conjecture that it was this deep alienation from her own feelings, including her sexual feeling, that enabled her to sustain the disorder of her early years even as long and as well as she did, and to speak of her awful childhood so simply and publicly. For most of us, the smallest "shame" in our past must be kept locked from others. We prefer that the least menacing of skeletons remain in the closet lest our current image of ourselves be violated by its emergence into the open. But Marilyn Monroe had no need for such reserves. She told the public the most gruesome facts of her personal history, for all the world as if we on the outside were worthy of such confidences—except that in some odd, generous response to her innocence, we exceeded ourselves in her instance and didn't take the advantage of her that we might have. Judged from the point of view of what we require of the artist, that he have the will and fearlessness to rise above the conventions which bind those of us with less gift, Marilyn Monroe's candor about her early life was something to be celebrated. But from another point of view her frankness was a warning that the normal barriers of self-protection were down or non-existent, leaving her grievously exposed to the winds of circumstance.

And indeed the very word "exposed" is a key word in the pattern of her life. She was an actress and she exposed her person and her personality to the public gaze. She was an exposed human being who told the truth about herself too readily, too publicly. And more than most actresses, she exposed her body, with but inadequate understanding of what this involved. We recall, for instance, the awkward little scandal about her having once posed naked for a calendar and the bewildered poise, the really untoward innocence and failure of comprehension, with which she met the dismay of her studio, as if to say, "But that was me yesterday when I needed money. That isn't me today; today I have money." Just as today and yesterday were discontinuous with each other, she was discontinuous with herself, held together, one feels, only and all too temporarily by her success.

And this success was perhaps more intimately connected with her awareness of her physical appeal than we always understood. It may well have been the fact that she was so much and so admiringly in the public eye that gave Marilyn Monroe the largest part of her sense of personal identity. Not long before her death, we now discover, she had herself photographed in the nude, carefully editing the many pictures as if to be certain she left the best possible record for posterity. The photographs leave, however, a record only of wasted beauty, at least of the famous body—while Marilyn Monroe's face is lovely as ever, apparently unscarred by her intense suffering, her body looked ravaged and ill, already drained of life. Recently the pictures have been published in an expensive magazine devoted to erotica. If their high price, prohibitive to the general buyer, could be interpreted as a precaution against their being too easily available to a sensation-seeking audience, the restraint was not really necessary. At the last, the nude Marilyn Monroe could excite no decent viewer to anything but the gentlest pity, and much fear.

But even before this ultimate moment the public success had been threatened. The great career was already failing. There had not been a Marilyn Monroe movie for a long time, and the last film she had worked on had had to be halted because she was unable to appear. And there was no private life to fall back upon, not even the formal structure of one: no marriage, no family, apparently not even friends. One had come, indeed, to think of her as the loneliest of people, so that it was not without bitterness that, on her death, one discovered that it was not only oneself who had wished to help her but many other strangers, especially women to whose protectiveness her extreme vulnerability spoke so directly. But we were the friends of whom she knew nothing, and among the people she knew it would seem that real relationships were out of reach across the desert emptiness that barricades whoever is out of touch with his feelings. One thinks of her that last evening of her life, alone and distraught, groping for human comfort and finding nothing but those endless bottles of medicine, and one confronts a pathos worse than tragedy.

Certainly it strains justice as well as imagination that the world's most glamorous woman should have been alone, with no date, on a Saturday night—for it was, in fact, a Saturday night when she killed herself. On other nights but Saturday, we are allowed our own company. Saturday night is when all American boys and girls must prove themselves sexually. This is when we must be "out," out in the world where we can be seen among the sexually chosen. Yet the American girl who symbolized sexual success for all of us spent her last Saturday night alone in despair. Every man in the country would have wanted to date Marilyn Monroe, or so he would say, but no man who knew her did.

Or, contemplating her loneliness, we think of her funeral, which, contrived to give her the peace and privacy that had so strenuously eluded her throughout her life, yet by its very restraint and limited attendance reminded us of the limitations of her actual connection with the world. Joe DiMaggio, who had been her husband for a few brief months earlier in her career, was the chief mourner. It was DiMaggio to whom, she had told us, it was impossible to be married because he had no conversation; at meals, instead of talking to her, he read the papers or looked at television. The more recent husband, *with* conversation, was not present, no doubt for his own inviolable reasons, but it was saddening. I do not know what, if anything, was read at the service, but I'd like to think it was of an elevated and literary kind, such as might be read at the funeral of a person of the first intellectual rank.

For of the cruelties directed at this young woman even by the public that loved her, it seems to me that the most biting, and unworthy of the supposedly enlightened people who were particularly guilty of it, was the mockery of her wish to be educated, or thought educated. Granting our right to be a bit confused when our sex idol protests a taste for Dostoevsky, surely the source of our discomfort must yet be located in our suspicions of Dostoevsky's worth for us and in our own sexual unease rather than in Marilyn Monroe. For what our mockery signifies is our disbelief that anyone who has enough sexuality needs to read Dostoevsky. The notion that someone with Marilyn Monroe's sexual advantages could have wanted anything except to make love robbed us of a prized illusion, that enough sexual possibility is enough everything.

I doubt that sex was enough anything for Marilyn Monroe, except the means for advancing herself in the world. One of the touching revelations of her early life was her description of how she discovered that somehow she was sexually different from other girls her age: the boys all whistled at her and crowded to her like bears to honey, so she came to realize that she must have something special about her, which she could use to rise above her poor circumstances. Her sexual awareness, that is, came to her from outside herself. It would be my guess that it remained outside her always, leaving a great emptiness, where a true sexuality would have supplied her with a sense of herself as a person with connection and content.

This void she tried to fill in every way available, with worldly goods, with fame and public attention and marriage, and also in ways that turned out to be unavailable, like children and domesticity—nothing could be more moving than the eagerness with which she seized upon a Jewish mother-in-law, even upon Jewish ceremonials and cooking, as if in the home life of her last husband's people she would find the secret of emotional plenitude. She also tried to fill her emptiness with books and learning. How mean-spirited can we be, to have denied her whatever might have added to her confidence that she was really a solid person and not just an uninhabited body?

And that she had the intellectual capacity for education there can be no question, had it but been matched with emotional capacity. No one without a sharp native intelligence could have spoofed herself as gracefully as she did or parried reporters with such finesse. If we are to judge by her interviews, she was as singularly lacking in the endemic off-stage dullness of actors and actresses, the trained courtesy and charm that is only another boring statement of their self-love, as she was deficient in the established defenses of her profession: one recalls no instance of even implied jealousy of her colleagues or of censure of others—directors, script-writers, husbands—for her own failures. Her generosity of spirit, indeed, was part of the shine that was on her. But unfortunately it spared everyone but herself; she had never studied self-justification. To herself she was not kind. She made fun of herself and of all that she had to go on in life: her biology. Certainly this added to her lovableness but it cut from under her the little ground that she could call her own. When she exhibited her sexual abundance with that wonderful, gay exaggeration of hers, or looked wide-eyed upon the havoc she wrought, it was her way of saying, "Don't be afraid. I don't take myself seriously so you don't have to take me seriously either." Her talent for comedy, in other words, was a public beneficence but a personal depredation, for, far more than most people, she precisely needed the assurance that she weighed in the scheme of human life, that she had substance and reality, that she had all the qualifications that make for a person we take seriously. Herself a supplicant, she gave us comfort. Herself a beggar, she distributed alms.

At her death, several writers of good will who undertook to deal with the tragedy of her suicide blamed it on Hollywood. In the industry that had made millions from her and in the methods by which Hollywood had exploited her, they found the explanation of her failed life; they wrote about her as the sacrificial lamb on the altar of American vulgarity and greed. I share their disgust with Hollywood and I honor their need to isolate Marilyn Monroe from the nastiness that fed on her, but I find it impossible to believe that this girl would have been an iota better off were Hollywood to have been other than what we all know it to be, a madness in our culture.

The self-destructiveness that Marilyn Monroe carried within her had not been put there by the "system," however overbearing in its ugliness. Just as her sweetness was her own, and immune to the influences of Hollywood, her terrors were also her own. They were not implanted in her, though undoubtedly they were increased, by the grandiosity of being a star. Neither for better nor worse, I feel, was she essentially falsified or distorted by her public role, though she must often have suffered cruelly from the inescapability of the public glare. In fact, it would be my conjecture that had she never gone into the movies and become rich and world-famous, her troubled spirit would long since have had its way with her. She would have been equally undone, and sooner, and with none of the many alleviations and compensations that she must have known in these years of success.

This doesn't mean that I don't think she was a "victim." But she was not primarily a victim of Hollywood commercialism, or exploitation, or of the inhumanity of the press. She was not even primarily a victim of the narcissistic inflation that so regularly attends the grim business of being a great screen personality. Primarily she was a victim of her gift, a biological victim, a victim of life itself. It is one of the excesses of contemporary thought that we like to blame our very faulty culture for tragedies that are inherent in human existence—at least, inherent in human existence in civilization. I think Marilyn Monroe was a tragedy of civilization, but this is something quite else again from, and even more poignant than, being a specifically American tragedy.

## SUGGESTIONS FOR DISCUSSION

1. Both these writers are addressing audiences in the early 1960s. From their essays, what can you infer about how these audiences might be different from contemporary audiences? What assumptions about celebrities do the writers seem to think their audiences will agree with that contemporary readers might not agree with? How have the past twenty or so years changed the definition of a celebrity?
2. Daniel Boorstin describes much of the machinery by which celebrities are created. In his profile of Lindbergh as a creation/victim of this machinery, he reveals its dangers for individuals caught in it. Diana Trilling contends, though, that Marilyn Monroe was not, like Lindbergh, a victim of this machinery, but "a victim of her gift, a biological victim, a victim of life itself." Can you remember Marilyn Monroe or do you know of the publicity surrounding her death? If not, are you convinced by Trilling's compassionate retrospective? Why is Trilling so eager to prove her thesis? What does she have to gain by proving it, and what do her readers have to gain by going along with her?
3. Most of the time, writers adopt *personae* which enable them to recruit a sympa-

thetic audience; they want their readers to identify with the mask they have assumed. Certainly both these writers try to do so. But to identify with Boorstin, a reader has to adopt a very different attitude toward him and his subject than to identify with Trilling. Describe these different attitudes as you experienced them, and try to locate the places in the texts that invited, nudged, or compelled you to become a sympathetic reader.

**4.** Analyze the sentence structure in the following passage: "The hero was distinguished by his achievement; the celebrity by his image or trademark. The hero created himself; the celebrity is created by the media. The hero was a big man; the celebrity is a big name." What rhetorical techniques is Boorstin using in this passage? Why are they effective?

**5.** Diana Trilling creates an intricate web of cause and effect in her effort to explain the suicide of Marilyn Monroe. Isolate and list some of these causes. How are they connected?

## SUGGESTIONS FOR WRITING

**1.** Analyze a current celebrity of your choice. What is his or her distinguishing image or trademark? Why is this figure popular with the public?

# 22

# Self-Fulfillment

*Ellen Goodman*
"SUCH EMPTY OPTIONS"

*John Ciardi*
"IS EVERYBODY HAPPY?"

Self-fulfillment is a goal even more elusive than fame and wealth, and one that is far more difficult to define. Ellen Goodman questions a popular approach to finding happiness in "Such Empty Options." She is doubtful about the ultimate value of avoiding personal commitment in order to keep one's options open. A person who potentially has everything, she concludes, "holds nothing in the palm of his hand." John Ciardi, however, does not think it is important to hold something in the palm of one's hand. His essay emphasizes that happiness is a process of becoming rather than a static state of being or having. In fact, an important component of happiness, according to Ciardi, is the deliberate choosing of difficulties.

## *Ellen Goodman*
## "SUCH EMPTY OPTIONS"

The man is keeping his options open. He has been doing it for some time now and it is, I suppose, what he does best.

Through the decade I have known him, he has let good women and great chances slip through his hands like water. But he has held onto his options like a lifeline.

In fact, you might say that at thirty his most long-lasting, deeply held commitment is to noncommitment. But perhaps that is too pat.

The option tender is, after all, a man of some charm. He wears the appropriate suit and air of interest. He carries the right briefcase and credentials. He has a good sense of taste and humor. And he travels light.

There is nothing wrong with him, nothing at all. Just something different. How can I explain it?

The option tender is a man who works carefully at his job, but always has a resume out. The option tender is a man who enjoys seeing a woman, but always has an eye out.

He doesn't get involved. He responds to affection with alarm and to praise with wariness. What one person calls connections, he calls bonds. And if one person values commitment—well, he values options.

The man is not unaware of himself. He once described life to me as a kind of one-plate buffet table. If you fill up your plate at the beginning, you won't have any more room at the end of the table. What, he asked earnestly, if the shrimp cocktail is in the last dish?

He prefers, you see, to leave some space for what might come next. So he serves himself only the stingiest spoonfuls. The option tender says that this way he is keeping his life open-ended.

He is not the only one. I am told that he belongs to a kind of subculture, a whole generation living in a permanent state of potential.

I am told, moreover, by people like Gail Sheehy that they have a label. They are called now the Postponing Generation, as if there were an Andromeda strain of delayed adolescence running through their age group. But I wonder if postponing can become incurably habit-forming.

The option tender had a father once. I knew the man. He had married at twenty-two, fathered at twenty-three, gone to war at twenty-four. By thirty he had three children, one mortgage, and a job which he turned into a vice-presidency after fifteen years of hard labor. By fifty-four he was dead.

"Locked in," the son had told me at his father's funeral. "He spent his whole life locked in." His father's plate was overloaded, and he had fallen under its weight.

So, the son mixed guilt with terror. He built his father's life story into his own life plan. Where his father was locked in, he would be open. Where his father had burdens, he would have space.

We all do that. Whatever else, we tell ourselves we won't make the same mistakes as our parents. We are much more conscious of what was missing in their lives than what was present. Much more conscious of what was bad than what was good.

We don't make their mistakes. We make our own.

The Workaholic Heart Attack Victim has become almost a cliché, a negative role-model, if you must, for a whole generation of sons.

He is, to young men, what the displaced homemaker is to young women: The Ghost of Christmas Future.

The man's sister, who watched her mother become a widow at fifty-one, also knows what she doesn't want to be when she grows up. An unemployed widow, an unemployable divorcée. Her protection against the ghosts is work. His protection is . . . keeping his options open.

The thirty-year-old man doesn't describe it this way. He says that where his father had obligations, he has freedom; where his father had responsibilities, he has opportunities; where his father had a wife, three children, a mortgage and a vice-presidency, he has. . . his options.

But what I wonder is simply this: Where is the line between being locked in and frozen out? When do options become emptiness? When do you realize that the only way to keep a full table of choices is to keep an empty plate?

When does the option tender who has everything in potential realize that he holds nothing in the palm of his hand?

## *John Ciardi*
# "IS EVERYBODY HAPPY?"

The right to pursue happiness is issued to Americans with their birth certificates, but no one seems quite sure which way it ran. It may be we are issued a hunting license but offered no game. Jonathan Swift seemed to think so when he attacked the idea of happiness as "the possession of being well-deceived," the felicity of being "a fool among knaves." For Swift saw society as Vanity Fair, the land of false goals.

It is, of course, un-American to think in terms of fools and knaves. We do, however, seem to be dedicated to the idea of buying our way to happiness. We shall all have made it to Heaven when we possess enough.

And at the same time the forces of American commercialism are hugely dedicated to making us deliberately unhappy. Advertising is one of our major industries, and advertising exists not to satisfy desires but to create them—and to create them faster than any man's budget can satisfy them. For that matter, our whole economy is based on a dedicated insatiability. We are taught that to possess is to be happy, and then we are made to want. We are even told it is our duty to want. It was only a few years ago, to cite a single example, that car dealers across the country were flying banners that read "You Auto Buy Now." They were calling upon Americans, as an act approaching patriotism, to buy at once, with money they did not have, automobiles they did not really need, and which they would be required to grow tired of by the time the next year's models were released.

Or look at any of the women's magazines. There, as Bernard DeVoto once pointed out, advertising begins as poetry in the front pages and ends as pharmacopoeia and therapy in the back pages. The poetry of the front matter is the dream of perfect beauty. This is the baby skin that must be hers. These, the flawless teeth. This, the perfumed breath she must exhale. This, the sixteen-year-old figure she must display at forty, at fifty, at sixty, and forever.

Once past the vaguely uplifting fiction and feature articles, the reader finds the other face of the dream in the back matter. This is the harness into which Mother must strap herself in order to display that perfect figure. These, the chin straps she must sleep in. This is the salve that restores all, this is her laxative, these are the tablets that melt away fat, these are the hormones of perpetual youth, these are the stockings that hide varicose veins.

Obviously no half-sane person can be completely persuaded either by such poetry or by such pharmacopoeia and orthopedics. Yet someone is obviously trying to buy the dream as offered and spending billions every year in the attempt. Clearly the happiness market is not running out of customers, but what is it trying to buy?

The idea "happiness," to be sure, will not sit still for easy definitions: the best one can do is to try to set some extremes to the idea and then work in toward the middle. To think of happiness as acquisitive and competitive will do to set the materialistic extreme. To think of it as the idea one senses in, say, a holy man of India will do to set the spiritual extreme. That holy man's ideal of happiness is in needing nothing from outside himself. In wanting nothing, he lacks nothing. He sits immobile, rapt in contemplation, free even of his own body. Or nearly free of it. If devout admirers bring him food he eats it: if not, he starves indifferently. Why be concerned? What is physical is an illusion to him. Contemplation is his joy and he achieves it through a fastastically demanding discipline, the accomplishment of which is itself a joy within him.

Is he a happy man? Perhaps his happiness is only another sort of illusion. But who can take it from him? And who will dare say it is more illusory than happiness on the installment plan?

But, perhaps because I am Western, I doubt such catatonic happiness, as I doubt the dreams of the happiness-market. What is certain is that his way of happiness would be torture to almost any Western man. Yet these extremes will still serve to frame the area within which all of us must find some sort of balance. Thoreau—a creature of both Eastern and Western thought—had his own firm sense of that balance. His aim was to save on the low levels in order to spend on the high.

Possession for its own sake or in competition with the rest of the neighborhood would have been Thoreau's idea of the low levels. The active discipline of heightening one's perception of what is enduring in nature would have been his idea of the high. What he saved from the low was time and effort he could spend on the high. Thoreau certainly disapproved of starvation, but he would put into feeding himself only as much effort as would keep him functioning for more important efforts.

Effort is the gist of it. There is no happiness except as we take on life-engaging difficulties. Short of the impossible, as Yeats put it, the satisfactions we get from a lifetime depend on how high we choose our difficulties. Robert Frost was thinking in something like the same terms when he spoke of "the pleasure of taking pains." The mortal flaw in the advertised version of happiness is in the fact that it purports to be effortless.

We demand difficulty even in our games. We demand it because without difficulty there can be no game. A game is a way of making something hard for the fun of it. The rules of the game are an arbitrary imposition of difficulty. When the spoilsport ruins the fun, he always does so by refusing to play by the rules. It is easier to win at chess if you are free, at your pleasure, to change the wholly arbitrary rules, but the fun is in winning within the rules. No difficulty, no fun.

The buyers and sellers at the happiness market seem too often to have lost their sense of the pleasure of difficulty. Heaven knows what they are playing, but it seems a dull game. And the Indian holy man seems dull to us, I suppose, because he seems to be refusing to play anything at all. The Western weakness may be in the illusion that happiness can be bought. Perhaps the Eastern weakness is in the idea that there is such a thing as perfect (and therefore static) happiness.

Happiness is never more than partial. There are no pure states of mankind. Whatever else happiness may be, it is neither in having nor in being, but in becoming. What the Founding Fathers declared for us as an inherent right, we should do well to remember, was not happiness but the *pursuit* of happiness. What they might have underlined, could they have foreseen the happiness market, is the cardinal fact that happiness is in the pursuit itself, in the meaningful pursuit of what is life-engaging and life-revealing, which is to say, in the idea of *becoming*. A nation is not measured by what it possesses or wants to possess, but by what it wants to become.

By all means let the happiness-market sell us minor satisfactions and even minor follies so long as we keep them in scale and buy them out of spiritual change. I am no customer for either puritanism or asceticism. But drop any real spiritual capital at those bazaars, and what you come home to will be your own poorhouse.

## SUGGESTIONS FOR DISCUSSION

1. Because Goodman's essay was written for her column in the *Boston Globe*, she had strict limitations on style and length. What techniques make her writing appropriate for a newspaper format? John Ciardi's audience, the readers of the *Saturday Review,* is quite different from Goodman's audience. How would you contrast the readers of the two essays?
2. Examine the analogy between life and the "one-plate buffet table" in the Goodman essay. Discuss the way this analogy changes in the course of the essay.
3. The following assertion by Oscar Wilde has bewildered many people: "In this world there are only two tragedies. One is not getting what one wants, and the other is getting it." Does Ciardi's essay shed any light on this statement?
4. Contrast Ciardi's view of self-fulfillment with that of Goodman. Readers who accept certain gender stereotypes might argue that Goodman's emphasis on commitment is a female view and that Ciardi's focus on pursuit of difficulty is a male view of happiness. How do both Goodman and Ciardi overcome these stereotypes and universalize their ideas?
5. Both Ciardi and Goodman implicitly accept the idea that complete happiness or total self-fulfillment is never possible. How does each writer account for the elusive or unattainable nature of happiness.

## SUGGESTIONS FOR WRITING

1. Ciardi's strategy for arriving at a definition of happiness is "to set some extremes to the idea and then work in toward the middle." He eventually suggests that happiness is midway between the materialistic extreme and the spiritual extreme.

   Using Ciardi's basic strategy, write an essay analyzing a human quality such as honesty, humor, loyalty, sympathy, or determination. Describe the results when that quality is lacking and when it is excessive. Then present your idea of the right balance.
2. Read the following short essay by Bertrand Russell. Then write an essay on

**"The Three Goals of My Life," using the same basic format that Russell uses: introduction, three main points, and conclusion. Be sure to include effective transitional sentences between your main points, as Russell does.**

WHAT I HAVE LIVED FOR

Three passions, simple but overwhelmingly strong, have governed my life: the longing for love, the search for knowledge, and unbearable pity for the suffering of mankind. These passions, like great winds, have blown me hither and thither, in a wayward course, over a deep ocean of anguish, reaching to the very verge of despair.

I have sought love, first, because it brings ecstasy—ecstasy so great that I would often have sacrificed all the rest of life for a few hours of this joy. I have sought it next, because it relieves loneliness—that terrible loneliness in which one shivering consciousness looks over the rim of the world into the cold unfathomable lifeless abyss. I have sought it, finally, because in the union of love I have seen, in a mystic miniature, the prefiguring vision of the heaven that saints and poets have imagined. This is what I sought, and though it might seem too good for human life, this is what—at last—I have found.

With equal passion I have sought knowledge. I have wished to understand the hearts of men. I have wished to know why the stars shine. And I have tried to apprehend the Pythagorean power by which number holds sway above the flux. A little of this, but not much, I have achieved.

Love and knowledge, so far as they were possible, led upward toward the heavens. But always pity brought me back to earth. Echoes of cries of pain reverberate in my heart. Children in famine, victims tortured by oppressors, helpless old people a hated burden to their sons, and the whole world of loneliness, poverty, and pain make a mockery of what human life should be. I long to alleviate the evil, but I cannot, and I too suffer.

This has been my life. I have found it worth living, and would gladly live it again if the chance were offered me.

Bertrand Russell,
*The Autobiography of Bertrand Russell, 1872–1914*

# 23

# Barriers To Success

*Loren Eiseley*

"OBITUARY OF A BONE HUNTER"

*Virginia Woolf*

"PROFESSIONS FOR WOMEN"

The final pair of essays explores some of the barriers that prevent people from reaching, or even pursuing, their chosen goals. Loren Eiseley's "Obituary of a Bone Hunter" deals with the problems that arise when a person's conscience stands in the way of success. Eiseley's narrative, with its subdued ironies, reminds us that it sometimes takes more nobility to choose failure than it does to achieve success. Virginia Woolf describes the subtle way in which society's limited expectations may become an integral part of a woman's self-image and so hinder her ability to accomplish serious work. Woolf blends figurative language and incisive analysis to produce a rich and searching assessment of social barriers.

## *Loren Eiseley*
## "OBITUARY OF A BONE HUNTER"

### I

The papers and the magazines reprint the stories endlessly these days—of Sybaris the sin city, or, even further back, that skull at Tepexpan. One's ears are filled with chatter about assorted magnetometers and how they are used to pick up the traces of buried objects and no one has to guess at all. They unearth the city, or find the buried skull and bring it home. Then everyone concerned is famous overnight.

I'm the man who didn't find the skull. I'm the man who'd just been looking twenty years for something like it. This isn't sour grapes. It's their skull and welcome to it. What made me sigh was the geophysics equipment. The greatest gambling game in the world—the greatest wit-sharpener—and now they do it with amplifiers and electronically mapped grids. An effete age, gentlemen, and the fun gone out of it.

There are really two kinds of bone hunters—the big bone hunters and the little bone hunters. The little bone hunters may hunt big bones, but they're little bone hunters just the same. They are the consistent losers in the most difficult game of chance that men can play: the search for human origins. Eugene Dubois, the discoverer of Pithecanthropus, hit the jackpot in a gamble with such stupendous odds that the most devoted numbers enthusiast would have had better sense than to stake his life on them.

I am a little bone hunter. I've played this game for a twenty-year losing streak. I used to think it all lay in the odds—that it was luck that made the difference between the big and little bone hunters. Now I'm not so sure any longer. Maybe it's something else.

Maybe sometimes an uncanny clairvoyance is involved, and if it comes you must act or the time goes by. Anyhow I've thought about it a lot in these later years. You think that way as you begin to get grayer and you see pretty plainly that the game is not going to end as you planned.

With me I think now that there were three chances: the cave of spiders, the matter of the owl's egg, and the old man out of the Golden Age. I muffed them all. And maybe the old man just came to show me I'd sat in the big game for the last time.

## II

In that first incident of the spiders, I was playing a hunch, a long one, but a good one still. I wanted to find Neanderthal man, or any kind of ice-age man, in America. One or two important authorities were willing to admit he *might* have got in before the last ice sheet; that he *might* have crossed Bering Strait with the mammoth. He might have, they said, but it wasn't likely. And if he had, it would be like looking for humming birds in the Bronx to find him.

Well, the odds were only a hundred to one against me, so I figured I'd look. That was how I landed in the cave of spiders. It was somewhere west out of Carlsbad, New Mexico, in the Guadalupe country. Dry. With sunlight that would blister cactus. We were cavehunting with a dynamiter and a young Harvard assistant. The dynamiter was to blow boulders away from fallen entrances so we could dig what lay underneath.

We found the cave up a side canyon, the entrance blocked with fallen boulders. Even to my youthful eyes it looked old, incredibly old. The waters and the frosts of centuries had eaten at the boulders and gnawed the cave roof. Down by the vanished stream bed a little gleam of worked flints caught our eye.

We stayed there for days, digging where we could and leaving the blasting till the last. We got the Basket Maker remains we had come to get—the earliest people that the scientists of that time would concede had lived in the Southwest. Was there anything more? We tamped a charge under one huge stone that blocked the wall of the cave and scrambled for the outside. A dull boom echoed down the canyon and the smoke and dust slowly blew away.

Inside the cave mouth the shattered boulder revealed a crack behind it. An opening that ran off beyond our spot lights. The hackles on my neck crawled. This might be the road to—something earlier? There was room for only one man to worm his way in. The dynamiter was busy with his tools. "It's probably nothing," I said to the assistant. "I'll just take a quick look."

As I crawled down that passage on my belly, I thought once or twice about rattlesnakes and what it might be like to meet one on its own level where it could look you in the eye. But after all I had met snakes before in this country, and besides I had the feeling that there was something worth getting to beyond.

I had it strong—too strong to turn back. I twisted on and suddenly dropped into a little chamber. My light shot across it. It was low and close, and this was the end of the cave. But there was earth on the floor beneath me, the soft earth that must be dug, that might hold something more ancient than the cave entrance. I couldn't stand up; the roof was too low. I would have to dig on hands and knees. I set the light beside me and started to probe the floor with a trench shovel. It was just then that the fear got me.

The light lay beside me shining on the ceiling—a dull, velvety-looking ceiling, different from the stone around. I don't know when I first sensed that something was wrong, that the ceiling was moving, that waves were passing over it like the wind in a stand of wheat. But suddenly I did; suddenly I dropped the shovel and thrust the light closer against the roof. Things began to detach themselves and drop wherever the light touched them. Things with legs. I could hear them plop on the soft earth around me.

I shut off the light. The plopping ceased. I sat on my knees in the darkness, listening. My mind was centered on just one thing—escape. I knew what that wavering velvet wall was. Millions upon millions of daddy-long-legs—packed in until they hung in layers. Daddy-long-legs, the most innocent and familiar of all the spider family. I wish I could say I had seen black widows there among them. It would help now, in telling this.

But I didn't. I didn't really see anything. If I turned on the light that hideous dropping and stirring would commence again. The light woke them. They disliked it.

If I could have stood up it would have been different. If they had not been overhead it would have been different. But they had me on my knees and they were above and all around. Millions upon millions. How they got there I don't know. All I know is that up out of the instinctive well of my being flowed some ancient, primal fear of the crawler, the walker by night. One clambered over my hand. And above they dangled, dangled. . . What if they all began to drop at once?

I did not light the light. I had seen enough. I buttoned my jacket close, and my sleeves. I plunged blindly back up the passage down which I had wriggled and which, luckily, was free of them.

Outside the crew looked at me. I was sweating, and a little queer. "Close air," I gasped; "a small hole, nothing there."

We went away then in our trucks. I suppose in due time the dust settled, and the fox found his way in. Probably all that horrible fecund mass eventually crept, in its single individualities, back into the desert where it frightened no one. What it was doing there, what evil unknown to mankind it was plotting, I do not know to this day. The evil and the horror, I think now, welled out of my own mind, but somehow that multitude of ancient life in a little low dark chamber touched it off. It did not pass away until I could stand upright again. It was a fear out of the old, four-footed world that sleeps within us still.

Neanderthal man? He might have been there. But I was young and that was only a first chance gone. Yes, there were things I might have done, but I didn't do them. You don't tell your chief dynamiter that you ran from a daddy-long-legs. Not in that country. But do you see, it wasn't *one* daddy-long-legs. That's what I can't seem to make clear to anyone. It wasn't just one daddy-long-legs. It was millions of them. Enough to bury you. And have you ever thought of being buried under spiders? I thought not. You begin to get the idea?

## III

I had a second chance and again it was in a cave I found. This time I was alone, tramping up a canyon watching for bones, and I just happened to glance upward in the one place where the cave could be seen. I studied it a long time—until I could feel the chill crawling down my back. This might be it; this might be the place. . . This time I would know. This time there would be no spiders.

Through the glasses I could make out a fire blackened roof, a projecting ledge above the cave mouth, and another one below. It was a small, strange hide-out, difficult to reach, but it commanded the valley on which the canyon opened. And there was the ancient soot-impregnated cave roof. Ancient man had been there.

I made that climb. Don't ask me how I did it. Probably there had been an easier route ages ago. But I came up a naked chimney of rock down which I lost my knapsack and finally the geologist's pick that had helped me hack out a foothold in the softening rock.

When I flung myself over the ledge where the cave mouth opened, I was shaking from the exhausting muscle tension and fear. No one, I was sure, had come that way for a thousand years, and no one after me would come again. I did not know how I would get down. It was enough momentarily to be safe. In front of me the cave mouth ran away darkly into the mountain.

I took the flashlight from my belt and loosened my sheath knife. I began to crawl downward and forward, wedging myself over sticks and fallen boulders. It was a clean cave and something was there, I was sure of it. Only, the walls were small and tight. . . .

They were tighter when the voice and the eyes came. I remember the eyes best. I caught them in my flashlight the same instant that I rammed my nose into the dirt and covered my head. They were big eyes and coming my way.

I never thought at all. I just lay there dazed while a great roaring buffeting thing beat its way out over my body and went away.

It went out into the silence beyond the cave mouth. A half minute afterward, I peered through my fingers and rolled weakly over. Enough is enough. But this time I wasn't going back empty-handed. Not I. Not on account of a mere bird. Not if I *had* thought it was a mountain lion, which it could just as well have been. No owl was going to stop me, not even if it was the biggest owl in the Rocky Mountains.

I twitched my ripped shirt into my pants and crawled on. It wasn't much farther. Over the heap of debris down which the great owl had charged at me, I found the last low chamber, the place I was seeking. And there in a pile of sticks lay an egg, an impressive egg, glimmering palely in the cavernous gloom, full of potentialities, and fraught, if I may say so, with destiny.

I affected at first to ignore it. I was after the buried treasures that lay beneath its nest in the cave floor. The egg was simply going to have to look after itself. Its parent had gone, and in a pretty rude fashion, too. I was no vandal, but I was going to be firm. If an owl's egg stood in the path of science—But suddenly the egg seemed very helpless, very much alone. I probed in the earth around the nest. The nest got in the way. This was a time for decision.

I know a primatologist who will lift a rifle and shoot a baby monkey out of its mother's arms for the sake of science. He is a good man, too, and goes home nights to his wife. I tried to focus on this thought as I faced the egg.

I knew it was a rare egg. The race of its great and lonely mother was growing scant in these mountains and would soon be gone. Under it might lie a treasure that would make me famed in the capitals of science, but suppose there was nothing under the nest after all and I destroyed it? Suppose . . .

Here in this high, sterile silence with the wind crying over frightful precipices, myself and that egg were the only living things. That seemed to me to mean something. At last and quietly I backed out of the cave and slipped down into the chasm out of which I had come. By luck I did not fall.

Sometimes in these later years I think perhaps the skull was there, the skull that could have made me famous. It is not so bad, however, when I think that the egg became an owl. I had had charge of it in the universe's sight for a single hour, and I had done well by life.

It is not the loss of the skull that torments me sometimes on winter evenings. Suppose the big, unutterably frightened bird never came back to its egg? A feeling of vast loss and desolation sweeps over me then. I begin to perceive what it is to doubt.

## IV

It was years later that I met the old man. He was waiting in my office when I came in. It was obvious from the timid glances of my secretary that he had been passed from hand to hand and that he had outwitted everybody. Someone in the background made a twisting motion at his forehead.

The old man sat, a colossal ruin, in the reception chair. The squirrel-like twitterings of the office people did not disturb him.

As I came forward he fished in a ragged wallet and produced a clipping. "You made this speech?" he asked.

"Why, yes,"I said.

"You said men came here late? A few thousands years ago?"

"Yes, you see—"

"Young man," he interrupted, "you are frightfully wrong."

I was aware that his eyes were contracted to pin points and seemed in some danger of protruding on stalks.

"You have ignored," he rumbled, "the matter of the Miocene period—the Golden Age. A great civilization existed then, far more splendid that this—degenerate time." He struck the floor fiercely with his cane.

"But," I protested, "that period is twenty million years ago. Man wasn't even in existence. Geology shows—"

"Nothing!" said the massive relic. "Geology has nothing to do with it. Sit down. I know all about the Golden Age. I will prove to you that you are wrong."

I collapsed doubtfully into a chair. He told me that he was from some little town in Missouri, but I never believed it for a moment. He smelled bad, and it was obvious that if he brought news of the Golden Age, as he claimed, he had come by devious and dreadful ways from that far era.

"I have here," he said, thrusting his head forward and breathing heavily into my face, "a human jaw. I will unwrap it a little and you can see. It is from a cave I found."

"It is embedded in stalactite drippings," I murmured, hypnotized against my will. "That might represent considerable age. Where did you find it?"

He raised a protesting hand. "Later, son, later. You admit then—?"

I strained forward. "Those teeth," I said, "they are large—they look primitive." The feeling I had had at the mouth of the owl's cave came to me again overpoweringly. "Let me see a little more of the jaw. If the mental eminence should be lacking, you may have something important. Just let me handle it a moment."

With the scuttling alacrity of a crab, the old man drew back and popped the papers over his find. "You admit, then, that it is important? That it proves the Golden Age was real?"

Baffled, I looked at him. He eyed me with an equal wariness.

"Where did you find it?" I asked. "In this light it seemed—it might be—a fossil man. We have been looking a long time. If you would only let me see—"

"I found it in a cave in Missouri," he droned in a rote fasion. "You can never find the cave alone. If you will make a statement to the papers that the Golden Age is true, I will go with you. You have seen the evidence."

Once more I started to protest. "But this has nothing to do with the Golden Age. You may have a rare human fossil there. You are denying science—"

"Science," said the old man with frightening dignity, "is illusion." He arose. "I will not come back. You must make a choice."

For one long moment we looked at each other across the fantastic barriers of our individual minds. Then, on his heavy oakwood cane, he hobbled to the door and was gone. I watched through the window as he crossed the street in a patch of autumn sunlight as phantasmal and unreal as he. Leaves fell raggedly around him until, a tatter among tatters, he passed from sight.

I rubbed a hand over my eyes, and it seemed the secretary looked at me strangely. How was it that I had failed this time? By unbelief? But the man was mad. I could not possibly have made such a statement as he wanted.

Was it pride that cost me that strange jaw bone? Was it academic dignity? Should I have followed him? Found where he lived? Importuned his relatives? Stolen if necessary, that remarkable fragment?

Of course I should! I know that now. Of course I should.

Thirty years have passed since the old man came to see me. I have crawled in many caverns, stooped with infinite aching patience over the bones of many men. I have made no great discoveries.

I think now that in some strange way that old man out of the autumn leaf-fall was the last test of the inscrutable gods. There will be no further chances. The egg and the spiders and the madman—in them is the obituary of a life dedicated to the folly of doubt, the life of a small bone hunter.

## *Virginia Woolf*
## "PROFESSIONS FOR WOMEN"*

When your secretary invited me to come here, she told me that your Society is concerned with the employment of women and she suggested that I might tell you something about my own professional experiences. It is true I am a woman; it is true I am employed; but what professional experiences have I had? It is difficult to say. My profession is literature; and in that profession there are fewer experiences for women than in any other, with the exception of the stage—fewer, I mean, that are peculiar to women. For the road was cut many years ago—by Fanny Burney, by Aphra Behn, by Harriet Martineau, by Jane Austen, by George Eliot—many famous women, and many more unknown and forgotten, have been before me, making the path smooth, and regulating my steps. Thus, when I came to write, there were very few material obstacles in my way. Writing was a reputable and harmless occupation. The family peace was not broken by the scratching of a pen. No demand was made upon the family purse. For ten and sixpence one can buy paper enough to write all the plays of Shakespeare—if one has a mind that way. Pianos and models, Paris, Vienna and Berlin, masters and mistresses, are not needed by a writer. The cheapness of writing paper is, of course, the reason why women have succeeded as writers before they have succeeded in the other professions.

But to tell you my story—it is a simple one. You have only got to figure to yourselves a girl in a bedroom with a pen in her hand. She had only to move that pen from left to right—from ten o'clock to one. Then it occurred to her to do what is simple and cheap enough after all—to slip a few of those pages into an envelope, fix a penny stamp in the corner, and drop the envelope into the red box at the corner. It

* A paper read to The Women's Service League.—Eds.

was thus that I became a journalist; and my effort was rewarded on the first day of the following month—a very glorious day it was for me—by a letter from an editor containing a cheque for one pound ten shillings and sixpence. But to show you how little I deserve to be called a professional woman, how little I know of the struggles and difficulties of such lives, I have to admit that instead of spending that sum upon bread and butter, rent, shoes and stockings, or butchers' bills, I went out and bought a cat—a beautiful cat, a Persian cat, which very soon involved me in bitter disputes with my neighbours.

What could be easier than to write articles and to buy Persian cats with the profits? But wait a moment. Articles have to be about something. Mine, I seem to remember, was about a novel by a famous man. And while I was writing this review, I discovered that if I were going to review books I should need to do battle with a certain phantom. And the phantom was a woman, and when I came to know her better I called her after the heroine of a famous poem, The Angel in the House. It was she who used to come between me and my paper when I was writing reviews. It was she who bothered me and wasted my time and so tormented me that at last I killed her. You who come of a younger and happier generation may not have heard of her—you may not know what I mean by the Angel in the House. I will describe her as shortly as I can. She was intensely sympathetic. She was immensely charming. She was utterly unselfish. She excelled in the difficult arts of family life. She sacrificed herself daily. If there was chicken, she took the leg; if there was a draught she sat in it—in short she was so constituted that she never had a mind or a wish of her own, but preferred to sympathize always with the minds and wishes of others. Above all—I need not say it—she was pure. Her purity was supposed to be her chief beauty—her blushes, her great grace. In those days—the last of Queen Victoria—every house had its Angel. And when I came to write I encountered her with the very first words. The shadow of her wings fell on my page; I heard the rustling of her skirts in the room. Directly, that is to say, I took my pen in hand to review that novel by a famous man, she slipped behind me and whispered: "My dear, you are a young woman. You are writing about a book that has been written by a man. Be sympathetic; be tender; flatter, deceive; use all the arts and wiles of our sex. Never let anybody guess that you have a mind of your own. Above all, be pure." And she made as if to guide my pen. I now record the one act for which I take some credit to myself, though the credit rightly belongs to some excellent ancestors of mine who left me a certain sum of money— shall we say five hundred pounds a year?—so that it was not necessary for me to depend solely on charm for my living. I turned upon her and caught her by the throat. I did my best to kill her. My excuse, if I were to be had up in a court of law, would be that I acted in self-defence. Had I not killed her she would have killed me. She would have plucked the heart out of my writing. For, as I found, directly I put pen to paper, you cannot review even a novel without having a mind of your own, without expressing what you think to be the truth about human relations, morality, sex. And all these questions, according to the Angel in the House, cannot be dealt with freely and openly by women; they must charm, they must conciliate, they must—to put it bluntly—tell lies if they are to succeed. Thus, whenever I felt the shadow of her wing or the radiance of her halo upon my page, I took up the inkpot and flung it at her. She died hard. Her fictitious nature was of great assistance to her. It is far harder to kill a phantom than a reality. She was always creeping back when I thought I had despatched her. Thought I flatter myself that I killed her in the end, the struggle was severe; it took much time that had better have been spent upon learning Greek grammar; or in roaming the world in search of adventures. But it was a real experience; it was an experience that was bound to befall all women writers at that time. Killing the Angel in the House was part of the occupation of a woman writer.

But to continue my story. The Angel was dead; what then remained? You may say that what remained was a simple and common object—a young woman in a bedroom with an inkpot. In other words, now that she had rid herself of falsehood, that young woman had only to be herself. Ah, but what is "herself"? I mean, what is a woman? I assure you, I do not know. I do not believe that you know. I do not believe that anybody can know until she has expressed herself in all the arts and professions open to human skill. That indeed is one of the reasons why I have come here—out of respect for you, who are in process of showing us by your experiments what a woman is, who are in process of providing us, by your failures and successes, with that extremely important piece of information.

But to continue the story of my professional experiences, I made one pound ten and six by my first review; and I bought a Persian cat with the proceeds. Then I grew ambitious. A Persian cat is all very well, I said; but a Persian cat is not enough. I must have a motor car. And it was thus that I became a novelist—for it is a very strange thing that people will give you a motor car if you will tell them a story. It is a still stranger thing that there is nothing so delightful in the world as telling stories. It is far pleasanter than writing reviews of famous novels. And yet, if I am to obey your secretary and tell you my professional experiences as a novelist, I must tell you about a very strange experience that befell me as a novelist. And to understand it you must try to imagine a novelist's state of mind. I hope I am not giving away professional secrets if I say that a novelist's chief desire is to be as unconscious as possible. He has to induce in himself a state of perpetual lethargy. He wants life to proceed with the utmost quiet and regularity. He wants to see the same faces, to read the same books, to do the same things day after day, month after month, while he is writing, so that nothing may break the illusion in which he is living—so that nothing may disturb or disquiet the mysterious nosings about, feelings round, darts, dashes and sudden discoveries of that very shy and illusive spirit, the imagination. I suspect that this state is the same both for men and women. Be that as it may, I want you to imagine me writing a novel in a state of trance. I want you to figure to yourselves a girl sitting with a pen in her hand, which for minutes, and indeed for hours, she never dips into the inkpot. The image that comes to my mind when I think of this girl is the image of a fisherman lying sunk in dreams on the verge of a deep lake with a rod held out over the water. She was letting her imagination sweep unchecked round every rock and cranny of the world that lies submerged in the depths of our unconscious being. Now came the experience, the experience that I believe to be far commoner with women writers than with men. The line raced through the girl's fingers. Her imagination had rushed away. It had sought the pools, the depths, the dark places where the largest fish slumber. And then there was a smash. There was an explosion. There was foam and confusion. The imagination had dashed itself against something hard. The girl was roused from her dream. She was indeed in a state of the most acute and difficult distress. To speak without figure she had thought of something, something about the body, about the passions which it was unfitting for her as a woman to say. Men, her reason told her, would be shocked. The consciousness of what men will say of a woman who speaks the truth about her passions had roused her from her artist's state of unconsciousness. She could write no more. The trance was over. Her imagination could work no longer. This I believe to be a very common experience with women writers—they are impeded by the extreme conventionality of the other sex. For though men sensibly allow themselves great freedom in these respects, I doubt that they realize or can control the extreme severity with which they condemn such freedom in women.

These then were two very genuine experiences of my own. These were two of the adventures of my professional life. The first—killing the Angel in the House—I think I solved. She died. But the second, telling the truth about my own experiences as a body, I do not think I solved. I doubt that any woman has solved it yet. The obstacles against her are still immensely powerful—and yet they are very difficult to define. Outwardly, what is simpler than to write books? Outwardly, what obstacles are there for a woman rather than for a man? Inwardly, I think, the case is very difficult; she has still many ghosts to fight, many prejudices to overcome. Indeed it will be a long time still, I think, before a woman can sit down to write a book without finding a phantom to be slain, a rock to be dashed against. And if this is so in literature, the freest of all professions for women, how is it in the new professions which you are now for the first time entering?

Those are the questions that I should like, had I time, to ask you. And indeed, if I have laid stress upon these professional experiences of mine, it is because I believe that they are, though in different forms, yours also. Even when the path is nominally open—when there is nothing to prevent a woman from being a doctor, a lawyer, a civil servant—there are many phantoms and obstacles, as I believe, looming in her way. To discuss and define them is I think of great value and importance; for thus only can the labour be shared, the difficulties be solved. But besides this, it is necessary also to discuss the ends and the aims for which we are fighting, for which we are doing battle with these formidable obstacles. Those aims cannot be taken for granted; they must be perpetually questioned and examined. The whole position, as I see it—here in this hall surrounded by women practising for the first time in history I know not how many different professions—is one of extraordinary interest and importance. You have won rooms of your own in the house hitherto exclusively owned by men. You are able, though not without great labour and effort, to pay the rent. You are earning your five hundred pounds a year. But this freedom is only a beginning; the room is your own, but it is still bare. It has to be furnished; it has to be decorated; it has to be shared. How are you going to furnish it, how are you going to decorate it? With whom are you going to share it, and upon what terms? These, I think are questions of the utmost importance and interest. For the first time in history you are able to ask them; for the first time you are able to decide for yourselves what the answers should be. Willingly would I stay and discuss those questions and answers—but not tonight. My time is up; and I must cease.

## SUGGESTIONS FOR DISCUSSION

1. How would Eiseley and Woolf define success? Is it strictly a matter of pursuing career objectives, or does it involve other dimensions as well?
2. Loren Eiseley and Virginia Woolf write in comparable forms in this pair of readings. Each focuses on key moral and/or imaginative experiences—Woolf two, Eiseley three—that make us believe that we understand who they are, that give us insight into their careers and lives. But the form is deceptively simple; it is not as if, after all, they could simply look back over their working years and know that the events they finally put in their essays were the key ones. Think about their purposes. Why did Eiseley select these three episodes? What do they have in common? Why are they appropriate for his purpose? Why does Woolf choose the Angel in the House and the fisherman metaphors? How do they help to clarify and dramatize the issues she is discussing?
3. Explain why Eiseley's bone hunter "muffed" each of his three chances: the cave of spiders, the owl's egg, and the old man. Was it personal inadequacy, or conflicting pressures, or something else entirely? Describe how a successful bone hunter would have handled the same set of opportunities.
4. Eiseley is known for his sensitive shifts in tone. Which passages did you find playful or humorous? Point out some of the serious, reflective passages.

   Consider this sentence: "What it [the mass of spiders] was doing there, what evil unknown to mankind it was plotting, I do not know." What is the point of such a ludicrous and hysterical statement? Is the author mocking someone or something? Explain.
5. Like so many of the other writers in this collection, this pair writes about barriers: forces or obstacles, both inside and outside of us, that shape us, control our destinies. What are the differences between Woolf's and Eiseley's barriers? How do they compare to Anne Morrow Lindbergh's "life of multiplicity"?

## SUGGESTIONS FOR WRITING

1. Choose one common notion of success and write an essay showing the inadequacy or superficiality of this orientation. In your essay choose two or three episodes, either from your reading or from your own experience, which suggest that it is better to be a failure, according to these standards, than to be a success.

   Or write an essay showing that the contemporary version of success is an unattainable one. If you select this subject, describe some of the barriers which prevent individuals from reaching their goals. Be sure to include two or three specific episodes from your reading or your experiences which defend your thesis.

# Appendix

# Essays on the Writing Process

**1. JOURNALS AND NOTEBOOKS:**
*Joan Didion,* "On Keeping a Notebook"

**2. PEER EVALUATION:**
*Ursula Le Guin,* "Fifteen Vultures, the Strop, and the Old Lady"

**3. WRITER'S BLOCK:**
*Jacques Barzun,* "A Writer's Discipline"
*Gail Godwin,* "The Watcher at the Gates"

**4. CLARITY AND CORRECTNESS:**
*Richard Mitchell,* "The Worm in the Brain"

**5. STYLE:**
*Walker Gibson,* "Hearing Voices: Tough Talk, Sweet Talk, Stuffy Talk"

# *Joan Didion*
# "ON KEEPING A NOTEBOOK"

"'That woman Estelle,'" the note reads, "'is partly the reason why George Sharp and I are separated today.' *Dirty crepe-de-Chine wrapper, hotel bar, Wilmington RR, 9:45 a.m. August Monday morning.*"

Since the note is in my notebook, it presumably has some meaning to me. I study it for a long while. At first I have only the most general notion of what I was doing on an August Monday morning in the bar of the hotel across from the Pennsylvania Railroad station in Wilmington, Delaware (waiting for a train? missing one? 1960? 1961? why Wilmington?), but I do remember being there. The woman in the dirty crepe-de-Chine wrapper had come down from her room for a beer, and the bartender had heard before the reason why George Sharp and she were separated today. "Sure," he said, and went on mopping the floor. "You told me." At the other end of the bar is a girl. She is talking, pointedly, not to the man beside her but to a cat lying in the triangle of sunlight cast through the open door. She is wearing a plaid silk dress from Peck & Peck, and the hem is coming down.

Here is what it is: the girl has been on the Eastern Shore, and now she is going back to the city, leaving the man beside her, and all she can see ahead are the viscous summer sidewalks and the 3 A.M. long-distance calls that will make her lie awake and then sleep drugged through all the steaming mornings left in August (1960? 1961?). Because she must go directly from the train to lunch in New York, she wishes that she had a safety pin for the hem of the plaid silk dress, and she also wishes that she could forget about the hem and the lunch and stay in the cool bar that smells of disinfectant and malt and make friends with the woman in the crepe-de-Chine wrapper. She is afflicted by a little self-pity, and she wants to compare Estelles. That is what that was all about.

Why did I write it down? In order to remember, of course, but exactly what was it I wanted to remember? How much of it actually happened? Did any of it? Why do I keep a notebook at all? It is easy to deceive oneself on all those scores. The impulse to write things down is a peculiarly compulsive one, inexplicable to those who do not share it, useful only accidentally, only secondarily, in the way that any compulsion tries to justify itself. I suppose that it begins or does not begin in the cradle. Although I have felt compelled to write things down since I was five years old, I doubt that my daughter ever will, for she is a singularly blessed and accepting child, delighted with life exactly as life presents itself to her, unafraid to go to sleep and unafraid to wake up. Keepers of private notebooks are a different breed altogether, lonely and resistant rearrangers of things, anxious malcontents, children afflicted apparently at birth with some presentiment of loss.

My first notebook was a Big Five tablet, given to me by my mother with the sensible suggestion that I stop whining and learn to amuse myself by writing down my thoughts. She returned the tablet to me a few years ago; the first entry is an account of a woman who believed herself to be freezing to death in the Arctic night, only to find, when day broke, that she had stumbled onto the Sahara Desert, where she would die of the heat before lunch. I have no idea what turn of a five-year-old's mind could have prompted so insistently "ironic" and exotic a story, but it does reveal a certain predilection for the extreme which has dogged me into adult life; perhaps if I were analytically inclined I would find it a truer story than any I might have told about Donald Johnson's birthday party or the day my cousin Brenda put Kitty Litter in the aquarium.

So the point of my keeping a notebook has never been, nor is it now, to have an accurate factual record of what I have been doing or thinking. That would be a different impulse entirely, an instinct for reality which I sometimes envy but do not possess. At no point have I ever been able successfully to keep a diary; my approach to daily life ranges from the grossly negligent to the merely absent, and on those few occasions when I have tried dutifully to record a day's events, boredom has so overcome me that the results are mysterious at best. What is this business about "shopping, typing piece, dinner with E, depressed"? Shopping for what? Typing what piece? Who is E? Was this "E" depressed, or was I depressed? Who cares?

In fact I have abandoned altogether that kind of pointless entry; instead I tell what some would call lies. "That's simply not true," the members of my family frequently tell me when they come up against my memory of a shared event. "The party was *not* for you, the spider was *not* a black widow, *it wasn't that way at all.*" Very likely they are right, for not only have I always had trouble distinguishing between what happened and what merely might have happened, but I remain unconvinced that the distinction, for my purposes, matters. The cracked crab that I recall having for lunch the day my father came home from Detroit in 1945 must certainly be embroidery, worked into the day's pattern to lend verisimilitude; I was ten years old and would not now remember the cracked crab. The day's events did not turn on cracked crab. And yet it is precisely that fictitious crab that makes me see the afternoon all over again, a home movie run all too often, the father bearing gifts, the child weeping, an exercise in family love and guilt. Or that is what it was to me. Similarly, perhaps it never did snow that August in Vermont; perhaps there never were flurries in the night wind, and maybe no one else felt the ground hardening and summer already dead even as we pretended to bask in it, but that was how it felt to me, and it might as well have snowed, could have snowed, did snow.

*How it felt to me:* that is getting closer to the truth about a notebook. I sometimes delude myself about why I keep a notebook, imagine that some thrifty virtue derives from preserving everything observed. See enough and write it down, I tell myself, and then some morning when the world seems drained of wonder, some day when I am only going through the motions of doing what I am supposed to do, which is write — on that bankrupt morning I will simply open my notebook and there it will all be, a forgotten account with accumulated interest, paid passage back to the world out there: dialogue overheard in hotels and elevators and at the hat-check counter in Pavillon (one middle-aged man shows his hat check to another and says, "That's my old football number"); impressions of Bettina Aptheker and Benjamin Sonnenberg and Teddy ("Mr. Acapulco") Stauffer; careful *aperçus* about tennis bums and failed fashion models and Greek shipping heiresses, one of whom taught me a significant lesson (a lesson I could have learned from F. Scott Fitzgerald, but perhaps we all must meet the very rich for ourselves) by asking, when I arrived to interview her in her orchid-filled sitting room on the second day of a paralyzing New York blizzard, whether it was snowing outside.

I imagine, in other words, that the notebook is about other people. But of course it is not. I have no real business with what one stranger said to another at the hat-check counter in Pavillon; in fact I suspect that the line "That's my old football number" touched not my own imagination at all, but merely some memory of something once read, probably "The Eighty-Yard Run." Nor is my concern with a woman in a dirty crepe-de-Chine wrapper in a Wilmington bar. My stake is always, of course, in the unmentioned girl in the plaid silk dress. *Remember what it was to be me:* that is always the point.

It is a difficult point to admit. We are brought up in the ethic that others, any others, all others, are by definition more interesting than ourselves; taught to be diffident, just this side of self-effacing. ("You're the least important person in the room and don't forget it," Jessica Mitford's governess would hiss in her ear on the advent of any social occasion; I copied that into my notebook because it is only recently that I have been able to enter a room without hearing some such phrase in my inner ear.) Only the very young and the very old may recount their dreams at breakfast, dwell upon self, interrupt with memories of beach picnics and favorite Liberty lawn dresses and the rainbow trout in a creek near Colorado Spings. The rest of us are expected, rightly, to affect absorption in other people's favorite dresses, other people's trout.

And so we do. But our notebooks give us away, for however dutifully we record what we see around us, the common denominator of all we see is always, transparently, shamelessly, the implacable "I." We are not talking here about the kind of notebook that is patently for public consumption, a structural conceit for binding together a series of graceful *pensées*, we are talking about something private, about bits of the mind's string too short to use, an indiscriminate and erratic assemblage with meaning only for its maker.

And sometimes even the maker has difficulty with the meaning. There does not seem to be, for example, any point in my knowing for the rest of my life that, during 1964, 720 tons of soot fell on every square mile of New York City, yet there it is in my notebook, labeled "FACT." Nor do I really need to remember that Ambrose Bierce liked to spell Leland Stanford's name "£eland $tanford" or that "smart women almost always wear black in Cuba," a fashion hint without much potential for practical application. And does not the relevance of these notes seem marginal at best?:

> In the basement museum of the Inyo County Courthouse in Independence, California, sign pinned to a mandarin coat: "This MANDARIN COAT was often worn by Mrs. Minnie S. Brooks when giving lectures on her TEAPOT COLLECTION."
>
> Redhead getting out of car in front of Beverly Wilshire Hotel, chinchilla stole, Vuitton bags with tags reading:

MRS LOU FOX
HOTEL SAHARA
VEGAS

Well, perhaps not entirely marginal. As a matter of fact, Mrs. Minnie S. Brooks and her MANDARIN COAT pull me back into my own childhood, for although I never knew Mrs. Brooks and did not visit Inyo County until I was thirty, I grew up in just such a world, in houses cluttered with Indian relics and bits of gold ore and ambergris and the souvenirs my Aunt Mercy Farnsworth brought back from the Orient. It is a long way from that world to Mrs. Lou Fox's world, where we all live now, and is it not just as well to remember that? Might not Mrs. Minnie S. Brooks help me to remember what I am? Might not Mrs. Lou Fox help me to remember what I am not?

But sometimes the point is harder to discern. What exactly did I have in mind when I noted down that it cost the father of someone I know $650 a month to light the place on the Hudson in which he lived before the Crash? What use was I planning to make of this line by Jimmy Hoffa: "I may have my faults, but being wrong ain't one of them"? And although I think it interesting to know where the girls who travel with the Syndicate have their hair done when they find themselves on the West Coast, will I ever make suitable use of it? Might I not be better off just passing it on to John O'Hara? What is a recipe for sauerkraut doing in my notebook? What kind of magpie keeps this notebook? *"He was born the night the Titanic went down."* That seems a nice enough line, and I even recall who said it, but is it not really a better line in life than it could ever be in fiction?

But of course that is exactly it: not that I should ever use the line, but that I should remember the woman who said it and the afternoon I heard it. We were on her terrace by the sea, and we were finishing the wine left from lunch, trying to get what sun there was, a California winter sun. The woman whose husband was born on the night the *Titanic* went down wanted to rent her house, wanted to go back to her children in Paris. I remember wishing that I could afford the house, which cost $1,000 a month. "Someday you will," she said lazily. "Someday it all comes." There in the sun on her terrace it seemed easy to believe in someday, but later I had a low-grade afternoon hangover and ran over a black snake on the way to the supermarket and was flooded with inexplicable fear when I heard the checkout clerk explaining to the man ahead of me why she was finally divorcing her husband. "He left me no choice," she said over and over as she punched the register. "He has a little seven-month-old baby by her, he left me no choice." I would like to believe that my dread then was for the human condition, but of course it was for me, because I wanted a baby and did not then have one and because I wanted to own the house that cost $1,000 a month to rent and because I had a hangover.

It all comes back. Perhaps it is difficult to see the value in having one's self back in that kind of mood, but I do see it; I think we are well advised to keep on nodding terms with the people we used to be, whether we find them attractive company or not. Otherwise they turn up unannounced and surprise us, come hammering on the mind's door at 4 A.M. of a bad night and demand to know who deserted them, who betrayed them, who is going to make amends. We forget all too soon the things we thought we could never forget. We forget the loves and the betrayals alike, forget what we whispered and what we screamed, forget who we were. I have already lost touch with a couple of people I used to be; one of them, a seventeen-year-old, presents little threat, although it would be of some interest to me to know again what it feels like to sit on the river levee drinking vodka-and-orange-juice and listening to Les Paul and Mary Ford and their echoes sing "How High the Moon" on the car radio. (You see I still have the scenes, but I no longer perceive myself among those present, no longer could even improvise the dialogue.) The other one, a twenty-three-year-old, bothers me more. She was always a good deal of trouble, and I suspect she will reappear when I least want to see her, skirts too long, shy to the point of aggravation, always the injured party, full of recriminations and little hurts and stories I do not want to hear again, at once saddening me and angering me with her vulnerability and ignorance, an apparition all the more insistent for being so long banished.

It is a good idea, then, to keep in touch, and I suppose that keeping in touch is what notebooks are all about. And we are all on our own when it comes to keeping those lines open to ourselves: your notebook will never help me, nor mine you. *"So what's new in the whiskey business?"* What could that possibly mean to you? To me it means a blonde in a Pucci bathing suit sitting with a couple of fat men by the pool at the Beverly Hills Hotel. Another man approaches, and they all regard one another in silence for a while. "So what's new in the whiskey business?" one of the fat men finally says by way of welcome, and the blonde stands up, arches one foot and dips it in the pool, looking all the while at the cabaña where Baby Pignatari is talking on the telephone. That is all there is to that, except that several years later I saw the blonde coming out of Saks Fifth Avenue in New York with her California complexion and a voluminous milk coat. In the harsh wind that day she looked old and irrevocably tired to me, and even the skins in the mink coat were not worked the way they were doing them that year, not the way she would have wanted them done, and there is the point of the story. For a while after that I did not like to look in the mirror, and my eyes would skim the newspapers and pick out only the deaths, the cancer victims, the premature coronaries, the suicides, and I stopped riding the Lexington Avenue IRT because I noticed for the first time that all the strangers I had seen for years — the man with the seeing-eye-dog, the spinster who read the classified pages every day, the fat girl who always got off with me at Grand Central — looked older than they once had.

It all comes back. Even that recipe for sauerkraut: even that brings it back. I was on Fire Island when I first made that sauerkraut, and it was raining, and we drank a lot of bourbon and ate the sauerkraut and went to bed at ten, and I listened to the rain and the Atlantic and felt safe. I made the sauerkraut again last night and it did not make me feel any safer, but that is, as they say, another story.

## *Ursula K. Le Guin*
# "FIFTEEN VULTURES, THE STROP, AND THE OLD LADY"

During the month of July 1971, I took the noon bus daily from Portland to Forest Grove, via Hillsboro and a lot of cow pastures, to meet my one o'clock Science Fiction Writing Workshop at Pacific University. The workshop consisted of me, three registered students, one unregistered student who just appeared, and one registered but disembodied student who never did appear. The atmosphere at Pacific in summer is exceedingly serene and relaxed. In fact, they frequently forgot to unlock our classroom building. My ingenious students picked the lock, or if it was sunny we sat out under the oaks, and batted ideas around and gnats away.

This was delightful, but it wasn't much preparation for Seattle in August. Seattle was different. Fifteen or twenty of 'em. Sharp. Razors, honed to a fine edge by Johnson, Russ, Ellison. And the Strop* himself sitting there with them, Samuel R. Delany, looking innocent, waiting for me to open my great big dull mouth. All perched around above and below me, vulturelike, in this ghastly black futuristic underground coffeeshop-mortuary which the University of Washington gave us for a classroom. All with piercing eyes. Some with English accents. Some with knives in their boots. All carrying sawed-off short stories and concealed MSS. Oh, Lord! Do not — I strongly recommend to you — do not undertake, in almost total ignorance, to teach the sixth week of a six-week workshop, following after four of the best performers in the business, to a set of people between the ages of sixteen and fifty who have been working like crazy for five weeks and are all tuned up to, or past, concert pitch, and who are probably brighter than you are to begin with.

I was supposed to *teach* these people something?

I don't think I ever did, but I ended up having a very good time not doing so. That was largely because of the infinitely welcome presence of the Strop, who could bring reassurance to a rabbit as it was disappearing down the python's throat. And also because the kids were not only sharp, but gentle. They forgave the confused little old pipe-smoking lady her presumption in "teaching" them anything; and they did, most of them, what was necessary. They wrote. They wrote hard, and often. They wrote too much, too fast. They wrote in class, on order. They wrote at odd hours of the night, and even ones. They wrote very well and very badly, in the same piece, in the same sentence. They did what writers do. They wrote.

The sessions of mutual criticism in such a course are fascinating to participate in. By the time I came the kids had had sound training and five weeks' practice, and they knew how to criticize a story much better than I did. I should like to record here my lasting gratitude to them all, for teaching me all I know about the Art of Workshopping.

If the leader wants, I'm sure that workshopping sessions could serve as a poor man's Esalen. Since neither Chip nor I was looking for that, they were mostly mild,

* strop—a device for sharpening razor blades.—Eds.

my week, emotionally speaking. Intellectually they were pretty surgical: deep, sharp, and skillful. If they caused pain, that wasn't their intent — only a by-product.

Workshopping is the finest blood sport I know. It is splendid intellectual exercise, and highly stimulating to the brain and the adrenals. It may also provide something which is genuinely necessary, even essential, to the development of a certain type of writer's personality; of this I am not sure. I am inclined, at this point, to question the nature of its real function.

It is a truism to say that a writer (or any artist) cannot depend, in any profound sense, on the judgment of others: he has got to see his own mistakes and his own virtues. But what is not said so often — and is very hard to say to the young, the ambitious, the impatient — is that this takes not only will, not only work, but *time.* An intellectual decision can be reached quickly, a rational perception can be made all at once, but in order to be useful to the artist, it has all got to get down into the unconscious, and ferment in the darkness, and work slowly back up into the light. The artist's judgment of his own work — upon which the value of his work depends — is made *with his entire personality;* and until the personality is formed, and the psychic processes are perfected, the judgment will be incomplete.

For example, the alternations of moral preachiness and savage cynicism that characterize (and always have characterized) most writing by young people are not going to be talked away. They are essential. They are part of being twenty. The young writer has to live through them — and *write* through them — in order to get on to the next level. He cannot be elevated to that next level by the efforts of others, even the best critics with the best intentions in the world. He has got to walk there.

I have never found anywhere, in the domain of art, that you don't have to walk to. (There is quite an array of jets, buses, and hacks which you can ride to Success; but that is a different destination.) It is a pretty wild country. There are, of course, roads. Great artists make the roads; good teachers and good companions can point them out. But there ain't no free rides, baby. No hitchhiking. And if you want to strike out in any new direction — you go alone. With a machete in you hand, and the fear of God in your heart.

I am not convinced, then, that the purpose of workshopping, of mutual criticism, is what it seems to be. I wonder if what it really does is this. It tells the writer whose story is being criticized: Your opening is awkward, page 6 is incoherent, Asimov used that idea in 1938, what kind of idiot doesn't know you can't have a low-mass planet with a high-density atmosphere, you don't spell reliable with an o, your characters are wooden, your prose is leaden, your story is rotten, you are a writer. . .

You are a writer, because here we sit, fifteen vultures, the Strop, and the Old Lady, and take your work seriously (rip, tear, shred).

You are a writer because you sat down and wrote it, last night. And tonight you're going to write another one. And tomorrow, and tomorrow. . .

Whether we can really teach any more than that, I'm not yet sure. Whether one should call that "teaching," I'm not yet sure. That it is worth doing, I am convinced.

# *Jacques Barzun*
# "A WRITER'S DISCIPLINE"

No writer has ever lived who did not at some time or other get stuck. Even the great producers such as Scott and Dickens suffered from the professional malady of being "for no good reason" (as we all say) unable to write. And for every writer in working trim there may be a dozen persons of great ability who are somehow self-silenced. At long intervals they turn out remarkable fragments — half-essays or embryo stories; but they cannot seem to pull themselves together and finish anything, much less begin at will.

Now writing is not an art in which one can succeed by the production of interesting ruins, and since the total or partial paralysis of the writer's will is a fearsome and mysterious blight, most writers come to recognize the need of a discipline, a set of ritual practices which will put the momentum of habit behind their refractory ego and push them over the obstacle. Scott confessed that he used his divided self in order to rule: hating the thought of commitment, he hardly ever wrote anything except to flee the necessity of writing something else. And Dickens tells of long mornings when he forced himself to stay at the desk making false starts, lest by giving up he should give up forever. For all his books already in print, he might just as well have been the common schoolboy who is told to write of his visit to Aunt Julia and who honestly finds nothing to say except that he arrived on Friday and left on Sunday.

It may be partly because we were all coerced in this fashion that writing on demand comes so hard later on. If so, the old experience contains its own corrective, provided we are willing to look into it, that is to say, look into ourselves. If we ask what is the literary impulse par excellence we are, I think, bound to say that it is a desire to pull together one's conscious self and project it into some tangible constructed thing made up of words and ideas. The written thing may serve ulterior ends, as in exposition or polemic, but its first intention is to transfer a part of our intellectual and emotional insides into an independent and self-sustaining outside. It follows that if we have any doubts about the strength, truth, or beauty of our insides, the doubt acts as an automatic censor which quietly forbids the act of exhibition. Johnny cannot write about the visit to his aunt not merely because he did not initiate the literary idea, but because he feels like a fool relating the trivial things that happen every weekend: "They don't want to hear about that." Generalizing from his dominant conviction, we may say that the antiliterary emotion par excellence is fear. It acts precisely as when one attempts to speak a foreign language; one feels too damn silly for words — and one shuts up.

Obviously, if one were starving or in danger of assault, words would come fast enough, the inner censorship lifted and all sense of affectation gone. This, then, is the desirable situation to create for oneself every morning at nine, or every evening at five. The hopelessly stuck would find it expensive but worth it to hire a gunman to pound on the door and threaten death as a spur to composition. Ideas would come thick and fast and yet be sorted out with wonderful clarity in that final message to one's literary executors.

The sober application of this principle suggests that the writer needs an equivalent of this urgency, this pressure. It cannot help being artificial, like any pulmotoring; but although it need have nothing to do with danger, it must generate some form of excitement. Most of those who have written extensively under varying conditions would say that the true healthful pressure and excitement come from a belief that the things one wants to say form a coherent whole and are in some way needed; that is, the urge is a mixture of the aesthetic and the utilitarian impulses. This seems to be borne out by the observation frequently made that if one can only get something down on paper — anything — one feels no further hindrance to working. The final product may not contain a single sentence of the original, but in the successive drafts one has only a sense of pleasure at molding a resistant lump of clay — cutting away here and adding there in the double light of utility and harmony. It is at the outset, before the matter exists, that the great void paradoxically objectifies one's fear, one's conviction that "they don't want to hear about it."

To know how to begin, then, is the great art — no very profound maxim — but since in any extended piece of work one must begin many times, this is the art which it is essential to master. There is only one way: to study one's needs and quirks, and circumvent one's tricks for escape. The guidebooks will tell you that you should be full of your subject — a very good notion but too abstract. Fullness requires moral and mechanical aids and stout controls. For nothing is more common than to feel a stream of excellent ideas racing past and never a hook to lure them out into the open. This is especially true if one has previously tried to capture them and failed. We may say that our ideas feel like a whole world which is too big and whirling too fast to be pulled out in one piece. True, and this is why first aid at this point consists in not trying to have it born whole. Convince yourself that you are working in clay not marble, on paper not eternal bronze: let that first sentence be as stupid as it wishes. No one will rush out and print it as it stands. Just put it down; then another. Your whole first paragraph or first page may have to be guillotined in any case after your piece is finished: it is a kind of "forebirth." But as modern mathematics has discovered, there can be no second paragraph (which contains your true beginning) until you have a first.

The alternative to beginning stupidly, with a kind of "Er-ah," is to pick out during the earliest mental preparation for the work some idea which will make a good beginning, whether for intrinsic or topical reasons, and let it pull the rest along. Thus I began this essay on the cheering note that those mighty engines, Scott and Dickens, also stalled, and I had this in mind long before I knew what would come next. The danger of this procedure is that a picturesque idea can lead one too far back of the true starting line, and the cleverness or the charm of the idea makes one unwilling to sacrifice it. Burke was rightly accused of beginning every speech by inviting the Speaker of the House to dance a minuet with him. Ruthless decapitation is the remedy; but note in passing that the error confirms our analysis of the writer's insidious desire to put a cozy padded vest between his tender self and that vague, hostile, roaming animal known as the audience.

Having begun, the writer of even moderate gifts will feel a certain warmth creeping into his veins and rising, as it should, to his head. (In writing, always keep your feet warm, unless you are a full-blooded Indian accustomed to thinking great thoughts while walking barefoot in icy streams.) This genial current, which might prove genius, must be maintained and a physical and mental circulation established, in which blood, ink, and thoughts perform their appointed roles. It is now more than ever important not to let the vigilant censor within freeze everything on a technicality. I refer to that sudden stoppage due to the lack of the right word. Some writers, it is true, are able once started to shape their sentences whole in their heads before putting them down — Gibbon was one of those. But most, I believe, do not. Hence it is fatal for them to feel the entire system of ideas, feelings, and tenuous associations which is now in motion come to a dead stop because some adjective which means "boring" and begins with *n* eludes them. Don't look for it. Leave a blank. The probability is that there is no such word; if there is, it will come up of itself during revision or be rendered unnecessary by it. This sets the rule, by the way, for revision itself: keep going at a reasonable pace to the end, skipping the impossible; then start afresh until you have solved the true problems and removed the insoluble. Remember Barrie's schoolboy who chewed a pencil to splinters and failed the examination because he sought a word halfway between mickle and muckle.

The same law of momentum applies to the search for transitions, to perfecting the rhythm and shape of sentences, even occasionally to the ordering of paragraphs. Don't haggle and fuss but reassure yourself with the knowledge that when you come back to settle these uncertainties and fill these blanks you will still have your mind with you. Especially for young writers who have experienced difficulty and discouragement, the proper aim is that of the learner on the bicycle — keep going, which means a certain speed. Cutting slow capers will come later.

**1**

More serious than being stopped by a word is the breakdown in ideas. This has to be judged and treated with an even sharper eye for evasion and fraud on the part of the writing self. For the possibilities are several: one is that you have written enough for one day and reached a natural stopping place. It is wise therefore to have not simply a set time for writing — it need not be daily and yet be regular — but also a set "stint" for the day, based on a true, not vainglorious estimate of your powers. Then, when you come to a natural stop somewhere near the set amount, you can knock off with a clear conscience.

Another cause of stoppage is that the work has reached a point of real difficulty — an intellectual decision has to be made, a turning taken, and your mind is balking at it from fatigue or other causes. Or again, it may be that by reason of faulty arrangement there is no obvious bridge from where you are to where you want to go. If the former is true, you must fight it out sooner or later, on the same principles that enabled you to make a beginning. If the latter, devices may help: go back to the beginning, or to some convenient break in the development and read ahead, making but few corrections — just enough to warrant the expense of time and eyesight, but not enough to bog you down. As you approach the halting place, you may suddenly see where you lost the true way and how to bypass the evil spot altogether; or conversely you may find that your fresh running start carries you straight on and over the hump.

Why not an outline? Well, for my taste, outlines are useless, fettering, imbecile. Sometimes, when you get into a state of anarchy, or find yourself writing in circles, it may help to jot down a sketchy outline of the topics (or in a story, of the phases) so far covered. You outline, in short, something that already exists in written form, and this may help to show where you started backstitching. To be sure, a memorandum listing haphazardly what belongs to a particular project is useful. In fact, if you would be a "full" man as you undertake a new piece of work, you should have before you a little stack of slips bearing the ideas that have occurred to you since the subject first came to life in your mind. Otherwise the effort and the sense of treasures just out of reach will be a drain and diversion of writing power. It is jottings of this sort that fill the "Notebooks" at the tail end of "The Works." When I say slips or notebooks, I mean any congenial form of memorandum, for I doubt whether a self-respecting man with a lively flow of ideas can constrain himself to a uniform style and shape of note taking until the sacred fires have begun to cool — say around the age of fifty-one.

In all such matters, I believe in humoring to the greatest extent the timid and stubborn censor which stops work on flimsy pretenses. Grant, by all means, its falsely innocent preferences as to paper, ink, furnishings, and quash its grievances forever. We know that Mark Twain liked to write lying in or on a bed; we know that Schiller needed the smell of apples rotting in his desk. Some like cubicles, others vasty halls. "Writers' requisites," if a Fifth Avenue shop kept them, would astound and demoralize the laity. Historically, they have included silk dressing gowns, cats, horses, pipes, mistresses, particular knickknacks, exotic headgear, currycombs, whips, beverages and drugs, porcelain stoves, and hair shirts. According to one of Bernard De Voto's novels, writing paper of a peculiar blue tint has remarkable properties, about which the author makes an excellent point very subtly: he shows his writer-hero as neurotically exigent on this "trivial" matter, but after we have mocked and put him down as a crank, his work turns out to be a masterpiece. Quite simply, by yielding on such apparently irrational details, the writer is really outwitting his private foe — the excuse-maker within each of us who says: "I can't work today because I haven't any blue paper." Nor is this weakness limited to the literary artist, whether genius or duffer. Before me is a letter just received from a distinguished scientific friend who says: "I have got down to honest work on my article, drawing up elaborate typed notes in what may be a desperate attempt to avoid the actual writing."

That is the true spirit: suspect all out-of-the-way or elaborate preparations. You don't have to sharpen your pencils and sort out paper clips before you begin — unless it be your *regular* warming up. Give yourself no quarter when the temptation strikes, but grab a pen and put down some words — your name even — and a title: something to see, to revise, to carve, to do over in the opposite way. And here comes the advantage of developing a fixation on blue tinted paper. When you have fought and won two or three bloody battles with the insane urge to clean the whole house before making a start, the sight of your favorite implements will speak irresistibly of victory, of accomplishment, of writing done. True, you are at the mercy of the paper mills, as Samuel Butler was the slave of a certain thick book which he used to prop up his writing board at the exact slope of his desire, but such attachments are changeable once they have become a way of tackling work. Even fundamental routines may be recast. I used to wonder how Jane Austen could possibly write in the midst of family conversation, when to me Crusoe's solitude was scarcely adequate. But I learned under necessity to compose (first drafts at least) while keeping a chattering and enterprising child out of mischief in my workroom. The one thing needful is to have an anchorage in some fixed habits and to deal with writer's cowardice precisely as one would with other kinds — facing pain or going over the top. For it is never the specifically literary faculty which balks; it is the affection for one's dear self seeking to protect it against the fearful dangers of laughter, criticism, indifference, and reprints in digest form.

Since habits are rooted in the physical part of us, some writers find it serviceable to begin by doing some act requiring no special thought but which insensibly leads to composition. This doing may be as simple as answering correspondence or (with Butler) "posting one's books" — i.e., transcribing notes. But most writers prefer not to spoil the day's freshness by a reminder that relatives exist, nor distract themselves with the scattered subject matter of their notes. The ideal situation perhaps is to awaken with the grand design in mind (it was the last thing thought of before falling asleep), to shave while a matching throng of ideas lathers up within, and to go straight to the blank sheet without exchanging words with anyone.

Here a natural analogy with other arts suggests a few scales and runs on the typewriter, and it may well be that the writer's lack of anything so pleasantly muscular is a real cause of his frequent impotence; even the painter can busy his hands, craftsmanlike. The momentous question behind this comparison is of course the familiar one — pen or typewriter? It is no hedging answer to say, take your choice. But your choice (as I keep repeating) must be thoroughly considered. Is it possible, for instance, that like me you find it discouraging not to see whole paragraphs at a time and not to be able to cross out whole sentences at a time? If so, stick to the pen and use the typewriter to do your first revision as you transcribe. The plastic aspect of written matter is important, and the best revision is undoubtedly made from a clean copy embodying previous revisions. One reason why so much nineteenth-century work is good is that printers' revises were cheap and the writer carved direct on cold print.

Many writers' liking to compose on the typewriter has to do with this clean look of near-print. Hence persons whose fingers are clumsy and whose typed odes are full of fractions and dollar signs should give up the instrument. According to biographers, what they usually take up instead is a short stubby pencil. I do not know why it must be stubby; I mention it only to be fair. Let us by all means have poems, even if written with skewers in goose fat: the point is: Suit Thyself, but pay for it, i.e., *work!*

2

Numberless other facts, tricks, and generalities could be added to this already overlong set of hints. Writers young or old who take an interest in the bare processes of their art (as painters more frequently do) would be well advised to read at large in the considerable literature of exhortation and confession about writing. Nine-tenths of it is pedantic or platitudinous, but the other tenth is often amusing and likely to contain particles of illuminating truth, especially if written by a practicing writer. But again, the reader's object being ultimately to make personal applications, he should be on the watch for statements — there must be more than one in the present essay — which make him exclaim: "What an idea! why, it's just the opposite."

The writer must indeed turn everything into grist for *his* mill and no other, as a result of which he acquires both self-knowledge and self-command. His last consideration is therefore his first: what is he afraid of? Only, after he has disciplined himself, he puts the question differently and asks: Whom am I writing for? The century of the common man makes this no easy question to answer, for the common man is a social and political ideal, admirable in the spheres indicated. As a buyer and reader of books he does not exist; one finds humanity instead, which is diverse. One will write for different kinds of people at different times but at any one time there must be some imagined interlocutor, some animated ear trumpet, into which we pour our words. This may be posterity or the children aged eight to ten, but either must be represented in our minds. In judging our own work, we "suit" this mythical person, and our original verdict, "they don't want to hear about that," takes on another meaning — critical yet productive — a kind of ideal collaboration.

This endless conversation in which the writer's censor turns into a helping representative of a given public, is of course most pleasantly realized when the writer has in truth "a reader" — a relative or friend whose judgment he can use. Notice I did not say "whose judgment he will take." For the last step in the writer's liberation through discipline is the discovering of judicial distance — distance from himself, from his work, from his critic, and even from that fickle tiger, his audience.

The practical rules that follow are obvious. Do not read what you have written — much less what you are writing — to whoever will listen; indeed never read unpublished work (except perhaps poems), but give it to be read at leisure. Never show a first draft — except to an old and tried reader who knows from the crude signs what your work may become. Above all, do not talk yourself out of good ideas by trying to expound them to haphazard gatherings. In general, never choose your critic from your immediate family circle: they have usually no knowledge of the processes of writing, however literary they may be as consumers; and in their best-natured act of criticism one may hear the unconscious grinding of axes sounding like a medieval tournament.

No, your special reader (or two or three at most) must be chosen from those who care for writing as much as for you — no writer wants his work to shine in a *charitable* light. And even from your critic-by-appointment you must take only what goes with the grain of your thought and intent. This calls for delicate decisions, since it is always easy to cut off dead tissue and always hard to cut into the living cells that are not true flesh but tumor. The basic principle here as always is to protect the work and not the self.

There is one thing more. A man who writes, as Hardy said, stands up to be shot at, but Hardy was wrong to resent the shooting. So-called established writers who after years of work still wince at criticism are certainly not established in their own souls. Nor does one have to be callous or stubborn about reproof in order to feel solid and to accept one's errors and limitations with a composure which one can then extend to the errors and injustices of critics. Doing so habitually makes one more and more able to *see the work,* which is the prerequisite to producing it, pruning it, and preserving it against the ravages of time.

## *Gail Godwin*
## "THE WATCHER AT THE GATE"

I first realized I was not the only writer who had a restraining critic who lived inside me and sapped the juice from green inspirations when I was leafing through Freud's "Interpretation of Dreams" a few years ago. Ironically, it was my "inner critic" who had sent me to Freud. I was writing a novel, and my heroine was in the middle of a dream, and then I lost faith in my own invention and rushed to "an authority" to check whether she could have such a dream. In the chapter on dream interpretation, I came upon the following passage that has helped me free myself, in some measure, from my critic and has led to many pleasant and interesting exchanges with other writers.

Freud quotes Schiller, who is writing a letter to a friend. The friend complains of his lack of creative power. Schiller replies with an allegory. He says it is not good if the intellect examines too closely the ideas pouring in at the gates. "In isolation, an idea may be quite insignificant, and venturesome in the extreme, but it may acquire importance from an idea which follows it. . . . In the case of a creative mind, it seems to me, the intellect has withdrawn its watchers from the gates, and the ideas rush in pell-mell, and only then does it review and inspect the multitude. You are ashamed or afraid of the momentary and passing madness which is found in all real creators, the longer or shorter duration of which distinguishes the thinking artist from the dreamer. . . you reject too soon and discriminate too severely."

So that's what I had: a Watcher at the Gates. I decided to get to know him better. I discussed him with other writers, who told me some of the quirks and habits of their Watchers, each of whom was as individual as his host, and all of whom seemed passionately dedicated to one goal: rejecting too soon and discriminating too severely.

It is amazing the lengths a Watcher will go to keep you from pursuing the flow of your imagination. Watchers are notorious pencil sharpeners, ribbon changers, plant waterers, home repairers and abhorrers of messy rooms or messy pages. They are compulsive looker-uppers. They are superstitious scaredy-cats. They cultivate self-important eccentricities they think are suitable for "writers." And they'd rather die (and kill your inspiration with them) than risk making a fool of themselves.

My Watcher has a wasteful penchant for 20-pound bond paper above and below the carbon of the first draft. "What's the good of writing out a whole page," he whispers begrudgingly, "if you just have to write it over again later? Get it perfect the first time!" My Watcher adores stopping in the middle of a morning's work to drive down to the library to check on the name of a flower or a World War II battle or a line of metaphysical poetry. "You can't possibly go on till you've got this right!" he admonishes. I go and get the car keys.

Other Watchers have informed their writers that:

"Whenever you get a really good sentence you should stop in the middle of it and go on tomorrow. Otherwise you might run dry."

"Don't try and continue with your book till your dental appointment is over. When you're worried about your teeth, you can't think about art."

Another Watcher makes his owner pin his finished pages to a clothesline and read them through binoculars "to see how they look from a distance." Countless other Watchers demand "bribes" for taking the day off: lethal doses of caffeine, alcoholic doses of Scotch or vodka or wine.

There are various ways to outsmart, pacify or coexist with your Watcher. Here are some I have tried, or my writer friends have tried, with success:

Look for situations when he's likely to be off-guard. Write too fast for him in an unexpected place, at an unexpected time. (Virginia Woolf captured the "diamonds in the dustheap" by writing at a "rapid haphazard gallop" in her diary.) Write when very tired. Write in purple ink on the back of a Master Charge statement. Write whatever comes into your mind while the kettle is boiling and make the steam whistle your deadline. (Deadlines are a great way to outdistance the Watcher.)

Disguise what you are writing. If your Watcher refuses to let you get on with your story or novel, write a "letter" instead, telling your "correspondent" what you are going to write in your story or next chapter. Dash off a "review" of your own unfinished opus. It will stand up like a bully to your Watcher the next time he throws obstacles in your path. If you write yourself a good one.

Get to know your Watcher. He's yours. Do a drawing of him (or her). Pin it to the wall of your study and turn it gently to the wall when necessary. Let your Watcher feel needed. Watchers are excellent critics after inspiration has been captured; they are dependable, sharp-eyed readers of things already set down. Keep your Watcher in shape and he'll have less time to keep you from shaping. If he's really ruining your whole working day sit down, as Jung did with his personal demons, and write him a letter. On a very bad day I once wrote my Watcher a letter. "Dear Watcher," I wrote, "What is it you're so afraid I'll do?" Then I held his pen for him, and he replied instantly with a candor that has kept me from truly despising him.

"Fail," he wrote back.

# *Richard Mitchell*
# "THE WORM IN THE BRAIN"

There's an outrageous but entertaining assertion about language and the human brain in Carl Sagan's *Dragons of Eden.* It is possible, Sagan says, to damage the brain in precisely such a way that the victim will lose the ability to understand the passive or to devise prepositional phrases or something like that. No cases are cited, unfortunately — it would be fun to chat with some victim — but the whole idea is attractive, because if it were true it would explain many things. In fact, I can think of no better way to account for something that happened to a friend of mine — and probably to one of yours too.

He was an engaging chap, albeit serious. We did some work together — well, not exactly work, committee stuff — and he used to send me a note whenever there was to be a meeting. Something like this: "Let's meet next Monday at two o'clock, OK?" I was always delighted to read such perfect prose.

Unbeknownst to us all, however, something was happening in that man's brain. Who can say what? Perhaps a sleeping genetic defect was stirring, perhaps some tiny creature had entered in the porches of his ear and was gnawing out a home in his cranium. We'll never know. Whatever it was, it had, little by little, two effects. At one and the same time, he discovered in himself the yearning to be an assistant dean pro tem, and he began to lose the power of his prose. Ordinary opinion, up to now, has always held that one of these things, either one, was the cause of the other. Now we can at last guess the full horror of the truth. *Both* are symptoms of serious trouble in the brain.

Like one of these Poe characters whose friends are all doomed, I watched, helpless, the inexorable progress of the disease. Gradually but inevitably my friend was being eaten from within. In the same week that saw his application for the newly created post of assistant dean pro tem, he sent me the following message: "This is to inform you that there'll be a meeting next Monday at 2:00." Even worse, much worse, was to come.

A week or so later it was noised about that he would indeed take up next semester a new career as a highranking assistant dean pro tem. I was actually writing him a note of congratulations when the campus mail brought me what was to be his last announcement of a meeting of our committee. Hereafter he would be frying fatter fish, but he wanted to finish the business at hand. His note read: "Please be informed that the Committee on Memorial Plaques will meet on Monday at 2:00."

I walked slowly to the window, his note in my hand, and stared for a while at the quad. The oak trees there had been decimated not long before by a leak in an underground gas line. The seeping poison had killed their very roots, but they had at least ended up as free firewood for the faculty. Pangloss* might have been right, after all, and, calamity that it was, this latest message spared me the trouble of writing the congratulatory note and even afforded me a glimpse of a remarkably attractive young lady straying dryad-fashion through the surviving oaks. Things balance out.

* Pangloss—a character in Voltaire's *Candide,* famous for his simple-minded optimism and his insistence on finding a good side to every disaster—Eds.

You would think, wouldn't you, that the worm or whatever had at last done its work, that the poor fellow's Hydification* was complete and his destruction assured. No. It is a happy mercy that most of us cannot begin to imagine the full horror of these ravaging disorders. To this day that man still sends out little announcements and memos about this and that. They begin like this: "You are hereby informed..." Of what, I cannot say, since a combination of delicacy and my respect for his memory forbid that I read further.

It's always a mistake to forget William of Occam and his razor. Look first for the simplest explanation that will handle the facts. I had always thought that perfectly normal human beings turned into bureaucrats and administrators and came to learn the language of that tribe through some exceedingly complicated combination of nature and nurture, through imitative osmosis and some flaw of character caused by inappropriate weaning. Piffle. These psychologists have captured our minds and led us into needless deviousness. The razor cuts to the heart of things and reveals the worm in the brain.

Admittedly, that may be a slight oversimplification. It may be that the decay of language and the desire to administrate are not merely concomitant symptoms of one and the same disease, but that *one* is a sympton and the other a symptom of the symptom. Let's imagine what deans, who like to imitate government functionaries, who, in their turn, like to imitate businessmen, who themselves seem to like to imitate show-business types, would call a "scenario."

There you sit, minding your own business and hurting no man. All at once, quite insensibly, the *thing* creeps into your brain. It might end up in the storage shelves of the subjunctive or the switchboard of the nonrestrictive clauses, of course, but in your case it heads for the cozy nook where the active and passive voices are balanced and adjusted. There it settles in and nibbles a bit here and a bit there. In our present state of knowledge, still dim, we have to guess that the active voice is tastier than the passive, since the destruction of the latter is very rare but of the former all too common.

So there you are with your active verbs being gnawed away. Little by little and only occasionally at first, you start saying things like: "I am told that..." and "This letter is being written because..." This habit has subtle effects. For one thing, since passives always require more words than actives, anything you may happen to write is longer than it would have been before the attack of the worm. You begin to suspect that you have a lot to say after all and that it's probably rather important. The suspicion is all the stronger because what you write has begun to sound — well, sort of "official." "Hmm," you say to yourself, "Fate may have cast my lot a bit below my proper station," or, more likely, "Hmm. My lot may have been cast by Fate a bit below my proper station."

Furthermore, the very way you consider the world, or the very way in which the world is considered by you, is subtly altered. You used to see a world in which birds ate worms and men made decisions. Now it looks more like a world in which worms are eaten by birds and decisions are made by men. It's almost a world in which

* Hydification—a coined word referring to Dr. Jekyll and Mr. Hyde.—Eds.

victims are put forward as "doers" responsible for whatever may befall them and actions are almost unrelated to those who perform them. But only almost. The next step is not taken until you learn to see a world in which worms are eaten and decisions made and *all* responsible agency has disappeared. Now you are ready to be an administrator.

This is a condition necessary to successful administration of any sort and in any calling. Letters are written, reports are prepared, decisions made, actions taken, and consequences suffered. These things happen in the world where agents and doers, the responsible parties around whose throats we like our hands to be gotten, first retreat to the remoter portions of prepositional phrases and ultimately disappear entirely. A too-frequent use of the passive is not just a stylistic quirk; it is the outward and visible sign of a certain weltanschauung.*

And now that it is *your* weltanschauung (remember the worm has been gnawing all this time), you discover that you are suited to the life of the administrator. You'll fit right in.

Therefore, we may say that it is not the worm in the skull that causes deans and managers and vice presidents, at least not directly. The worm merely causes the atrophy of the active and the compensatory dominance of the passive. (Through a similar compensatory mechanism, three-legged dogs manage to walk, and the language of the typical administrator is not very different from the gait of the three-legged dog, come to think of it.) The dominance of the passive causes in the victim an alteration of philosophy, which alteration is itself the thing that both beckons him to and suits him for the work of administration. And there you have it. Thanks to Carl Sagan and a little help from William of Occam, we understand how administrators come to be.

You may want to object that a whole view of the world and its meanings can hardly be importantly altered by a silly grammatical form. If so, you're just not thinking. Grammatical forms are *exactly* the things that make us understand the world the way we understand it. To understand the world, we make propositions about it, and those propositions are both formed and limited by the grammar of the language in which we propose.

To see how this works, let's imagine an extreme case. Suppose there *is* after all a place in the brain that controls the making and understanding of prepositional phrases. Suppose that Doctor Fu Manchu has let loose in the world the virus that eats that very place, so that in widening circles from Wimbledon mankind loses the power to make and understand prepositional phrases. Now the virus has gotten you, and to you prepositional phrases no longer make sense. You can't read them, you can't write them, you can't utter them, and when you hear them you can only ask "Wha?" Try it. Go read something, or look out the window and describe what you see. Tell the story of your day. Wait . . . you can't exactly do that . . . tell, instead, your day-story. Recite how you went working . . . how morning you went . . . no . . . morning not you . . . morning went . . . how you morning went . . . The rest will be silence.

* Weltanschauung—world view; philosophy.—Eds.

Only through unspeakable exertion and even ad hoc invention of new grammatical arrangements can we get along at all without the prepositional phrase, as trivial as that little thing seems to be. It's more than that. Should we lose prepositional phrases, the loss of a certain arrangement of words would be only the visible sign of a stupendous unseen disorder. We would in fact have lost *prepositionalism,* so to speak, the whole concept of the kind of relationship that is signaled by the prepositional phrase. We'd probably be totally incapacitated.

Try now to imagine the history of mankind without the prepositional phrase, or, if you're tired of that, the relative clause or the distinction between subject and object. It would be absurd to think that lacking those and other such things the appearance and growth of human culture would have been merely hindered. It would have been impossible. *Everything* that we have done would have been simply impossible. The world out there is made of its own stuff, but the world that we can understand and manipulate and predict is made of discourse, and discourse is ruled by grammar. Without even so elementary a device as the prepositional phrase we'd be wandering around in herds right now, but we wouldn't know how to name what we were doing.

We're inclined to think of things like prepositional phrases as though they were optional extras in a language, something like whitewall tires. This is because we don't spend a lot of time dwelling on them except when we study a language not our own. We study German, and here comes a lesson on the prepositional phrase. Great, now we can *add* something to our German. That's the metaphor in our heads; we think — there *is* German, it exists, and when you get good at it you can add on the fancy stuff like prepositional phrases. All we have to do is memorize the prepositions and remember which ones take the dative and which ones take the accusative and which ones sometimes take the one and sometimes the other and when and why and which ones are the exceptions. Suddenly it becomes depressing. How about we forget the whole thing and settle for your stripped-down basic model German without any of the fancy stuff? If you do that, of course, you'll never find the *Bahnhof.** You'll be stymied in Stuttgart.

Like prepositional phrases, certain structural arrangements in English are much more important than the small bones of grammar in its most technical sense. It really wouldn't matter much if we started dropping the *s* from our plurals. Lots of words get along without it anyway, and in most cases context would be enough to indicate number. Even the distinction between singular and plural verb forms is just as much a polite convention as an essential element of meaning. But the structures, things like passives and prepositional phrases, constitute, among other things, an implicit system of moral philosophy, a view of the world *and* its presumed meanings, and their misuse therefore often betrays an attitude or value that the user might like to disavow.

Here's an example from the works of a lady who may also have a worm in her brain. She is "the chair" of the Equal Employment Opportunity Commission. It's very short and seems, to those willing to overlook a "small" grammatical flaw,

* *Bahnhof*—railroad station—Eds.

almost too trivial to be worthy of comment. She writes: "Instead of accepting charges indiscriminately and giving them docket numbers, charging parties are counseled immediately."

"Charging parties" are probably faster than landing parties and larger than raiding parties, but no matter. She means, probably, people who are bringing charges of some sort, but there are many kinds of prose in which people become parties. It's not really meant to sound convivial, though: it's meant to sound "legal." What's important is that the structure of her sentence leads us to expect that the people (or parties) named first after that comma will also be the people (or parties) responsible for doing the "accepting." We expect something like: "Instead of doing *that,* we now do this." That's not because of some *rule;* it's just the way English works. It both reflects and generates the way the mind does its business in English. We, the readers, are disappointed and confused because somebody who ought to have shown up in this sentence has in fact not appeared. What has become of the *accepting* parties? Are they hanging around the water cooler? Do they refuse to accept? Are they at least hoping that no one will remember that they are *supposed* to accept? We can guess, of course, that they are the same people who make up the counseling parties, who have also disappeared into a little passive. It's as though we went charging down to the EEOC and found them all out to lunch.

Well, that could have been a slip of the mind, the mind of the chair, of course, but later we read: "Instead of dealing with charging parties and respondents through formalistic legal paper, the parties are called together within a few weeks . . ."

It's the same arrangment. Who does that dealing, or, since that's what they did before the "instead," who *did* that dealing through "formalistic" paper? Wouldn't they be the same parties who ought to do the calling together? Where have they all gone?

A schoolteacher would call those things examples of dangling modifiers and provide some rules about them, but that's not important. What's important is that those forms are evocations of that imagined world in which responsible agency is hardly ever visible, much to the comfort of responsible agency. Since that is the nature of the world already suggested by the passive voice, you would expect that this writer, or chair, would be addicted to the passive. You'd be right. Here are the bare skeletons of a few consecutive sentences:

. . . staff is assigned . . .
. . . cases are moved . . .
. . . parties are contacted . . .
. . . files are grouped . . . and prioritized . . .
. . . steps are delineated . . . and time frames established . . .
. . . discussions are encouraged . . .

You have to wonder how much of a discussion you could possibly have with these people. They're never around.

Admittedly, it does these bureaucrats some credit that in their hearts they are ashamed to say that they actually do those things that they do. After all, who would want to tell the world that he, himself, in his very flesh, goes around grouping and prioritizing?

The dangling modifiers go well with the passives, and, in suggesting the nature of the world as seen by bureaucrats, they even add something new. The passives are sort of neutral, verbal shoulder-shrugs — these things happen — what can I tell you? The danglers go the next obvious and ominous step and suggest subtly that those charging parties have caused a heap of trouble and really ought to be handed the job of sorting things out for themselves, which, grammatically, is exactly what happens. In the first example the people who do the accepting and the counseling ought to appear right after the comma, but they don't. In the second, the people who do the dealing and the calling ought to appear right after the comma, but they don't. In both cases the people who *do* appear are the clients on whose behalf someone is supposed to accept, counsel, deal, and call. Does that mean something about the way in which those clients are regarded by this agency? They seem to have been put in some kind of grammatical double jeopardy, which is probably unconstitutional.

The poor lady, or chair, has inadvertently said what she probably meant. Working for the government would be so pleasant if it weren't for those pesky citizens. A waspish psychiatrist might observe that she has taken those charging parties and has "put them in their place" with a twist of grammar, thus unconsciously expressing her wish that they ought to be responsible for all the tedious labor their charges will cost her and her friends. She herself, along with the whole blooming EEOC, has withdrawn behind a curtain of cloudy English from the clash of charging parties on the darkling plain. "Ach so, sehr interessant, nicht wahr, zat ze patzient ist immer py ze Wort 'inshtead' gonvused. Es gibt, vielleicht, a broplem of, how you zay, Inshteadness." And indeed, the result of the dangling modifiers is to put the charging parties forth *instead* of someone else, as though the word had been chosen to stand out in front of the sentence as a symbol of the latent meaning.

Surely this lady, or chair, is an educated person, or chair, perfectly able to see and fix dangling modifiers of the sort they used to deal with in the early grades. After all, she has been hired as a chair, and for such a position we can assume some pretty high standards and stringent requirements. All right, so she doesn't know the difference between "formal" and "formalistic"— big deal. When such a high-ranking official of our government apparatus makes a mistake in structure, and habitually at that, it's not much to the point to underline it and put an exclamation mark in the margin. In a small child these would be mistakes; in a chair they are accidental revelations of a condition in the mind. To put the name of the thing modified as close as possible to the modifier is not a "rule" of English; it is a sign of something the mind does in English. When the English doesn't do that thing, it's because the mind hasn't done it.

It would be fatuous for us to say that we don't understand those sentences because of the disappearance of the people who are supposed to do all those things. It is a schoolteacher's cheap trick to say that if you don't get your grammar right people won't understand you. It's almost impossible to mangle grammar to that point where you won't be understood. We understand those sentences. In fact, we understand them better than the writer; we understand both what she thought she was saying and something else that she didn't think she was saying.

Many readers, of course, would "understand" those sentences without even thinking of the problem they present, and they might think these comments pedantic and contentious. Oh, come on, what's all the fuss? A couple of little mistakes. What does it matter? We all know what she means, don't we?

Such objections come from the erroneous idea that the point of language is merely to communicate, "to get your ideas across," whatever that means. Furthermore, such objectors may think that they are defending a hardworking and well-meaning chair, but she is little likely to be grateful for their partisanship if she figures out what it means. They say, in effect, that her little mistakes are just that, little mistakes rather than inadvertent and revealing slips of the mind. In the latter case, however, we can conclude that she is merely a typical bureaucrat with an appropriately managerial twist in the brain; in the former we would simply have to conclude that she is not well enough educated to be allowed to write public documents. Which of these conclusions do you suppose she would prefer? It seems that we must choose one or the other. Those are either mistakes made in ignorance or mistakes made in something other than ignorance.

The mind, thinking in English, does indubitably push modifiers and things modified as close together as possible. Can there really be a place in the brain where that happens, a function that might be damaged or dulled? It doesn't matter, of course, because there is surely a "place" in the mind analogous to the imagined place in the brain.

Whether by worms or world-views, it does seem sometimes to be invaded and eaten away. The malfunctions we can see in this chair and in my erstwhile friend, now an assistant dean pro tem, are small inklings of a whole galaxy of disorders that has coalesced out of the complicated history of language, of our language in particular, and out of the political history of language in general.

*Walker Gibson*

## "HEARING VOICES: TOUGH TALK, SWEET TALK, STUFFY TALK"

When a writer selects a style, however unconsciously, and so presents himself to a reader, he chooses certain words and not others, and he prefers certain organizations of words to other possible organizations. I take it that every choice he makes is significant in dramatizing a personality or voice, with a particular center of concern and a particular relation to the person he is addressing. Such self-dramatizations in language are what I mean by style. The Tough Talker, in these terms, is a man dramatized as centrally concerned with himself — his style is I-talk. The Sweet Talker goes out of his way to be nice to us — his style is *you*-talk. The Stuffy Talker expresses no concern either for himself or his reader — his style is *it*-talk. These are three extreme possibilities: the way we write at any given moment can be seen as an adjustment or compromise among these three styles of identifying ourselves and defining our relation with others.

. . . . . . . . . . . . . . . . . . . . . . . . . . . . . .

In what follows, I shall be asking how writers introduce themselves in those crucial opening paragraphs of prose works. How, that is to say, they present to us a *self,* the assumed author, not to be confused with that complex mass of chaotic experience making up the writer as human being. The procedure can be simple enough. Of the beginnings of assorted prose works, let us ask: (1) Who's talking? Who is being introduced? (2) To whom is he being introduced? Who are *we* expected to be as we read this prose sympathetically? (3) By what magic was all this done? How were words chosen and arranged in order to make these effects possible, without physical voice, or gesture, or facial expression?*

. . . . . . . . . . . . . . . . . . . . . . . . . .

Suppose we begin to read—to expose ourselves to an introduction. Suppose we pick up, for instance, a magazine, the *Saturday Review.* We riffle its pages. Already we are taking on some attributes of an assumed reader: we have some experience of this magazine and its general personality, and we know vaguely the sort of person we are expected to be as we read it. We are not, at any rate, at this moment, the assumed reader of *The Hudson Review,* or *The New Yorker,* or *House Beautiful,* or *Frisky Stories*. The eye lights on a title. Just our subject. Who's speaking here?

THE PRIVATE WORLD OF A MAN WITH A BOOK

> The temptation of the educator is to explain and describe, to organize a body of knowledge for the student, leaving the student with nothing to do. I have never been able to understand why educators do this so often, especially where books are concerned. Much of this time they force their students to read the wrong books at the wrong time, and insist that they read them in the wrong way. That is, they lecture to the students about what is in the books, reduce the content to a series of points that can be remembered, and, if there are discussions, arrange them to deal with the points.
>
> Schools and colleges thus empty books of their true meaning, and addict their students to habits of thought that often last for the rest of their lives. Everything must be reduced to a summary, ideas are topic sentences, to read is to prepare for a distant text. This is why so many people do not know how to read. They have been taught to turn books into abstractions.†

Everything depends on the *personality* to whom we have just been introduced. His message can never be divorced from that personality, that speaking voice — or at least not without becoming essentially another message. The question I am asking is not "What is he saying?" but "Who is he? What sort of person am I being asked to *be,* as I experience these words?" A difficulty immediately arises. We can hardly describe with justice the fellow talking except by quoting his own words. He is what he says, precisely. The minute we lift an assumed "I" out of the text and start to describe or reproduce his personality in *our* language, or in language that we infer might be his, we are admittedly altering him, mangling him, killing him perhaps. But it is the only way. The biologist studying cellular structure has to dye his specimen under the microscope so he can see its parts, but the dye kills the living tissue, and what he sees is dead and gone. It is a familiar intellectual dilemma, and there is

* From the Preface and Introduction of Gibson's book, *Tough, Sweet and Stuffy.*—Eds.
p. 375a Appendix

† *Saturday Review,* XLIV (January 7, 1961). The author is Mr. Harold Taylor.—Au.

nothing to do but be cheerful about it, applying one's dye as liberally as necessary while recognizing its poisonous possibilities.

With that proviso, then, who's talking, in the first two paragraphs of "The Private World of a Man with a Book"? What assumptions is he sharing with his ideal reader? What follows is, as I hear it, a between-the-lines communication between the assumed author and the assumed reader:

> You and I know all about the shoddy academic situation, where lazy and wrongheaded teachers do so much harm to the true meaning of books. You and I share a true knowledge of true meanings, and can recognize instantly when wrong books are taught at the wrong time in the wrong way. I am a rugged no-nonsense character, for all my academic connections, and you, thrusting out your jaw, couldn't agree more.

Now it is clear from this effort that I (the assumed author of this essay) do not very successfully engage myself as the ideal assumed reader of these two paragraphs. It is clear that when I have the speaker saying "You and I share a true knowledge of true meanings" I am not writing a paraphrase at all, but a parody. I am exaggerating what I take to be a sort of arrogance in the speaker, with a view to ridicule. How did I reach this curious position?

I reached it because, as I read the two paragraphs, I suffered a conflict. I was aware, on the one hand, of the person I was supposed to be (one who knows what "true meanings" are, for instance). But I was also aware, much too aware, that I was *not* that person, and, more important, didn't want to pretend to be. This is not a question of changing one's beliefs for the sake of literary experience — that is easy enough. One can "become" a Hindu or a Hottentot if the speaker is sufficiently persuasive and attractive. But that's the rub: the speaker must be attractive to us. And in this case, because of qualities I have called "arrogance" and "rugged no-nonsense," I have become not the assumed reader at all, but a hostile reader.* Consider one moment where hostility, at least in this reader, was aroused. It is the second sentence — "I have never been able to understand why educators do this. . . ." The difficulty here is that we sense hypocrisy in that remark. Just how is the assumed reader being addressed? Is it this?

> I've tried and tried to understand why teachers go at books this way, but I just can't get it.

Or is it this?

> The trouble with teachers is that they're either too dim-witted or too lazy to teach books the right way. Oh I understand it all right!

Now which is it? Let's admit it could be either (a fault in itself?), but insofar as we may strongly suspect it's the second, then the actual phrasing ("I have never been able to understand") seems falsely prevaricating in its covert antagonism.

I have used such expressions as "rugged no-nonsense," "covert antagonism," and "thrusting out your jaw." In the next-to-last sentence of our passage we can

* This has of course absolutely nothing to do—or almost nothing to do—with the writer as an actual person.—Au.

illustrate one rhetorical technique by which impressions like these are conveyed. "This is why so many people do not know how to read." We have here, to anticipate, some rhetoric of Tough Talk. The phrasing does not allow the possibility that not so many people are so benighted after all. No doubts are permitted. By placing its "many people do not know how to read" in a subordinate clause, the voice assumes a *fact* from what is at best an extreme statement of an arguable position. The independent clause ("This is why") merely speculates on the cause of the "fact." The reader is pushed around by a tough-talking voice.

But insofar as we can divorce the utterance here from the utterer — and I have said that this is strictly impossible — then what is being said in this paragraph seems to me both true and important. Indeed, I would personally agree, books *are* too often taught as abstractions, and in any vote in any faculty meeting, the assumed author and this reader would vote together on this issue. But we do not take pleasure in reading for such reasons as that. In fact it may have been this very agreement, this sense that I personally did not need persuading, that led me to read no further in the article than the two paragraphs I have quoted. But surely it was not only that. I read no more because I felt that the assumed author was browbeating me, and changing me over in ways I did not like. I don't care how "right" he is: he's got to be *nice* to me!

But unfortunately, it is not enough to be nice. Life is very hard. Let us consider now another assumed author — same magazine, a few years earlier, same general subject — and listen to a voice that goes out of its way to be nice.

### UNREQUIRED READING

The title of this essay may strike you as a typographical error. You may be saying to yourself that the writer really means required reading, and the phrase conjures up for you, I suspect, lists distributed on the first days of college courses: Volume One of this distinguished scholar's work on the Byzantine empire in the fourth century, that brochure on the economic interpretation of the Constitution, this pundit's principles of economics, that pedant's source book.

Or, perhaps, still under the apprehension that I mean required reading, you are reminded of what by now is one of the more maddening isolences of criticism, or at any rate of book reviewing. "This," says Mr. Notability, "is a *must* book." This in the atomic age is compulsory reading. In a world of anxiety this uneasy novel is not to be passed by.

I beg of you to forget such obligations and responsibilities. To this day you have to forget that you *had* to read "Macbeth" in order to begin to remember how perturbingly moving a play it is. Hardly anyone would reread Burke's "Speech on Conciliation" if he recalled how he had to make an abstract of it in high school.*

Once again let us try to assess the sort of person addressing us here, remembering that this person bears no necessary connection with its author. In listening to this voice, we become aware as always of an ideal listener, a "you," whose characteristics we are expected to adopt as we read.

I am a sweet professorish sort of fellow, full of big words but simple at heart — you are younger than I, and though you have of course been through college, you are by no means an

* *Saturday Review*, XXXIII (November 4, 1950). By Irwin Edman.—Au.

academic professional like me. My charm is based on an old-fashioned sort of formality ("I beg of you") combined with a direct conversational approach that I trust you find attractive. I wear my learning lightly, occasionally even offering you a tricky phrasing (*pundit's principles, pedant's source book*) or a modern cliché (*world of anxiety*) to show you I'm human. But we share, you and I, a knowledgeable experience of literature; we both recognize for example how "perturbingly moving" *Macbeth* really is.

It is easy to identify at least one rhetorical device by which the professional voice is often dramatized. It is the device of parallel structure. A pattern of balanced phrasings suggests a world similarly balanced, well ordered, academic. The first paragraph's list is an example: *this distinguished scholar, that brochure, this pundit, that pedant.* A somewhat similar effect occurs later: *this is a must book, this is compulsory reading, this is not to be passed by.* Triplets like that are characteristic of the fancier tones. In the last two sentences we have the balanced device of chiasmus, a criss-cross relation of parallel ideas. The clauses there are arranged in an order of time past, time present, time present, time past.

> You have to forget that you *had* to read to remember how perturbingly moving it *is*.
>
> Hardly anyone *would reread* Burke (now) if he recalled how he *had* to make an abstract.

Very neat, literary, elegant. Parallel structure alone, of course, could not produce a sweet-professorish voice. But it can support the meanings of the words, as it does here.

The assumed reader, here as always, is a sympathetic yes man, responding uncritically (yet of course intelligently) to the speaker's invitations. When a reader responds critically, in the negative sense, and begins to disagree, he forsakes his role as assumed reader and lets his Real-Life Self take over. If this goes on very long, he will simply stop reading, unless he has some strong motive for swallowing his irritation and continuing.

We can imagine a sympathetic conversation going on between speaker and assumed reader in our passage, something like this:

> The title of this essay may strike you as a typographical error. [Why, yes, as a matter of fact it did.] You may be saying to yourself that the writer really means required reading [I did rather think that, yes], and the phrase conjures up for you, I suspect, lists distributed on the first days of college courses [Oh yes, those dreadful things]: Volume one of this etc. [You certainly have it down pat! And I do appreciate your gentle scorn of pundits and pedants.]

But suppose, once again, that one does not enjoy playing the part of this particular assumed reader. Suppose one is uncomfortably aware of an insupportable gap between one's Own True Self and the role one is here being asked to adopt. Again it is probably obvious that I (still the assumed author of this essay) suffer from just such an uncomfortable awareness. The mechanical and prissy straight man that I have constructed out of the assumed reader reveals my own antagonism, both to him and to the sweet talk of the speaker. Suppose we were to play it my way, and invent a conversation between the speaking voice and a hostile reader who refused to take on the required qualities:

The title of this essay may strike you as a typographical error. [Why, no, as a matter of fact that never occurred to me.] You may be saying to yourself that the writer really means required reading [Don't be silly. I would be more surprised to see a title so trite. In fact your title embodies just the sort of cute phrase I have learned to expect from this middlebrow magazine.] and the phrase conjures up for you, I suspect, lists distributed on the first days of college courses [That's a dim memory at best. How old do you think I am?]: Volume one of this distinguished etc. etc. [You bore me with this lengthy list and your affected effects of sound-play.]

Or, perhaps, still under the apprehension that I mean required reading ["Perhaps" is good. How *could* I be "still" under such an apprehension?], you are reminded of what by now is one of the more maddening insolences of criticism [You're maddened, not I. Calm down.], or at any rate of book reviewing. "This," says Mr. Notability, "is a *must* book." [Do even book reviewers use such language?] This in the atomic age is compulsory reading. In a world of anxiety this uneasy novel is not to be passed by. [I appreciate that you are ironically repeating these tired phrases, but they're still tired.]

Now of course this mean trick can be worked by anybody against almost anything. The assumed reader of this essay, for example, may so far forget himself as to try it on *me,* though I deeply hope he doesn't. Again it is important to emphasize that the argument here is not between two people disagreeing about an issue. I agree with the educational stand taken here about reading, just as I did with the similar stand taken in our first passage. *The argument is between two people disagreeing about one another.* And this time it is not a case of the Tough Talker pushing the reader around, but a case of the Sweet Talker who condescends and irritates in a totally different way.

The general subject our two writers have been discussing comes down to something we could call The Teaching of Reading. It is a subject that can easily be confronted in some other voice, of course; in fact it seems to me doubtful that there can be *any* subject which by definition *requires* any particular voice. To illustrate the third of my triumvirate of styles, and to exhibit The Teaching of Reading as attacked with a very different voice, I offer the passage that follows. Again it presents a thesis with which I am quite in agreement — as who is not?

## TEACHING LITERATURE

Rapid and coherent development of programs in modern literature has led to the production of excellent materials for study from the earliest years of secondary education through the last of undergraduate study. The sole danger — if it be one, in the opinion of others — lies in easy acceptance of what is well done. The mechanics of mass production can overpower and drive out native creativeness in reflecting on literature and so stop individual interpretation in teaching. We hear a good deal of the dangers to imaginative experience in youth from excesses of visual exposure, and we know that they therefore read much less, in quantity, from longer works of prose and poetry. It may prove to be true, therefore, that in the study of literature the critical authority of the printed page will seem an easy substitute for individual analysis of original texts, first for the teacher and next inevitably for students who have never learned to read, with conscious effort in thinking, through verbal symbols.*

* David H. Stevens, *The Changing Humanities* (New York, 1953), p. 173. Title added.—Au.

After making necessary allowances for a passage ripped from context (for I have had to choose this time a paragraph from inside a work rather than an introduction), the fact remains that this is a Stuffy voice. It is by no means an extreme example of Stuffy Talk, but it is Stuffy enough to be marked off as distinct from the Toughness of "Private World" and the Sweetness of "Unrequired Reading." We become, as we read, solemn; the brow furrows; perhaps we are a little Stuffy ourselves. This transformation is the direct result of certain habits of vocabulary and sentence structure by which the Stuffiness is conveyed. I put off identification of these habits until we have examined the Tough Talker and Sweet Talker more thoroughly. Meanwhile, my point is that a *style* is not simply a response to a particular kind of subject-matter, nor is it entirely a matter of the writer's situation and his presumed audience. It is partly a matter of sheer individual will, a desire for a particular kind of self-definition no matter what the circumstances.

The point can be further illuminated by trying just one more introduction, asking ourselves what sort of voice this is:

## ON TEACHING THE APPRECIATION OF POETRY

I hold no diploma, certificate, or other academic document to show that I am qualified to discuss this subject. I have never taught anybody of any age how to enjoy, understand, appreciate poetry, or how to speak it. I have known a great many poets, and innumerable people who wanted to be told that they were poets. I have done some teaching, but I have never "taught poetry." My excuse for taking up this subject is of a wholly different origin. I know that not only young people in colleges and universities, but secondary school children also, have to study, or at least acquaint themselves with, poems by living poets; and I know that my poems are among those studied, by two kinds of evidence. My play *Murder in the Cathedral* is a set book in some schools: there is an edition of the English text published in Germany with notes in German, and an edition published in Canada with notes in English. The fact that this play, and some of my other poems, are used in schools brings some welcome supplement to my income; and it also brings an increase in my correspondence, which is more or less welcome, though not all letters get answered. These are letters from the children themselves or more precisely, the teenagers. They live mostly in Britain, the United States, and Germany, with a sprinkling from the nations of Asia. It is in a spirit of curiosity, therefore, that I approach the subject of the teaching of poetry: I should like to know more about these young people and about their teachers and the methods of teaching.*

This is an interesting case, unlike our other three passages but not uncommon in expository prose, where the assumed reader simply has to know who the real author *is* if he *is* to understand the message at all. In this instance, he is the late T. S. Eliot. Implicit in the speaker's words is the knowledge, on the part of both his reader and himself, that he is speaking for one specific human being, and that the most distinguished literary figure of his time. How pleasant to meet Mr. Eliot. This knowledge is modest (or is it smug?) on the speaker's part, deferential on the reader's part — but it is *there.* We may imagine messages going out from speaker to assumed reader something like this:

* *The Critic*, XVIII (1960). By T. S. Eliot.—Au.

How pleasant it is for me to acknowledge my academic deficiencies when you know exactly who I am! (Besides, *are* they deficiencies? You and I know better, don't we?) When I start in to attack an educational method, my own method can assume the mild forms of amateurishness, good humor, and mere "spirit of curiosity." My words can be so light because my reputation is so weighty. You, surely an admirer of my long career, can smile knowingly when I say that I "should like to know more about" these teachers and this method. *You* know that I'm going to tear them apart, but gently, deftly, without losing an ounce of my urbanity. They are scarcely worth my heavier weapons.

The assumed author of this essay finds that voice very hard to deny. This is not Tough Talk at all, nor is it exactly Sweet Talk, nor is it Stuffy. Some readers may find it overly self-conscious, possibly condescending, possibly banking too much on the reader's swooning before this great reputation. But I do not find it so. The spectacle offered here, of the great man unbending, seems to me not unattractive, and I am won more than lost by such carefully human touches as the reference to his income, or the amused use of the slight vulgarism "teenagers." The blunt repetition of "I" and the simple structure of the opening sentences seem candid and there is some deliberately comic hypocrisy in the modest admissions. (I hold no diploma, true, but you know I don't need to!)

We have — or at least I have — a trust in this speaker. Why? Is it because of his overpowering reputation? In large measure, probably. This is a speaker with an enormous advantage, and he takes advantage of his advantage. But it is more than that. The personality that emerges here, with his wit, his urbanity, his refusal to be ruffled, is simply a personality I am willing to go on listening to. The fact that he is about to take a general stand about teaching that is more or less in agreement with all three of our previous voices, and myself, is neither here nor there. The fact that he may also tread on some educational methods I myself espouse (or have been guilty of) is mildly disturbing, but not seriously. It is the character I meet here that makes the difference. He is not pushing me around, like the Tough Talker. He is not cuddling up to me, like the Sweet Talker. He is not holding me off, like the Stuffy Talker. He respects me. I return the compliment.

# Notes on Contributors

**Ilse Aichinger** (1921–    )
Austrian novelist and short-story writer, whose fiction often has a dreamlike atmosphere and strongly symbolic overtones. She is the author of the novel *Herod's Children* and a collection of stories entitled *The Bound Man*.

**Alan Alda** (1936–    )
American actor, writer, and director, best known for his starring role in the television series MASH. He appeared in the films *California Suite, Same Time Next Year,* and *The Four Seasons,* which he also directed. Alda is also known for his active involvement in feminist issues.

**Maya Angelou** (1924–    )
American author, actress, and civil rights worker. She has written two volumes of poetry, *Just Give Me a Cool Drink of Water 'fore I Die* and *Oh Pray My Wings Are Gonna Fit Me Well.* Angelou's most celebrated work is her autobiography, *I Know Why the Caged Bird Sings,* which depicts the experiences of a black girl growing up in an Arkansas town.

**Aristotle** (384–322 B.C.)
One of the most influential of the ancient Greek philosophers, famous for a wide range of contributions. He placed great emphasis on direct observation and logical, systematic thinking. His works consist mostly of notes made on his lectures by his students. Among them are the *Rhetoric, Poetics, Physics, Discourse on Conduct, Metaphysics,* and *Organum,* a treatise on logic.

**Jacques Barzun** (1907–    )
French-American writer and educator. He has served at Columbia University as professor, dean of faculties, and provost. Barzun has written books on a wide variety of subjects, including *Race: A Study of Modern Superstition, Romanticism and the Modern Ego, The Teacher in America, The House of Intellect, Science: The Glorious Entertainment,* and *The Use and Abuse of Art.*

**Daniel J. Boorstin** (1914–    )
American lawyer, educator, and historian, currently serving as Librarian of Congress. Boorstin has written numerous books, including *The Mysterious Science of the Law, The Image, The Americans, The Sociology of the Absurd, Democracy and Its Discontents,* and *The Republic of Technology.*

**Brigid Brophy** (1929–    )
Irish author, literary critic, and social commentator, noted for her independent views. She is the author of *Black Ship to Hell, Mozart the Dramatist, The Snow Ball,* and *The King of a Rainy Country.*

**Andrew Carnegie** (1835–1919)
American industrialist and philanthropist, who acquired enormous wealth from steel

production. His benefactions include Carnegie Hall in New York, the Carnegie Institute in Washington, the Carnegie Endowment for International Peace, the Carnegie Foundation for the Advancement of Teaching, and hundreds of grants for free public libraries and church organs.

**Winston Churchill** (1874–1965)
English statesman and author, one of the most famous public figures of the twentieth century. He served as prime minister of England during World War II and was honored for his brilliant leadership and stirring speeches. Churchill was awarded the Nobel Prize in Literature for his writing and his oratory. He is the author of an autobiography, *My Early Life: A Roving Commission,* and several historical works, such as *World Crisis, The Second World War,* and *A History of the English-Speaking Peoples.*

**John Ciardi** (1916– )
American poet, teacher, and critic, also known for his regular column in *Saturday Review,* "Manner of Speaking." His volumes of poetry include *Homeward to America, Live Another Day, In the Stoneworks,* and *Lives of X.* He has written a book of criticism called *How Does a Poem Mean?*

**Eldridge Cleaver** (1935– )
American political activist and former leader of the Black Panther Party. He is the author of *Soul on Ice* and *Soul on Fire.* Cleaver currently owns a boutique in Hollywood, California.

**Simone de Beauvoir** (1908– )
French writer with an international reputation, whose most famous book, *The Second Sex,* analyzes the societal forces that influence the development of women. She has written several novels, including *She Came to Stay, The Blood of Others,* and *All Men Are Mortal.* Some of her noted nonfictional works are *The Ethics of Ambiguity, America Day by Day,* and *The Coming of Age.*

**Joan Didion** (1934– )
American novelist, essayist, and screenplay writer, whose works explore the neurotic emptiness of modern American life. Her best-known works are the novels *Run River, Play It As It Lays, A Book of Common Prayer,* and a collection of essays entitled *Slouching Toward Bethlehem.*

**Loren Eiseley** (1907–1977)
American anthropologist, naturalist, and educator, who received many writing awards for his highly original reflective prose. He served as professor and academic administrator at the University of Pennsylvania for thirty years. His books include *Darwin's Century, The Firmament of Time, The Immense Journey, The Night Country,* and *All the Strange Hours.*

**Nora Ephron** (1941– )
American writer and magazine editor, noted for her satirical social observations. Her essays are collected in three books, *Wallflower at the Orgy, Crazy Salad,* and *Scribble Scribble.*

**Joseph Epstein** (1937– )
American writer, editor of *The American Scholar,* and visiting lecturer at Northwestern University. His books include *Divorced in America, Familiar Territory,* and *Ambition.*

**Walker Gibson**
American educator and writer. He has taught at Amherst College, New York Univer-

sity, and is currently professor of English at the University of Massachusetts. Gibson has written several books on writing, including *Persona* and *Tough, Sweet and Stuffy.*

**Gail Godwin** (1937– )
American writer, whose stories and essays have appeared in numerous periodicals. She is the author of five novels, *The Perfectionists, Glass People, The Odd Woman, Violet Clay,* and *A Mother and Two Daughters.*

**Ellen Goodman** (1941– )
American journalist who writes a regular column for the *Boston Globe.* Her column usually explores the relationship between public issues and personal lives. Goodman won the Pulitzer Prize in 1980. She is the author of *Turning Points, Close to Home,* and *At Large.*

**Margaret Halsey** (1910– )
American writer, whose first book, *With Malice Toward Some,* became a bestseller. Since then, she has written a number of books on political and social subjects. Among them are *The Pseudo-Ethic, Color Blind,* and *The Folks at Home.*

**Lillian Hellman** (1907– )
American dramatist whose plays are often chilling studies of human malice. Her best-known dramas are *The Children's Hour, Watch on the Rhine, The Little Foxes,* and *Toys in the Attic.* She has also written two autobiographical works, *An Unfinished Woman* and *Pentimento.* Hellman is also known for her long personal association with Dashiell Hammett, the detective novelist.

**Muriel James/Dorothy Jongeward**
American psychologists and educators, known primarily for their work in transactional analysis and for their best-selling book, *Born to Win.*

**Samuel Johnson** (1709–1784)
English author, moralist, and leading literary scholar of his time. He was also celebrated for his brilliant conversation and witty sayings, many of which are still remembered. Johnson's classical values, acute mind, and strong personality guided English taste and helped establish many English literary traditions. He wrote *The Vanity of Human Wishes, Rasselas, Lives of the Poets,* and two collections of essays, *The Idler* and *The Rambler.* Johnson is also famous as the author of the first English dictionary.

**Suzanne Britt Jordan**
American college teacher and occasional free-lance writer. She currently teaches at North Carolina State University.

**Jean Kerr** (1923– )
American author, playwright, and humorist. Her plays include *Mary, Mary, Poor Richard,* and *Finishing Touches.* Kerr is also known for her amusing autobiographical sketches of family life, such as *Please Don't Eat the Daisies* and *The Snake Has All the Lines.*

**Martin Luther King, Jr.** (1929–1968)
American clergyman and leader in the civil rights movement. King was a pacifist who sought racial equality through non-violent means. He was awarded the Nobel Peace Prize in 1964. His writings include *Stride Toward Freedom, Strength to Love,* and *Why We Can't Wait.* King was assassinated in Memphis, Tennessee.

**Ring Lardner** (1885–1933)
American short-story writer known chiefly for his humorous and satirical sketches of

ordinary people. His fictional works appear in several collections, including *How to Write Short Stories, The Love Nest and Other Stories,* and *Round Up.*

**Susan Lee** (1944– )
American novelist and journalist.

**Ursula LeGuin** (1929– )
American novelist who has received wide recognition and several awards for her science fiction. Some of her novels are *A Wizard of Earthsea, The Left Hand of Darkness, Orsinian Tales, The Language of the Night,* and *Hard Words.*

**C. S. Lewis** (1898–1963)
English scholar and writer, known equally well for his intellectual treatises and for his allegorical fantasies with Christian overtones. His scholarly works include *The Allegory of Love, The Screwtape Letters,* and *Studies in Medieval and Renaissance Literature.* His most famous work of fiction is the "Chronicles of Narnia," a series of fantasies that includes *The Lion, the Witch and the Wardrobe* and *The Silver Chair.*

**Anne Morrow Lindbergh** (1906– )
American writer and aviator. Her works include *North to the Orient* and *Listen! the Wind,* both accounts of flights she made with her famous husband, Charles Lindbergh. Most of her other writings are highly personal sketches and poems. Among them are *Gift from the Sea, The Unicorn and Other Poems, Dearly Beloved,* and *Earth Shine.*

**D. Keith Mano** (1942– )
American novelist, magazine editor, and vice president of a building-materials firm. His books include *Bishop's Progress, War Is Heaven!, The Proselytizer,* and *The Bridge.*

**Milton Mayer** (1908– )
American journalist, lecturer, and teacher, an independent commentator on social, political, and ethical issues. Mayer has been a controversial figure on several occasions, most notably for his pacifist stance during World War II and his later refusal to take a Communist-disclaimer oath. He is the author of *They Thought They Were Free, If Men Were Angels, The Nature of the Beast,* and co-author of *The Revolution in Education,* with Mortimer Adler.

**Mary McCarthy** (1912– )
American novelist, short-story writer, and critic, noted for her intellect and wit. Among her novels are *The Company She Keeps, The Oasis, The Group,* and *The Groves of Academe.* McCarthy's nonfictional works include *Vietnam* and *The Mask of State: Watergate Portraits.*

**H. L. Mencken** (1880–1956)
American editor, journalist, and critic, famous for his biting satire and criticism of complacent middle-class attitudes. His essays have been collected in a six-volume series entitled *Prejudices.* He wrote a monumental study of philology, *The American Language.* Among his other works are *In Defense of Women, Treatise of the Gods,* and *George Bernard Shaw: His Plays.*

**John Stuart Mill** (1806–1873)
English philosopher, economist, and advocate of progressive social reforms. He served as a member of Parliament from 1865 to 1868. Mill's writings explore ethical problems, logical processes, and political theory. His most famous works are *A System of Logic, Principles of Political Economy, Utilitarianism,* and *On Liberty.*

**Richard Mitchell** (1929– )
American educator, editor of *The Underground Grammarian,* and professor of English at Glassboro State College. He is the author of two books, *Less Than Words Can Say* and *The Graves of Academe.*

**Tillie Olsen** (1912– )
American writer, whose fictional works deal primarily with the theme of wasted potential and unfulfilled lives. Olsen has spent most of her life working at tedious jobs and raising children, and her career as a writer has been curtailed by the necessities of a working-class life. Her writings consist of four short stories, collected in the volume *Tell Me a Riddle,* one novel entitled *Yonnondio,* and a collection of essays.

**Dorothy Parker** (1893–1967)
American columnist, short-story writer, and poet, celebrated for her wry and sardonic wit. Most of her writings are concise and satirical commentaries on modern life. Her collections of poetry include *Enough Rope* and *Death and Taxes.* Parker's stories are collected in *Laments for the Living, Here Lies,* and *Collected Stories.*

**William G. Perry, Jr.** (1913– )
American educator and psychologist. Perry has been a member of the Harvard faculty for over thirty years. He is the author of *Forms of Intellectual and Ethical Development in the College Years.*

**Adrienne Rich** (1929– )
American poet and political activist. Her writings explore the changing possibilities brought about by women's rights, student activism, and black power, as well as the unchanging aspects of personal relationships. Among her volumes of poetry are *A Change of World, Necessities of Life, Will to Change, The Diamond Cutters,* and *Diving into the Wreck.*

**Lissa Rotundo**
American homemaker and former biology teacher.

**Dorothy Sayers** (1893–1957)
English scholar and writer, known primarily for her brilliant detective stories featuring the character Lord Peter Wimsey. She is the author of ten novels, including *The Nine Tailors* and *Gaudy Night,* and numerous short stories, which have been collected in a book called *Lord Peter.* Sayers has also written several religious essays and studies of Dante.

**Manuel J. Smith** (1934– )
American psychologist, a pioneer in assertiveness training. He is currently a professor of clinical psychology at UCLA. Smith is the author of the best-selling book, *When I Say No, I Feel Guilty.* He has also written *Kicking the Fear Habit.*

**Robert Paul Smith** (1915–1977)
American writer, who gained recognition when his book, *"Where Did You Go?" "Out." "What Did You Do?" "Nothing."* became a best seller. Among his other works are a book of poetry called *And Another Thing,* a play (with Max Shulman) called *The Tender Trap,* which later became a motion picture, *So It Doesn't Whistle,* and *How to Do Nothing with Nobody, All Alone by Yourself.*

**Susan Sontag** (1933– )
American writer and philosopher, known chiefly for her critical essays on modern

culture and radical politics. Her best-known collections of essays are *Against Interpretation* and *Styles of Radical Will.* She has written and directed several motion pictures, including *Duet for Cannibals* and *Brother Carl.* Her fictional works include the novels *Death Kit* and *The Benefactor.*

**Diana Trilling** (1905– )
American writer and editor, who has contributed numerous essays of literary criticism and social analysis. Her articles have appeared in *Atlantic, Esquire, Harpers,* and the *New York Times Book Review.* She is the author of *Claremont Essays, We Must March My Darlings,* and *Mrs. Harris: The Death of the Scarsdale Diet Doctor.*

**Esther Vilar** (1935– )
German writer and former physician. Her best-known work is a scathing critique of sex roles entitled *The Manipulated Man.*

**E. B. White** (1899– )
American essayist and fiction writer, widely acclaimed for his prose style, which is both clear and evocative. He began his career by writing a regular column for the *New Yorker* magazine. His essays are collected in several books, including *The Wild Flag, One Man's Meat, The Points of My Compass,* and *The Second Tree from the Corner.* White is also the author of three well-known stories for children, *Stuart Little, Charlotte's Web,* and *The Trumpet of the Swan.*

**Virginia Woolf** (1882–1941)
English novelist, essayist, and critic, famous for her poetic prose style and subtle interplay of images. As a novelist, she emphasized the individual consciousness rather than plot or characterization. Her most famous novels are *Mrs. Dalloway, The Waves,* and *To the Lighthouse.* Her collections of essays include *The Common Reader, The Second Common Reader,* and *The Death of the Moth and Other Essays.*

**William Zinsser** (1922– )
American writer, educator, and film critic, who taught at Yale University from 1971 to 1979. His books include *Any Old Place With You, Seen Any Good Movies Lately?, The City Dwellers, The Lunacy Boom,* and *On Writing Well.*